DAVID W. OWENS & ADAM S. LOVELADY

CHAPTER 160D

A NEW LAND USE LAW FOR NORTH CAROLINA

UNC | SCHOOL OF GOVERNMENT

The School of Government at the University of North Carolina at Chapel Hill works to improve the lives of North Carolinians by engaging in practical scholarship that helps public officials and citizens understand and improve state and local government. Established in 1931 as the Institute of Government, the School provides educational, advisory, and research services for state and local governments. The School of Government is also home to a nationally ranked Master of Public Administration program, the North Carolina Judicial College, and specialized centers focused on community and economic development, information technology, and environmental finance.

As the largest university-based local government training, advisory, and research organization in the United States, the School of Government offers up to 200 courses, webinars, and specialized conferences for more than 12,000 public officials each year. In addition, faculty members annually publish approximately 50 books, manuals, reports, articles, bulletins, and other print and online content related to state and local government. The School also produces the *Daily Bulletin Online* each day the General Assembly is in session, reporting on activities for members of the legislature and others who need to follow the course of legislation.

Operating support for the School of Government's programs and activities comes from many sources, including state appropriations, local government membership dues, private contributions, publication sales, course fees, and service contracts.

Visit sog.unc.edu or call 919.966.5381 for more information on the School's courses, publications, programs, and services.

Michael R. Smith, DEAN
Thomas H. Thornburg, SENIOR ASSOCIATE DEAN
Jen Willis, ASSOCIATE DEAN FOR DEVELOPMENT
Michael Vollmer, ASSOCIATE DEAN FOR ADMINISTRATION

FACULTY

Whitney Afonso
Trey Allen
Gregory S. Allison
David N. Ammons
Ann M. Anderson
Maureen Berner
Frayda S. Bluestein
Mark F. Botts
Anita R. Brown-Graham
Peg Carlson
Leisha DeHart-Davis
Shea Riggsbee Denning
Sara DePasquale
Jacquelyn Greene
Norma Houston
Cheryl Daniels Howell
Willow S. Jacobson
Robert P. Joyce
Diane M. Juffras
Dona G. Lewandowski
Adam Lovelady
James M. Markham

Christopher B. McLaughlin
Kara A. Millonzi
Jill D. Moore
Jonathan Q. Morgan
Ricardo S. Morse
C. Tyler Mulligan
Kimberly L. Nelson
David W. Owens
William C. Rivenbark
Dale J. Roenigk
John Rubin
Jessica Smith
Meredith Smith
Carl W. Stenberg III
John B. Stephens
Charles Szypszak
Shannon H. Tufts
Aimee N. Wall
Jeffrey B. Welty (on leave)
Richard B. Whisnant

Printed in the United States of America

24 23 22 21 20   1 2 3 4 5

ISBN 978-1-56011-976-0

Contents

Foreword   vii

1. Context for Chapter 160D   1

   I. Overview   1

      A. Reorganization   1

      B. Consensus Reforms   3

      C. Implementation and Transition   3

   II. Legislative History   4

      A. Statutory Context   4

      B. The 160D Proposal   7

   III. Framework for Development Regulations   9

      A. Development Definitions   9

      B. Decision Types   11

      C. Clarifying Site-Specific Approvals   13

2. Organization and Administration of Development Regulations   15

   I. Geographic Jurisdiction   15

   II. Boards   17

   III. Administration of Development Regulations   18

      A. General Administration   19

      B. Enforcement of Development Regulations   21

3. Substance of Development Regulations   25

   I. Substance of Zoning Regulations   25

      A. Exactions and Zoning   25

      B. Maps   26

      C. Zoning Districts   27

      D. Zoning Standards   29

   II. Substance of Additional Development Regulations   30

      A. Moratoria   30

      B. Subdivision Regulations   30

      C. Regulation of Particular Land Uses and Particular Areas   32

      D. Development Agreements   33

      E. Building and Housing Codes   34

      F. Specialized Development Regulations   35

4. Planning and Development Decisions   37

I.   Planning   37
A. Planning Requirement   37
B. Advisory   38
C. Plan Process and Content   39

II.   Legislative Decisions   40
A. Hearings   40
B. Planning Board Review   41
C. Plan Consistency and Reasonableness Statements   41
D. Voting   43
E. Administrative Minor Modifications to Conditional Zoning Decisions   44
F. Limits on Legislative Zoning Decisions   45

III.   Quasi-Judicial Decisions   45
A. Uniform Terminology   46
B. Uniform Procedures   46
C. Presentation of Evidence by Non-Parties   47
D. Advisory Reviews   47
E. Other Modifications   48

IV.   Administrative Decisions   50
A. Development Approvals   50
B. Determinations   51
C. Appeals of Administrative Decisions   52

5. Rights and Review   53

I.   Vested Rights and Permit Choice   53
A. Process to Claim and Appeal   53
B. Types and Terms   54
C. Runs with the Land   55
D. Continuing Review   55
E. Exceptions   56
F. Permit Choice   56

II.   Judicial Review   57
A. Declaratory Judgments and Other Civil Actions   57
B. Appeals of Quasi-Judicial Decisions   58
C. Subdivision Decisions   59
D. Attorneys' Fees   60
E. Statutes of Limitation   60
F. Additional Judicial Rules   60

Appendix A. G.S. Chapter 160D Checklist of Changes to Local Ordinances, Policies, and Practices 63

Appendix B. Location of Prior Statutes in G.S. Chapter 160D 77

Appendix C. Location of G.S. Chapter 160D Provisions in Prior Statutes 83

Appendix D. Reviews Solicited and Comments Received on Proposed Chapter 160D Legislation 91

Appendix E. Annotated Text of Chapter 160D 97

Foreword

Chapter 160D of the North Carolina General Statutes is the first major recodification and modernization of city and county development regulations since 1905. The endeavor was initiated by the Zoning and Land Use Section of the N.C. Bar Association in 2013 and emanated from the section's rewrite of the city and county board of adjustment statute earlier that year. This bill summary and its many footnotes are intended to help citizens and local governments understand and navigate these changes.

This recodification effort was not without setbacks and challenges. First introduced as H.B. 483 in 2015, it passed the House unanimously but failed to achieve Senate approval. Reintroduced as S.B. 419 in 2017, it passed the Senate unanimously but failed to achieve passage in the House. Reintroduced yet again in 2019 as S.B. 355, the bill passed both chambers and was signed into law by the governor on July 11, 2019.

This five-year undertaking, Herculean in hindsight, was always transparent and inclusive. From the beginning, drafts were routinely circulated among section members, city and county planners, developers, city and county attorneys, private attorneys, and various development groups. Updated drafts were posted on multiple websites. Consensus changes were included, while problematic or controversial changes were not. The result is more efficient regulations, clearer language, logical structure, changes that accommodate established case law, and a consolidation of city and county regulations. All changes were footnoted to explain the drafting committee's reasoning.

Moving from inspiration to session law took the work of numerous people, not the least of whom are the hundreds of citizens who provided edits or input on various drafts, helping us to harness the insights of many experiences and perspectives. Naming them all is not possible, but their fingerprints are obvious (and appreciated). Special thanks to Representative Paul Stam and Senators Michael Lee, Floyd McKissick, and Paul Newton for their leadership as each bill moved through their respective chambers. The N.C. Bar Association; numerous Zoning, Planning, and Land Use Section chairs; the N.C. League of Municipalities; and the N.C. Homebuilders Association provided invaluable feedback as we translated an uncommonly long and detailed bill for a busy legislature.

Finally, this effort would not have been possible without the dedication, knowledge, experience, countless work hours, and unquestioned integrity of UNC School of Government Professor David W. Owens, a member of the committee and the true draftsman of this bill. Professor Owens is known by most and trusted by all. Working with him has been among our highest personal and professional honors.

The Drafting Committee:
LeAnn Nease Brown
Robin Tatum
Thomas E. Terrell, Jr.

1. Context for Chapter 160D

I. Overview

In 2019, the North Carolina General Assembly adopted the long-debated complete reorganization of the state's planning and development regulation statutes. Originally introduced as Senate Bill 422 and House Bill 448, the legislation was adopted as Part II of S.L. 2019-111 (Senate Bill 355). To conform to this new statutory framework, every city and county development regulation in the state will need to be updated by January 1, 2021.

This publication includes an overview of the law, its legislative history, and an analysis of how the law amends existing statutes. The appendixes include a checklist of amendments that need to be made to local ordinances, tables that provide cross-references to where the existing statutes are located in the new Chapter 160D, and an annotated edition of the bill that identifies the changes it makes to previous law and provides footnotes explaining those changes.

A. Reorganization

Consolidation. The new Chapter 160D consolidates the previous county enabling statutes (now in Article 18 of Chapter 153A of the North Carolina General Statutes (hereinafter G.S.) and the city enabling statutes (now in Article 19 of G.S. Chapter 160A) into a single, unified new Chapter 160D. Related statutes on city and county development regulation previously scattered throughout the General Statutes are also relocated to Chapter 160D. These include, for example, provisions for land use regulation of adult businesses and family care homes. The existing statutory provisions are repealed and replaced by the relocated provisions in Chapter 160D. In addition, statutes remaining in other chapters, such as the seldom-used 1941 Model Airport Zoning Act in G.S. Chapter 63, are amended to use the procedures for ordinance adoption, administration, and enforcement that are set out in Chapter 160D.

The intent of this consolidation is to have a uniform set of statutes applicable to cities and counties and common to all development regulations. In most instances, previous parallel systems of city and county statutes produced the same statutory authority for both cities and counties. As development regulation statutes were adopted, the same language was usually added to both G.S. Chapter 153A for counties and Chapter 160A for cities. However, over the decades, modest and often unintentional differences in the city and county statutes evolved. For example, when first enacted in 2005, the language on adopting a plan consistency statement prior to voting on a zoning amendment was identical for cities and counties, but in 2006, a clarification was made to the city statute, while the county statute was left unchanged (and in 2017, the city statute was again amended to bring it more into sync with the county version). Over the decades, similar scenarios played out for various provisions in the development regulation statutes, leaving confusion and uncertainty as to whether differences in the city and county language, sometimes subtle and sometimes substantial, were intentional or merely a result of drafting oversight. Differences also led to confusion among developers and planners who worked with both cities and counties, as they often assumed, sometimes incorrectly, that the version of the statute they were most familiar with was equally applicable to cities and counties. Intentional differences between city and county authority, principally the exemption of agricultural uses from county zoning coverage, are retained in Chapter 160D, but otherwise the default is to have a unitary statute for both cities and counties. Similarly, the intent of Chapter 160D is to use the same ordinance adoption, administration, and enforcement procedures for all development regulations, with only a few intentional differences remaining for individual types of ordinances (such as specialized appeals of building code interpretations to the state rather than to the board of adjustment).

Reorganization. Chapter 160D also places the development regulation statutes into a more logical, coherent organization. In addition to being scattered in other statutory locations, the provisions within the land use regulatory articles themselves could be confusing and hard to find. For example, the administrative provisions related to inspections, stop work orders, and enforcement for zoning were buried in the building permit parts in G.S. Chapters 153A and 160A. The provisions on development moratoria, which applied to all development regulations, were codified in the middle of the zoning part but applied to moratoria on subdivision plats or other development approvals. Notice and hearing provisions applicable to the same decision were in two different parts, as with the requirement for published notice of a rezoning hearing being in a different part from the mailed and posted notice requirements.[1] This body of statutes grew organically and sporadically over the course of a century, with each amendment and new program grafted on to the pre-existing organizational structure. The result was a convoluted organization that even experienced practitioners found challenging to navigate.

Chapter 160D places all of the statutes on development regulation into a more user-friendly organization. Provisions that affect all development regulations (such as definitions and provisions related to moratoria, vested rights, and conflicts of interest) are grouped in one article, followed by articles that address geographic jurisdiction, creation and duties of boards, administration of regulations, the process for adoption and amendment of regulations, and judicial review of regulations. There are also detailed articles for each major type of development regulation, including planning, zoning, subdivision, building and housing codes, environment, historic preservation, and community development.

Chapter 160D is organized under fourteen articles:

- Article 1. General Provisions
- Article 2. Planning and Development Regulation Jurisdiction
- Article 3. Boards and Organizational Arrangements
- Article 4. Administration, Enforcement, and Appeals
- Article 5. Planning
- Article 6. Process for Adoption of Development Regulations
- Article 7. Zoning Regulation
- Article 8. Subdivision Regulation
- Article 9. Regulation of Particular Uses and Areas
- Article 10. Development Agreements

---

1. The published notice requirements for municipal rezonings are in G.S. 160A-364, while the mailed and posted notice requirements are in G.S. 160A-384. County requirements are similarly separated.

- Article 11. Building Code Enforcement
- Article 12. Minimum Housing Codes
- Article 13. Additional Authorities
- Article 14. Judicial Review

As an aid to statutory navigation, Chapter 160D uses a numbering convention for individual statutory sections. As adopted, each section number used this convention: Chapter number-Article number-Section number. For example, the first statutory section in Article 7 on zoning regulations was G.S. 160D-7-1. When codified, a similar but slightly different numbering convention will be used, adapting the Chapter 160D numbering to the convention used in other chapters of the G.S. Instead of a three-part number, there will be a two-part number: Chapter number-Section number. However, each section number will start with the relevant article number. For example, the first section in Article 7 on zoning regulations will be G.S. 160D-701, while the first section in Article 10 on development agreements will be G.S. 160D-1001. For clarity going forward, this publication uses the statutory numbering convention for the bill as codified rather than the version in S.L. 2019-111.

Appendix B is a chart that shows where the previous statutory provisions in Article 19 of G.S. Chapter 160A and Article 18 of Chapter 153A are located in Chapter 160D. The annotated edition of Chapter 160D, set out as Appendix E, footnotes the original location in the statutes of each provision included in Chapter 160D.

B. Consensus Reforms

While not making major policy changes or shifts in the scope of authority granted to local governments, Chapter 160D includes many clarifying amendments and consensus reforms in the statutes. Because some of these statutes were first adopted nearly a century ago, archaic terminology needed to be modernized. Superfluous and redundant language was deleted, and gender-neutral language was employed. More readable sentence structures and lengths were used to replace confusing and overly legalistic language. If reviewers objected that a proposed language modernization changed the meaning or scope of regulatory authority, then the bill drafters reverted to the existing statutory language as a default. Only consensus modernization of the existing language was included in Chapter 160D.

Chapter 160D also includes many modest substantive changes to previous law. These amendments clarify and reform the law without making major policy changes. For example, Chapter 160D reduces confusion by eliminating the 1980s tool of special and conditional use districts, leaving legislative conditional zoning and quasi-judicial special use permits in the statute (and employing uniform terminology for the names of these tools). Form-based zoning districts are explicitly authorized, plan consistency statements are simplified, and required statements of reasonableness for zoning-map amendments are clarified. There are dozens of other consensus reforms in the new law, which are discussed below.

C. Implementation and Transition

Delayed effective date. In order to provide time for the development, consideration, and adoption of necessary amendments to conform local ordinances to this new law, Chapter 160D is not effective until January 1, 2021. All city and all county unified development ordinances, including zoning, subdivision, and other development regulations, will need to be updated by that date to conform to the new law. Many of the needed amendments can be made now, but the authority to adopt a few of the changes will not exist until Chapter 160D is effective.[2]

Incorporation of other statutory amendments. This delayed effective date also allows time for other legislation enacted in 2019[3] to be incorporated into the new Chapter 160D framework during the 2020 legislative session. Just as amendments to the existing statutes incorporated into Chapter 160D that were adopted in the 2015 and 2017 legislative sessions were incorporated into the version of Chapter 160D that was introduced in 2019, changes made by other bills adopted in 2019 will also be incorporated into Chapter 160D before it becomes effective.[4]

A number of the provisions of Part I of S.L. 2019-111 will need to be added to Chapter 160D, as will provisions in the other legislation enacted that affect other development regulations. Many of the provisions of Part I and other 2019 legislation are briefly noted in the discussion below where appropriate. Exactly how these provisions will be incorporated into Chapter 160D will be determined by 2020 legislation.

Effect on prior local acts and charters. G.S 160D-111 provides that Chapter 160D does not amend or repeal charters or local acts in effect when this new law was enacted. Ordinances and individual permits in effect when the law becomes effective do not have to be readopted or reapproved. However, any provisions in local regulations that are inconsistent with Chapter 160D (such as the use of conditional use districts or the reference to special use permits as *conditional use permits*) need to be amended to conform to the new law.

II. Legislative History

A. Statutory Context

Original enactment of enabling statutes. North Carolina's planning and development regulation statutes have evolved over the past century. Statutes authorizing individual planning and development regulations were adopted one by one over the course of the past century. The statutes on building standards date to 1905,[5] the planning statutes date to 1919,[6] and municipal zoning was first authorized in 1923.[7] Over the decades, others were added, such as authorization for housing codes in 1939[8] and

---

2. Examples of ordinance amendments that cannot become effective prior to the effective date of Chapter 160D include the authority for two cities to agree that one of them will exercise exclusive development regulation jurisdiction for an entire parcel that lies partially in each of the jurisdictions (G.S. 160D-203), and the authority to provide that appeals of historic district commissions on certificates of appropriateness go directly to court rather than initially to the board of adjustment (G.S. 160D-947).

3. Other 2019 legislation is described in more detail in Adam Lovelady & David W. Owens, *2019 North Carolina Legislation Related to Planning and Development Regulation*, Plan. & Zoning L. Bull. No. 28 (UNC School of Government, Sept. 2019).

4. S.L. 2019-111, § 2.10.

5. S.L. 1905-506. This law required all cities to designate fire districts, which were to include the principal business area of the city. No new frame or wooden buildings were to be erected there. Construction and fire safety standards were set, building permits required, and provision made for local inspectors to ensure that new construction complied with the building safety standards.

6. S.L. 1919-23.

7. S.L. 1923-250.

8. S.L. 1939-287.

municipal subdivision regulation in 1955.[9] In 1959, many of the city enabling statutes were extended to counties.[10] Municipal extraterritorial jurisdiction was also authorized in 1959. Specialized provisions were added in more recent decades, including open space protection in 1963, historic preservation and landmark protection in 1971,[11] community appearance in 1971, floodplain zoning in 1979, and authority to negotiate and approve development agreements in 2005. In addition to enacting new statutes, the legislature made many individual amendments to these statutes over the decades.

Creation of planning and development regulation articles. The basic statutory framework for county government was first enacted in 1905 and for city government in 1917. In the late 1960s, the General Assembly used a local government study commission to examine and modernize the statutes affecting cities and counties.[12] As part of this effort, the various statutes affecting municipal planning and development regulation were collected as Article 19 of G.S. Chapter 160A when that chapter was created in 1971.[13] The same was done in Article 18 of Chapter 153A when that chapter was created in 1973.[14]

As is the case with Chapter 160D, this effort was intended to provide a more coherent organizational structure for various planning and development regulation statutes. Over the course of the nearly five decades since this framework was created, however, hundreds of amendments have added sections that have obscured the original organizational clarity. Further, these early 1970s laws did not attempt to coordinate administrative, enforcement, or other aspects common to differing regulatory functions.

Beyond this early 1970s collection of related statutes into individual articles within the city and county statutes, there has been no attempt to integrate and consolidate these various separate laws into a coherent whole.

2005 modernization. Prior to the enactment of Chapter 160D, the most significant update to the state's planning and development regulation statutes came in 2005. This effort, initiated by the North Carolina chapter of the American Planning Association, used a legislation development process that was later employed in the Chapter 160D initiative. A nonprofit group with substantial interest and experience in planning and development regulation carefully considered the issues, developed a draft

9. S.L. 1955-1334.

10. County planning boards were first authorized in 1945. S.L. 1945-1040. County zoning and subdivision regulation were authorized in 1959. S.L. 1959-1006 (zoning); S.L. 1959-1007 (subdivision). Several more urban counties had previously been authorized to exercise this authority by local bills.

11. S.L. 1971-884. Winston-Salem, Edenton, Bath, and Halifax secured authorization to require certificates of appropriateness for exterior alterations to historic structures in 1965. Several additional jurisdictions secured approval for similar regulation between 1965 and 1971. S.L 1965-504. Regulations to authorize protection of individual landmark buildings were also enacted in 1971. S.L. 1971-885.

12. The Local Government Study Commission was created by the 1967 General Assembly to conduct a thorough study of the entire local government system in the state. S.L. 1967-Res. 76. Institute of Government faculty members were the principal staff members for the commission. The commission made recommendations for state constitutional amendments regarding local governments in 1969. In the two following legislative sessions, the commission made recommendations for statutory amendments regarding city and county government.

13. S.L. 1971-698. This 1971 recodification was the first such comprehensive revision since 1917. This act recodified significant portions of G.S. Chapter 160 into a new Chapter 160A. It also made numerous amendments and reorganized statutes within the new chapter, just as was done with Chapter 160D.

14. S.L. 1973-822. This law, which created G.S. Chapter 153A, largely aligned county planning and development regulation statutes with the city statutes adopted in 1971 as Chapter 160A. Like Chapter 160D, this law had a delayed effective date in order to allow counties time to amend their ordinances and for the next session of the General Assembly to enact any subsequently identified corrective legislation. It was enacted on May 24, 1973, but was not effective until February 1, 1974.

comprehensive reform bill, and then it engaged all affected interest groups in an intensive review process prior to bill introduction. The principal sponsor of the 2005 legislation in the Senate was Dan Clodfelter, a former member of the Charlotte-Mecklenburg Planning Commission and Charlotte city council. The principal sponsor in the House of Representatives was Lucy Allen, a former mayor of Louisburg and past president of the N.C. League of Municipalities.

The result was the near-unanimous legislative approval of two bills, one making technical and clarifying changes to the statutes[15] and a second modernizing the statutes with more-substantive additions.[16] These two bills focused on reforms to the zoning and subdivision statutes; neither bill attempted to reorganize the overall statutory framework for development regulation statutes. Among the reforms added to the planning and development regulation statutes by these two laws were the following: (1) authorization of purely legislative conditional zoning; (2) a requirement for a plan consistency analysis and statement for all zoning amendments; (3) a requirement for a statement of reasonableness for any spot zoning; (4) allowance of the combination of ordinances into a "unified development ordinance"; (5) authorization of development moratoria and setting a process for adoption of development moratoria; (6) authorization of the use of development agreements and authorization of sketch plans and preliminary plats in subdivision review; (7) clarification of the use of performance guarantees to assure completion of subdivision improvements; (8) allowance for sale of lots after approval of a preliminary plat; and (9) codification of conflict of interest rules for legislative, advisory, and quasi-judicial decisions. The bills also included numerous more-technical reforms, such as requiring a posted notice for rezoning hearings, clarifying how votes are computed when board members have a conflict of interest, and clarifying qualifying zoning protest petitions.

Earlier NCBA reform legislation. Chapter 160D originated as a proposal developed by the Zoning, Planning, and Land Use Law section (ZPLU) of the North Carolina Bar Association (NCBA). In prior years, this group developed several legislative proposals to clarify the state land use law. In each instance, the NCBA proposed reforms that clarified and simplified the law without making major policy changes. These bills were eventually adopted with near-unanimous, bipartisan legislative support.

The first proposal put forward by the ZPLU was a reform of the process for judicial review of quasi-judicial land use decisions. It was first proposed in 2005,[17] again in 2007,[18] and eventually enacted in 2009.[19] This law created G.S. 160A-393, which clarified the rules on filing a petition for writ of certiorari, standing, intervention, the record on appeal, the standard for review, and the decisions the trial court could make.

---

15. S.B. 518, enacted as S.L. 2005-418. The bill was unanimously approved in the Senate and had only a single dissenting vote in the House of Representatives.

16. S.B. 814, enacted as S.L. 2005-426. The bill was approved with a single dissenting vote in the Senate and by a 104–12 majority in the House of Representatives. The two bills are summarized in NORTH CAROLINA LEGISLATION 2005 37–43 (Martha H. Harris ed., UNC School of Government, 2006).

17. S.B. 970. The bill was approved by the Senate but not considered by the House of Representatives. The bill's primary sponsor was Ellie Kinnaird, former mayor of Carrboro. The bill's principal drafter was Mike Brough, Carrboro's town attorney and a founding member of the ZPLU in 2005.

18. S.B. 212. The bill was substantially the same as the 2005 version. The proposal was again approved by the Senate but not considered by the House of Representatives.

19. S.B. 44, enacted as S.L. 2009-421. The bill was unanimously approved in both the House of Representatives and the Senate.

The second reform proposal by the ZPLU was an update of the statute on quasi-judicial land use decision making and boards of adjustment. It was proposed and enacted in 2013 as a revised G.S. 160A-388.[20] This new statute

- codified judicial provisions regarding quasi-judicial decisions;
- clarified a number of statutory process requirements;
- clarified who can make appeals to the board of adjustment and the time period for making an appeal;
- set uniform procedures for notice of hearings and the conduct of the evidentiary hearing;
- explicitly required written decisions to be based on competent, substantial, and material evidence;
- required timely decisions;
- specified how decisions should be delivered; and
- clarified the standards for granting variances.

B. The 160D Proposal

Development of initial proposal. Based on this track record of success with policy-neutral legislation, the NCBA in 2013 embarked on a more audacious undertaking—a complete reorganization and modernization of the entire body of state laws on local planning and development regulation, what is now Article 19 of G.S. Chapter 160A (for cities) and Article 18 of G.S. Chapter 153A (for counties). The objective was to develop a new organizational structure for these statutes that was coherent and easy to follow, allowing seasoned professionals and newcomers to quickly find applicable laws. In addition, the group proposed to edit the entire body of law to secure greater clarity, removing archaic, obsolete, and confusing language and recommending greater uniformity and consistency among the various statutes. Finally, where consensus among the various affected parties was possible, the group sought to incorporate commonsense reforms and solutions to nagging problems and ambiguities in the statutes.

A small drafting committee worked in the summer of 2013 to the fall of 2014 to prepare a draft bill for broader discussion.[21] The initial drafting committee members were attorneys Tom Terrell,[22] LeAnn Nease Brown,[23] Mike Brough,[24] and David Owens,[25] all of whom had been directly involved in drafting the legislative reforms adopted in the previous decade. Robin Currin[26] joined the drafting committee upon Mike Brough's retirement in 2015.

The initial draft of the Chapter 160D proposal was completed in October 2014. It was circulated as a discussion draft to all city and county attorneys, planners, and zoning administrators. Copies were shared with key government and development interest groups—homebuilders, commercial and industrial developers, planners, zoning officials, city and county government associations, attorneys,

---

20. H.B. 276, enacted as S.L. 2013-126. The principal sponsor was Paul "Skip" Stam, a former city attorney. The bill was unanimously approved in both the House of Representatives and the Senate.

21. The drafting committee was initially organized in 2012 to prepare drafts of the bill enacted in 2013 to revise the quasi-judicial statute. That committee continued its statutory reform work with an initial meeting on what became the 160D proposal on June 4, 2013.

22. Partner, Fox Rothschild, Greensboro; former chair, ZPLU.

23. Brown & Bunch, Chapel Hill; former chair, ZPLU; current president, NCBA.

24. Brough Law Firm, Chapel Hill (retired); former chair, ZPLU.

25. Gladys Coates Professor, School of Government, University of North Carolina at Chapel Hill.

26. City attorney, City of Raleigh; former city attorney, City of Asheville; former chair, ZPLU.

state agencies, the Government and Public Sector section of the NCBA, and others. Listservs and web postings were used as well as direct mailings and individual meetings. In all, some 4,000 individuals and organizations were asked to review and comment on the draft. A distribution list for the various editions of the bill, and a list of commenters, appears in Appendix D.

In January 2015, an updated draft bill that responded to these initial reviews was recirculated for review and comment, a process that was repeated in February and again in March. During this period, the proposed bill also went through the NCBA's legislative review process. These multiple reviews resulted in hundreds of edits to the original draft of the bill. Some new ideas were added, and some provisions were dropped when it became clear there was not broad consensus support for a particular idea or that more detailed study and discussion were needed before the law should be amended.

Consideration in 2015 and 2017. The legislation was introduced as House Bill 548 in 2015. The primary sponsors were Paul Stam (a former town attorney who was the lead sponsor of the bill to revise G.S. 160A-388 in 2013), Susie Hamilton (a former planner and past executive director of Wilmington Downtown), Dan Bishop (a former member of the Mecklenburg County Board of Commissioners), and Rob Bryan (chair of the House Judiciary IV Committee). A companion bill was not introduced in the Senate. As the deadline for bills to pass the chamber of introduction approached in April 2015, there was consensus on most of the bill, but the development community still had several unresolved issues. The bill sponsors converted the bill to a study of these issues, with a report to be made in the 2016 session. The expectation was that the remaining issues in contention would be worked out either later in the 2015 session or between the 2015 and 2016 sessions. That did not occur, and no further consideration was given to the bill.

An updated version of the bill was introduced in 2017 as Senate Bill 419. The principal sponsors were Michael Lee (a land use lawyer in Wilmington) and Floyd McKissick (an attorney in Durham who also has a graduate degree in city planning). There was not a companion bill in the House. After further review and modest edits, the Senate passed the bill in April 2017. However, despite the efforts of the Senate sponsors, the House did not consider the bill in either 2017 or 2018.

Enactment in 2019. An updated version of the bill was introduced in 2019 as Senate Bill 422 and House Bill 448. The updated bill incorporated all amendments made to the affected statutes in the 2015 to 2018 period, as well as many of the suggestions made by the many reviewers of earlier drafts of the bill. The principal sponsors of the bill in the Senate were Paul Newton (an attorney from Cabarrus County and president of Duke Energy North Carolina) and Floyd McKissick (who had been a lead sponsor in 2017).[27]

Given the extensive review, vetting, and editing of the legislation in earlier sessions, the bill moved through the 2019 General Assembly with virtually no amendments. The Senate Judiciary Committee, which had several bills affecting this same subject matter under consideration, merged this relatively noncontroversial reorganization bill (Senate Bill 422) with the more controversial set of amendments proposed by the N.C. Home Builders Association (Senate Bill 355) based on the rationale that neither bill should be enacted without the other. Although merged into a single bill (Parts I and II of Senate Bill 355), the individual parts were debated independently throughout the legislative process. As a result, the more controversial Part I was substantially amended as it progressed through the legislative process, while the reorganization bill in Part II was largely unchanged. The Senate passed the

---

27. The House bill was sponsored by Sarah Stevens and Lee Zachary, although there was an early agreement that the Senate members would take the lead on Chapter 160D in 2019. Thus, the House bill was not taken up.

reorganization bill exactly as introduced as Part II of Senate Bill 355. The House also passed the bill as introduced, with only minor technical edits to the telecommunications provisions to conform the bill to existing statutes. The governor signed the legislation on July 11, 2019. It is S.L. 2019-111.

III. Framework for Development Regulations

Chapter 160D clarifies the terminology for development regulations and the types of decisions made pursuant to those regulations. The definitions and distinctions will bring more consistency to regulations and approvals across the state and will reduce unnecessary legal risks and practical confusion.

A. Development Definitions

Article 1 of Chapter 160D provides clarifying definitions for many significant terms and gathers existing definitions that were previously scattered throughout the planning and development regulation statutes. Several are highlighted in this section, and more are set forth in the statute. In addition, definitions limited to specific articles are left within those articles.

The terms *development*, *development approval*, and *development regulations* are broad terms that encompass many specifics. They are also terms used frequently throughout Chapter 160D. The definitions outlined in Article 1 provide a clear scope for each term.

Development. Chapter 160D draws upon prior definitions from G.S. Chapter 113A, Chapter 153A, and Chapter 160A to craft a new definition for *development*, as follows:

> Development. Unless the context clearly indicates otherwise, the term means any of the following:
>   a. The construction, erection, alteration, enlargement, renovation, substantial repair, movement to another site, or demolition of any structure.
>   b. The excavation, grading, filling, clearing, or alteration of land.
>   c. The subdivision of land as defined in G.S. 160D-802.
>   d. The initiation or substantial change in the use of land or the intensity of use of land.[28]

The statute emphasizes that "this definition does not alter the scope of regulatory authority granted" by Chapter 160D.

Development approval. *Development approval* is a flexible term applicable to a range of permits, plats, certificates, and other approvals. A development approval, as defined, is an administrative or quasi-judicial approval. A legislative decision, such as amendments to the ordinance or adoption of conditional zoning, is a legislative act, not a development approval as defined. Types of decisions—administrative, quasi-judicial, and legislative—are discussed more in the next section. Chapter 160D defines development approval as follows:

> Development approval. An administrative or quasi-judicial approval made pursuant to this Chapter that is written and that is required prior to commencing development or undertaking a specific activity, project, or development proposal. Development approvals include, but are not limited to, zoning permits, site plan approvals, special use permits, variances, and certificates of appropriateness. The term also includes all

---

28. G.S. 160D-102.

other regulatory approvals required by regulations adopted pursuant to this Chapter, including plat approvals, permits issued, development agreements[29] entered into, and building permits issued.[30]

Determination. Another term, *determination*, is closely related to, but distinct from, *development approval*. Determination is a "written, final, and binding order, requirement, or determination regarding an administrative decision."[31] Whereas development approvals are the permits and certificates for development to move forward, determinations are the stop work orders and notices of violation to force development to halt. Some decisions may fall in the gray area between development approval and determination. An affirmative determination of vested rights (or nonconforming status) or an interpretation allowing an activity to proceed has characteristics of both development approval and determination. Determinations are discussed more in Chapter 2: Organization and Administration of Development Regulations.

Development regulation. *Development regulation* is a broad term referring to the ordinances, regulations, and codes concerning the use and development of land. This includes zoning and subdivision regulations as well as those pertaining to the State Building Code, housing codes, stormwater control, telecommunications ordinances, and much more. The breadth of these regulatory topics is an important element of the structure and authority outlined in Chapter 160D. The procedures and administrative authority outlined in Chapter 160D apply broadly to all development regulations, not just to zoning and subdivision. *Development regulation* is defined as follows:

> Development regulation. A unified development ordinance, zoning regulation, subdivision regulation, erosion and sedimentation control regulation, floodplain or flood damage prevention regulation, mountain ridge protection regulation, stormwater control regulation, wireless telecommunication facility regulation, historic preservation or landmark regulation, housing code, State Building Code enforcement, or any other regulation adopted pursuant to this Chapter, or a local act or charter that regulates land use or development.[32]

Site plan. The *site plan* is an essential document for development regulations. A technical drawing is used to show compliance with a range of regulatory requirements, from grading and stormwater to parking and building design. Site plans have long been used in administrative approvals, such as zoning and stormwater permits; quasi-judicial decisions, such as special use permits and certificates of appropriateness; and legislative approvals, such as conditional zoning and development agreements. Even so, there has not been a general definition of the term.[33] Chapter 160D defines *site plan* as follows:

> Site plan. A scaled drawing and supporting text showing the relationship between lot lines and the existing or proposed uses, buildings, or structures on the lot. The site plan may include site-specific details such as building areas, building height and floor area, setbacks from lot lines and street rights-of-way, intensities, densities, utility lines

---

29. As adopted by S.L. 2019-111, G.S. 160D-102 includes development agreements in the list of permits that are administrative or quasi-judicial development approvals. G.S. 160D-1005, however, states that development agreements are legislative decisions. This discrepancy will be resolved as a technical correction in future legislative sessions, so "development agreement" may be struck from this definition.

30. G.S. 160D-102.

31. *Id.*

32. *Id.*

33. G.S. 153A-344.1 and 160A-385.1 defined *site-specific development plan* for vested rights purposes, and some local legislation defined and authorized *site plan review*.

and locations, parking, access points, roads, and stormwater control facilities that are depicted to show compliance with all legally required development regulations that are applicable to the project and the site plan review. A site plan approval based solely upon application of objective standards is an administrative decision, and a site plan approval based in whole or in part upon the application of standards involving judgment and discretion is a quasi-judicial decision. A site plan may also be approved as part of a conditional zoning decision.[34]

Additional definitions. Chapter 160D provides additional definitions for specific terms. The definitions for types of approvals and hearings are discussed more below. Other terms are discussed in relevant sections of this book.

In addition to the definitions of Chapter 160D, S.L. 2019-111 (S.B. 355), Section 1.17 added language about certain terms in local zoning and other development regulation ordinances that will be incorporated into Chapter 160D. Within local development regulations, the definitions of specified terms—*building, dwelling, dwelling unit, bedroom,* and *sleeping unit*—may not be inconsistent with definitions in a statute or in a rule adopted by a state agency, including the N.C. Building Code Council.[35]

B. Decision Types

North Carolina case law and statutory provisions have long established three distinct types of development decisions: legislative, quasi-judicial, and administrative. And the type matters. For each development decision, the authority, procedures, and standards depend upon the type of decision. Chapter 160D defines each type of development decision and differentiates between the type of hearing applicable for each. Chapter 160D also provides clarification for and changes to the procedural requirements for each type of decision. Those are discussed further in Chapter 4: Planning and Development Decisions, which includes a section on each type of decision.

Legislative decision. A *legislative decision* is a decision by the governing board to adopt, amend, or repeal an ordinance. The hearings that accompany such decisions are legislative hearings[36] seeking public comment and opinion on the proposed policy change. Legislative hearings are distinguished from hearings on quasi-judicial and administrative decisions, which are focused on evidence and fact-finding. The relevant definitions in Chapter 160D are as follows:

> Legislative decision. The adoption, amendment, or repeal of a regulation under this Chapter or an applicable local act. The term also includes the decision to approve, amend, or rescind a development agreement consistent with the provisions of Article 10 of this Chapter.[37]

---

34. G.S. 160D-102.

35. While other state statutes and rules have other definitions, Section 202 of the 2018 State Building Code provides the following definitions: "BUILDING. Any structure used or intended for supporting or sheltering any use or occupancy." "DWELLING. A building that contains one or two *dwelling units* used, intended or designed to be used, rented, leased, let or hired out to be occupied for living purposes." "DWELLING UNIT. A single unit providing complete, independent living facilities for one or more persons, including permanent provisions for living, sleeping, eating, cooking and sanitation." "SLEEPING UNIT. A room or space in which people sleep, which can also include permanent provisions for living, eating, and either sanitation or kitchen facilities but not both. Such rooms and spaces that are also part of a *dwelling unit* are not sleeping units."

36. For clarity and differentiation, Chapter 160D avoids the term *public hearing* in favor of *legislative hearing, quasi-judicial hearing,* and *administrative hearing.*

37. G.S. 160D-102.

Legislative hearing. A hearing to solicit public comment on a proposed legislative decision.[38]

Quasi-judicial decision. The definition of *quasi-judicial decision* in Chapter 160D is retained from prior law with modest clarifications. One noteworthy change is the addition of certificates of appropriateness for historic preservation regulations to the list of quasi-judicial decisions. This confirms the implication from prior law. Chapter 160D provides a definition of *evidentiary hearing*, reiterating the distinction between hearings for quasi-judicial decisions and hearings for legislative decisions. The relevant definitions in Chapter 160D are as follows:

> Evidentiary hearing. A hearing to gather competent, material, and substantial evidence in order to make findings for a quasi-judicial decision required by a development regulation adopted under this Chapter.[39]

> Quasi-judicial decision. A decision involving the finding of facts regarding a specific application of a development regulation and that requires the exercise of discretion when applying the standards of the regulation. The term includes, but is not limited to, decisions involving variances, special use permits, certificates of appropriateness, and appeals of administrative determinations. Decisions on the approval of subdivision plats and site plans are quasi-judicial in nature if the regulation authorizes a decision-making board to approve or deny the application based not only upon whether the application complies with the specific requirements set forth in the regulation, but also on whether the application complies with one or more generally stated standards requiring a discretionary decision on the findings to be made by the decision-making board.[40]

Administrative decision. An *administrative decision*, sometimes called a *ministerial decision*, is the most common decision in development regulations: zoning permits, notices of violation, ordinance interpretations, and more. Under prior law, these decisions were implied but not defined. The new definitions—and related authorities—clarify the administration powers and procedures for development regulations. Most administrative decisions do not require a hearing. For certain administrative decisions, however, there is an option or requirement for the administrative staff to hold a hearing to gather facts and make determinations. Housing code administration is an example. The applicable terms are defined as follows:

> Administrative decision. Decisions made in the implementation, administration, or enforcement of development regulations that involve the determination of facts and the application of objective standards set forth in this Chapter or local government development regulations. These are sometimes referred to as ministerial decisions or administrative determinations.[41]

> Administrative hearing. A proceeding to gather facts needed to make an administrative decision.[42]

---

38. *Id.*
39. *Id.*
40. *Id.*
41. *Id.*
42. *Id.*

Table 1.1 Land Use Decisions and Hearings

Decision Type	Hearing Type
Legislative	Legislative hearing
Quasi-judicial	Evidentiary hearing
Administrative (or ministerial)	Generally no hearing needed; administrative hearing in some cases

C. Clarifying Site-Specific Approvals

Chapter 160D provides a notable and substantive clarification for the types of site-specific conditional development approvals authorized in North Carolina. Under Chapter 160D, quasi-judicial decisions for a particular use in a district are *special use permits*. Legislative map amendment decisions with site-specific conditions are *conditional zoning*. The two-step decision combining legislative rezoning with a quasi-judicial permit, *conditional use district zoning*, is no longer permitted. This change provides clarity in terminology, reaffirms the role of conditional zoning, and avoids the legal and practical confusion of a combined legislative and quasi-judicial decision.

Quasi-judicial site-specific approvals have been part of the regulatory framework from the earliest days of zoning. Communities have used terms including *conditional use permit*, *special use permit*, and *special exception* for these types of decisions. The varying terminology—and especially the similarity to related terms such as *conditional zoning* and *conditional use district zoning*—was a source of confusion.[43] Chapter 160D establishes that *special use permit* shall be the term used for these quasi-judicial decisions. *Special use permit* is defined as follows:

> Special use permit. A permit issued to authorize development or land uses in a particular zoning district upon presentation of competent, material, and substantial evidence establishing compliance with one or more general standards requiring that judgment and discretion be exercised, as well as compliance with specific standards. The term includes permits previously referred to as conditional use permits or special exceptions.[44]

The concept of special use district zoning or conditional use district zoning was incorporated into the zoning statutes in the 1980s as a work-around to avoid contract zoning when individualized site-specific conditions were deemed to be needed. The conditional use district concept required a concurrent legislative rezoning and quasi-judicial conditional use permit. That concurrent consideration of a legislative decision and a quasi-judicial decision was legally complicated and the source of considerable confusion for local governments, landowners, and neighbors.

Subsequent case law and statutory authority allowed purely legislative conditional zoning in place of the complicated legislative/quasi-judicial conditional use district zoning. The definitions of Chapter 160D confirm that *conditional zoning* is "[a] legislative zoning-map amendment with site-specific conditions incorporated into the zoning-map amendment." As it is no longer needed, the conditional use district zoning process is eliminated by Chapter 160D. The implementation provisions of Chapter

---

43. David W. Owens, *A Conditional What? Clarifying Some Confusing Zoning Terminology*, COATES' CANONS: NC LOC. GOV'T L. blog (Nov. 13, 2012), https://canons.sog.unc.edu/a-conditional-what-clarifying-some-confusing-zoning-terminology/.

44. G.S. 160D-102.

160D address the transition of existing approvals that are inconsistent with the new terminology. Existing conditional use district approvals are converted automatically to conditional zoning. Existing conditional use permits and special exceptions are converted automatically to special use permits.[45]

Limits on conditions. Part I of S.L. 2019-111, which will be incorporated into Chapter 160D, provides that the petitioner for a conditional rezoning must consent in writing to the conditions in order for those conditions to be effective. Unless the petitioner consents in writing, the zoning may not include any conditions or requirements not otherwise authorized by law.[46] Notably, the amended language affirms the authority and flexibility for local governments and petitioners to negotiate appropriate conditions for conditional-zoning approvals. With written consent from the petitioner, such conditions may go beyond the basic zoning authority to address additional fees, design requirements, and other development considerations.

Additionally, Part I of S.L. 2019-111 specifies stricter limits on conditions imposed through special use permits. It provides that special use permit conditions "shall not include requirements for which the [local government] does not have authority under statute to regulate nor requirements for which the courts have held to be unenforceable if imposed directly by the [local government], including, without limitation, taxes, impact fees, building design elements within the scope of subsection (h) of this section, driveway-related improvements in excess of those allowed in G.S. 136-18(29) and G.S. 160A-307, or other unauthorized limitations on the development or use of land." Arguably, design restrictions may still be imposed in compliance with G.S. 153A-340(*l*) and 160A-381(h), which allow design restrictions for commercial and multifamily development, in historic districts, or with written consent from the owner.

---

45. S.L 2019-111, § 2.9(b).

46. "Unless consented to by the petitioner in writing, in the exercise of the authority granted by this section, including the establishment of special or conditional use districts or conditional zoning, a [local government] may not require, enforce, or incorporate into the zoning regulations or permit requirements any condition or requirement not authorized by otherwise applicable law, including, without limitation, taxes, impact fees, building design elements within the scope of G.S. 160A-381(h), driveway-related improvements in excess of those allowed in G.S. 136-18(29) and G.S. 160A-307, or other unauthorized limitations on the development or use of land." S.L. 2019-111, § 1.4; S.L. 2019-111, § 1.5.

2. Organization and Administration of Development Regulations

I. Geographic Jurisdiction

In North Carolina, jurisdiction for planning and development regulation is assigned to cities or counties, with no overlap in authority. Cities have jurisdiction within their corporate limits and may, if proper procedures are followed, have jurisdiction for a defined extraterritorial area immediately surrounding the city.[1] This extraterritorial jurisdiction is generally referred to as the "ETJ" area. Counties have jurisdiction for unincorporated areas that have not been included in a city's corporate limits or extraterritorial area.

This basic allocation of geographic jurisdiction for planning and development regulation is not changed by Chapter 160D.[2] The provisions on city and county geographic jurisdiction are collected into Article 2 of Chapter 160D. The new law will, however, make several modest changes related to jurisdiction.

County authority within a municipal extraterritorial area. Under previous law, when a city establishes extraterritorial planning jurisdiction, the city gains authority to apply all of its land development regulations that are authorized by Article 19 of Chapter 160A of the North Carolina General Statutes (hereinafter G.S.). Conversely, the county loses jurisdiction for all of its development regulations adopted under Article 18 of G.S. Chapter 153A.

A question arises if a city with ETJ elects to extend some, but not all, of its development regulations in the extraterritorial area. For example, a city might apply its zoning and subdivision regulations in the ETJ area but elect to apply its housing code only within the corporate limits. This is legally permissible as there is no mandate in previous law that a city apply all of its development regulations in the extraterritorial area. The statutes say a city may not apply a regulation in the ETJ that it does not apply inside the city, but it does not go on to say that if the regulation is applied in the city it must

---

1. Extraterritorial planning and development regulation jurisdiction is granted to cities by G.S. 160A-360. This authority was initially provided to cities in 1959 (with several cities getting this authority earlier by local legislation). A number of local acts grant additional extraterritorial jurisdiction or, in a few instances, prohibit its use by specified cities.

2. G.S. 153A-342(d) previously allowed a county to zone less than its entire jurisdiction but required each zoned area to have at least 640 acres, at least 10 parcels, and at least 10 separate landowners. G.S. 160D-201(b) authorizes county planning and development regulations in any area not subject to municipal jurisdiction and does not carry forward the minimum size of areas subject to county zoning regulations. This provides additional flexibility to counties with partial-county zoning coverage. While formerly common, only twelve counties had partial-county zoning as of January 2019.

also be applied in the ETJ. However, once the city establishes an ETJ, the county loses its jurisdiction for all county development regulations there, whether or not a comparable city regulation is being applied. So, in the example above, both the city and county may have a housing code, but if the city elects not to apply it in the ETJ, property in the ETJ is subject to neither the city nor the county housing code—the proverbial hole in the doughnut.

Various solutions to this issue were discussed in the Chapter 160D deliberations. One option considered was to require cities to apply all of their development regulation to the ETJ. Another possibility discussed was to automatically apply any county regulation if the city did not extend its comparable regulation. G.S. 160D-202(b) adopts an intermediate approach. It provides that if a city does not extend a particular type of development regulation to the ETJ, then the county may elect to exercise that development regulation in the ETJ. The county is not mandated to do so, but the prohibition of doing so is removed, leaving it to the county's discretion.

As with previous law, the municipal extraterritorial authority is only for development regulations. Cities may not, previously or under Chapter 160D, enforce their general police power ordinances (nuisance lot, junk car, or noise ordinances) in the extraterritorial area.

Notice of ETJ boundary ordinance hearing. Before a city may adopt or expand its ETJ area, it must hold a public hearing and provide mailed notice of the hearing to all property owners in the affected area. G.S. 160D-202(d) amends the mailed notice requirement by stating that it must be sent thirty days prior to the hearing (currently, it is four weeks). However, G.S. 160D-602(a), the provision on mailed notice for the hearing on the proposed municipal zoning for the new ETJ area, provides that one hearing may be held on the ETJ boundary amendment and the proposed zoning, with a single mailed notice provided at least thirty days prior to the hearing.

Hearings in anticipation of jurisdiction shifts. When land is being considered for a shift in jurisdiction from one city or county to another, there are often development proposals for that property involved as well. For example, a landowner in the unincorporated area of the county may petition for annexation by a city and seek to have the property rezoned from a county to a city district at the same time. In fact, such landowners often only want to be annexed if the city is going to approve their proposed development. However, a question arises as to whether the property first would have to be annexed in order for the city to begin to process development applications. Does the city have the legal authority to accept an application and application fees, hold hearings on the application, and otherwise process the application before it has jurisdiction over the land involved?

G.S. 160D-204 answers this question in the affirmative. It provides that a jurisdiction can begin the process of applying its development regulations and may accept and process applications for development in anticipation of a jurisdiction shift. This can only be done after the process to change jurisdiction has been formally proposed. Final decisions on ordinance adoption or on permit applications can only be made after the jurisdiction changes. Acceptance of jurisdiction, adoption of regulations, and decisions on permit applications may be made at the same time and have a common effective date.

Split jurisdiction. City and county jurisdictional boundaries do not have to follow property lines. It is not unusual for part of a parcel of land to be in one jurisdiction and the remainder in another. One part of the parcel may be subject to city development regulations while the remainder is subject to county regulation or the regulations of another city. When this happens, a number of questions arise. Which jurisdiction handles the development regulations? What if the use of the land requires land in the other jurisdiction to meet development standards (such as having a building in Jurisdiction A but the required off-street parking or stormwater management area for the building is located on the same parcel of land but in Jurisdiction B)?

One solution is to change the boundary between the two jurisdictions so that it matches the property boundary. This change is relatively straightforward to accomplish if it is an ETJ boundary being moved. If there are de-annexations or county boundaries involved, however, this process is quite complicated and time-consuming, as such changes literally require an act of the legislature to move the boundary line.

G.S. 160D-203 provides a simple solution. If the landowner and both units of government agree, exclusive planning and development regulation jurisdiction for the entire parcel may be assigned to one jurisdiction. That agreement does not change the jurisdictions' boundary lines, taxation, or any other nonregulatory matter. The agreement on development regulation must be approved by a resolution formally adopted by both governing boards and be recorded with the register of deeds within fourteen days of adoption of the last required resolution.

II. Boards

Chapter 160D collects the statutory provisions regarding boards established for planning and development regulation purposes into a single article. The statutory provisions for the various boards that are authorized—planning boards, boards of adjustment, historic preservation commissions, and so forth—are all placed in Article 3 of Chapter 160D. The statutory provisions for each board then use a common format setting out requirements regarding board composition and duties. In addition to this reorganization, Chapter 160D provides clarification on several points regarding appointed boards.

Planning boards. The potential duties of the planning board are modernized by G.S. 160D-301. The board may prepare, review, maintain, monitor, update, and make recommendations regarding the comprehensive plan and any other plans deemed appropriate. The statute for the first time recognizes that the planning board may be assigned the role of facilitating and coordinating citizen engagement in planning. The responsibility to comment on all zoning text and map amendments is expressly noted. Also, for the first time, the statute provides that the board may provide a preliminary forum for review of and comment on quasi-judicial decisions (discussed in more detail in the section above on quasi-judicial decisions).

Boards of adjustment. G.S. 160D-302 clarifies that the board of adjustment may hear and decide matters under any development regulation, not just the zoning regulation. It also clarifies that if any board other than the board of adjustment is assigned quasi-judicial decision making, then that board must follow all of the quasi-judicial procedures required for those decisions.

Housing appeals board. G.S. 160D-305 explicitly allows a board of adjustment to be assigned the duties of a housing appeals board.

Other advisory boards. G.S. 160D-306 explicitly allows a city or county to establish any additional advisory boards it deems appropriate. Local governments are not limited to the use of boards specifically mentioned in the statutes.

Extraterritorial members of boards. Previous law requires cities with extraterritorial jurisdiction to appoint ETJ members to the planning board and to the board of adjustment. G.S. 160D-307 extends this requirement to historic preservation commissions if there are historic districts or designated landmarks in the ETJ.

G.S. 160D-307 simplifies the calculation of the number of extraterritorial members required and the process for their appointment. The law deletes the confusing formulation that was to be used to calculate the number of ETJ members required, replacing it with a simple directive that the number be proportional based on the population of the ETJ area relative to the population inside the corporate limits of the city. It adds a directive that the population estimate for the ETJ area be updated at least as frequently as every decennial census. The requirement that the county commissioners hold a public hearing on their selection of ETJ appointments is removed, and the time for the commissioners to make an appointment is extended from forty-five days to ninety days (matching the time after which the city governing board can make the appointments if the county commissioners fail to do so).

Rules of procedure. G.S. 160D-308 confirms that each board may have its own detailed rules of procedure. The governing board is authorized to adopt these rules for any or all of its appointed boards. If the governing board does not adopt rules of procedure for its boards, then the individual boards can adopt their own rules. All rules must be consistent with the provisions of Chapter 160D. A copy of the current edition of all rules of procedure must be maintained by the city or county clerk (or by such other officer as set by the ordinance). A copy of the rules must also be posted on the local government's website, if it has one. Each board is also directed to keep minutes of its proceedings.

Oath of office. G.S. 160D-309 requires that board members take an oath of office before starting their duties. Some boards already did so, but this will be mandatory for all board members.[3]

Process for appointments. G.S. 160D-310 clarifies that appointments to all boards are made by the governing board of the city or county unless a statute or ordinance provides otherwise. Thus, some flexibility in appointment authority is retained, but if the governing board wants to delegate any appointment authority, then it must do so by ordinance. This statute also acknowledges that the governing board may establish reasonable procedures to solicit, review, and make appointments. This is intended to encourage an open, clear appointment process but not to mandate the particular details or methods that must be followed.

Conflicts of interest. G.S. 160D-109 collects the provisions on conflicts of interest that apply to boards involved with development regulations. As noted in more detail below,[4] the prohibition on governing board and advisory board members voting on legislative decisions is broadened. In addition to not voting in cases in which the outcome would have a direct, substantial, and readily identifiable financial impact, members are also directed not to vote on legislative decisions involving a family member or someone with whom the member has a close business or associational relationship.

III. Administration of Development Regulations

Under prior law—G.S. Chapter 160A, Article 19 and Chapter 153A, Article 18—there were no provisions for general administration of development regulations. There were administrative provisions for specific activities, such as building code and housing code enforcement. Zoning inspectors were authorized under the provisions for building inspections, which sometimes made zoning and subdivision administrative authority ambiguous. Many of the essential activities of administering development regulations—things like reviewing site plans, interpreting the ordinance, revoking zoning

---

3. G.S. 11-7 provides a standard form for an oath of office. That oath is as follows: "I, _____, do solemnly and sincerely swear that I will support the Constitution of the United States; that I will be faithful and bear true allegiance to the State of North Carolina, and to the constitutional powers and authorities which are or may be established for the government thereof; and that I will endeavor to support, maintain and defend the Constitution of said State, not inconsistent with the Constitution of the United States, to the best of my knowledge and ability; so help me God."

4. See the section on voting and advice on legislative decisions in Chapter 4.

permits, and issuing notices of violation—had to be drawn from implied authority or references in the building inspections statutes.[5] Article 4 of Chapter 160D remedies this problem. The article draws together authority from the old building inspections statutes, formerly scattered enforcement authorities, and newly crafted clarifications to make plain the authority and procedures for administering development regulations in North Carolina.

The administrative provisions outlined in Article 4 of Chapter 160D apply to all development regulations adopted under 160D and any other local ordinance substantially affecting land use and development. Additionally, local governments may apply these administrative provisions to any general police power ordinances.[6] This allowance aligns with the language of general applicability at G.S. 160D-101. As was the case under prior law, development regulations may be consolidated into a unified development ordinance, and such consolidation does not change the scope of the statutory authority for those regulations.[7]

The general administrative provisions are supplemental to any specific administrative provisions for particular development types, such as building code and housing code matters. When there is difference between provisions, the more specific provision controls. So, for example, the mandatory qualification requirements for building code inspectors provided at G.S. 160D-1103 are still required.

A. General Administration

Procedures and fees. Under Chapter 160D, "[t]he local government shall have the authority to enact ordinances, procedures, and fee schedules relating to the administration and the enforcement of this Chapter."[8] Local governments retain the authority to charge "reasonable fees for support, administration, and implementation of programs authorized by this Chapter, and all such fees shall be used for no other purposes."[9] That section also provides for the refund of building inspection fees when required because inspections are performed by an inspector from the state pool of inspectors.

If a court determines a local government illegally imposed a tax or fee for development, then the local government must pay back the amount of the tax plus 6 percent interest. Chapter 160D clarifies that this refund goes to the person who made the payment or as directed by court if the entity entitled payment is no longer in existence.[10]

Staff and duties. Drawing on the language from the prior statutes for building inspections administration, G.S. 160D-402 affirms that local governments may appoint "administrators, inspectors, enforcement officers, planners, technicians, and other staff to develop, administer, and enforce development regulations." Designated administrative staff members may be required to take an oath of office.[11]

Possible duties of administrative staff are provided in a nonexclusive list:[12]

- drafting and implementing plans and development regulations to be adopted pursuant to Chapter 160D;
- determining whether applications for development approvals are complete;

---

5. Homebuilders Ass'n of Charlotte, Inc. v. City of Charlotte, 336 N.C. 37, 442 S.E.2d 45 (1994).
6. G.S. 160D-401.
7. G.S. 160D-103.
8. G.S. 160D-402(b).
9. G.S. 160D-402(d).
10. G.S. 160D-106.
11. G.S. 160D-402(b).
12. *Id.*

- receiving and processing applications for development approvals;
- providing notices of applications and hearings;
- making decisions and determinations regarding development regulation implementation;
- determining whether applications for development approvals meet applicable standards as established by law and local ordinance;
- conducting inspections;
- issuing or denying certificates of compliance or occupancy;
- enforcing development regulations, including issuing notices of violation and orders to correct violations, and recommending bringing judicial actions against actual or threatened violations;
- keeping adequate records; and
- performing any other duties that may be required in order to adequately enforce the laws and development regulations under their jurisdiction.

As was the case under prior law, local governments may establish interlocal agreements to handle staffing and administration of local development regulations.[13]

Decision making. Chapter 160D provides notable clarity to the terminology, standards, and procedures for making decisions related to development regulations. The specifics are discussed in other chapters. Chapter 1 describes terminology and definitions for decision making. Chapter 4 outlines the standards and procedures for decisions, including legislative, quasi-judicial, and administrative decisions.

Conflicts of interest for staff. Chapter 160D clarifies and strengthens the statutory conflict of interest standard applicable to administrative staff. It applies a new conflict of interest standard for when administrative staff handle development approvals. First, a staff person may not make a decision if the outcome would have a direct, substantial, and readily identifiable financial impact on that person. Second, a staff person may not make a decision if that person has a close familial, business, or other associational relationship with the applicant or other person subject to the decision.[14]

Additionally, the conflict of interest standard under the prior building inspections statutes—a standard that already applied to planning and zoning staff—is preserved. This standard prevents staff from having a financial or employment interest in a business with a financial interest in a development in the jurisdiction. An exception is provided for when the staff person is the owner of the property. The conflict standard also prohibits administrative staff from engaging in work that is inconsistent with their duties or the interest of the local government.[15] Local government policy can help clarify those expectations.

---

13. G.S. 160D-402(c).

14. G.S. 160D-109(c). "No staff member shall make a final decision on an administrative decision required by this Chapter if the outcome of that decision would have a direct, substantial, and readily identifiable financial impact on the staff member or if the applicant or other person subject to that decision is a person with whom the staff member has a close familial, business, or other associational relationship. If a staff member has a conflict of interest under this section, the decision shall be assigned to the supervisor of the staff person or such other staff person as may be designated by the development regulation or other ordinance."

15. G.S. 160D-109(c). "No staff member shall be financially interested or employed by a business that is financially interested in a development subject to regulation under this Chapter unless the staff member is the owner of the land or building involved. No staff member or other individual or an employee of a company contracting with a local government to provide staff support shall engage in any work that is inconsistent with his or her duties or with the interest of the local government, as determined by the local government."

The conflict of interest provisions apply to actions for which the administrator is a decision maker, but what about recommendations and advisory decisions? While the statute does not explicitly refer to staff recommendations, it is prudent to apply the same conflict of interest standards as when the administrator is the decision maker. Local policy can clarify that staff persons should not issue a recommendation for a project for which they have a conflict of interest.

B. Enforcement of Development Regulations

Inspections. Chapter 160D makes clear that the permit inspections authority covers all development regulations and provides clarity for the scope.[16] Local administrative staff may inspect work done pursuant to a development approval to ensure it is done in accordance with state law, local law, and the terms of the approval. As was the case under prior law, staff may enter the premises during reasonable hours and upon presenting credentials. Clarifying language in Chapter 160D states that the inspector must have consent or an administrative search warrant to inspect areas that are not open to the public. Inspections remain mandatory for building permits;[17] local governments may choose to inspect work under other development permits.

The inspections provisions of G.S. 160D-403(e) are specifically related to inspections of work pursuant to a development approval (a permit). Enforcement of development regulations, though, is not limited to permit inspections; many violations relate to unpermitted work or unauthorized activities. Administrative staff is authorized by the broad list of general staff duties to make inspections of existing conditions.[18]

Certificates of occupancy. At the conclusion of work under a development approval, a local government may make final inspections to ensure the work complies with applicable laws and the terms of the approval before issuing a certificate of compliance or occupancy.[19] For projects requiring a building permit, a certificate of occupancy is required prior to occupying the structure. For other development approvals, local governments have the option to require a certificate of occupancy or compliance at the conclusion of the work.

Stop work orders. Chapter 160D clarifies and aligns the prior authority for cities and counties to issue stop work orders.[20] The revised authority for stop work orders includes a notable clarification of the scope: Stop work orders may be issued for illegal or dangerous work *or activity*. Stop work orders are not limited to work under a building permit. Rather, they are a general enforcement tool to stop illegal or dangerous development and activities on land. The broadened scope is further clarified by the placement of the stop work authority under the general enforcement statute (G.S. 160D-404) rather than the permitting statute (160D-403).

Under the new provision, if any work or activity subject to a local development regulation or state regulation delegated for local enforcement is undertaken in substantial violation of state or local law or in a manner that endangers life or property, then staff may issue a stop work order for the part of the work or activity creating the violation or hazard. Upon issuance of a stop work order, no further work or activity shall take place in violation of the order. Violation of the order constitutes a Class 1 misdemeanor.

---

16. G.S. 160D-403(e).

17. G.S. 160D-1113.

18. G.S. 160D-402(b). Duties include "conducting inspections; . . . and any other actions that may be required in order adequately to enforce the laws and development regulations under their jurisdiction."

19. G.S. 160D-403(g).

20. G.S. 160D-404(b).

A stop work order must be in writing and directed to the person doing the work or activity. It must state the work or activity to be stopped, the reasons for the order, and the conditions under which the work or activity may be resumed. The stop work order must be delivered by hand delivery, electronic mail, or first-class mail to the holder of the development approval and the property owner, if different. The administrator providing the stop work order shall certify for the file the timing and content of the stop work order, and such certification shall be deemed conclusive in the absence of fraud.

Generally, appeals of stop work orders go to the board of adjustment, but appeals of stop work orders under the building code or housing code follow the appeal provisions for those articles.

Notice of violation. The issuance of a notice of violation (NOV) is an integral tool in development regulation enforcement—and one that was not explicitly spelled out under prior law. Chapter 160D resolves that.

Under G.S. 160D-404(a), an NOV may be issued when it is determined that work or activity is in violation of a local development regulation or development approval, or in violation of a state law delegated to the local government for enforcement (such as building code enforcement or certain environmental permits). The NOV shall be delivered to the holder of the development approval and the landowner, if different. The NOV may also be delivered to the occupant or person undertaking the work or activity. Delivery shall be delivered by personal delivery, electronic delivery, or first-class mail. The NOV may also be posted on the property. The administrator providing the NOV shall certify for the file the timing and content of the NOV, and such certification shall be deemed conclusive in the absence of fraud. Aside from building permits and housing code violations, which have their own appeal processes, NOVs are appealed to the board of adjustment under G.S. 160D-405.

Revocation of development approvals. In addition to other general enforcement actions, a local government may revoke a development approval.[21] A revocation must follow the same notice, review, and decision process as the granting of the development approval. The local government must provide written notice to the permit holder stating the reason for revocation. A local government *shall* revoke a development approval for

- any substantial departure from the approved application, plans, or specifications;
- refusal or failure to comply with the requirements of any applicable local development regulation or any state law delegated to the local government for enforcement purposes in lieu of the state; or
- false statements or misrepresentations made in securing the approval.

If a development approval is mistakenly issued in violation of a state or local law, then the local government *may* revoke the development approval.

Note that revocation is an option in addition to stop work orders and notices of violation. An enforcement official might issue a stop work order or NOV as an immediate administrative action and then go through a full revocation process if the owner fails to take corrective action.

A revocation by a staff person may be appealed as an administrative decision under G.S. 160D-405, including applicable provisions on stays of enforcement.

Separate sections have specific provisions for the revocation of development agreements[22] and building permits.[23]

---

21. G.S. 160D-403(f).
22. G.S. 160D-1008.
23. G.S. 160D-1115.

General enforcement. As authorized under prior law, Chapter 160D continues the general enforcement of development regulations.[24] Development regulations may be enforced under general ordinance enforcement authority outlined at G.S. 160A-175 and 153A-123. That includes civil penalties, fines, court-ordered action, and treating the violation as a misdemeanor. Additionally, a local government may institute "appropriate action or proceedings" to prevent work or activity in violation of development regulations.

Historic preservation enforcement. Enforcement authority previously outlined under the historic preservation statutes is now codified with the general enforcement authority.[25] For properties designated as local historic landmarks or properties in a local historic district, the local government, the local historic preservation commission, or a party aggrieved "may institute any appropriate action or proceeding" to prevent an unlawful demolition (by neglect or otherwise), destruction, alteration, or other illegal act. The other general enforcement authorities are also available for enforcement of historic preservation requirements.

Statute of limitations. A prior legislative change continues to apply to enforcement of development regulations. S.L. 2017-10 amended G.S. 1-51 and 1-49 to establish statutes of limitation for bringing legal action to enforce a development regulation. The details are described in a blog on the topic,[26] but the short summary is as follows: A local government has five years to bring court action starting when "[t]he facts constituting the violation are known to the governing body, an agent, or an employee of the unit of local government" or when "[t]he violation can be determined from the public record of the unit of local government." Additionally, the local government has seven years to bring a court action starting when "[t]he violation is apparent from a public right-of-way" or when "[t]he violation is in plain view from a place to which the public is invited."

---

24. G.S. 160D-404(c).
25. G.S. 160D-404(c)(3).
26. Adam Lovelady, *Tick Tock! The Clock Is Now Running for Zoning Enforcement*, COATES' CANONS: NC LOC. GOV'T L. blog (Sept 26, 2017), https://canons.sog.unc.edu/tick-tock-the-clock-is-now-running-for-zoning-enforcement/.

3. Substance of Development Regulations

I. Substance of Zoning Regulations

A. Exactions and Zoning

An exaction is a condition upon a development approval for the private developer to provide to the public some property, improvement, or fee in order to address the community impacts of the project. Chapter 160D of the North Carolina General Statutes (hereinafter G.S.) clarifies the authority for exactions relating to zoning decisions, making it parallel to the explicit authority under prior law for subdivision ordinances. G.S. 160D-702 provides that "[w]here appropriate, a zoning regulation may include requirements that street and utility rights-of-way be dedicated to the public, that provision be made of recreational space and facilities, and that performance guarantees be provided, all to the same extent and with the same limitations as provided for in G.S. 160D-804."

Under prior law the statutes had a patchwork of exaction authority. Statutes authorizing subdivision regulations allowed broad exactions and performance guarantees. Statutes authorizing special use permits and conditional zoning had distinct exaction authority. Statutes for special use permits had language similar to the authority for subdivisions concerning streets, utilities, and recreation space. Conditional zoning approvals could require reasonable conditions to address the impacts of development. Authority for exactions for administrative approvals arguably was implied through the general regulatory authority and related provisions such as driveway permits, but there was ambiguity about the scope of exaction authority.

This old statutory framework resulted in confusion and uncertainty in two respects. First, do modest differences in terminology create legal differences in the scope of authority for exactions required under zoning approvals as distinct from subdivision approvals? Second, is there a difference between the scope of authority for exactions for different types of zoning approvals, such as those required for a site plan approval versus a special use permit approval or a conditional zoning?

G.S. 160D-702(a) simplifies and clarifies. Using the prior language for special use permit exactions as a starting point, Chapter 160D authorizes common exactions for all types of zoning approvals. Thus the same basic exaction authority applies for conditional rezonings, special use permits, and site plan approvals: "[w]here appropriate, a zoning regulation may include requirements that street and utility rights-of-way be dedicated to the public, that provision be made of recreational space and facilities, and that performance guarantees be provided, all to the same extent and with the same limitations as provided for in G.S. 160D-804." Other exactions may be possible for conditional rezonings and special use permits with written consent from the applicant. Additionally, Chapter 160D makes the authority parallel to the subdivision authority ("to the same extent and with the same limitations as provided for" subdivisions).[1]

B. Maps

Chapter 160D provides that duly adopted zoning maps must be maintained for public inspection by the local government clerk or another office specified by the development regulation.[2] The local government must also maintain for public inspection the currently effective version of any map incorporated by reference (an option discussed more below). This new map recordkeeping provision aligns with similar requirements for county and municipal clerks to maintain township and municipal maps[3] and to maintain incorporated technical codes.[4] Current and prior maps may be maintained in a paper or digital format approved by the local government. As has been established in case law, local governments must maintain current *and* past zoning maps.[5]

A copy of a map is admissible as evidence in a legal proceeding when the copy is certified by the local government clerk in accordance with G.S. 153A-50 or 160A-79.[6]

Development regulations may incorporate certain maps by reference, including flood insurance rate maps (FIRMs), watershed boundary maps, and other maps officially adopted by state or federal agencies. The ordinance may incorporate a specific map (the 2017 version, for example) or the most recent officially adopted version of the map. It was already the case that G.S. 153A-47 and 160A-76 allowed incorporation by reference into local ordinances "any published technical code or any standards or regulation promulgated by any public agency." This new provision of Chapter 160D clarifies that maps officially adopted by state or federal agencies, including approved updates to those maps, can be incorporated by reference into local development regulations.

This provision to permit incorporation of updated maps is especially notable for floodplain maps. Local government flood regulations must use state and federally approved flood hazard delineations. And local governments must amend their local flood hazard ordinances within six months of the date of the federal final determination for revised maps. Prior to final determination, the FIRM has gone through significant review and public comment. Once approved, local governments must adopt FIRMs without amendment. Thus, if a local government is required to go through the full zoning-map amendment process to incorporate the FIRM, then it is going through a costly process for a map that is already substantially vetted and cannot be amended.

The provision in Chapter 160D allows (but does not require) updated flood hazard delineations to be automatically incorporated into local ordinances, preventing inadvertent use of outdated and inaccurate maps or zoning district delineations. Chapter 160D also confirms that when zoning district boundaries are based upon incorporated maps, the local ordinance may provide that the zoning

---

1. While G.S. 160D-702 provides that exactions and performance guarantees under zoning authority are authorized "all to the same extent and with the same limitations" as for plat approvals, some modest ambiguity remains, as the simplified list of types and purposes of exactions in G.S. 160D-702(a) and the more detailed provisions in 160D-804 do not match exactly.
2. G.S. 160D-105.
3. G.S. 153A-19, 160A-22.
4. G.S. 153A-47, 160A-76.
5. Shearl v. Town of Highlands, 236 N.C. App. 113, 762 S.E.2d 877 (2014).
6. G.S. 160D-105(c).

district boundaries are automatically amended to remain consistent with the incorporated map, provided the clerk maintains the incorporated map for public inspection. This saves time and money to allow incorporation by reference without any impact on timely public input.

C. Zoning Districts

Eliminate conditional use district zoning. Understanding the difference between conditional zoning, conditional use districts, and conditional use permits has long been a major source of confusion in North Carolina zoning law. The fact that three very different types of decisions, with significantly different procedural requirements, have such similar names has befuddled elected officials, board members, zoning staff, and land use lawyers for decades.

Chapter 160D adopts several measures to reduce this confusion. One is nomenclature. As discussed in Section III of Chapter 2, "Framework for Development Regulations," the term *conditional zoning* is applied exclusively to legislative decisions, and the term *special use permit* is the exclusive term for quasi-judicial decisions (removing further use of the term *conditional use permit*). A more substantive change is elimination of authority to have conditional use district zoning.

Conditional use districts were created in North Carolina zoning statutes in the 1980s as a way to avoid illegal contract zoning. At that time, purely legislative conditional zoning was not allowed by the state's statutes or case law. Conditional use districts were an ingenious way around this prohibition. The concept was that a parcel would be rezoned to a new zoning district that had no permitted uses at all—only conditional uses. The standard practice was to use a conventional district but make all of its permitted uses conditional uses in a parallel conditional use district. For example, a highway business district might have twenty permitted uses. The highway business conditional district would have those same twenty uses allowed, but none of them would be permitted by right and all of them would be subject to getting a conditional use permit. Concurrently with a rezoning to the conditional use district, the local government would consider a conditional use permit application for the desired project. All of the site-specific conditions for development would be placed on the conditional use permit, thus avoiding legal problems that would have arisen with conditions on the rezoning itself. While this practice was sanctioned by the courts and eventually written into the statutes, it is a cumbersome process rife with opportunities for legal missteps. Concurrently making a legislative rezoning and a quasi-judicial permit decision, which have very different legal process requirements, is difficult at best. Despite the cumbersome process, most of the state's more populous jurisdictions adopted this process in the 1980s.

In 2001 and 2002, courts held that purely legislative conditional zoning was legal in North Carolina.[7] The authority to adopt legislative conditional zoning was then added to the state's zoning statutes in 2005. However, the authority to use conditional use district zoning was left in the statutes. While some cities and counties that had adopted conditional use district zoning in the 1980s and 1990s amended their ordinances to shift to purely legislative conditional zoning, other jurisdictions retained the hybrid legislative/quasi-judicial conditional use districts.

---

7. Massey v. City of Charlotte, 145 N.C. App. 345, 550 S.E.2d 838 (finding statutory authority for conditional zoning), *review denied*, 354 N.C. 219, 554 S.E.2d 343 (2001); Summers v. City of Charlotte, 149 N.C. App. 509, 562 S.E.2d 18 (finding conditional zoning to be constitutional), *review denied*, 355 N.C. 758, 566 S.E.2d 482 (2002).

G.S. 160D-703 simplifies matters and promotes greater uniformity around the state by eliminating the authority for conditional use districts. A zoning ordinance may have legislative conditional zoning. It may also have quasi-judicial special use permits. But it may no longer combine the two into one process and decision.

Section 2.9(b) of S.L. 2019-111 addresses the transition for existing conditional use districts. Any conditional use district or special use district in effect on January 1, 2021, becomes a conditional district. Any special or conditional use permit issued as part of those approvals remains valid and is deemed a special use permit after that date.

Allow form-based codes. In the past decade, several North Carolina jurisdictions have amended their zoning regulations to focus on the physical form of proposed development rather than on the proposed use of the land. A "form-based" code typically addresses the form and mass of buildings and the scale and types of streets and blocks. Building heights, building placement, the design of building fronts, and the relation of buildings to streets, sidewalks, and public open space become the focus of the regulation, as opposed to the focus on the use of land and buildings that is typical of traditional zoning regulation. A form-based code can be incorporated within a more traditional use-based zoning code, such as a form-based overlay district for an area or street corridor or a form-based district for parts of the jurisdiction and traditional districts for other areas. In a 2018 survey of all North Carolina cities and counties, nearly 30 percent of the responding jurisdictions reported some use of form-based codes.

Most aspects of a form-based code are within the expressly authorized scope of zoning regulations, which currently authorize regulation of the height and size of buildings, the location of buildings and structures, and the size of open spaces. But there have been some questions as to whether North Carolina cities and counties could adopt a form-based zoning regulation or zoning district. Chapter 160D confirms that local governments have this authority. G.S. 160D-703(a)(3) authorizes use of form-based zoning districts that "address the physical form, mass, and density of structures, public spaces, and streetscapes."

Even though this provision clarifies that use of form-based standards in a zoning regulation is permissible, it is important to remember that Chapter 160D does not remove the statutory limits adopted in 2015 that limit regulation of "building design elements" for structures subject to the one- and two-family residential building code. Those limits, which are relocated to G.S. 160D-702(b), prohibit zoning regulation of exterior building color, type or style of exterior cladding material, and other design elements for these residential structures. Chapter 160D continues to provide exceptions if the design standards are consented to as part of a zoning approval. Design standards agreed to by the owners of all affected property can still be incorporated into conditional zoning, special use permits, or development agreements. Also, as in prior law, design standards for residential structures are also allowed in historic district and floodplain regulations. In addition to these limits on regulation of residential building design, prohibition of zoning regulation of the minimum square footage of structures subject to the one- and two-family building code that was adopted in 2019[8] will be incorporated into Chapter 160D before its effective date.

---

8. S.L. 2019-174.

D. Zoning Standards

Allow administrative minor modifications of prior approvals. Chapter 160D provides significant procedural efficiency by explicitly authorizing administrative minor modifications for legislative conditional zoning, quasi-judicial special use permits, and other development approvals.[9]

The number of local land use decisions, along with the substantive and procedural complexity of those decisions, has created administrative challenges for handling amendments and revisions. Under prior law, any change to a site plan or condition had to go through the full relevant approval process. Once a development was approved, the standards for that development were set. Even a modest change would require a substantial process.

Consider legislative conditional zoning. Many local governments have incorporated conditional zoning in their development regulations. In a 2018 School of Government survey of all cities and counties in the state, over half of the responding jurisdictions reported that they use conditional zoning. The practice is particularly common in jurisdictions with higher populations. Over 75 percent of cities with populations of more than 25,000 use conditional zoning. Commonly in more populous cities well over half of all rezonings in a given year are now conditional zoning.

Given this high use of conditional zoning, the question increasingly arises as to how the standards for development in a conditional zone are amended. Because the development standards are part of the zoning ordinance itself, any amendment is legally a zoning-text amendment. Amending the site plan that is a part of a conditional zoning amendment; adjusting the setback, buffer, or parking requirements; or modifying landscaping conditions would all require a zoning-text amendment no matter how modest the scale of the proposed amendment.[10] Under previous law, each adjustment is a zoning-text amendment that requires the same public notice, hearing, planning board review, and governing board action as any other zoning amendment.

The demand for tweaks in a rapidly increasing number of conditional zoning approvals threatens to impose a substantial burden on both landowners and local governments. G.S. 160D-703(b) addresses this concern by giving local governments the option of processing minor amendments administratively. To use this option, the ordinance itself must define what constitutes a "minor modification." For example, it could allow up to X percent change in a dimensional requirement. A minor modification cannot include a change in permitted uses or in the density of the overall development. Once defined, staff can be authorized to approve minor modifications administratively. Any other modification must follow the same process for approval as is required for a zoning-map amendment. Also, if the conditional zoning applies to multiple parcels of property, the conditions may be modified for individual parcels without the necessity of obtaining the consent of all property owners within the conditional zoning (but in those instances the modification will only apply to the parcels whose owners consent).

Allow zoning standards that apply jurisdiction-wide. A question occasionally arises as to whether zoning regulations can include standards that apply jurisdiction-wide in addition to standards that apply in specific zoning districts. For example, some jurisdictions have proposed requiring a uniform setback for new development from all perennial streams, no matter the zoning district in which the stream flows. G.S. 160D-703(d) expressly authorizes this practice.

---

9. G.S. 160D-703(b), -705(c), -430(d).

10. *See, e.g.,* McDowell v. Randolph Cty., ___ N.C. App. ___, 808 S.E.2d 513 (2017) (amendment of site plan for prior conditional zoning is a zoning-text amendment and a legislative decision).

Development in navigable waters. Counties currently have zoning authority to regulate development over navigable waters, including floating homes. The municipal statute is silent on this issue. G.S. 160D-702(a) makes this authority uniform by providing that all local governments may regulate development over estuarine and navigable waters owned by the state.

Temporary uses. The pending 2019 Regulatory Reform Act creates G.S. 160A-383.6 (and 153A-341.4) and would allow, but not require, cities and counties to adopt regulations to permit temporary-event venues.[11] The event may be considered an accessory use in any zoning district. The approval is not to be considered a zoning-map amendment, nor can a special use permit be required. The statute specifies that if these venues are permitted, then the ordinance is to set forth the zoning districts where they are allowed, the permit process to be followed, the criteria for approval of event permits, the types of events that qualify, the duration allowed for the events, the venue's capacity limits, and the permit fee to be charged. The permit fee is capped at $100 for the initial permit and $50 for an annual renewal. A site inspection is required, and the N.C. Building Code Council is directed to prepare an inspection checklist for use by cities and counties. The site inspection must address the general structural stability of the venue, its fire safety, and whether it has sufficient toilet capacity. A building permit under the State Building Code is not required for the construction, installation, repair, replacement, or alteration of a temporary-event venue, but the local approval may require reasonable measures to address any safety or public-health concerns identified by the local inspection.

II. Substance of Additional Development Regulations

A. Moratoria

The authority and limits for development moratoria are carried over, with little change, to G.S. 160D-107 from the prior statute at G.S. 153A-340 and 160A-381. One notable clarification is provided. A moratorium does not affect rights established under the permit choice rule outlined at G.S. 160D-108.

B. Subdivision Regulations

The subdivision enabling statute is relocated to Article 8 of Chapter 160D. The sections within Article 8 are reordered for a more logical flow. Also, some of the sections are reorganized for clarity; for example, the provisions related to exactions in G.S. 160D-804 are grouped by purpose (transportation and utilities, recreation areas and open space, community service facilities, and school sites). The scope of exaction authority is, however, unchanged from previous law. Recent legislative changes, such as the 2017 requirement for expedited review for certain minor plats,[12] are incorporated into Chapter 160D.

---

11. A *temporary event* is defined as an event lasting no more than seventy-two hours. Temporary events can be public or private entertainment events, educational events, marketing events, meetings, sales, trade shows, or any other events that an ordinance might address. Only one temporary event may be allowed on a parcel at one time, and no more than twenty-four temporary events may be conducted on a parcel in a calendar year.

12. S.L. 2017-10; *See also* Adam Lovelady, *Subdivision Legislation: An Old Exemption and a New Expedited Review*, Coates' Canons: N.C. Loc. Gov't L. blog (June 13, 2017), https://canons.sog.unc.edu/subdivision-legislation-old-exemption-new-expedited-review/.

S.L. 2019-79 (Senate Bill 313) amended prior statutes—and will be incorporated into Chapter 160D—to further clarify and limit the scope of performance guarantees. The discussion below outlines some of the existing parameters of the law and highlights the recent additions. Performance guarantees allow a developer to obtain final subdivision plat approval and begin selling lots before the required infrastructure for the development is complete. The performance guarantee is a financial commitment from the developer to ensure that the local government will have funds available to complete the required infrastructure in the event that the developer fails to do so. The authority for performance guarantees has been refined by legislation and litigation over the last decade.

Completion, not maintenance. As was already the law, performance guarantees are only for completion of required infrastructure, not repairs or maintenance after completion.

Parties with rights. As previously required, only three parties may have or claim rights under a performance guarantee: the local government to whom the guarantee is provided, the developer, and the entity issuing the financial instrument. Specifically excluded from that list are purchasers of the lots in the subdivision, future developers who may acquire the development, and other local governments who may get jurisdiction over the development (through annexation or adjustment of extraterritorial jurisdiction). In the event of a transition in the development—a change in ownership or jurisdiction—new guarantees may be needed to ensure that the proper parties are named.

Type of financial instrument. As was the case under prior law, the developer gets to elect the type of performance guarantee from the following menu of options:

- a surety bond issued by any company authorized to do business in North Carolina,
- a letter of credit issued by any financial institution licensed to do business in North Carolina, or
- another form of guarantee that provides equivalent security to a surety bond or letter of credit.

Amount. Performance guarantees must not exceed 125 percent of the reasonably estimated cost to complete the improvements. The local government may determine the estimate or use a cost estimate determined by the developer. Where applicable, costs should be based on unit pricing. The additional 25 percent over the estimated cost is for inflation and administrative costs. Any extension or new guarantees issued also must not exceed 125 percent of the reasonably estimated cost to complete remaining improvements.

Timing for issuance. The local government may determine whether a performance guarantee must be provided at the time of plat recordation or at a time subsequent to plat recordation.

Multiple guarantees. A developer may elect to post only one performance guarantee for a development project rather than multiple guarantees for different types of infrastructure. But the local government may still require separate guarantees for erosion- and stormwater-control measures.

Duration. The initial term of the performance guarantee is one year unless the developer elects a longer term. Moreover, when the financial instrument is a bond, the completion date for the bonded obligation is one year from the date the bond is issued, unless the developer elects a longer term.

Extension. The developer must make reasonable, good-faith progress toward completion of the required improvements, but if the performance guarantee is likely to expire before completion of the improvements, then the developer must secure an extension on the guarantee or a new guarantee. The extension (or new guarantee) must be in an amount based only on the remaining improvements and only for the duration necessary to complete the remaining improvements.

Release. Once the improvements are built to the local government specifications or accepted by the local government, the local government must release the performance guarantee. Letters of credit and escrowed funds must be returned. In the case of performance bonds, the local government must provide written acknowledgment that the improvements are complete. There is no specification about the frequency of requests for such release.

C. Regulation of Particular Land Uses and Particular Areas

Article 9 of Chapter 160D collects specialized statutory provisions that deal with local land development regulation of particular land uses and particular land areas. Some of these statutes were previously included in Article 18 of G.S. Chapter 153A and Article 19 of G.S. Chapter 160A, but others were scattered throughout the G.S. Pulling them together in a single chapter is intended to make the statutes more user-friendly and ensure that these individual statutory requirements are not overlooked. For the most part, the substance of the provisions, other than relocation and minor clarifications, is unchanged. Some modifications promote greater uniformity across the state, such as creating a single process to be used by cities and counties of all population sizes or making a provision that has applied only to specified cities applicable to all local governments.

Agricultural uses. Chapter 160D retains the long-standing policy choice in North Carolina statutes that bona fide farm uses are exempt from county zoning but not from city zoning. Chapter 160D simplifies the provision regarding regulation of farms in municipal ETJ areas. The previous statute exempted those lands from all municipal development regulation jurisdiction. G.S. 160D-903(c) amends this to more simply and directly provide that bona fide farming activities in the municipal ETJ are exempt from city zoning to the same extent they would be exempt from county zoning. This section also extends statewide the provision on municipal authority to exempt accessory farm buildings from zoning.

The pending 2019 Farm Act, Senate Bill 315, amends G.S. 99E-30(a) and 153A-340(b)(2a) to expand the range of uses that can be considered agritourism on a qualified farm. It adds hunting, fishing, shooting sports, and equestrian activities to agritourism uses.[13] The Farm Act also provides that cities and counties may not require regulatory approval (other than health and safety rules) for a business that provides on-premise or off-premise catering from a bona fide farm.

Manufactured homes. G.S. 160D-909 codifies prior case law holding that a city or county may not exclude manufactured homes from its entire zoning jurisdiction based on the age of the home.

Historic preservation. G.S. 160D-947 makes several clarifying amendments regarding certificates of appropriateness required for the alteration or demolition of landmarks and structures in designated historic districts.

The term "guidelines" in G.S. 160D-947(c) regarding new construction, alterations, moving, and demolition of structures is replaced with the term "standards" to guide the determinations of congruency. The intent is to clarify that these are not suggestions or advice but binding, mandatory standards for decision. This section also promotes uniformity and clarity by replacing the specific hearing and notice requirements for certificates of appropriateness with a declaration that these are quasi-judicial decisions and the procedural requirements of G.S. 160D-406 are to be followed, thus creating a uniform process for all local government quasi-judicial development regulation decisions.

Chapter 160D gives local governments a new option for handling appeals of decisions on certificates of appropriateness. Previous law requires that an appeal of a decision of a historic district commission

---

13. To qualify as agritourism for zoning purposes, a shooting range must be in a county with a population less than 110,000 in the last census and comply with guidelines for design and site evaluation set by the Wildlife Resources Commission. The statute requires the full board of county commissioners to vote on whether the shooting range meets the Wildlife Resources Commission guidelines.

must first go to the board of adjustment, and then the decision of the board of adjustment can be appealed to court. The board of adjustment does not conduct a new hearing on these appeals and is only reviewing questions of law. This limited and legalistic role for a lay board of adjustment often proves problematic for both the applicant and the local government. G.S. 160D-947(e) allows a local government to retain this process, but it gives cities and counties the option of eliminating board of adjustment review and having appeals of decisions on certificates of appropriateness go directly to superior court, as is the case with appeals of all other quasi-judicial development regulation decisions.

D. Development Agreements

The statute on development agreements is relocated to Article 10 of Chapter 160D. Several modest clarifications and simplifications are made to the statute.

Parties. Previous law allows development agreements to be entered into by "local governments and agencies." This has prompted some confusion as to whether local agencies, such as a water and sewer authority, could enter into development agreements. G.S. 160D-1001(b) clarifies this by deleting the term "agencies," confirming that only cities and counties may enter these agreements. G.S. 160D-1006(b) allows a local or regional utility authority to be a party to the agreement, which is often useful if the agreement includes cost-sharing and timing agreements on provision of water and sewer services, but it cannot enter into a development agreement independently of a city or county.

Regulation and plan consistency. G.S. 160D-1001(d) confirms that the development approved in a development agreement must be consistent with the development regulations in effect at the time of the agreement. But because comprehensive plans are advisory rather than having independent regulatory effect, the requirement that the development also be consistent with the comprehensive plan is removed. G.S. 160D-1003(b) specifically allows a development agreement to be considered concurrently with a zoning-text or map amendment, subdivision plat, or site plan affecting the property and the development allowed upon it. This section also recognizes the increasingly common practice of using a development agreement and conditional zoning together, with the development agreement being incorporated into the conditional zoning. It provides that in this scenario, in the event of the developer's subsequent bankruptcy, the development agreement is considered a part of the development regulation, not an individual permit subject to bankruptcy modification.

Notice and hearing. The previous statutes state that a "public hearing" is required prior to local government approval of a development agreement. G.S. 160D-1005 clarifies that this is a legislative hearing, not a quasi-judicial hearing, and requires the same published, mailed, and posted notice for the hearing that is required for a zoning-map-amendment hearing.

Mandated contents of agreement. G.S. 160D-1006 simplifies the mandated contents of a development agreement. It removes the requirement to list all permits that will be required for the development. It allows, but no longer mandates, inclusion of a schedule for the development.

Mitigation measures and provision of facilities. One of the critical features of many development agreements, in addition to locking in regulatory requirements for the duration of the development, are agreements on what infrastructure and other public improvements will be made, when they will be provided, and how they will be paid for. Developers may offer to provide more in the way of public facilities than could be required as a mandatory exaction under development regulations. For example, the developer may offer to donate land for a school site, contribute more parkland than regulations require, or pay for transportation improvements that will serve more than the development being approved. G.S. 160D-1006(d) clarifies that as long as these provisions are mutually agreed to by the local government and the developer, they can be included in the agreement. However, if terms for provision of facilities and their funding exceed that which could be mandated, then those terms must be expressly listed in the agreement. Also, the agreement may not include a tax or impact fee not otherwise authorized by law.

Enforcement. The previous statute defines what constitutes a breach of a development agreement and allows the agreement to be terminated in the event of a breach. G.S. 160D-108 adds additional enforcement provisions. It allows an ordinance setting the procedures for development agreements or an individual development agreement to specify the penalties for a breach of the agreement. It also allows either party, the local government or the developer, to bring suit seeking an injunction to enforce the terms of the agreement.

Recordation and permitting. G.S. 160D-1011 retains the requirement that development agreements must be recorded with the register of deeds. It clarifies that the fourteen-day deadline for recordation runs from the execution of the agreement, not the vote of the governing board to approve it. It also clarifies that no development permits for work under the agreement may be issued until the agreement is recorded.

E. Building and Housing Codes

Statutory provisions on local government enforcement of the State Building Code and provisions for addressing dangerous and unsafe buildings are relocated to Article 11 of Chapter 160D.[14] Statutory provisions on local housing codes are relocated to Article 12 of Chapter 160D. For the most part, these articles contain very few amendments to the previous statutory provisions for building and housing codes. There are a few clarifying and simplifying amendments.

Periodic inspections. In 2011, the General Assembly placed limits on periodic inspection of residential properties, largely in reaction to residential rental registration and inspection programs initiated by Raleigh and several other cities. This statute, G.S. 153A-364 and 160A-424, was placed in the building code part of the statutes even though it dealt with existing housing rather than new construction. Chapter 160D clarifies matters by relocating this section, G.S. 160D-1207, to the housing code article rather than the building code article. A more general provision allowing periodic inspection of all buildings, not just residential ones, for unsafe, unsanitary, or hazardous conditions, remains in the building code article as G.S. 160D-1117.

Uniform process for abandonment of intent to repair. After a dilapidated residential structure has been ordered vacated and closed, previous law allows a local government to take steps to require demolition of the structure if timely repairs are not made, thereby improving public safety and preventing boarded-up abandoned buildings from harming neighboring properties. The previous statute had multiple procedures that local governments were required to follow to determine the owner's intent to repair the abandoned structure and whether demolition should be required. G.S. 160D-1203(6) simplifies this determination by providing a uniform process, which was previously required for large population municipalities, for all local governments.

---

14. G.S. 160A-439.1, dealing with receivership for vacant buildings, was created by S.L. 2018-65. It was inadvertently omitted when the draft bill for Chapter 160D was updated for 2019 introduction. It is to be added to Chapter 160D in 2020.

F. Specialized Development Regulations

In 1941, a time when no counties and few small towns had zoning ordinances, the General Assembly enacted a Model Airport Zoning Act, now codified as Article 4 of G.S. Chapter 63. This statute allowed those cities and counties without zoning to adopt regulations pertaining to land uses and the height of structures and trees that could affect airport operations. Several of these airport zoning regulations are still in effect. Sections 2.5(c) through 2.5(g) of S.L. 2019-111 retain this article in Chapter 63, but they replace its specific procedural, enforcement, variance, and judicial review provisions with requirements to follow the provisions of Chapter 160D. This ensures uniform provisions for all development regulations.

Additional subsections of Section 1.5 of S.L. 2019-111 make similar conforming amendments to statutes on floodplain zoning, sanitary district zoning, water supply watershed regulation, and mountain ridge protection ordinances.

The provisions in Article 19 of Chapter 160A relative to open space acquisition, applicable to both cities and counties, were relocated to Article 13 of Chapter 160D without substantive amendment. Similarly, the provisions from G.S. 160A-456 and 153A-376 regarding community development and redevelopment and the provisions of G.S. 160A-459.1 and 153A-455 regarding financing energy improvements were also relocated to Article 13 of Chapter 160D without substantive amendment.

4. Planning and Development Decisions

I. Planning

Under Chapter 160D, a local government must have an adopted comprehensive plan in order to have zoning in the jurisdiction. Article 5 outlines elements that may be included in a comprehensive plan, describes the approval process for comprehensive plans, and confirms that the plans remain advisory.

A. Planning Requirement

Since zoning was first authorized in the North Carolina statutes, the state law called for zoning to be "in accordance with a comprehensive plan."[1] North Carolina courts, though, interpreted that to require a systematic approach to the zoning regulations, not a formal comprehensive plan document.[2] Since 1974, the Coastal Area Management Act (CAMA) has mandated land use plans for local governments along North Carolina's coast, and other state and federal funding and regulatory requirements called for some level of planning.[3] Beginning in 2006, state law required local governing boards to consider plan consistency for any zoning amendment and adopt a plan consistency statement,[4] but there was still no state mandate that cities or counties adopt a comprehensive plan.

Now, local governments must have a comprehensive plan to have zoning. G.S. 160D-501(a) states that "[a]s a condition of adopting and applying zoning regulations under this Chapter, a local government shall adopt and reasonably maintain a comprehensive plan that sets forth goals, policies, and programs intended to guide the present and future physical, social, and economic development of the jurisdiction."

Most local governments already have an adopted comprehensive plan, and many are relatively recent. A 2018 survey conducted by the School of Government found that 68 percent of responding cities (and 94 percent of cities with populations of more than 25,000) and 78 percent of responding counties had adopted a comprehensive plan.[5] Some local governments, though, will need to craft and adopt a plan. A grace period for planning is provided: A local government with zoning but without a comprehensive plan must adopt a plan by July 1, 2022, in order to continue zoning regulations.[6]

---

1. G.S. 153A-341, 160A-383.

2. Shuford v. Town of Waynesville, 214 N.C 135, 198 S.E. 585 (1938); A-S-P Assocs. v. City of Raleigh, 298 N.C. 207, 258 S.E.2d 444 (1979).

3. G.S. ch. 113A, art. 7.

4. G.S. 153A-341, 160A-383

5. David W. Owens, *Plan-Consistency Statements*, PLAN. & ZONING L. BULL. No. 27 (UNC School of Government, Nov. 2018).

6. S.L.2019-111 (S.B. 355), § 2.9(c).

What is zoning? Chapter 160D requires a local government to adopt a comprehensive plan in order to have zoning, but what counts as zoning? For most jurisdictions, this is a non-issue. They have adopted a zoning ordinance or unified development ordinance that plainly applies the land use zoning regulations authorized under the zoning statutes. Those local governments plainly must adopt a comprehensive plan to continue the zoning regulation past July 2022.

Some local regulations, though, may be adopted as zoning regulations *or* as police power regulations. A jurisdiction without zoning might have a high impact land use ordinance, a manufactured home ordinance, a sign ordinance, an adult business ordinance, and/or another regulation of land uses that is framed as a police power ordinance rather than zoning. Do these regulations amount to zoning such that the jurisdiction needs to adopt a comprehensive plan to continue the regulations?

North Carolina courts have allowed that some single-purpose, land use-related ordinances may be adopted under the general ordinance authority (not as zoning).[7] But, North Carolina courts have also made clear that ordinances that substantially affect land use may be treated as zoning when considering the statutory authority and procedural requirements.[8]

With that in mind, if a community has a single-purpose, land use–related ordinance adopted under the general ordinance authority, there likely is no requirement for a comprehensive plan. If, however, a community has an ordinance that substantially affects land use, or if a community has a set of ordinances that addresses a range of land uses, those ordinances may be treated as zoning. The community would need to adopt a comprehensive plan to continue those regulations.

Flood damage prevention ordinances commonly raise the question: Is it zoning? A single stand-alone flood damage prevention ordinance may be adopted under the general ordinance authority and would not require a comprehensive plan. But a flood damage prevention ordinance combined with several other land use–related ordinances may trigger the need for a comprehensive plan.

Plan must be reasonably maintained. In order to adequately guide future growth, a plan must be reasonably up to date. Data and priorities from ten or fifteen years ago may be of little use for a fast-growing and fast-changing jurisdiction. But growth patterns and community planning priorities vary greatly across the state. Previously, CAMA plans were required to be updated every five years, and drafters of Chapter 160D discussed a similar requirement for comprehensive plans, but the final legislation leaves the timing of plan updates to local discretion. Given the diversity of communities and situations around the state, Chapter 160D does not set a specific time frame for updating the comprehensive plan, but it does call for plans to be "reasonably maintained."[9] Factors determining reasonableness would include rate of growth and change as well as physical, economic, and social conditions. Notably, the requirement is for reasonable *maintenance*; there is no mandate for a complete rewrite of the comprehensive plan.

B. Advisory

Plan is still advisory. Comprehensive plans are advisory in nature; they are not regulatory documents, and the governing board is not bound by them.[10] Moreover, topics addressed in a plan do not change the scope of authority for development regulations. Still, the planning board and governing

---

7. PNE AOA Media, L.L.C. v. Jackson Cty., 146 N.C. App. 470, 554 S.E.2d 657 (2001).

8. Vulcan Materials Co. v. Iredell Cty., 103 N.C. App. 779, 407 S.E.2d 283 (1991); Thrash Ltd. P'ship v. Cty. of Buncombe, 195 N.C. App. 727, 673 S.E.2d 689 (2009).

9. G.S. 160D-501(a).

10. G.S. 160D-501(c).

board must consider the comprehensive plan—and other adopted plans—when considering amendments to the zoning regulations under G.S. 160D-604 and -605. That process and the role of consistency statements is addressed in the following section, which covers legislative decisions.

C. Plan Process and Content

Plan adoption process. Prior law did not mandate any particular process for adoption of a comprehensive plan. With no specific requirement, plans might be adopted like an ordinance, passed by resolution, or merely accepted as a recommendation from the planning board or planning staff. Chapter 160D provides clarity and uniformity for the plan adoption process. Under the new law, a plan must be adopted the same as any other legislative decision.

Pursuant to Chapter 160D, during plan preparation the local government must allow for citizen engagement.[11] At the time of plan adoption, the local government follows the same process as a legislative zoning decision outlined at G.S. 160D-601,[12] including recommendation from the planning board, public notice, and a public hearing. Local governments do not need to re-adopt plans adopted under prior legislation; such plans remain effective even if the local government did not follow the new procedures.[13]

Plan contents. Given the diversity of communities in the state, the new planning requirement allows flexibility. Chapter 160D does not specifically require elements for a comprehensive plan, but it provides a notable list of topics that may be addressed at the discretion of the local government.[14] This is a permissive, not mandatory, list. These topics may include the following:

1. issues and opportunities facing the local government, including consideration of trends, values expressed by citizens, community vision, and guiding principles for growth and development;
2. the pattern of desired growth and development and civic design, including the location, distribution, and characteristics of future land uses, urban form, utilities, and transportation networks;
3. employment opportunities, economic development, and community development;
4. acceptable levels of public services and infrastructure to support development, including water, waste disposal, utilities, emergency services, transportation, education, recreation, community facilities, and other public services, including plans and policies for provision of and financing for public infrastructure;
5. housing with a range of types and affordability to accommodate persons and households of all types and income levels;
6. recreation and open spaces;
7. mitigation of natural hazards such as flooding, winds, wildfires, and unstable lands;
8. protection of the environment and natural resources, including agricultural resources, mineral resources, and water and air quality;

---

11. G.S. 160D-501(a).
12. G.S. 160D-501(c).
13. S.L. 2019-111 (S.B. 355).
14. G.S. 160D-501(b).

9. protection of significant architectural, scenic, cultural, historical, or archaeological resources; and

10. analysis and evaluation of implementation measures, including regulations, public investments, and educational programs.

Additional plans. The comprehensive plan may be crafted and adopted as part of or in conjunction with other required plans, such as CAMA plans. Additionally, the statute recognizes that local governments can and do adopt related plans, such as land use plans, small area plans, neighborhood plans, hazard mitigation plans, transportation plans, housing plans, and recreation and open space plans. If those plans are formally adopted in the same manner as the comprehensive plan, then those plans must also be considered in zoning amendments.[15]

Optional plan coordination. A local government may undertake planning processes in coordination with other local governments, state agencies, or regional agencies.[16]

II. Legislative Decisions

Chapter 160D amends and clarifies the process for adopting, amending, or repealing development regulations. As noted in Section III of Chapter 1, Chapter 160D defines legislative decisions and legislative hearings as being distinct from quasi-judicial and administrative decisions and hearings. The process for these legislative decisions is set out in Article 6 of Chapter 160D. The same process is applied to all development regulations, though additional requirements are still imposed for zoning amendments (mandatory planning board review and plan consistency statements for all zoning amendments, plus mailed hearing notice and statement of rationale for zoning-map amendments).

A. Hearings

Hearing required. G.S. 160D-601 requires that a legislative hearing before the governing board be held prior to the decision to adopt, amend, or repeal any development regulation. This has always been required for most development regulations, and the new statute confirms that this basic requirement applies to all regulations. Every development regulation, whether previously called an ordinance, a regulation, a code, or a guideline, must be adopted by ordinance (not as a more informal resolution). The requirement for two newspaper published notices of the hearing before the governing board is unchanged.

Notice of hearing. G.S. 160D-602 retains the requirement for mailed notice of the hearing for all zoning-map amendments. This section clarifies what constitutes an abutting property that must be provided a mailed notice of the hearing. This includes not only property that actually touches the property being rezoned but also property separated from the rezoned property by a street, railroad, or other transportation corridor.

If a city zoning-map amendment is being proposed as part of an expansion of the city's extraterritorial jurisdiction (ETJ), a single mailed notice may be made for the hearing on the ETJ boundary ordinance amendment and the zoning-map amendment that applies city zoning to the property. If a combined ETJ/rezoning hearing notice is mailed, then it must go out at least thirty days prior to the hearing (as is required by G.S. 160D-202(d) for the mailing of the notice for the ETJ boundary amendment).

---

15. G.S. 160D-501(a).
16. G.S. 160D-503(a).

Posted notice. Since 2005, existing law has required a posted notice of hearings on zoning-map amendments. The law has not, however, specified when that posting had to be made. G.S. 160D-602(c) adds a provision to require that the posting be made in the same time period as the mailing of the notice—at least ten but not more than twenty-five days prior to the date of the hearing.

Optional notice requirement. A fairly common practice has developed over the last decade of requiring landowners or developers proposing some rezonings to provide notice to neighbors prior to submission of the rezoning request. This is most often done when an ordinance requires the developer to conduct a neighborhood meeting prior to submitting a conditional rezoning request. The intent of these requirements is to encourage a landowner–neighborhood dialogue that identifies concerns early in the project design process, allowing at least the opportunity to address these concerns prior to initiation of the more formal governmental review process.

G.S. 160D-602(e) explicitly allows a city or county to require that someone proposing a rezoning communicate with the neighbors prior to submitting a rezoning petition. Rather than specify that the communication come in the form of a neighborhood meeting, the authorization is written broadly to encompass requirements for a mailing, a meeting, or some other means of engaging the neighbors. The ordinance may also require that the rezoning application include a report on the neighborhood communication.

B. Planning Board Review

Under previous law, all zoning amendments must be submitted to the planning board for review and comment. Chapter 160D continues this requirement and clarifies several points regarding planning board reviews.

G.S. 160D-604(c) clarifies the question of whether the planning board is to review development regulations other than zoning. It provides that the adoption and amendment of other development regulations may also be referred to the planning board for review and comment but is mandatory only for zoning.

G.S. 160D-604(e) clarifies that while the ordinance can assign some duties of the planning board to the governing board, review and comment on ordinance amendments cannot be assigned to the governing board (otherwise the board would be making a recommendation to itself). As a practical matter, this means each jurisdiction with zoning must have a planning board or other appointed board that conducts these reviews and makes recommendations on ordinance amendments to the governing board.

G.S. 160D-604(d) clarifies that when making a comment of plan consistency, the planning board is to consider any plan that has been adopted following the plan adoption process required by G.S. 160D-501.

C. Plan Consistency and Reasonableness Statements

Plan consistency statements. Legislation enacted in 2005 requires that local governments consider their adopted plan prior to amending zoning ordinances.[17] Planning boards must provide written comments on plan consistency to governing boards, and governing boards must, in turn, approve written statements documenting their consideration of the plans when making decisions

---

17. Article 5 of Chapter 160D includes substantial updates to statutory provisions on plan content and the plan adoption process. These are discussed in the prior section.

on proposed zoning amendments. The plans do not dictate the decisions to be made, but the concept was that deliberate consideration of the plans would produce more thoughtful decisions about proposed ordinance amendments. This relatively simple concept proved to be somewhat complicated and contentious in its implementation.[18]

G.S. 160D-605 simplifies the plan consistency statement that must be approved by the governing board in several ways.

First, it clarifies that the consistency statement does not have to be adopted as a separate motion prior to acting on the proposed zoning amendment. It does so by removing the language saying the statement must be approved "prior to" action on the amendment and replacing it with a direction that the statement be approved "when" making the decision. A similar amendment was made to the municipal statute in 2006,[19] but that municipal clarification was reversed by later legislation in 2017.[20] G.S. 160D-605(a) applies the "when adopting" formulation uniformly to cities and counties.

Second, it addresses the situation in which a governing board complies with the spirit of the plan consideration requirement but fails to approve a formal plan consistency statement. If the governing board explicitly approves a written plan consistency statement when it considers a zoning amendment, then the statutory mandate is met. But what if the governing board discusses and debates the plan consistency statement, but the motion to approve or reject the zoning amendment fails to explicitly include approval of the plan consistency statement? G.S. 160D-605(a) provides that if the minutes of the board meeting in which the zoning amendment was acted upon show the governing board was aware of and actually considered the plan, then the failure to formally adopt a written statement does not invalidate the action taken. In effect, the statutory mandate is that the governing board consider the plan before acting—not vote on a particular form of a motion. The intent of this amendment is to encourage compliance with the concept of real consideration of adopted plans—not to provide a litigation trap for those who fail to make their motions in a prescribed format. While clear governing board approval of a written plan consistency statement is preferable and the legally safest course of action, actual board discussion about plan consistency that is fully reflected in the minutes will suffice.

Third, G.S. 160D-605 simplifies the required statement by eliminating the 2017 requirement that it take one of three specified forms. G.S. 160D-605(a) requires only a "brief statement describing whether its action is consistent or inconsistent" with approved plans. A simple conclusion or checklist is still inadequate. The statement must *describe* how the action taken is or is not consistent. Formal findings and elaborate analysis are not required, but a brief description is.

Fourth, it simplifies the provision that a plan is deemed to be amended if a zoning amendment is made that is inconsistent with the plan. Currently, the statute says a zoning amendment that is inconsistent with the plan amends the plan, without specifying what that means. This requirement has been confusing to implement, particularly in determining which policies in an adopted plan were deemed amended by a zoning-text amendment or rezoning of an individual parcel. For example, are the policies set out in the plan deemed amended? Did the change apply to all of the jurisdiction or only for the property covered by a rezoning?

G.S. 160D-605(a) simplifies and clarifies this provision by specifying that the zoning decision only amends any future land use map in the plan, and that land use map is deemed amended to conform

---

18. See David W. Owens, *Plan-Consistency Statements*, PLAN. & ZONING L. BULL. No. 27 (UNC School of Government, Nov. 2018), for a summary of related litigation and legislative amendments.

19. S.L. 2006-259, § 28. The request to make this amendment was initiated by the City of Charlotte.

20. S.L. 2017-10, § 2.4(e).

it to the zoning action taken. As under previous law, no separate application for a plan amendment may be required in this situation. The new statute specifically allows concurrent consideration of requests for plan amendments and zoning amendments, reflecting the practice in some jurisdictions to require anyone proposing a zoning amendment that is inconsistent with the plan to also submit a plan amendment so both can be adopted or approved at the same time. Also, G.S. 160D-501 requires that if the future land use map is deemed amended by adoption of an inconsistent zoning action, then that amendment must be noted in the plan itself, helping to ensure that the plan itself is updated for those consulting it after the zoning amendment is made. G.S. 160D-501 also clarifies that if the plan being amended is a plan mandated by CAMA, then the plan amendment is not effective until it goes through the plan review and approval process required by CAMA.

Statements of reasonableness. Since 2005, the statutes have required the governing board to adopt a statement of reasonableness for each conditional rezoning or other small-scale rezoning.[21] This requirement was designed to assist cities and counties in assessing the case law requirement that spot zoning must be "reasonable."[22] In addition, G.S. 153A-341(b) and 160A-383(a) require the governing board to approve a statement for all zoning-text and zoning-map amendments of why the action taken was reasonable and in the public interest.

G.S. 160D-605(b) simplifies and clarifies this requirement in several ways. First, the statement is required for only zoning-map amendments. A local government can still do the reasonableness analysis for text amendments, but it is not required. Second, the statute lists the factors that should be considered in this analysis. The factors are suggested and not mandated, as not all factors will be relevant to all rezoning decisions. The factors to be addressed, generally adapted from *Chrismon v. Guilford County,*[23] the leading North Carolina case on spot zoning, are as follows:

1. the size and physical attributes of the site;
2. the benefits and detriments to the landowner, the neighbors, and the community;
3. how the actual and previously permitted uses of the site relate to newly permitted uses;
4. any changed conditions warranting the amendment; and
5. other factors affecting the public interest.

G.S. 160D-605(c) provides that the statement of reasonableness and the plan consistency statement can be approved as a single, combined statement.

D. Voting

Simple majority. One of the differences in previous law between cities and counties is the voting requirement for adoption of zoning amendments. The previous city voting statutes require a two-thirds majority to adopt any ordinance at the meeting it is first voted upon. If an ordinance amendment receives majority approval, but not a two-thirds majority, then it must voted on a second time at a subsequent meeting. By contrast, the county voting statute only requires a simple majority to adopt an ordinance on its first reading if the statutes required a public hearing on that matter prior to the vote.

The Chapter 160D legislation amends the city statute to conform to the county practice, at least when development regulations are involved. Section 2.5(n) of S.L. 2019-111 amends G.S. 160A-75

---

21. G.S. 153A-342(b), 160A-382(b).
22. Chrismon v. Guilford Cty., 322 N.C. 611, 628, 370 S.E.2d 579, 589 (1988).
23. *Id.*

to provide that the supermajority vote required to adopt an ordinance on first reading does not apply to any ordinance that requires a public hearing under G.S. 160D-601. This includes zoning and all other development regulations in Chapter 160D.

Conflicts of interest. A provision was added to the zoning statute in 2005 to codify the rule that members of a governing board must not vote on any legislative decision if the outcome would have a direct, substantial, and readily identifiable financial impact on the member. That same restriction was placed on planning board members making a recommendation on a zoning amendment. More-stringent conflict-of-interest provisions were placed on board members making a quasi-judicial decision. The intent of those changes was to codify due process limits on board members, clarify the scope of the need to abstain, and protect public confidence in the integrity of governmental decision making on development regulation issues.

Chapter 160D collects the various conflict-of-interest provisions that apply to governing boards, advisory boards, boards making quasi-judicial decisions, and staff administering development regulations. The consolidated provision is G.S. 160D-109.

The revised statute adds new restrictions with the intent of avoiding both actual conflicts of interest and the appearance of conflicts.[24] In addition to not voting on matters that would have a direct, substantial financial interest on the member, G.S. 160D-109(a) and (b) expand the prohibition to require that board members not vote on any zoning amendment if the landowner of property subject to a rezoning petition or the applicant for a text amendment has a close family, business, or associational relationship to the member. This standard is currently applicable only for quasi-judicial decisions. The new statute extends this limitation to legislative decisions and advisory recommendations on legislative decisions. For the purposes of this section, a close family relationship is defined to mean a spouse, parent, child, brother, sister, grandparent, or grandchild (including step, half, and in-law relationships).

G.S. 160D-109(e) also extends the process for resolving objections regarding conflicts of interest that previously applied to quasi-judicial decisions to all conflict-of-interest objections regarding board members. Board members may recuse themselves in response to such objections. If a member chooses not to do so, then the remaining members of the board are to vote on the member's participation.

E. Administrative Minor Modifications to Conditional Zoning Decisions

G.S. 160D-703(b) gives local governments the option of processing minor amendments to legislative conditional zoning decisions administratively. To use this option, the ordinance itself must define what constitutes a "minor modification." For example, it could allow up to X percent change in a dimensional requirement. A minor modification cannot include a change in permitted uses or in the density of the overall development. Once defined, staff can be authorized to approve minor modifications administratively. Any other modification must follow the same process for approval as is required for a zoning-map amendment. Also, if the conditional zoning applies to multiple parcels of property, the conditions may be modified for individual parcels without the necessity of obtaining the consent of all property owners within the conditional zoning (but in those instances the modification will only apply to the parcels whose owners consent).

---

24. It also for the first time extends the prohibition against acting when there is a financial conflict of interest or a close relation to a party to staff making administrative decisions. That requirement is discussed above in Chapter 2.

F. Limits on Legislative Zoning Decisions

Other 2019 amendments. Other bills were enacted in 2019 that affect legislative development regulations decisions. All will be incorporated into Chapter 160D prior to its effective date.[25]

Two amendments regarding legislative zoning decisions made by Part I of S.L. 2019-111 are particularly noteworthy. First, it amends G.S. 153A-343 and 160A-384 to prohibit third-party downzonings without consent from the property owners. A neighbor, for example, cannot request that property be rezoned for reduced density unless the property owner has consented to that requested reduction. Property owners may petition for downzoning of their own properties. The local government may initiate and adopt a downzoning without an owner's consent. A neighbor could request for the local government to initiate a downzoning, but the neighbor could not initiate the downzoning request unilaterally. This amendment applies to zoning applications submitted on or after July 11, 2019.

Part I of S.L. 2019-111 also amends G.S. 153A-342 and 160A-382 to provide that the petitioner for a conditional rezoning must consent in writing to the conditions in order for those conditions to be effective. Unless the petitioner consents in writing, the zoning may not include any conditions or requirements not otherwise authorized by law.[26] Notably, the amended language affirms the authority and flexibility for local governments and petitioners to negotiate appropriate conditions for conditional-zoning approvals. With written consent from the petitioner, such conditions may go beyond the basic zoning authority to address additional fees, design requirements, and other development considerations.

III. Quasi-Judicial Decisions

Given the relatively recent update of G.S. 160A-388, Chapter 160D makes only modest amendments to the statutory provisions on quasi-judicial development regulation decisions. These provisions apply to all quasi-judicial decisions made under any development regulation.[27] As provided in G.S. 160D-102(28), these include decisions on variances, special use permits, certificates of appropriateness, and appeals of administrative determinations. Decisions on the approval of subdivision plats and site plans are also quasi-judicial if they include discretionary standards. As discussed in Section III of Chapter 1, Chapter 160D defines quasi-judicial decisions and evidentiary hearings as being distinct from legislative and administrative decisions and hearings.

---

25. Section 2.10 of S.L. 2019-111 expresses that intent and directs the General Statutes Commission to study the need for legislation to accomplish the incorporation and make recommendations for that legislation upon the convening of the 2020 session of the General Assembly. This 2019 legislation is described in more detail in Adam Lovelady & David W. Owens, *2019 Legislation Related to Planning and Development Regulation*, Plan. & Zoning L. Bull. No. 28 (UNC School of Government, Sept. 2019).

26. "Unless consented to by the petitioner in writing, in the exercise of the authority granted by this section, including the establishment of special or conditional use districts or conditional zoning, a [local government] may not require, enforce, or incorporate into the zoning regulations or permit requirements any condition or requirement not authorized by otherwise applicable law, including, without limitation, taxes, impact fees, building design elements within the scope of G.S. 160A-381(h), driveway-related improvements in excess of those allowed in G.S. 136-18(29) and G.S. 160A-307, or other unauthorized limitations on the development or use of land." S.L. 2019-111, § 1.4.; S.L. 2019-111, § 1.5.

27. See the discussion regarding decision types in Chapter 1.

A. Uniform Terminology

Zoning regulations describe uses that are automatically permitted in a particular zoning district. These permitted uses are often referred to as "uses by right." Most zoning regulations also allow additional uses in each district that are permitted only if specified standards are met. The regulation sets out the standards that must be met to secure approval for these uses. If those standards require application of some degree of judgment and discretion, as opposed to permitted uses in which only objective standards are applied, then the decision is quasi-judicial.

The original Standard State Zoning Enabling Act and the original North Carolina zoning-enabling act used the term *special exception* for these permits and assigned decision making on them to the board of adjustment. Contemporary zoning regulations usually term these *conditional uses* or *special uses*. These terms are interchangeable, having the same legal consequence. Whether the application concerns a special use permit, conditional use permit, or special exception, the decision on the application must be assigned to a board, and the board making the decision must follow quasi-judicial procedures.

Chapter 160D retains the authority to use these permits and continues to allow decisions on them to be assigned to the governing board, the board of adjustment, the planning board, or any combination of these boards. However, G.S. 160D-102(30) simplifies matters by assigning a single standard name, "special use permit," for these types of permits that is to be used by all cities and counties. This terminology is intended to distinguish quasi-judicial special use permits from legislative conditional zoning and to secure uniform terminology among the hundreds of zoning regulations around the state. Section 2.9(b) of S.L. 2019-111 provides that any valid "conditional use permit" issued prior to the effective date of Chapter 160D becomes known as a "special use permit" after the effective date.

B. Uniform Procedures

G.S. 160D-406 simplifies the statutes by setting uniform procedural requirements for all quasi-judicial decisions in a single statutory section. These procedures apply to any and all boards making quasi-judicial decisions under any development regulation. For the most part, the required procedures are the same as previously required under G.S. 160A-388. An evidentiary hearing must be conducted by the board to gather competent, material, and substantial evidence to establish the facts of the case. Testimony is under oath and subject to cross-examination. Written findings of fact and conclusions of law are required. Chapter 160D does, however, make several modest clarifications to the mandated process.

Continuations. G.S. 160D-406(b) clarifies that an evidentiary hearing on a quasi-judicial matter may be continued in the same manner as currently allowed for legislative hearings. If the time, date, and place of the continued hearing is announced at a duly noticed hearing that has been convened, then no additional notice of the continuation is required. Also, if a quorum of the board is not present at the announced date and time of a properly noticed evidentiary hearing, then the hearing is automatically continued to the next regular meeting of the board and no additional notice of the hearing is required.[28]

Meeting packets. It is common for a packet of information about pending quasi-judicial cases to be distributed to the board prior to the evidentiary hearing. This allows board members to read the application and supporting materials in advance so that they are prepared at the outset of the hearing.

---

28. This provision for an automatic continuance to the next meeting if no quorum is present is currently in the statutes for public hearings conducted by governing boards. *See* G.S. 160A-81.

This is particularly useful if there are lengthy technical documents or reports that need to be read prior to the hearing. This practice has raised questions as to whether this is appropriate, given the limits on ex parte evidence, unsworn testimony, and the like. G.S. 160D-406(c) addresses this question by explicitly allowing, but not requiring, the distribution of meeting packets to board members prior to the hearing. The law requires the staff to transmit to the board all administrative materials relative to the pending case—the application, reports, and other written materials received by the staff. The materials can be distributed in advance of the hearing, provided that copies of all of the materials are also provided to the applicant and the landowner at the same time they are distributed to the board members. If these materials are not distributed prior to the hearing, then they must be presented at the hearing. These administrative materials then become a part of the official hearing record. The law does not address the mechanics of exactly how this is to be done, but a standard practice of having the staff member responsible for the case appear as a witness and offer the administrative materials as an exhibit to be entered into the hearing record will suffice.

Parties may make objections to the inclusion or exclusion of administrative materials before or at the hearing. Rulings on any objections are to be made by the board at the hearing. G.S. 160D-406(d) provides that the board chair rules on any objections and that the ruling may be appealed to the full board. Evidentiary rulings are also subject to judicial review on appeal to the courts.

C. Presentation of Evidence by Non-Parties

In a judicial case, only the parties to the case actively participate in the hearing. In more informal quasi-judicial cases, a standard practice has been to allow anyone present at the hearing to offer relevant evidence to the board. Persons appearing at the evidentiary hearing do not have as much latitude as a would be the case in a legislative hearing. They are presenting evidence, not offering opinions about a policy decision to be made. They must be under oath, subject to cross-examination, and limited to presentation of relevant evidence.

Given statutory and case law directives, the more frequent appearance of legal counsel, and the increasing financial stakes involved, the quasi-judicial process in North Carolina over the past few decades has become increasingly formal. The unit of government, the applicant, and other parties to a quasi-judicial matter have the legal right to appear at the hearing and present evidence, cross-examine witnesses, object to evidence proposed to be presented, and make legal arguments. Increasingly, however, questions have arisen about the scope and propriety of allowing non-parties to participate in these hearings.

G.S. 160D-406(d) provides a simple and uniform answer. While parties to the case may fully participate, non-parties are limited to presentation of competent, material, and substantial evidence that is not repetitive. Further, they may do so only as allowed by the board. It would be prudent for boards to have clear and uniformly applied rules of procedure specifying whether non-parties may present evidence, but that is not mandated by the statute.

D. Advisory Reviews

North Carolina zoning statutes have long required legislative zoning matters (zoning-text and zoning-map amendments) to be presented to the planning board for review and comment prior to a decision by the governing board. A majority of the state's cities and counties decided to extend these advisory reviews to some quasi-judicial matters, typically sending a special use permit application to the planning board for review prior to the evidentiary hearing on the case by the governing board.[29] This practice, though widespread, was not addressed by the statutes. It also raised substantial legal questions regarding the advisory review in terms of ex parte evidence and other due process concerns.

Chapter 160D addresses these issues by allowing, but not mandating, advisory reviews. G.S. 160D-301 authorizes planning board review and comments on pending quasi-judicial matters but limits the practice. The statute clarifies that such reviews are a "preliminary forum." A planning board making an advisory review is not conducting a formal evidentiary hearing but is allowing an informal, preliminary discussion of the application. Given this informality, the statute goes on to provide that "no part of the forum or recommendation" may be used as the basis for a decision by the board making the quasi-judicial decision. The decision must still be based on competent evidence presented at the evidentiary hearing held by the decision-making board.

These informal advisory reviews can identify issues and concerns and provide the parties with informal guidance about particular evidence that should be presented at a forthcoming evidentiary hearing. But they do not constitute evidence that can be used by the decision-making board.

E. Other Modifications

Minor modifications to special use permits. As with conditional zoning, Chapter 160D allows local governments the option of approving minor modifications of quasi-judicial decisions administratively. G.S. 160D-705(c), however, provides that this is only possible if the ordinance defines a "minor modification," which may not include a change in permitted uses or in the overall density of the development. Once defined, qualified applications may be approved by the staff without the necessity of going through the quasi-judicial process. As with conditional zoning, if multiple parcels of land are included within a special use permit, then the permit may be modified for individual parcels at the request of the owners of those parcels.

Recordation. Some local zoning regulations require that special use permits be recorded in the chain of title to provide notice to future purchasers of the property of the existence of the permit and its conditions for development. The previous statutes are silent as to the authority to impose this requirement. G.S. 160D-705(c) specifically authorizes, but does not require, this practice.

Variances for reasonable accommodation. Chapter 160D makes an important change to the mandatory standards for making decisions about applications for zoning variances. Previous law prohibits granting a variance based on the personal circumstances of the applicant. Because the variance runs with the land and is not a personal right of the landowner, the law requires that the need for the variance be based on the physical conditions of the property itself.

The Federal Fair Housing Act requires that local development regulations make reasonable accommodations for persons with disabilities. For example, a request might be made for a modest relaxation of a side-yard setback to allow construction of a wheelchair ramp that meets appropriate design standards in order to accommodate a resident with a disability. A few North Carolina cities and counties have a specific process in their development regulations that allows exceptions to zoning rules in order to make such accommodations. But most jurisdictions process these accommodation requests

---

29. A 2005 School of Government survey indicated that 69 percent of responding jurisdictions send special use permits to the planning board for an advisory review. David W. Owens, *Special Use Permits in North Carolina Zoning*, Special Series No. 22 (UNC School of Government, Apr. 2007), at 9.

as variance requests. Doing so poses a legal question because the statutes provide that a personal circumstance—the condition of the person with a disability—is not a legitimate factor that can be considered in a variance request.

G.S. 160D-705(c) remedies this problem by explicitly allowing a variance that is "necessary and appropriate" to make a reasonable accommodation under the Federal Fair Housing Act.

Uniform time to appeal administrative decisions. For many years, the statutes allowed each development regulation to set time limits for making appeals and required only appeals to the board of adjustment to be made within a reasonable time. The 2013 amendments to G.S. 160A-388 moved toward uniformity by setting the time to make an appeal to the board of adjustment at thirty days from receipt of notice of a zoning determination. G.S. 160D-405(c) now clarifies that this thirty-day period to file an appeal applies to all appeals of any final, written determination under any development regulation. It also clarifies that if the notice of the administrative determination is sent by mail, then the notice is deemed to have been received on the third business day after deposit of the notice in the mail.

Defining family relationships. Previous statutes provide that members of boards making quasi-judicial decisions may not participate in decisions if the member has a close family, business, or associational relationship to a party to the decision. G.S. 160D-109(f) clarifies that standard by adding a definition of what constitutes a *close family relationship*. It is defined to mean a spouse, parent, child, brother, sister, grandparent, or grandchild (including step, half, and in-law relationships).

Other 2019 amendments. Other bills were enacted in 2019 that affect quasi-judicial decisions. All will be incorporated into Chapter 160D prior to its effective date.[30] These additional amendments affecting quasi-judicial decisions include more explicit limits on special use permit conditions.

> Part I of S.L. 2019-111 amends G.S. 153A-340 and 160A-381 to specify limits on conditions imposed through special use permits. It provides that special use permit conditions shall not include requirements for which the [local government] does not have authority under statute to regulate nor requirements for which the courts have held to be unenforceable if imposed directly by the [local government], including, without limitation, taxes, impact fees, building design elements within the scope of subsection (h) of this section, driveway-related improvements in excess of those allowed in G.S. 136-18(29) and G.S. 160A-307, or other unauthorized limitations on the development or use of land.

Design restrictions may still be imposed in compliance with G.S. 153A-340(*l*) and 160A-381(h), which allow them for commercial and multifamily development, in historic districts, or with written consent from the owner.

---

30. Section 2.10 of S.L. 2019-111 expresses that intent and directs the General Statutes Commission to study the need for legislation to accomplish the incorporation and make recommendations for that legislation upon the convening of the 2020 session of the General Assembly. This 2019 legislation is described in more detail in Adam Lovelady & David W. Owens, *2019 Legislation Related to Planning and Development Regulation*, PLAN. & ZONING L. BULL. No. 28 (UNC School of Government, Sept. 2019).

IV. Administrative Decisions

As discussed in Section III of Chapter 1, Chapter 160D defines certain types of administrative decisions and identifies administrative decisions and hearings as being distinct from legislative and quasi-judicial decisions and hearings.

A. Development Approvals

Chapter 160D defines a *development approval* to be

> [a]n administrative or quasi-judicial approval made pursuant to this Chapter that is written and that is required prior to commencing development or undertaking a specific activity, project, or development proposal. Development approvals include, but are not limited to, zoning permits, site plan approvals, special use permits, variances, and certificates of appropriateness. The term also includes all other regulatory approvals required by regulations adopted pursuant to this Chapter, including plat approvals, permits issued, development agreements entered into, and building permits issued.[31]

G.S. 160D-403 states that a person may not proceed with development without first obtaining the required development approvals. This language—which previously appeared in the statutes concerning building code administration—now clarifies that the rule is applicable across all development regulations. Development approvals must be written but may be in print or electronic form. If electronic, the development approval must be in a format protected from further editing.[32]

Applications for development approvals may be made by the property owner, a person leasing the property, a person with an option or contract to purchase or lease the property, or a person with an easement on the property (provided the development is within the scope of the easement).[33] The rights and obligations of development approvals run with the land, unless provided otherwise by law.[34] This confirms that development approvals are project- and site-specific and connected to the property; they are not personal rights separate from the property itself.

Chapter 160D-403(h) clarifies that a development regulation may require community notice, informational meetings, or both as part of the decision-making process for administrative development approvals. Quasi-judicial and legislative approvals already had (and continue to have) notice and hearing requirements.

Part I of S.L. 2019-111, which will be incorporated into Chapter 160D, offers a slightly different term and definition. For purposes of permit choice rule, Part I defines *development permit* to include the permits that Chapter 160D includes in *development approval*, but Part I adds "[d]riveway permits," "[e]rosion and sedimentation control permits," and "[s]ign permit." Those likely are encompassed in Chapter 160D as "other regulatory approvals required by regulations adopted pursuant to this Chapter." Notably, the Part I definition also includes "[s]tate agency permits for development"—not just local permits—within the definition of *development permit*. That broader definition to encompass state permits may be limited to permit choice rule—an issue that will be resolved as Part I is incorporated into Chapter 160D.

---

31. G.S. 160D-102.
32. G.S. 160D-403(a).
33. *Id.*
34. G.S. 160D-104.

Duration. As outlined at G.S. 160D-403(c), by default a development approval is valid twelve months (with an option for local or state rules to shorten or lengthen that time frame). If after one year the development has not been substantially commenced, then the development approval expires. Additionally, if after a development is commenced it is discontinued for twelve months, then the development approval expires. Section 1.3 of S.L. 2019-111 sets the duration period for discontinuation at twenty-four months. This discrepancy will be resolved when Part I is incorporated into Chapter 160D. The time period is tolled during any appeal.

The general period of validity may be adjusted by the state statute or local decision or development regulation. The statute governing building permits, for example, states that they are valid for six months. A local development regulation may have shorter validity for temporary uses or longer validity for other development types. Development approvals that qualify as site-specific vesting plans are valid for two years. Similarly, a local ordinance, conditional zoning decision, or quasi-judicial decision may specify a validity period other than twelve months. For example, a zoning regulation may provide that special use permits are valid for two years. Additionally, owners may still claim common law or statutory vested rights provided they have made substantial expenditures in reliance on a valid permit approval and would suffer detriment if required to comply with newly enacted regulations.

Modifications. After an owner obtains a development approval, the owner is obligated to adhere to the specifications of the development as approved. A local government may define by ordinance minor modifications that may be approved administratively by staff. Major modifications must be approved in the same manner as the original approval. Local governments have discretion to define minor modifications and major modifications according to the local context and policies.

In addition to minor modifications on administrative development approvals, Chapter 160D authorizes staff to approve minor modifications for legislative conditional zoning decisions and quasi-judicial special use permits. G.S. 160D-703(b) gives local governments the option of processing minor amendments to conditional zoning approvals administratively. G.S. 160D-705(c) gives comparable authority for minor modifications to special use permits. For each authorization, "minor modification" must be defined in the ordinance and cannot include a change in permitted uses or the density of the overall development. Modifications that do not qualify as minor must follow the same process for approval as is required for the original approval.

B. Determinations

A *determination* is "[a] written, final, and binding order, requirement, or determination regarding an administrative decision."[35] It could be an interpretation of an ordinance, an affirmation of nonconforming status, a notice of violation, or some other binding order concerning a development regulation.

A local government may designate by ordinance a staff person to make determinations under a particular development regulation.[36] The staff person must provide written notice of the determination to the property owner and the party seeking the determination, if different from the owner. Notice is provided by personal delivery, electronic mail, or first-class mail to the last address of the owner in county tax records and the address provided by the applicant if different from that of the owner. Additionally, an owner or applicant may post a zoning notice sign on the affected property for ten days

---

35. G.S. 160D-102.
36. G.S. 160D-403(b).

to establish constructive notice of the determination to neighboring parties. Unless a local ordinance requires such posted notice, it is at the option of the owner or applicant. These provisions for staff determinations are a clarification and restatement from the prior version codified at 160A-388(b1).

Determination is closely related to, but distinct from, *development approval*. In general, a determination is a decision about interpretation and fact-finding. (What does the ordinance mean? Does the owner have vested rights? Is the use lawfully nonconforming? Is there a violation of the ordinance?) A development approval is a permit for future land use or land development. This may be a distinction without a difference, but for some circumstances it may be meaningful. The expiration for development approvals, for example, is set at one year. There is no explicit expiration for determinations.

C. Appeals of Administrative Decisions

The provisions for appeals of administrative decisions are, for the most part, carried over from the prior law outlined at G.S. 160A-388. The language is broadened to clarify that these provisions apply for appeals of administrative decisions under any development regulation, unless an alternate appeal is provided by statute or local ordinance. Appeals of administrative decisions follow quasi-judicial procedures as outlined at G.S. 160D-406. If an appeal is assigned to a board other than the board of adjustment, then that alternate board still must follow the quasi-judicial procedures required for the board of adjustment. Appeals of decisions relating to erosion and sedimentation control, stormwater control, or housing code violations are not made to the board of adjustment unless specified by local ordinance.

G.S. 160D-405 now allows a notice of appeal to be filed with the local government clerk *or* another local government official as designated by the local ordinance. A party with standing has thirty days from receipt of notice to file an appeal. A new provision clarifies that unless there is evidence to the contrary, a person is deemed to receive notice on the third business day following deposit of notice for mailing with the United States Postal Service. G.S. 160D-406 continues the requirement that the official who made the decision being appealed must participate as a witness in the appeal. The statute now clarifies that if the individual who made the decision is no longer employed by the local government, then the individual currently occupying that position must participate as a witness in the appeal. During an appeal, enforcement actions—including fines—are stayed and do not accrue.

As discussed more in the Judicial Review section, a person may file a separate and original civil action to challenge the constitutionality of or statutory authority for a development regulation. That person does not have to bring that challenge before the board of adjustment prior to going to court. Part I of S.L. 2019-111, Section 1.7, clarifies that if the challenge concerns the interpretation of the ordinance, then the appeal must go to the board of adjustment prior to going to court.

5. Rights and Review

I. Vested Rights and Permit Choice

A vested right is the right of a landowner to continue a development as permitted even if the applicable regulations were amended after the permit was issued in a way that would prevent or limit that development. A landowner may go to court to establish a common law vested right by showing that he or she has a valid governmental permit, made substantial expenditures in good-faith reliance on that permit, and would suffer detriment to comply with regulations adopted after obtaining the permit. In addition to common law vested rights, North Carolina state law has established a set of statutory vested rights—vesting standards and periods for specific types of permits.

The permit choice rule is a relatively recent addition to the statutes granting applicants a right to choose the regulations in effect at the time of application. In general, if an applicant submits a complete application for a development approval and then the local government changes the regulations applicable to that approval, then the applicant may choose for the application to be reviewed under the old rules or under the new rules.

Guidance for statutory vested rights and permit choice has been scattered across the planning and development statutes (and beyond). Chapter 160D gathers those provisions and recodifies them as G.S. 160D-108. Part I of S.L. 2019-111, which will be incorporated into Chapter 160D, also provided notable amendments to the statutes concerning vested rights and permit choice. Those are noted, where appropriate, in the discussion below.

A. Process to Claim and Appeal

A person claiming a common law or statutory vested right may seek an administrative determination by submitting evidence to the zoning administrator or other authorized official.[1] One critical question for some vesting determinations is whether work has substantially commenced. This is a fact-specific inquiry. There is no state standard for that determination, but case law concerning common law vested rights provides a useful guide. As with other determinations, the vested rights determination may be appealed to the board of adjustment and then to superior court pursuant to G.S. 160A-405. Such appeals are reviewed de novo.

In lieu of seeking an administrative determination, the person claiming vested rights may bring an original civil action under G.S. 160D-405(c).

---

1. G.S. 160D-108(c).

B. Types and Terms

Building permits (six months). As was the case under prior law, a building permit is valid for six months unless work under the permit has commenced.[2] Once work is begun, the permit expires if work is discontinued for a period of twelve months.

Development approvals (one year). This new section sets a default rule that development approvals are valid for one year, unless specified otherwise by statute or local ordinance.[3] After one year, the approval expires if the applicant has not substantially commenced work.

This one-year vesting does not limit longer vesting that may be established by other statutory vested rights or by common law vested rights. Also, if desired by the local government, a local ordinance can specify terms for development approvals, such as subdivision plats, site plans, or special use permits, and treat them as site-specific development plans (discussed below).

Site-specific vesting plans (two to five years). Site-specific vesting plans—formerly called site-specific development plans—continue under Chapter 160D.[4] The standards and processes for site-specific vesting plans remain mostly the same as under prior law. These approvals vest for at least two years and may vest for up to five years at the local government's discretion. At the end of the vesting period, the vested rights terminate for any buildings for which no valid building permit applications have been submitted. For buildings with valid building permit applications, the permit choice rule and vesting considerations for building permits continue to apply.

As under prior law, the local government specifies what constitutes a site-specific vesting plan, but if the local government does not specify vesting plans, then any development approval constitutes a site-specific vesting plan. Such vesting plans must describe with reasonable certainty the type and intensity of use for a specific property. Examples include planned unit development, a subdivision plat, a site plan, a preliminary or general development plan, a special use permit, a conditional zoning, or other development approval. The statute specifies the details to be included in these vested plans, including boundaries, topography, and site-planning details, such as buildings and infrastructure. Variances are not site-specific vesting plans; sketch plans may not be site-specific vesting plans if they lack sufficient certainty of development details.

Chapter 160D provides notable clarifications for the process of approving vesting plans. When the ordinance defines a type of approval as constituting a site-specific vesting plan, there is no need to identify the approval as such in the approval process. (Prior law called for the vesting to be identified "at the time of approval.") If the site-specific vesting plan is based on a standard approval outlined in the ordinance (a special use permit or a subdivision plat, for example), then the local government follows the standard notice and hearing procedures for the underlying approval. There is no need for additional notice or hearing for the vesting plan. (Prior law implied that separate notice and hearing may have been required.) Alternatively, if the site-specific vesting plan is a stand-alone approval, meaning it is not based on another standard approval, then it is treated as a legislative approval.

Amendments to site-specific vesting plans are allowed with approval from the owner and the local government. Substantial modifications must follow the same process as the original approval. Minor modifications may be approved by staff if allowed by local regulation.

---

2. G.S. 160D-108(d)(1).
3. G.S. 160D-108(d)(2).
4. G.S. 160D-108(d)(3).

Multi-phase developments (seven years). A multi-phase development is a development at least twenty-five acres in size;[5] is subject to a master development plan with committed elements, including dedication of land; and is developed in phases (multiple site plans). A multi-phase development is vested for seven years from the time of initial site-plan approval. With regard to scope, a multi-phase development is vested in the zoning regulations, subdivision regulations, and unified development ordinances in place at the time of the first site-plan approval. These provisions are mostly unchanged from prior law.

The previously authorized "phased development plans" are deleted as obsolete because of the authority for multi-phase development, development agreements, and extended site-specific vesting plans.[6]

Development agreements (per agreement). In addition to addressing complex development design and finance issues, development agreements are used to create extended vested rights for large-scale and long-term projects. The term and scope of vested rights under a development agreement are set forth in the agreement itself.[7] The provisions for development agreements, outlined in Article 10 of Chapter 160D, are mostly unchanged from prior law. The few changes are outlined in Chapter 3, Section II.D, and include an explicit allowance for a development agreement to be incorporated into conditional zoning, a simplification of the required content in the agreement, and clarification of the permissible conditions.

C. Runs with the Land

G.S. 160D-108(g) affirms that vested rights run with the land. When property ownership changes, the new owner steps into the shoes of the prior owner—the new owner has all of the rights and obligations as the prior owner. Part I of S.L. 2019-111 provides a limitation. The use of land for outdoor advertising governed by G.S. 136-131.1 and G.S. 136-131.2 is deemed a personal right that runs with the owner of the permit—not the owner of the land.

D. Continuing Review

Local governments may make subsequent reviews and require approvals to ensure compliance with the terms and conditions of the original approval, provided such reviews and approvals are consistent with the original approval.[8] The local government may revoke the original approval for failure to comply with applicable terms, conditions, or development regulations. Additionally, G.S. 160D-401 addresses discontinuation of work under an approved permit. Unless a longer period is provided by state or local law or by the development approval, then a development approval expires after twelve months of discontinuation. (Part I of S.L. 2019-111 sets that expiration at twenty-four months of discontinuation. The difference will be resolved when Part I is incorporated into Chapter 160D.)

---

5. The change in minimum size from 100 to 25 acres was made by S.L. 2019-111, Part 1, and will be incorporated into Chapter 160D.

6. G.S. 160D-108(d)(4).

7. G.S. 160D-108(d)(5).

8. G.S. 160D-108(e).

E. Exceptions

G.S. 160D-108(f) preserves and clarifies the specific circumstances under which amended ordinances apply to development despite vested rights under a site-specific vesting plan or multi-phase development. These include the following:

- by written consent of the affected landowner;
- upon findings based on an evidentiary hearing that natural or man-made hazards would pose a serious threat to public health, safety, and welfare if the project proceeded as approved;
- upon compensation to the owner for the loss;
- upon findings based on an evidentiary hearing that the applicant intentionally supplied inaccurate information or made material misrepresentations that made a difference in the approval by the local government; and
- upon findings based on an evidentiary hearing that the enactment or promulgation of a state or federal law or regulation that precludes the development as approved and has a fundamental effect on the plan, in which case the local government may modify the affected provisions.

G.S. 160D-108(f)(2) continues the provision that a development with vested rights under a site-specific vesting plan or multi-phase development may still be subject to overlay zoning and other development regulations that impose additional requirements but do not affect the type or intensity of use, as well as other generally applicable regulations such as building code requirements.

Local governments may still adopt development regulations concerning nonconforming situations.

F. Permit Choice

The statutes concerning the permit choice rule for local regulations are recodified at G.S. 160D-108(b), alongside the vested rights provisions.[9] The statute maintains the existing rule: If an application is made in accordance with local regulation and then an applicable development regulation is changed, then the applicant may choose which version of the regulation applies to the application. The revised version of the rule clarifies that if the applicant chooses the former rule, then the local government cannot require the applicant to wait for final action on the proposed change.

Part I of S.L. 2019-111 added additional provisions for permit choice that are to be incorporated into Chapter 160D.[10] If a permit application is on hold for six consecutive months, then the permit choice rule is waived. This may occur if the applicant voluntarily places the application on hold or if the applicant fails to respond to comments or reasonable requests for additional information for six months. If an applicant resumes an application after six months of discontinuation, then the rules in effect at the time of resuming consideration of the application apply.

One application serves as a placeholder for permit choice for all related development regulations for that project. When an applicant submits an initial application for a development approval, the applicant can choose the development regulations applicable at that time for development approvals applicable to the project. This provision recognizes that many developments require multiple local and state permits that may be sequenced for approval. With this permit choice provision, the project is considered as a whole, allowing the entire project to be reviewed under the regulations in effect at

---

9. G.S. 143-755 also addresses the permit choice rule and applies more broadly to state permits. The alignment of Part I of S.L. 2019-111 into Chapter 160D may provide some additional clarification about the scope of the permit choice rule.

10. S.L. 2019-111 (S.B. 355), § 1.1.

the time of application if desired by the applicant. This broadened permit choice rule is available for eighteen months after the approval of the initial development approval. An erosion and sedimentation control permit or a sign permit may not be considered an initial development approval for purposes of this expanded permit choice.

If an application for a development approval is wrongfully denied or an illegal condition is imposed, then after appeal the applicant can choose the development regulations in effect at the time of the original application or the currently applicable rules. Any provision determined to be illegal will not apply.

An applicant may seek a court order compelling compliance. Such requests are set for immediate hearing, and subsequent proceedings are given priority.

II. Judicial Review

A. Declaratory Judgments and Other Civil Actions

G.S. 160D-1401 provides new statutory language to confirm that individuals may bring a declaratory judgment action to challenge certain development decisions. In particular, the section authorizes declaratory judgment actions for legislative zoning decisions, vested rights claims, and challenges to land use authority related to administrative decisions. The procedural rules outlined at Article 26 of G.S. Chapter 1 apply. The governmental unit making the challenged decision must be named a party to the action.

Legislative decisions. Under G.S. 160D-1401, a person may seek a declaratory judgment to challenge a legislative decision by a governing board, including a challenge to the validity or constitutionality of the development regulation. A challenge to a map adoption or amendment must be brought within sixty days of adoption.[11] A challenge to the validity of a development regulation (a challenge to text adoption of amendment) must be brought within one year of accrual of the action. Such action accrues when the party has standing to bring the action. A challenge to ordinance adoption on the basis of a procedural defect must be brought within three years after the adoption of the ordinance.[12]

Vested rights determinations. As discussed in the section on vested rights, a person claiming a common law or statutory vested right may seek an administrative determination by submitting evidence to the zoning administrator or other authorized official.[13] That decision may be appealed to the board of adjustment and then the superior court in the nature of certiorari, as discussed more below.

In addition to that authority, G.S. 160D-108(c) and (g) authorize a person to bring an original civil action to determine statutory or common law vested rights in lieu of seeking that determination from a zoning administrator and appealing to the board of adjustment. G.S. 160D-1401 reaffirms that such action is brought as a declaratory judgment action. Part I of S.L. 2019-111, which will be incorporated into Chapter 160D, states that such challenges must be commenced within one year after the date on which written notice of the final decision is delivered to the party.[14]

---

11. G.S. 160D-1405.
12. *Id.*
13. G.S. 160D-108(c).
14. S.L. 2019-111, § 1.7.

Authority for administrative decisions. G.S. 160D-405 outlines the authority and procedures for appeals of administrative decisions. Such appeals commonly go to the board of adjustment and then to superior court in the nature of certiorari (discussed more below). A new statutory provision authorizes a person to bring an original civil action to challenge the constitutionality of a development regulation or to challenge whether a development regulation is ultra vires, preempted, or otherwise in excess of statutory authority. Such a challenge may go straight to court without an appeal to the board of adjustment. There are a couple of reasons for this clarification. First, a local board of adjustment is tasked with reviewing variances and administrative decisions; a board of adjustment is not authorized to rule on questions of constitutionality or state authority. So, on questions of constitutionality and statutory authority, there is no need to go to the board of adjustment. Allowing for an original civil action will improve efficiency. Second, the local board of adjustment typically is not equipped to answer questions of law such as constitutionality and statutory authority. Those issues are more appropriate in court.

There are still plenty of disputes that are best handled through an administrative appeal process through the board of adjustment. Questions of ordinance interpretation or a determination of facts about a violation are still handled through the board of adjustment.

S.L. 2019-111, Section 1.7, which will be incorporated into Chapter 160D, clarifies that a challenge based on ordinance interpretation must still go to the board of adjustment before it is appealed to court. Part I also provides a statute of limitations for such challenge: one year after the date on which written notice of the final decision is delivered to the party.[15]

Other civil actions. G.S. 160D-1404 makes clear that parties may bring other civil actions authorized by law. Chapter 160D does not limit that availability of other civil actions except as expressly stated.

B. Appeals of Quasi-Judicial Decisions

G.S. 160D-1402 restates the provisions for appeals in the nature of certiorari previously codified at G.S. 153A-349 and 160A-393 with a few clarifications.

Stays, enforcement, and work. G.S. 160D-1402(e) clarifies that on appeal, a party may request a stay of the approval or enforcement action that is being appealed. The court has discretion to grant that stay and to require conditions to provide for the security of the adverse party. A stay in favor of a local government cannot require a bond or other security. G.S. 160D-1402(*l*) makes clear that in the absence of a stay, a person with a development approval may commence work while the approval is on appeal. If, however, that approval is reversed on appeal, then the person does not have any vested rights based on actions taken during appeal and must proceed as if no development approval was granted.

Preservation certificates of appropriateness. A person cannot commence development work within a local historic district or affecting a local historic landmark without first obtaining a certificate of appropriateness (COA) from the historic preservation commission. Under prior law, appeals of COA decisions went to the local board of adjustment, which had to review the matter in the nature of certiorari. This process provides for a local appeal before parties go to court, but most boards of adjustment are not accustomed to sitting as an appellate tribunal reviewing a decision from another board. In that scenario, the board of adjustment cannot take new evidence and is greatly limited in overturning the preservation commission. This step commonly adds time and cost to a case that is heading to court anyway.

---

15. S.L. 2019-111, § 1.7.

G.S. 160D-947 allows for local governments to choose to continue with COA appeals going to the board of adjustment. Notably, the new statute also allows local governments to opt for COA appeals to go straight to superior court, like appeals of all other quasi-judicial decisions. The default rule now is that the appeals go to superior court. If a local government opts for appeals to the board of adjustment prior to judicial review, then that provision must be made in the development regulations.

Whether the appeal goes to the board of adjustment or directly to superior court, the procedures and standards set forth at G.S. 160D-1402 for appeals in the nature of certiorari apply. Appeals of COA decisions must be filed within thirty days after the decision is effective or written notice is provided—the same as other quasi-judicial matters.[16]

Supplementing the record. Previously, G.S. 160A-393 gave courts discretion to allow parties to supplement the record in superior court cases when needed. Now, with amendment by S.L. 2019-111, Section 1.9, which will be incorporated into Chapter 160D, courts must allow the record to be supplemented with affidavits, testimony of witnesses, documentary evidence, or other evidence if the petition raises questions of standing, conflicts of interest, constitutional violations, or actions in excess of statutory authority.[17]

Standard of review for prima facie case. S.L. 2019-111, Section 1.9, affirms that the question of whether a record contains competent, material, and substantial evidence is a conclusion of law to be reviewed by the court de novo.

Incompetent evidence. S.L. 2019-111, Section 1.9, clarifies that even if there is no objection before the local decision-making board, opinion testimony from a lay witness shall not be considered competent evidence concerning projected property-value impacts, projected traffic impacts, or other matters requiring technical expertise.

Judicial instructions. S.L. 2019-111, Section 1.9, clarifies the decisions that a court may make when handling an appeal from a quasi-judicial decision. When the court determines that a permit was wrongfully denied, "[it] shall remand with instructions that the permit be issued, subject to any conditions expressly consented to by the permit applicant as part of the application or during the board of adjustment appeal or writ of certiorari appeal." Additionally, the statute now includes language to address wrongful zoning enforcement: "If the court concludes that a zoning board decision upholding a zoning enforcement action was not supported by substantial competent evidence or was otherwise based on an error of law, the court shall reverse the decision."

C. Subdivision Decisions

G.S. 160D-1403 recodifies and clarifies the rules of appeals of subdivision plat decisions. Most subdivision decisions are administrative in nature. As defined in G.S. 160D-102, administrative decisions are those that involve the determination of facts and the application of objective standards set forth in the development regulation. Administrative decisions may be made by a staff person, committee, board, or governing body—the status as administrative is determined by the objective standards, not by the person or board making the decision. G.S. 160D-1403 restates the prior rule that administrative subdivision decisions are appealed to superior court. Such an appeal must be filed within thirty days of receipt of the written notice of the decision. As was the case under prior law, a local government can also establish rules for an administrative subdivision decision to be appealed to the local board of adjustment under G.S. 160D-405.

---

16. G.S. 160D-947, -1405.
17. G.S. 160A-393(j).

Some subdivision decisions are based on quasi-judicial standards, which require the decision-making board to apply judgment and discretion. Quasi-judicial subdivision decisions are appealed to superior court in the nature of certiorari and subject to the procedures outlined at G.S. 160D-1402, just like other quasi-judicial decisions.

D. Attorneys' Fees

Part I of S.L. 2019-111, legislation that will be incorporated into Chapter 160D, amends G.S. 6-21.7 to make attorneys' fees mandatory for some local government litigation. If a court finds "that the city or county violated a statute or case law setting forth unambiguous limits on its authority, the court shall award reasonable attorneys' fees and costs." The statute defines *unambiguous* to mean "that the limits of authority are not reasonably susceptible to multiple constructions." If a court finds "that the city or county took action inconsistent with, or in violation of, [the Permit Choice and Vested Rights statutes] . . . , the court shall award reasonable attorneys' fees and costs." In other matters of local government litigation, the courts maintain discretion and "may award reasonable attorneys' fees and costs to the prevailing private litigant."

E. Statutes of Limitation

G.S. 160D-1405 consolidates several of the applicable statutes of limitation for appeals of zoning decisions. The substance of the limits remains the same as under prior law, for the most part. Notably, Chapter 160D adds language to include development agreements alongside rezoning decisions with a sixty-day limit. Conditional zoning decisions similarly are subject to the sixty-day limit because those decisions are zoning-map amendments. Specific amendments in Part 1 of S.L. 2019-111 will be incorporated into the Chapter 160D provisions on statutes of limitation.

Prior law included specific provisions preserving certain rights to raise ordinance invalidity as a defense against enforcement actions. Note that those provisions are preserved in 160D-1405(c).

Table 5.1 below is a summary of the applicable statutes of limitation.

F. Additional Judicial Rules

Joinder. G.S. 160D-1402(m) clarifies that a civil action challenging an ordinance may be joined with an appeal in the nature of certiorari challenging a quasi-judicial decision. Part I of S.L. 2019-111 included similar joinder provisions that will be incorporated in Chapter 160D.

Estoppel and conditions. North Carolina courts have long recognized that when an applicant enjoys the benefits of a permit approval, the applicant cannot then challenge the conditions of that approval.[18] In other words, the applicant that begins the development and enjoys the benefits of the permit is estopped from challenging the rules of the permit or the conditions imposed. That rule remains, but Part I of S.L. 2019-111, legislation that will be incorporated into Chapter 160D, provides an important clarification and limitation. If the applicant did not consent to the condition in writing, and the applicant is challenging the unconsented condition, then the applicant may proceed with the development, and the local government may not assert the defense of estoppel against the applicant. This new statutory language is further incentive for local governments to ensure written consent from the applicant for any and all conditions.

---

18. *See, e.g.,* Convent of the Sisters of Saint Joseph v. City of Winston-Salem, 243 N.C. 316, 90 S.E.2d 879 (1956); River Birch Assocs. v. City of Raleigh, 326 N.C. 100, 388 S.E.2d 538 (1990).

Table 5.1. Statutes of Limitation

Challenge	Statute of Limitations	Citation
Ordinance text adoption or amendment: Procedural defect	Three years from adoption of the ordinance	G.S. 160D-1405(b)
Ordinance text adoption or amendment: Question of authority or constitutionality	One year from party having standing to challenge	G.S. 160D-1405(b); 1-54(10)
Vested rights: Civil action	One year after receipt of written notice of decision	S.L. 2019-111, § 1.7 (to be added to Chapter 160D)
Administrative decision: Civil action regarding authority or constitutionality	One year after receipt of written notice of decision	S.L. 2019-111, § 1.7 (to be added to Chapter 160D)
Validity of zoning-map adoption or amendment	Sixty days from adoption	G.S. 160D-1405(a); 1-54.1
Quasi-judicial decision	Thirty days after the decision is effective or after notice is provided to the party	G.S. 160D-1405(d)
Subdivision decision (quasi-judicial)	Thirty days after the decision is effective or after notice is provided to the party	G.S. 160D-1403
Subdivision decision (administrative): Appeal to superior court or board of adjustment	Thirty days after receipt of written notice of decision	G.S. 160D-1403
Administrative decision: Appeal to board of adjustment	Thirty days after receipt of notice of decision	G.S. 160D-405

Mootness. Part I of S.L 2019-111, which will be incorporated into Chapter 160D, establishes a specific mootness rule. For appeals in the nature of certiorari and original civil actions, an action is not rendered moot if the party loses the relevant property interest as a result of the local government action being appealed, and exhaustion of an appeal is required to preserve a claim for damages under G.S. 160A-393.1.[19] This provision is "[s]ubject to the limitations in the State and federal constitutions and State and federal case law," and these limitations may raise issues of case-or-controversy jurisprudence.

---

19. G.S. 160A-393(d)(4).

Appendix A. G.S. Chapter 160D Checklist of Changes to Local Ordinances, Policies, and Practices

This checklist outlines provisions in the new Chapter 160D of the North Carolina General Statutes (hereinafter G.S.) as well as related statutory changes that will be incorporated into Chapter 160D. The changes to the statutes affect the language of local ordinances, the options for local decision processes, and the administrative practices related to development regulations.

This checklist is one piece of a larger set of resources and training materials, including an explanatory book, *Chapter 160D: A New Land Use Law for North Carolina.* Each item on this checklist is described more thoroughly in those additional resources. Section headers in this checklist note the corresponding chapter and section of the Chapter 160D book [in brackets]. Check nc160D.sog.unc.edu for additional resources and training.

The checklist has specific notations, which are accompanied by specific icons, as follows:

☐ Denotes **legislative changes** for which local governments ***must*** take action (statutory citations are in parentheses)

○ Denotes **permissive legislative changes** for which local governments ***may*** take action

△ Denotes **notable legislative changes** that do not require local action but of which local governments must ***be aware***

*For items noted with an asterisk, local governments do not have authority for the change until January 1, 2021, unless legislation authorizes earlier effectiveness. Noted changes may be incorporated into ordinances and policies, but they must not be effective until 2021. All other changes may be adopted and effective immediately.

I. Terminology and Citations [Chapter 1, Section III]

☐ **Must** update any references to provisions in G.S. Chapter 160A or 153A to indicate relevant provisions in Chapter 160D. (*See* appendixes B and C in the Chapter 160D book.)

☐ **Must** align ordinance terminology with Chapter 160D terminology for *conditional zoning* and *special use permits*; must delete use of the terms *conditional use permit, special exception, conditional use district zoning,* and *special use district zoning.* (*See* G.S. 160D-102.)

☐ **Must** ensure that ordinance definitions for the following terms are not inconsistent with definitions provided in state law and regulation: *building, dwelling, dwelling unit, bedroom,* and *sleeping unit.* (S.L. 2019-111, § 1.17.)

○ **May** align ordinance terminology with Chapter 160D terminology, including for the following terms: *administrative decision, administrative hearing, determination, developer, development, development approval, development regulation, dwelling, evidentiary hearing, legislative decision, legislative hearing, planning and development regulation jurisdiction,* and *quasi-judicial decision.* (G.S. 160D-102.)

II. Geographic Jurisdiction [Chapter 2, Section I]

☐ *For extension of extraterritorial jurisdiction (ETJ), a municipality **must** provide mailed notice thirty days prior to ETJ hearing; municipality **may** hold one hearing (with single mailed notice) regarding ETJ and initial zoning amendment. (G.S. 160D-202(d).)

○ Municipality **may** hold hearings in anticipation of change in jurisdiction. (G.S. 160D-204.)

○ *For a parcel in two jurisdictions, the owner and the jurisdictions **may** agree for development regulations from one jurisdiction to apply to the entire parcel. (G.S. 160D-203.)

○ *In ETJ, the county **may** elect to exercise development regulations that the municipality is not exercising. (G.S. 160D-202(b).)

III. Boards [Chapter 2, Section II]

A. In General

☐ **Must** adopt broadened conflict-of-interest standards for governing and advisory boards. (G.S. 160D-109.)

☐ **Must** keep minutes of proceedings of each board. (G.S. 160D-308.)

☐ **Must** have each board member take an oath of office before starting his or her duties. (G.S. 160D-309.)

☐ **Must** update ETJ population estimate, at least with each decennial census (also calculation for proportional representation is simplified and process for appointment is clarified). (G.S. 160D-307.)

☐ **Must** provide proportional representation for ETJ on preservation commission if any districts or landmarks are designated in the ETJ. (G.S. 160D-307.)

○ **May** have detailed rules of procedure for each board; **may** be adopted by governing board; if not, then **may** be adopted by individual board; if adopted, **must** maintain board rules of procedure (by clerk or other officer as set by ordinance) and **must** post board rules of procedure to website, if the jurisdiction has a website. (G.S. 160D-308.)

○ **May** establish reasonable procedures to solicit, review, and make appointments; governing board typically makes appointments but may delegate that appointment-making authority. (G.S. 160D-310.)

○ **May** establish additional advisory boards related to development regulations. (G.S. 160D-306.)

B. Planning Board

○ **May** assign to planning board the coordination of citizen engagement for planning. (G.S. 160D-301.)

○ **May** assign planning board to serve as preliminary forum for review and comment on quasi-judicial decisions, provided that no part of the preliminary forum or recommendation may be used as a basis for the deciding board. (G.S. 160D-301.)

C. Board of Adjustment

○ **May** assign board of adjustment to hear and decide matters under any development regulation, not just zoning. (G.S. 160D-302.)

○ **May** assign duties of housing appeals board to board of adjustment. (G.S. 160D-305.)

IV. Land Use Administration [Chapter 2, Section III]

A. In General

☐ **Must** incorporate new staff conflict-of-interest standards into ordinance or policy. (G.S. 160D-109.)

☐ **Must** maintain in paper or digital format current and prior zoning maps for public inspection. (G.S. 160D-105.)

☐ **Must** maintain in paper or digital format any state or federal agency maps incorporated by reference into the zoning map. (G.S. 160D-105.)

○ **May** enact ordinances, procedures, and fee schedules relating to administration and enforcement of development regulations. (G.S. 160D-402(b).)

○ **May** charge reasonable fees for support, administration, and implementation of development regulation; **must** use any such fees for that purpose, not for other purposes. (G.S. 160D-402(d).)

B. Enforcement

☐ **Must** issue notices of violation (NOVs) in conformance with statutory procedures (must deliver to permittee and landowner if different; may deliver to occupant or person undertaking the activity; delivery by hand, email, or first-class mail; may be posted onsite; administrator to certify NOV for the file.) (G.S. 160D-404(a).)

☐ If inspecting, **must** enter the premises during reasonable hours and upon presenting credentials; **must** have consent of premises owner or an administrative search warrant to inspect areas not open to the public. (G.S. 160D-403(e).)

☐ For revocation of development approval, **must** follow the same process as was used for the approval. (G.S. 160D-403(f).)

○ **May** perform inspections for other development approvals to ensure compliance with state law, local law, and the terms of the approval; **must** perform (or contract for) inspections for building permits. (G.S. 160D-1113; -403(e).)

○ **May** perform inspections for general code compliance and enforcement (inspections unrelated to a development approval). (G.S. 160D-402(b).)

○ **May** require a certificate of compliance or occupancy to confirm that permitted work complies with applicable laws and terms of the permit; still **must** require certificate of occupancy for work requiring a building permit. (G.S. 160D-403(g).)

○ **May** issue stop-work orders for illegal or dangerous work or activity, whether related to a permit or not. (G.S. 160D-404(b).)

○ **May** continue to use general enforcement methods, including civil penalties, fines, court-ordered actions, and criminal prosecution. (G.S. 160D-404(c).)

△ Be aware that a local government must bring a court action in advance of the applicable five- and seven-year statutes of limitation. (G.S. 1-51 and -49; established prior to Chapter 160D.)

V. Substance of Zoning Ordinance [Chapter 3, Section I]

☐ **Must** maintain current and prior zoning maps for public inspection (local government clerk or other office may be the responsible office); **may** adopt and maintain in paper or digital format. (G.S. 160D-105.)

☐ **Must** eliminate conditional-use-district zoning; existing conditional-use-district zoning converts to conditional district on January 1, 2021. (G.S. 160D-703; S.L. 2019-111, § 2.9(b).)

○ ***May** incorporate maps officially adopted by state or federal agencies (such as flood-insurance rate maps (FIRMs)) into the zoning map; **may** incorporate *the most recent officially adopted version* of such maps so that there is no need for ordinance amendment for subsequent map updates; **must** maintain current effective map for public inspection; **may** maintain in paper or digital format. (G.S. 160D-105.)

○ ***May** require certain dedications and performance guarantees for zoning approvals to the same extent as for subdivision approvals. (G.S. 160D-702.)

○ **May** use form-based codes. (G.S. 160D-703(a)(3).)

○ **May** allow administrative minor modification of conditional zoning, special use permits, and other development approvals; if allowed, **must** define "minor modification" by ordinance, **must** not include modification of use or density, and major modifications **must** follow standard approval process. (G.S. 160D-403(d), -703(b), -705(c).)

○ **May** apply zoning standards jurisdiction-wide, not just on a zoning-district-by-zoning-district basis. (G.S. 160D-703(d).)

○ ***May** regulate development over navigable waters, including floating homes. (G.S. 160D-702(a).)

VI. Substance of Other Development Ordinances [Chapter 3, Section II]

☐ **Must** conform subdivision performance guarantee requirements with statutory standards. (S.L. 2019-79 (S.B. 313), to be incorporated into G.S. Chapter 160D.)

☐ **Must** conform subdivision procedures for expedited review of certain minor subdivisions. (G.S. 160D-802, established prior to G.S. Chapter 160D.)

☐ **Must** exempt farm use on bona fide farm in ETJ from city zoning to the same extent it would be exempt from county zoning; Chapter 160D clarifies that other municipal development regulations may still apply. (G.S. 160D-903(c).)

☐ **Must** not exclude manufactured homes based on the age of the home. (G.S. 160D-910.)

☐ ***Must** follow standardized process for housing-code enforcement to determine owner's abandonment of intent to repair and need for demolition. (G.S. 160D-1203(6).)

○ **May** adopt moratoria for development regulations (subject to limitation on residential uses); moratoria do not affect rights established by permit choice rule. (G.S. 160D-107.)

A. Historic Preservation

☐ **Must** follow standard quasi-judicial procedures for preservation certificates of appropriateness. (G.S. 160D-947(c).)

☐ **Must** frame preservation district provisions as "standards" rather than "guidelines." (G.S. 160D-947(c).)

☐ ***May** choose for appeals of preservation commission decisions to go directly to superior court rather than to board of adjustment. (G.S. 160D-947(e).)

B. Development Agreements

☐ **Must** process a development agreement as a legislative decision. (G.S. 160D-105.)

☐ **Must** have a local government as a party to a development agreement (a water and sewer authority may enter an agreement as a party, but not independently). (G.S. 160D-1001(b).)

○ **May** consider a development agreement concurrently with a rezoning, subdivision, or site plan; **may** consider a development agreement in conjunction with a conditional zoning that incorporates the development agreement. (G.S. 160D-1001(d).)

○ ***May** address fewer topics in development agreement content (list of mandated topics is shortened). (G.S. 160D-1006.)

○ **May** mutually agree with a developer for the developer to provide public improvements beyond what could have been required, provided such conditions are included in the development agreement. (G.S. 160D-1006(d).)

○ **May** include penalties for breach of a development agreement in the agreement or in the ordinance setting the procedures for development agreements; either party may bring legal action seeking an injunction to enforce a development agreement. (G.S. 160D-1008.)

VII. Comprehensive Plan [Chapter 4, Section I]

- ☐ **Must** adopt a comprehensive plan by July 1, 2022, to maintain zoning (no need to re-adopt a reasonably recent plan). (G.S. 160D-501(a).)

- ☐ **Must** adopt a plan or a plan update following the procedures used for a legislative decision. (G.S. 160D-501(c).)

- ☐ **Must** reasonably maintain a plan. (G.S. 160D-501(a).)

- ○ **May** coordinate a comprehensive plan with other required plans, such as Coastal Area Management Act (CAMA) plans. (G.S. 160D-501(a).)

- ○ **May** coordinate with other local governments, state agencies, or regional agencies on planning processes. (G.S. 160D-503(a).)

VIII. Legislative Decisions [Chapter 4, Section II]

A. Notice

- ☐ **Must** follow applicable procedures for legislative decisions under any development regulation authorized under Chapter 160D, not just zoning; **must** adopt any development regulation by ordinance, not by resolution. (G.S. 160D-601.)

- ☐ For zoning-map amendments, **must** provide notice not only to immediate neighbors but also to properties separated from the subject property by street, railroad, or other transportation corridor. (G.S. 160D-602.)

- ☐ For zoning-map amendments, **must** provide posted notice during the time period running from twenty-five days prior to the hearing until ten days prior to the hearing. (G.S. 160D-602(c).)

- ○ For extension of ETJ, **may** use single mailed notice for ETJ and zoning-map amendment pursuant to statutory procedures. (G.S. 160D-202.)

- ○ For zoning-map amendments, **may** require applicant to notify neighbors and hold a community meeting and **may** require report on the neighborhood communication as part of the application materials. (G.S. 160D-602(e).)

B. Planning Board Comment

- ☐ **Must** refer zoning amendments to the planning board for review and comment; **must** not have governing board handle planning board duty to review and comment on zoning amendments. (G.S. 160D-604(c), (e).)

- ☐ **Must** have planning board consider any plan adopted according to G.S. 160D-501 when making a comment on plan consistency. (G.S. 160D-604(d).)

- ○ **May** refer development regulation amendments (other than zoning) to the planning board for review and comment. (G.S. 160D-604(c).)

C. Plan Consistency

☐ When adopting an amendment to the zoning ordinance, **must** adopt a brief statement describing whether the action is consistent or inconsistent with approved plans. (G.S. 160D-605(a).) (*This eliminates the 2017 requirement that statements take one of three particular forms.*)

○ **May** adopt plan-consistency statement when acting upon the zoning amendment or as a separate motion. (G.S. 160D-605(a).)

○ ***May** meet the requirement for plan consistency even without formal adoption of a written statement if the minutes of the governing board meeting reflect that the board was fully aware of and considered the plan. (G.S. 160D-605(a).)

○ **May** concurrently consider a comprehensive plan amendment and a zoning amendment; must not require a separate application or fee for plan amendment. (G.S. 160D-605(a).)

☐ **Must** note on the applicable future land use map when a zoning-map amendment is approved that is not consistent with the map; the future land use map is deemed amended when an inconsistent rezoning is approved. (G.S. 160D-605(a).) (*This clarifies that a rezoning inconsistent with a plan does not amend the text of the plan, but it does amend the future land use map.*)

☐ *For a future land use map that is deemed amended, if it is a CAMA plan, then such amendment is not effective until it goes through the CAMA plan-amendment process. (G.S. 160D-501.)

☐ **Must** adopt a statement of reasonableness for zoning-*map* amendments; for such statements, **may** consider factors noted in the statutes; ***may** adopt a statement of reasonableness for zoning-*text* amendments. (G.S. 160D-605(b).)

○ **May** consider and approve a statement of reasonableness and a plan-consistency statement as a single, combined statement. (G.S. 160D-605(c).)

D. Voting

☐ *Must permit adoption of a legislative decision for development regulation on first reading by simple majority; no need for two-thirds majority on first reading, as was required for cities under prior law. (G.S. 160A-75; S.L. 2019-111, § 2.5(n).)

E. Certain Legislative Decisions

☐ **Must** prohibit third-party down-zonings; **may** process local government–initiated down-zonings (S.L. 2019-111, Pt. I.)

☐ **Must** obtain applicant's/landowner's written consent to conditions related to a conditional-zoning approval to ensure enforceability. (S.L. 2019-111, Pt. I.)

○ **May** use purely legislative conditional zoning and/or quasi-judicial special use permitting; **must** not use combined legislative and quasi-judicial process, such as conditional-use-district zoning. (G.S. 160D-102.)

○ With applicant's written consent, **may** agree to conditional-zoning conditions that go beyond the basic zoning authority to address additional fees, design requirements, and other development considerations. (S.L. 2019-111, Pt. I.)

○ **May** allow administrative minor modification of conditional zoning, special use permits, and other development approvals; if allowed, **must** define "minor modification" by ordinance, **must** not include modification of use or density, and major modifications **must** follow standard approval process. (G.S. 160D-403(d), -703(b), -705(c).)

IX. Quasi-Judicial Decisions [Chapter 4, Section III]

A. Procedures

☐ **Must** follow statutory procedures for all quasi-judicial development decisions, including variances, special use permits, certificates of appropriateness, and appeals of administrative determinations. (G.S. 160D-102(28).)

☐ **Must** hold an evidentiary hearing to gather competent, material, and substantial evidence to establish the facts of the case; the evidentiary hearing **must** have testimony under oath; **must** establish written findings of fact and conclusions of law. (G.S. 160D-406.)

☐ Board chair **must** rule at the evidentiary hearing on objections to inclusion or exclusion of administrative material; such ruling **may** be appealed to the full board. (G.S. 160D-406(d).)

☐ **Must** allow parties with standing to participate fully in the evidentiary hearing, including presenting evidence, cross-examining witnesses, objecting to evidence, and making legal arguments; **may** allow non-parties to present competent, material, and substantial evidence that is not repetitive. (G.S. 160D-406(d).)

○ **May** continue an evidentiary hearing without additional notice if the time, date, and place of the continued hearing is announced at a duly noticed hearing that has been convened; if quorum is not present at a meeting, the evidentiary hearing is automatically continued to the next regular meeting of the board with no notice. (G.S. 160D-406(b).)

○ **May** distribute meeting packet to board members in advance of the evidentiary hearing; if this is done, then **must** distribute the same materials to the applicant and landowner at the same time; **must** present such administrative materials at the hearing and make them part of the hearing record. (G.S. 160D-406(c).)

○ **May** have the planning board serve as a preliminary forum for review in quasi-judicial decisions; if this is done, the planning board must not conduct a formal evidentiary hearing but must conduct an informal preliminary discussion of the application; the forum and recommendation must not be used as the basis for the decision by the board—the decision must still be based on evidence presented at the evidentiary hearing. (G.S. 160D-301.)

○ **May** require recordation of special use permits with the register of deeds. (G.S. 160D-705(c).)

△ **Be aware** that the definition of *close family relationship* as used for conflicts of interest includes spouse, parent, child, brother, sister, grandparent, or grandchild (including step, half, and in-law relationships). (G.S. 160D-109(f).)

△ **Be aware** that even if there is no objection before the board, opinion testimony from a lay witness shall not be considered competent evidence for technical matters such as property value and traffic impacts. (S.L. 2019-111, § 1.9.)

B. Certain Quasi-Judicial Decisions

☐ **Must** not impose conditions on special use permits that the local government does not otherwise have statutory authority to impose. (S.L. 2019-111, Pt. I.)

☐ **Must** obtain applicant's/landowner's written consent to conditions related to a special use permit to ensure enforceability. (S.L. 2019-111, Pt. I.)

☐ **Must** set a thirty-day period to file an appeal of any administrative determination under a development regulation; **must** presume that if notice of determination is sent by mail, it is received on the third business day after it is sent. (G.S. 160D-405(c).)

○ ***May** adjust variance standards to provide for reasonable accommodation under the federal Fair Housing Act. (G.S. 160D-705(c).)

○ **May** use purely legislative conditional zoning and/or quasi-judicial special use permitting; **must** not use combined legislative and quasi-judicial process, such as conditional-use-district zoning. (G.S. 160D-102.)

○ **May** allow administrative minor modification of conditional zoning, special use permits, and other development approvals; if allowed, **must** define "minor modification" by ordinance, **must** not include modification of use or density, and major modifications **must** follow standard approval process. (G.S. 160D-403(d), -703(b), -705(c).)

X. Administrative Decisions [Chapter 4, Section IV]

A. Development Approvals

☐ **Must** provide development approvals in writing; **may** provide in print or electronic form; if electronic form is used, then it **must** be protected from further editing. (G.S. 160D-403(a).)

☐ **Must** provide that applications for development approvals must be made by a person with a property interest in the property or a contract to purchase the property. (G.S. 160D-403(a).)

☐ **Must** provide that development approvals run with the land. (G.S. 160D-104.)

☐ For revocation of development approval, **must** follow the same process as was used for the approval. (G.S. 160D-403(f).)

○ **May** require community notice or informational meetings as part of the decision-making process for administrative development approvals (quasi-judicial and legislative decisions already had notice and hearing requirements). (G.S. 160D-403(h).)

○ **May** set expiration of development approvals if work is not substantially commenced; default rule is twelve months, unless altered by state or local rule. (G.S. 160D-403(c).) **Be aware** that legislation will clarify the provisions on duration of development approvals. (G.S. 160D-403(c); S.L. 2019-111, § 1.3.)

○ **May** set expiration of development approvals if work is discontinued; default rule is twelve months, unless altered by state or local rule. (G.S. 160D-403(c).)

○ **May** authorize administrative staff to approve minor modifications of development approvals and conditional-zoning approvals; if this is done, then **must** define "minor modifications" by ordinance and **must** not include modification of permitted use or density of development; major modifications **must** go through full applicable approval process. (G.S. 160D-403(d); -703(b); -705(c).)

B. Determinations

☐ **Must** provide written notice of determination by personal delivery, electronic mail, or first-class mail to the property owner and party seeking determination, if different from the owner. (G.S. 160D-403(b).)

○ **May** designate an official to make determinations for a particular development regulation. (G.S. 160D-403(b).)

○ **May** require owner to post notice of determination on the site for ten days; if such is not required, then owner has option to post on the site to establish constructive notice. (G.S. 160D-403(b).)

C. Appeals of Administrative Decisions

☐ **Must** allow administrative decisions of any development regulations (not just zoning) to be appealed to the board of adjustment, unless provided otherwise by statute or ordinance. (Appeals relating to erosion and sedimentation control, stormwater control, or building-code and housing-code violations are not made to the board of adjustment unless specified by local ordinance.) (G.S. 160D-405.)

☐ **Must** set a thirty-day period to file an appeal of any administrative determination under a development regulation; must presume that if notice of determination is sent by mail, it is received on the third business day after it is sent. (G.S. 160D-405(c).)

☐ **Must** require the official who made the decision (or his or her successor if the official is no longer employed) to appear as a witness in the appeal. (G.S. 160D-406.)

☐ **Must** pause enforcement actions, including fines, during the appeal. (G.S. 160D-405.)

○ **May** assign the duty of hearing appeals to another board; if this is done, such board must follow quasi-judicial procedures. (G.S. 160D-405.)

○ **May** designate that appeals be filed with the local government clerk *or* another official. (G.S. 160D-405.)

XI. Vested Rights and Permit Choice [Chapter 5, Section I]

A. Vested Rights

☐ **Must** recognize that building permits are valid for six months, as under prior law. (G.S. 160D-108(d)(1).)

☐ **Must** recognize the default rule that development approvals are valid for twelve months, unless adjusted by statute or local rule. (G.S. 160D-108(d)(2).)

☐ **Must** identify site-specific vesting plans (formerly site-specific development plans) with vesting for two to five years, as under prior law, except for specified exceptions. (G.S. 160D-108(d)(3); -108(f).)

☐ **Must** recognize multi-phase developments—long-term projects of at least 25 acres—with vesting up to seven years, except for specified exceptions (160D-108(d)(4); -108(f).) (The previously authorized phased-development plan is obsolete and should be deleted from ordinance.)

○ **May** provide for administrative determination of vested rights and for appeal to the board of adjustment. (G.S. 160D-108(c), -405.)

△ **Be aware** that a person claiming vested rights may bring an original civil action in court, skipping administrative determination and board of adjustment consideration. (G.S. 160D-405(c).)

△ **Be aware** that vested rights run with the land, except for state-permitted outdoor advertising permits that run with the owner of the permit. (G.S. 160D-108(g); S.L. 2019-111, Pt. I.)

B. Permit Choice

☐ **Must** not make an applicant wait for final action on the proposed change before proceeding if the applicant elected determination under prior rules. (G.S. 160D-108(b).)

△ **Be aware** that if a local development regulation changes after an application is submitted, the applicant may choose the version of the rule that applies; but **may** require the applicant to comply with new rules if the applicant delays the application for six months. (G.S. 160D-108(b); S.L. 2019-111, Pt. I.)

△ **Be aware** that an application for one development permit triggers permit choice for permits under any development regulation; such permit choice is valid for eighteen months after approval of the initial application. (S.L. 2019-111, Pt. I.)

XII. Judicial Review [Chapter 5, Section II]

A. Declaratory Judgments

△ **Be aware** that an individual may bring a declaratory judgment action to challenge legislative zoning decisions, vested rights claims, and challenges to land use authority related to administrative decisions, subject to specified procedures. (G.S. 160D-1401.)

△ **Be aware** that other civil actions may be authorized—Chapter 160D does not limit availability of other actions. (G.S. 160D-1404.)

B. Appeals of Quasi-Judicial Decisions

☐ ***Must** update ordinance to address appeals of certificates of appropriateness for historic landmarks and historic districts; default rule is that such appeals go straight to court; local government may opt for such appeals to go to the board of adjustment, as under prior statutes. (G.S. 160D-947.)

☐ **Must** provide that appeals of certificates of appropriateness must be filed within thirty days after the decision is effective or written notice is provided, the same as for appeals of other quasi-judicial decisions. (G.S. 160D-947; -1405.)

△ **Be aware** that on appeal a party may request a stay of the approval or enforcement action. (G.S. 160D-1402(e).)

△ **Be aware** that a local government may seek a stay in favor of itself (to prevent development under an approval). (G.S. 160D-1402(e).)

△ **Be aware** that if, in the absence of a stay, an applicant proceeds with development, the person does so at his or her own risk. (G.S. 160D-1402(*l*).)

△ **Be aware** that on appeal, the superior court now must allow for supplementing the record on questions of standing, conflicts of interest, constitutional violations, or actions in excess of statutory authority. (S.L. 2019-111, § 1.9.)

△ **Be aware** that even if there is no objection before the board, opinion testimony from a lay witness shall not be considered competent evidence for technical matters such as property value and traffic impacts. (S.L. 2019-111, § 1.9.)

△ **Be aware** of specific judicial instructions for decisions of appeals of quasi-judicial decisions. (S.L. 2019-111, § 1.9.)

C. Subdivision Decisions

○ **May** establish a rule that administrative subdivision decisions are appealed to the board of adjustment. (G.S. 160D-1405.)

△ **Be aware** that appeals of administrative subdivision decisions may be appealed directly to superior court. (G.S. 160D-1403.)

△ **Be aware** that quasi-judicial subdivision decisions are appealed to superior court in the nature of certiorari. (G.S. 160D-1402.)

D. Attorneys' Fees

△ **Be aware** that a court *shall* award attorneys' fees if the court finds that a city or county violated a statute or case law setting forth unambiguous limits on its authority. (G.S. 6-21.7; S.L. 2019-111, Pt. I.)

△ **Be aware** that a court *shall* award attorneys' fees if the court finds that a local government took action inconsistent with, or in violation of, the permit choice and vested rights statutes. (G.S. 6-21.7; S.L. 2019-111, Pt. I.)

△ **Be aware** that a court may award attorneys' fees in other matters of local government litigation. (G.S. 6-21.7; S.L. 2019-111, Pt. I.)

E. Additional Judicial Rules

△ **Be aware** that a court may join a civil action challenging an ordinance with an appeal in the nature of certiorari. (G.S. 160D-1402(m).)

△ **Be aware** that a local government **must** not assert the defense of estoppel to enforce conditions to which an applicant did not consent in writing. (S.L. 2019-111, Pt. I.)

△ **Be aware** that an action is not rendered moot if the party loses the relevant property interest as a result of the local government action being appealed, subject to applicable case law limits. (S.L 2019-111, Pt. I.)

Appendix B. Location of Prior Statutes in G.S. Chapter 160D

CHAPTER 160A	CHAPTER 153A	CHAPTER 160D[1]
ARTICLE 1 ***Definitions and Statutory Construction (most also retained in 160A/153A)***	**ARTICLE 1**	
§ 160A-1. Application and meaning of terms.	153A-1	160D-102
§ 160A-2. Effect upon prior laws.	153A-2	160D-111
§ 160A-3. General laws supplementary to charters.	153A-3	160D-102; -111
§ 160A-4. Broad construction.	153A-4	160D-110
§ 160A-4.1. Notice of new fees and fee increases; public comment period.	--	160D-800
§ 160A-5. Statutory references deemed amended to conform to Chapter 160D.	153A-5	160D-111
ARTICLE 19 ***Planning and Regulation of Development***	**ARTICLE 18**	
Part 1. General Provisions		
§ 160A-360. Territorial jurisdiction.	153A-320	160D-200; -202; -903
§ 160A-360.1. Permit choice.		160D-108(b)
§ 160A-361. Planning boards.	153A-321	160D-301
§ 160A-362. Extraterritorial representation.	--	160D-307
§ 160A-363. Supplemental powers.	153A-322	160D-102; -103; -106; -502
§ 160A-364. Procedure for adopting, amending, or repealing ordinances under Article.	153A-323	160D-601
§ 160A-364.1. Statute of limitations.	153A-348	160D-1405
§ 160A-365. Enforcement of ordinances.	153A-324	160D-106; -404(c)
§ 160A-366. Validation of ordinance.	--	160D-111
§§ 160A-367 through 160A-370. Reserved.	153A-327 to -329	--

---

1. The numbering for Chapter 160D sections follows the version as codified rather than the version as adopted. See the annotated bill in Appendix E for the original and revised section numbers.

CHAPTER 160A	CHAPTER 153A	CHAPTER 160D
Part 2. Subdivision Regulations		**ARTICLE 8**
§ 160A-371. Subdivision regulation.	153A-330	160D-801
§ 160A-372. Contents and requirements of ordinance.	153A-331	160D-804
§ 160A-373. Ordinance to contain procedure for plat approval; approval prerequisite to plat recordation; statement by owner.	153A-332	160D-803
§ 160A-374. Effect of plat approval on dedications.	153A-333	160D-806
§ 160A-375. Penalties for transferring lots in unapproved subdivisions.	153A-334	160D-807
§ 160A-376. Definition.	153A-335	160D-802
§ 160A-377. Appeals of decisions on subdivision plats.	153A-336	160D-808; -1403
§ 160A-378 through 160A-380. Reserved.	153A-337 to -339	--

CHAPTER 160A	CHAPTER 153A	CHAPTER 160D
Part 3. Zoning		**ARTICLE 7**
§ 160A-381. Grant of power.	153A-340	160D-107; -109; -406; -702; -704; -705; -903; -908
§ 160A-382. Districts.	153A-342	160D-502; -605(b); -703; -909
§ 160A-383. Purposes in view.	153A-341	160D-604(d); -605(a); -701
§ 160A-383.1. Zoning regulations for manufactured homes.	153A-341.1	160D-910
§ 160A-383.2. Voluntary agricultural districts.	--	160D-903
§ 160A-383.3. Reasonable accommodation of amateur radio antennas.	153A-341.2	160D-905
§ 160A-383.4. Local energy efficiency incentives.	--	160D-704
§ 160A-383.5. Temporary health care facilities.	153A-341.3	160D-915
§ 160A-384. Method of procedure.	153A-343	160D-601
§ 160A-385. Changes.	--	160D-102; -18(d); -603
§ 160A-385.1. Vested rights.	153A-344.1	160D-102; -100(d)
§ 160A-386. Protest petition; form; requirements; time for filing.	--	160D-603
§ 160A-387. Planning board; zoning plan; certification to city council.	153A-344	160D-604
§ 160A-388. Board of adjustment.	153A-345.1	160D-1-9(d); -302; -403(b); -405; -406; -702; -705; -1405
§ 160A-389. Remedies.	--	160D-404(c)
§ 160A-390. Conflict with other laws.	153A-346	160D-706
§ 160A-391. Other statutes not repealed.	--	--
§ 160A-392. Part applicable to buildings constructed by State and its subdivisions; exception.	153A-347	160D-913
§ 160A-393. Appeals in the nature of certiorari.	153A-349	160D-1-2; -1402
§ 160A-394. Reserved.	--	--
§§ 160A-395 through 160A-399: Repealed.	--	--
§§ 160A-399.1 through 160A-400: Repealed.	--	--

CHAPTER 160A	CHAPTER 153A	CHAPTER 160D
Part 3C. Historic Districts and Landmarks	--	*ARTICLE 9, PART 4*
§ 160A-400.1. Legislative findings.	--	160D-940
§ 160A-400.2. Exercise of powers by counties as well as cities.	--	--
§ 160A-400.3. Character of historic district defined.	--	160D-944
§ 160A-400.4. Designation of historic districts.	--	160D-944
§ 160A-400.5. Designation of landmarks; adoption of an ordinance; criteria for designation.	--	160D-945
§ 160A-400.6. Required landmark designation procedure.	--	160D-946
§ 160A-400.7. Historic Preservation Commission.	--	160D-303; -941
§ 160A-400.8. Powers of the Historic Preservation Commission.	--	160D-942
§ 160A-400.9. Certificate of appropriateness required.	--	160D-102; -947
§ 160A-400.10. Conflict with other laws.	--	160D-951
§ 160A-400.11. Remedies.	--	160D-404(c)
§ 160A-400.12. Appropriations.	--	160D-943
§ 160A-400.13. Certain changes not prohibited.	--	160D-948
§ 160A-400.14. Delay in demolition of landmarks and buildings within historic district.	--	160D-949
§ 160A-400.15. Demolition by neglect to contributing structures outside local historic districts.	--	160D-950
§ 160A-400.16 through 160A-400.19. Reserved.	--	--

CHAPTER 160A	CHAPTER 153A	CHAPTER 160D
Part 3D. Development Agreements		*ARTICLE 10*
§ 160A-400.20. Authorization for development agreements.	153A-349.1	160D-101
§ 160A-400.21. Definitions.	153A-349.2	160D-102; -102
§ 160A-400.22. Local governments authorized to enter into development agreements; approval of governing board required.	153A-349.3	160D-1-2; -103
§ 160A-400.23. Developed property must contain certain number of acres; permissible durations of agreements.	153A-349.4	160D-104
§ 160A-400.24. Public hearing.	153A-349.5	160D-105; -106
§ 160A-400.25. What development agreement must provide; what it may provide; major modification requires public notice and hearing.	153A-349.6	160D-106
§ 160A-400.26. Law in effect at time of agreement governs development; exceptions.	153A-349.7	160D-107
§ 160A-400.27. Periodic review to assess compliance with agreement; material breach by developer; notice of breach; cure of breach or modification or termination of agreement.	153A-349.8	160D-108
§ 160A-400.28. Amendment or cancellation of development agreement by mutual consent of parties or successors in interest.	153A-349.9	160D-109
§ 160A-400.29. Validity and duration of agreement entered into prior to change of jurisdiction; subsequent modification or suspension.	153A-349.10	160D-1010

CHAPTER 160A	CHAPTER 153A	CHAPTER 160D
§ 160A-400.30. Developer to record agreement within 14 days; burdens and benefits inure to successors in interest.	153A-349.11	160D-1011
§ 160A-400.31. Applicability to local government of constitutional and statutory procedures for approval of debt.	153A-349.12	160D-1012
§ 160A-400.32. Relationship of agreement to building or housing code.	153A-349.13	160D-101(c)

Part 3E. Wireless Telecommunication Facilities		*ARTICLE 9, PART 3*
§ 160A-400.50. Purpose and compliance with federal law.	153A-349.50	160D-930
§ 160A-400.51. Definitions.	153A-349.51	160D-931
§ 160A-400.51A. Local authority.	153A-349.52	160D-932
§ 160A-400.52. Construction of new wireless support structures or substantial modifications of wireless support structures.	153A-349.53	160D-933
§ 160A-400.53. Collocation and eligible facilities requests of wireless support structures.	153A-349.54	160D-934
§ 160A-400.54 through 160A-400.58. Reserved.		

Part 4. Acquisition of Open Space		*ARTICLE 13, PART 1*
§ 160A-401. Legislative intent.	--	160D-1301
§ 160A-402. Finding of necessity.	--	160D-1302
§ 160A-403. Counties or cities authorized to acquire and reconvey real property.	--	160D-1303
§ 160A-404. Joint action by governing bodies.	--	160D-1304
§ 160A-405. Powers of governing bodies.	--	160D-1305
§ 160A-406. Appropriations authorized.	--	160D-1306
§ 160A-407. Definitions.	--	160D-1307
§§ 160A-408 through 160A-410. Reserved.	--	--

Part 5. Building Inspection		*ARTICLE 11*
"Building" defined.	153A-350	160D-1101
Tribal lands.	153A-350.1	160D-1101
§ 160A-411. Inspection department.	153A-351	160D-402(b); -404(c); -1102
§ 160A-411.1. Qualifications of inspectors.	153A-351.1	160D-1103
§ 160A-412. Duties and responsibilities.	153A-352	160D-402(b); -1104
§ 160A-413. Joint inspection department; other arrangements.	153A-353	160D-402(c); -1105
§ 160A-414. Financial support.	153A-354	160D-402(d)
§ 160A-415. Conflicts of interest.	153A-355	160D-109(c); -1106
§ 160A-416. Failure to perform duties.	153A-356	160D-1107
§ 160A-417. Permits.	153A-357	160D-403; -1108
§ 160A-418. Time limitations on validity of permits.	153A-358	160D-403(c); -1109

CHAPTER 160A	CHAPTER 153A	CHAPTER 160D
§ 160A-419. Changes in work.	153A-359	160D-403(d); -1110
§ 160A-420. Inspections of work in progress.	153A-360	160D-403(e); -1111
§ 160A-421. Stop orders.	153A-361	160D-404(b); -1112
§ 160A-422. Revocation of permits.	153A-362	160D-403(f); -1113
§ 160A-423. Certificates of compliance.	153A-363	160D-403(g); -1114
§ 160A-424. Periodic inspections.	153A-364	160D-1115; -1207
§ 160A-425. Defects in buildings to be corrected.	153A-365	160D-1116
§ 160A-425.1. Repealed.	--	--
§ 160A-426. Unsafe buildings condemned in localities.	153A-366	160D-1117
§ 160A-427. Removing notice from condemned building.	153A-367	160D-1118
§ 160A-428. Action in event of failure to take corrective action.	153A-368	160D-1119
§ 160A-429. Order to take corrective action.	153A-369	160D-1120
§ 160A-430. Appeal; finality of order if not appealed.	153A-370	160D-1121
§ 160A-431. Failure to comply with order.	153A-371	160D-1122
§ 160A-432. Enforcement.	153A-372	160D-1123
§ 160A-433. Records and reports.	153A-373	160D-1124
§ 160A-434. Appeals in general.	153A-374	160D-1125
§ 160A-435. Establishment of fire limits.	153A-375	160D-1126
§ 160A-436. Restrictions within primary fire limits.	--	160D-1126
§ 160A-437. Restriction within secondary fire limits.	--	160D-1126
§ 160A-438. Failure to establish primary fire limits.	--	160D-1126
§ 160A-439. Ordinance authorized as to repair, closing, and demolition of nonresidential buildings or structures; order of public officer.	153A-372.1	160D-1127
§ 160A-440. Reserved.	--	--

Part 6. Minimum Housing Standards		*ARTICLE 12*
§ 160A-441. Exercise of police power authorized.	--	160D-1201
§ 160A-442. Definitions.	--	160D-102; -1101; -1202
§ 160A-443. Ordinance authorized as to repair, closing, and demolition; order of public officer.	--	160D-1203
§ 160A-443.1. Heat source required.	--	160D-1204
§ 160A-444. Standards.	--	160D-1205
§ 160A-445. Service of complaints and orders.	--	160D-1206
§ 160A-446. Remedies.	--	160D-305; -1208
§ 160A-447. Compensation to owners of condemned property.	--	160D-1209
§ 160A-448. Additional powers of public officer.	--	160D-1210
§ 160A-449. Administration of ordinance.	--	160D-1211
§ 160A-450. Supplemental nature of Part.	--	160D-1212

CHAPTER 160A	CHAPTER 153A	CHAPTER 160D
Part 7. Community Appearance Commissions		*ARTICLE 9, PART 5*
§ 160A-451. Membership and appointment of commission; joint commission.	--	160D-304
§ 160A-452. Powers and duties of commission.	--	160D-960
§ 160A-453. Staff services; advisory council.	--	160D-961
§ 160A-454. Annual report.	--	160D-962
§ 160A-455. Receipt and expenditure of funds.	--	160D-963
Part 8. Miscellaneous Powers		
§ 160A-456. Community development programs and activities.	153A-376	160D-1311
§ 160A-457. Acquisition and disposition of property for redevelopment.	153A-377	160D-1312
§ 160A-457.1. Urban Development Action Grants.	--	160D-1313
§ 160A-457.2. Urban homesteading programs.	--	160D-1314
§ 160A-458. Erosion and sedimentation control.	--	160D-922
§ 160A-458.1. Floodway regulations.	--	160D-923
§ 160A-458.2. Mountain ridge protection.	153A-448	160D-924
§ 160A-458.3. Downtown development projects.	--	160D-1315
§ 160A-458.4. Designation of transportation corridor official maps.	--	160D-916
§ 160A-458.5. Restriction of certain forestry activities prohibited.	153A-452	160D-921
§ 160A-459. Stormwater control.	153A-454	160D-925
§ 160A-459.1. Program to finance energy improvements.	153A-455	160D-1320
Low- and moderate-income housing programs	153A-378	160D-1316
Others		
§ 160A-181.1. Adult businesses.	--	160D-902
§ 160A-199. Outdoor advertising.	153A-143	160D-912
§ 160A-201. Solar collectors.	153A-143	160D-914
§ 160A-20 to -22. Family care homes.	--	160D-907

Appendix C. Location of G.S. Chapter 160D Provisions in Prior Statutes

CHAPTER 160D[1]	CHAPTER 153A	CHAPTER 160A
ARTICLE 1 *General Provisions*		
§ 160D-101. Application.	--	--
§ 160D-102. Definitions.	153A-344.1(b) 153A-349.2	160A-1(3) 160A-385(a)(2) 160A-385.1(b) 160A-393(a) 160A-400.9 160A-400.21 160A-442
§ 160D-103. Unified development ordinance.	153A-322(d)	160A-363(d)
§ 160D-104. Development approvals run with the land.	--	--
§ 160D-105. Maps.	--	--
§ 160D-106. Refund of illegal fees.	153A-324(b)	160A-363(e
§ 160D-107. Moratoria.	153A-340(h)	160A-381(e)
§ 160D-108. Vested rights and permit choice.	153A-320.1 153A-344 153A-344.1	160A-360.1 160A-385 160A-385.1
§ 160D-109. Conflicts of interest.	153A-340(g) 153A-355	160A-381(d) 160A-388(e) 160A-415
§ 160D-110. Chapter construction.	--	--
§ 160D-111. Effect on prior laws.	153A-2	160A-2 160A-5 160A-366
ARTICLE 2 *Planning and Development Regulation Jurisdiction*		
§ 160D-201. Planning and development regulation jurisdiction.	153A-320	160A-360
§ 160D-202. Municipal extraterritorial jurisdiction.	--	160-360
§ 160D-203. Split jurisdiction.	--	--
§ 160D-204. Pending jurisdiction.	--	--

---

1. The numbering for Chapter 160D sections follows the version as codified rather than the version as adopted. See the annotated bill in Appendix E for the original and revised section numbers.

CHAPTER 160D	CHAPTER 153A	CHAPTER 160A
ARTICLE 3 ***Boards and Organizational Arrangements***		
§ 160D-301. Planning boards.	153A-361	160A-321
§ 160D-302. Boards of adjustment.	--	160A-388
§ 160D-303. Historic preservation commission.	--	160A-400.7
§ 160D-304. Appearance commission.	--	160A-451
§ 160D-305. Housing appeals board.	--	160A-446
§ 160D-306. Other advisory boards.	--	--
§ 160D-307. Extraterritorial representation on boards.	--	160A-362
§ 160D-308. Rules of procedure.	--	--
§ 160D-309. Oath of office.	--	--
§ 160D-310. Appointments to boards.	--	--
ARTICLE 4 ***Administration, Enforcement, and Appeals***		
§ 160D-401. Application.	--	--
§ 160D-402. Administrative staff.	153A-351 153A-352 153A-353 153A-354	160A-411 160A-412 160A-413 160A-414
§ 160D-403. Administrative development approvals and determinations.	153A-357 153A-358 153A-359 153A-360 153A-362 153A-363	160A-388 160A-417 160A-418 160A-419 160A-420 160A-422 160A-423
§ 160D-404. Enforcement.	153A-324 153A-361	160A-365 160A-389 160A-400.11 160A-421
§ 160D-405. Appeals of administrative decisions.	--	160A-388
§ 160D-406. Quasi-judicial procedure.	--	160A-388
ARTICLE 5 ***Planning***		
§ 160D-501. Plans.	--	--
§ 160D-502. Grants, contracts, and technical assistance.	153A-322	160A-363
§ 160D-503. Coordination of planning.	--	--
ARTICLE 6 ***Development Regulation***		
§ 160D-601. Procedure for adopting, amending, or repealing development regulations.	153A-323	160A-364
§ 160D-602. Notice of hearing on proposed zoning map amendments.	153A-343	160A-384
§ 160D-603. Citizen comments.	--	160A-385 160A-386
§ 160D-604. Planning board review and comments.	153A-344 153A-341	160A-387 160A-383

CHAPTER 160D	CHAPTER 153A	CHAPTER 160A
§ 160D-605. Governing board statement.	153A-341 153A-342	160A-382 160A-383

ARTICLE 7
Zoning Regulation

CHAPTER 160D	CHAPTER 153A	CHAPTER 160A
§ 160D-701. Purposes.	153A-341	160A-383
§ 160D-702. Grant of power.	153A-340	160A-381
§ 160D-703. Zoning districts.	153A-342	160A-382
§ 160D-704. Incentives.	153A-340	160A-381 160A-383.4
§ 160D-705. Quasi-judicial zoning decisions.	--	160A-388
§ 160D-706. Zoning conflicts with other development standards.	153A-346	160A-390

ARTICLE 8
Subdivision Regulation

CHAPTER 160D	CHAPTER 153A	CHAPTER 160A
§ 160D-801. Authority.	153A-330	160A-371
§ 160D-802. Applicability.	153A-335	160A-376
§ 160D-803. Review process, filing, and recording of subdivision plats.	153A-332	160A-373
§ 160D-804. Contents and requirements of regulation.	153A-331	160A-372
§ 160D-805. Notice of new subdivision fees and fee increases; public comment period.	153A-102.1	160A-4.1
§ 160D-806. Effect of plat approval on dedications.	153A-333	160A-374
§ 160D-807. Penalties for transferring lots in unapproved subdivisions.	153A-334	160A-375
1§ 60D-808. Appeals of decisions on subdivision plats.	153A-336	160A-377

ARTICLE 9
Regulation of Particular Uses and Areas

CHAPTER 160D	CHAPTER 153A	CHAPTER 160A
Part 1. Particular Land Uses	--	
§ 160D-901. Regulation of particular uses and areas.	--	
§ 160D-902. Adult businesses.	--	160A-181.1
§ 160D-903. Agricultural uses.	153A-340	160A-360 160A-383.2
§ 160D-904. Airport zoning.	--	--
§ 160D-905. Amateur radio antennas.	153A-341.2	160A-383.3
§ 160D-906. Bee hives.[2]	--	--
§ 160D-907. Family care homes.	--	168-20 168-21 168-22
§ 160D-908. Fence wraps.	153A-340	160A-381
§ 160D-909. Fraternities and sororities.	153A-340	160A-382
§ 160D-910. Manufactured homes.	153A-341.1	160A-383.1
§ 160D-911. Modular homes.	--	--
§ 160D-912. Outdoor advertising.	153A-143	160A-199
§ 160D-913. Public buildings.	153A-347	160A-392

---

2. Adopted as 160D-9-16, reordered by Revisor of Statutes to maintain alphabetical order of listed particular uses.

CHAPTER 160D	CHAPTER 153A	CHAPTER 160A
§ 160D-914. Solar collectors.	153A-144	160A-201
§ 160D-915. Temporary health care structures.	153A-341.3	160A-383.5
§ 160D-916. Streets and transportation.	--	160A-458.4

Part 2. Environmental Regulations

CHAPTER 160D	CHAPTER 153A	CHAPTER 160A
§ 160D-920. Local environmental regulations.	--	--
§ 160D-921. Forestry activities.	153A-452	160A-458.5
§ 160D-922. Erosion and sedimentation control.	--	160A-458
§ 160D-923. Floodplain regulations.	--	160A-458.1
§ 160D-924. Mountain ridge protection.	153A-448	160A-458.2
§ 160D-925. Stormwater control.	153A-454	160A-459
§ 160D-926. Water supply watershed management.	--	--

Part 3. Wireless Telecommunication Facilities

CHAPTER 160D	CHAPTER 153A	CHAPTER 160A
§ 160D-930. Purpose and compliance with federal law.	153A-349.50	160A-400.50
§ 160D-931. Definitions.	153A-349.51	160A-400.51
§ 160D-932. Local authority.	153A-349.51A	160A-400.51A
§ 160D-933. Construction of new wireless support structures or substantial modifications of wireless support structures.	153A-349.52	160A-400.52
§ 160D-934. Collocation and eligible facilities requests of wireless support structures.	153A-349.53	160A-400.53
§ 160D-935. Collocation of small wireless facilities.	--	160A-400.54
§ 160D-936. Use of public rights-of-way.	--	160A-400.55
§ 160D-937. Access to city utility poles to install small wireless facilities.	--	160A-400.56
§ 160D-938. Applicability.	--	160A-400.57

Part 4. Historic Preservation

CHAPTER 160D	CHAPTER 153A	CHAPTER 160A
§ 160D-940. Legislative findings.	--	160A-400.1
§ 160D-941. Historic preservation commission.	--	160A-400.7
§ 160D-942. Powers of the historic preservation commission.	--	160A-400.8
§ 160D-943. Appropriations.	--	160A-400.12
§ 160D-944. Designation of historic districts.	--	160A-400.3 160A-400.4
§ 160D-945. Designation of landmarks.	--	160A-400.5
§ 160D-946. Required landmark designation procedure.	--	160A-400.6
§ 160D-947. Certificate of appropriateness required.	--	160A-400.9
§ 160D-948. Certain changes not prohibited.	--	160A-400.13
§ 160D-949. Delay in demolition of landmarks and buildings within historic district.	--	160A-400.14
§ 160D-950. Demolition by neglect in contributing structures outside local historic districts.	--	160A-400.15
§ 160D-951. Conflict with other laws.	--	160A-400.10

Part 5. Community Appearance Commission

CHAPTER 160D	CHAPTER 153A	CHAPTER 160A
§ 160D-960. Powers and duties of commission.	--	160A-452
§ 160D-961. Staff services; advisory board.	--	160A-453

CHAPTER 160D	CHAPTER 153A	CHAPTER 160A
§ 160D-962. Annual report.	--	160A-454
§ 160D-963. Receipt and expenditure of funds.	--	160A-455

ARTICLE 10
Development Agreements

§ 160D-1001. Authorization.	153A-349.1	160A-400.20
§ 160D-1002. Definitions.	153A-349.2	160A-400.21
§ 160D-1003. Approval of governing board required.	153A-349.3	160A-400.22
§ 160D-1004. Size and duration.	153A-349.4	160A-400.23
§ 160D-1005. Public hearing.	153A-349.5	160A-400.24
§ 160D-1006. Content and modification.	153A-349.6	160A-400.25
§ 160D-1007. Vesting.	153A-349.7	160A-400.26
§ 160D-1008. Breach and cure.	153A-349.8	160A-400.27
§ 160D-1009. Amendment or termination.	153A-349.9	160A-400.28
§ 160D-1010. Change of jurisdiction.	153A-349.10	160A-400.29
§ 160D-1011. Recordation.	153A-349.11	160A-400.30
§ 160D-1012. Applicability of procedures to approve debt.	153A-349.12	160A-400.31

ARTICLE 11
Building Code Enforcement

§ 160D-1101. Definitions.	153A-350; -350.1	160A-442
§ 160D-1102. Building code administration.	153A-351	1160A-411
§ 160D-1103. Qualifications of inspectors.	153A-351.1	160A-411.1
§ 160D-1104. Duties and responsibilities.	153A-352	160A-412
§ 160D-1105. Other arrangements for inspections.	153A-353	160A-413
§ 160D-1106. Alternative inspection method for component or element.	--	160A-413.5
§ 160D-1107. Mutual aid contracts.	--	160A-413.6
§ 160D-1108. Conflicts of interest.	153A-355	160A-415
§ 160D-1109. Failure to perform duties.	153A-356	160A-416
§ 160D-1110. Building permits.	153A-357	160A-417
§ 160D-1111. Expiration of building permits.	153A-358	160A-418
§ 160D-1112. Changes in work.	153A-359	160A-419
§ 160D-1113. Inspections of work in progress.	153A-360	160A-420
§ 160D-1114. Appeals of stop orders.	153A-361	160A-421
§ 160D-1115. Revocation of building permits.	153A-362	160A-422
§ 160D-1116. Certificates of compliance.	153A-363	160A-423
§ 160D-1117. Periodic inspections.	153A-364	160A-424
§ 160D-1118. Defects in buildings to be corrected.	153A-365	160A-425
§ 160D-1119. Unsafe buildings condemned.	153A-366	160A-426
§ 160D-1120. Removing notice from condemned buildings.	153A-367	160A-427
§ 160D-1121. Action in event of failure to take corrective action.	153A-368	160A-428
§ 160D-1122. Order to take corrective action.	153A-369	160A-429
§ 160D-1123. Appeal; finality of order if not appealed.	153A-370	160A-430
§ 160D-1124. Failure to comply with order.	153A-371	160A-431
§ 160D-1125. Enforcement.	153A-372	160A-432

CHAPTER 160D	CHAPTER 153A	CHAPTER 160A
§ 160D-1126. Records and reports.	153A-373	160A-433
§ 160D-1127. Appeals.	153A-374	160A-434
§ 160D-1128. Fire limits.	153A-375	160A-435 160A-436 160A-437 160A-438
§ 160D-1129. Regulation authorized as to repair, closing, and demolition of nonresidential buildings or structures; order of public officer.	--	160A-439
§ 160D-1130 [2020 addition to come]	--	160A-439.1

ARTICLE 12
Minimum Housing Codes

CHAPTER 160D	CHAPTER 153A	CHAPTER 160A
§ 160D-1201. Authorization.	--	160A-441
§ 160D-1202. Definitions.	--	160A-442
§ 160D-1203. Ordinance authorized as to repair, closing, and demolition; order of public officer.	--	160A-443
§ 160D-1204. Heat source required.	--	160A-443.1
§ 160D-1205. Standards.	--	160A-444
§ 160D-1206. Service of complaints and orders.	--	160A-445
§ 160D-1207. Periodic inspections.	153A-364	160A-424
§ 160D-1208. Remedies.	--	160A-446
§ 160D-1209. Compensation to owners of condemned properties.	--	160A-447
§ 160D-1210. Additional powers of public officer.	--	160A-448
§ 160D-1211. Administration of ordinance.	--	160A-449
§ 160D-1212. Supplemental nature of Article.	--	160A-450

ARTICLE 13
Additional Authority

CHAPTER 160D	CHAPTER 153A	CHAPTER 160A
Part 1. Open Space Acquisition	--	
§ 160D-1301. Legislative intent.	--	160A-401
§ 160D-1302. Finding of necessity.	--	160A-402
§ 160D-1303. Local governments authorized to acquire and reconvey real property.	--	160A-403
§ 160D-1304. Joint action by governing body.	--	160A-404
§ 160D-1305. Powers of governing body.	--	160A-405
§ 160D-1306. Appropriations authorized.	--	160A-406
§ 160D-1307. Definitions.	--	160A-407

Part 2. Community Development

CHAPTER 160D	CHAPTER 153A	CHAPTER 160A
§ 160D-1311. Community development programs and activities.	153A-376	160A-456
§ 160D-1312. Acquisition and disposition of property for redevelopment.	153A-377	160A-457
§ 160D-1313. Urban Development Action Grants.	--	160A-457.1
§ 160D-1314. Urban homesteading programs.	--	160A-457.2
§ 160D-1315. Downtown development projects.	--	160A-458.3
§ 160D-1316. Low- and moderate-income housing programs.	153A-378	--

CHAPTER 160D	CHAPTER 153A	CHAPTER 160A
Part 3. Miscellaneous		
§ 160D-1320. Program to finance energy improvements.	153A-455	160A-459.1
Article 14 Judicial Review		
§ 160D-1401. Declaratory judgments.	--	--
§ 160D-1402. Appeals in the nature of certiorari.	153A-349	160A-393
§ 160D-1403. Appeals of decisions on subdivision plats.	153A-336	160A-377
§ 160D-1404. Other civil actions.	--	--
§ 160D-1405. Statutes of limitation.	153A-348	160A-364.1

Appendix D. Reviews Solicited and Comments Received on Proposed Chapter 160D Legislation

I. Presentations and Solicitations of Comments

Date	Groups/Persons or Event	Submitted
June 2013	Initial N.C. Bar Association (NCBA), Zoning, Planning, and Land Use section (ZPLU) discussion; drafting committee work commenced	
Spring, summer 2014	ZPLU section council; N.C. Homebuilders Association (NCHBA); N.C. Chapter, American Planning Association (APA-NC); N.C. Association of Zoning Officials (NCAZO)	Discussion of concept, purposes, process for bill draft
Sept. 15–30, 2014	Chair, NCBA, Government and Public Sector (GPS) section; leadership and government affairs staff for N.C. League of Municipalities; APA-NC; NCHBA, wireless communication association; Triad and Charlotte building industry coalition (Triad Real Estate and Building Industry Coalition (TREBIC) and Real Estate and Building Industry Coalition (REBIC))	Summary, outline of bill, draft table of contents
Oct. 1–15, 2014	N.C. League of Municipalities; NCHBA; Triad and Charlotte building industry coalition; presentation at APA-NC annual conference	Preliminary draft bill
Oct. 20–30, 2014	ZPLU membership; APA-NC membership; NCAZO membership; N.C. League of Municipalities; N.C. Association of County Commissioners (NCACC); all city and county attorneys, planning directors, and zoning administrators; NCHBA; Triad and Charlotte building industry coalition; office and industrial park development association; SOG Local Government Law and N.C. Planning (NCPlan) listserves (approximately 4,000 individuals plus interest-group leadership)	Letter describing effort, purpose, general contents, with link to review draft of full bill; request comments by Dec. 31, 2014
Jan. 8–15, 2015	N.C. League of Municipalities; APA-NC; NCHBA; Triad and Charlotte building industry coalition; commenting local governments (Charlotte, Raleigh, Winston-Salem, Durham, Cary, Chapel Hill, Catawba County); commenting ZPLU and GPS section members; ZPLU and GPS membership	Updated bill draft reflecting comments and edits through Dec. 31, 2014
Jan. 20, 2015	Asheville city attorney and attorney for development industry	Detailed bill review/discussion
Jan. 23, 2015	GPS section council; N.C. League of Municipalities; NCACC; local governments	Detailed bill review/discussion
Feb. 5, 2015	ZPLU section council	Discussion
Feb. 6, 2015	County attorneys conference	Overview
Feb. 19, 2015	N.C. Department of Insurance (DOI); N.C. Building Inspectors Association	Bill review/discussion
Feb. 23, 2015	NCAZO conference	Bill review/discussion
March 19, 2015	Joe Padilla (REBIC)	Bill review/discussion

Date	Groups/Persons or Event	Submitted
March 19, 2015	Marlene Sanford (TREBIC)	Bill review/discussion
March 20, 2015	Municipal attorneys conference	Bill review/discussion
March 24, 2015	ZPLU section council	Bill review/discussion
March 27, 2015	ZPLU continuing legal education (CLE) program	Bill review/discussion
July 27, 2015	NCAZO summer conference	Bill review/discussion
Oct. 21, 2015	APA-NC annual conference	Bill review/discussion
Nov. 6, 2015	N.C. Permitting Personnel Association	Bill review/discussion
Jan. 6, 2016	Mark Matheny (N.C. Council of Code Officials)	Bill review/discussion
Feb. 22, 2016	NCAZO winter conference	Bill review/discussion
March 8, 2016	Randolph Cloud, Amy Nelson (APA-NC)	Bill review/discussion
July 25, 2016	NCAZO summer conference	Bill review/discussion
Aug. 5, 2016	Municipal attorneys summer conference	Bill review/discussion
Sept. 15, 2016	APA-NC annual conference	Bill review/discussion
Sept. 16, 2016	ZPLU section council	Bill review/discussion
Sept. 19–20, 2016	ZPLU membership; GPS section council chair; N.C. League of Municipalities staff; NCACC staff; Raleigh city attorney; NCHBA; TREBIC; REBIC; SOG NCPlan and Local Government Law listserves; NCAZO listserve; post on ZPLU and SOG web pages	Distribution of updated bill for 2017 session
Dec. 6, 2016	ZPLU membership; N.C. League of Municipalities staff; NCACC staff; NCHBA; TREBIC; REBIC; SOG NCPlan and Local Government Law listserves; NCAZO listserve; post on ZPLU and SOG web pages	Distribution of updated bill for 2017 session
March 28–30, 2017	ZPLU membership; TREBIC; REBIC; SOG NCPlan and Local Government Law listserves; NCAZO listserve; post on ZPLU and SOG web pages	Distribution of S. 419
April 6, 2017	ZPLU annual CLE program and section meeting	Update on S. 419
June 8–12, 2017	Updated annotated edition of S. 419, 2d ed., posted on ZPLU and SOG websites; notice to SOG NCPlan and Local Government Law listserves, NCAZO listserve	Update on S. 419
July 27, 2017	Updated annotated edition of S. 419, 3d ed., posted to ZPLU and SOG websites, notice to SOG and NCAZO listserves	Update on S. 419 as approved by Senate, 2018
Dec. 8, 2017	ZPLU section council	Bill review/discussion of technical amendments
Feb. 15, 2018	ZPLU section council	Update on S. 419
Sept. 12, 2018	APA-NC annual conference	Update on S. 419
Sept. 21, 2018	ZPLU section council	Update on Chapter 160D
Nov. 2, 2018	NCBA legislative advisory committee	Update on Chapter 160D for 2019
Nov. 8, 2018	APA-NC legislative committee	Update on Chapter 160D
Feb. 8, 2019	ZPLU section council	Update on Chapter 160D edits/tweaks
Feb. 19, 2019	NCAZO winter conference	Update on Chapter 160D
Feb. 27, 2019	Posting on ZPLU and SOG websites	Updated draft Chapter 160D for 2019 introduction
April 5, 2019	ZPLU annual CLE program	Update on Chapter 160D

II. Comments Received

Date	Party/Parties Submitting Comments
2014	
Oct. 20	Jim Scarborough (ZPLU)
Oct. 27	James Bryan (ZPLU)
Oct. 21	Bob Hagemann (Charlotte)
Oct. 30	Mark Locklear (Harnett County)
Oct. 30	Susan Burkhardt
Oct. 30	Ed Muir (Rowan County)
Oct. 31	Randy Mundt (N.C. Division of Emergency Management (DEM))
Oct. 31	Craig Justus, Bill Bryan (ZPLU)
Oct. 31	Scott Davis (New Bern)
Nov. 3	Tom King (Hillsborough)
Nov. 3	Hal Johnson (Randolph County)
Nov. 4	Dan Porter (Camden County)
Nov. 12	Sam Shames (Gaston County)
Nov. 12	Amy Nelson (Burlington)
Nov. 14	Ralph Karpinos (Chapel Hill)
Nov. 17	Chuck Kitchen (GPS)
Nov. 15	Debra Bechtel (Catawba County)
Nov. 24	Chad Meadows (APA-NC)
Nov. 26	Chris Murphy (Winston-Salem)
Nov. 26	Ginny Faust (N.C. Department of Commerce)
Dec. 1	Adam Lovelady (SOG)
Dec. 1	Ron Satterfield (Wilmington)
Dec. 9	Ira Botvinick (Raleigh)
Dec. 11	Chuck Kitchen (GPS)
Dec. 16	Rich Ducker (SOG)
Dec. 17	Lisa Glover/Chris Simpson (Cary)
Dec. 17	Rebecca Harper (Iredell County)
Dec. 17	Mike Sheidy (Andrews)
Dec. 18	Eric Gooby (Pitt County)
Dec. 19	Don O'Toole (Durham)
Dec. 23	Chad Meadows (APA-NC)
Dec. 23	John Cort (Cort Architecture)
Dec. 23	Ramona Bartos (N.C. State Historic Preservation Office (SHPO))
Dec. 29	Kyle Breuer (Pender County)
Dec. 31	Ira Botvinick (Raleigh)
Dec. 31	Richard Flowe (N-Focus Planning)
Dec. 31	Mike Carpenter (NCHBA)
Dec. 31	Bob Hagemann (Charlotte)

Date	Party/Parties Submitting Comments
2015	
Jan. 12	Ira Botvinick (Raleigh)
Jan. 14	Rodger Lentz (Wilson)
Jan. 15	Chad Meadows (APA-NC)
Jan. 15	Chad Essick (ZPLU)
Jan. 15	Robin Currin (Asheville)
Jan. 20	Craig Justus (ZPLU)
Jan. 20	Robin Currin (Asheville, ZPLU)
Jan. 22	Ralph Karpinos (Chapel Hill)
Jan. 22	Don O'Toole (Durham)
Jan. 23	GPS section reps (NCBA)
Jan. 27	Randy Mundt (DEM)
Jan. 27	Ben Hitchings (APA-NC, Morrisville)
Feb. 3	Dan McLawhorn (Raleigh)
Feb. 6	County attorney association membership
Feb. 9	Dan McLawhorn (Raleigh)
Feb. 11	John Morck (APA-NC)
Feb. 11	Ramona Bartos (SHPO)
Feb. 11	J. Smith (Pitt County)
Feb. 13	Nicollet Fulton (Raleigh)
Feb. 16	Dan McLawhorn, Nicolette Fulton (Raleigh)
Feb. 16	Don O'Toole (Durham
Feb. 16	Ira Botvinick (Raleigh)
Feb. 18	Lisa Glover (Cary)
Feb. 18	Chris Noles (DOI)
Feb. 19	Chris Noles (DOI), officers of N.C. Association of Building Inspectors
Feb. 20	Ramona Bartos (SHPO)
Feb. 20	Nicollet Fulton (Raleigh)
Feb. 23	NCAZO membership/comments at workshop
Feb. 24	Don O'Toole (Durham)
Feb. 26	Randy Mundt (DEM)
March 4	Don O'Toole (Durham)
March 6	Chris Noles (DOI)
March 6	Randy Mundt (DEM)
March 6	Tom Miller
March 6	Sadler Barnhardt
March 6	Bob Hagemann (Charlotte)
March 9	Chad Essick (ZPLU)
March 10	Craig Justus (NCHBA)
March 13	Don O'Toole (Durham)
March 15	Nicolette Fulton (Raleigh)
March 15	Lisa Glover (Cary)
March 16	Michael Thomas (Oak Ridge)
March 25	Craig Justus (NCHBA)

Date	Party/Parties Submitting Comments

2015, cont'd

April 1	Pat Crawford (UNC-CH)
April 10	Mike Carpenter (NCHBA)
April 13	Jim Scarborough (NCHBA)
April 21	Marlene Sanford (TREBIC)
April 23	Ira Botvinick (Raleigh)
April 23	Nicolette Fulton (Raleigh)
April 23	Lisa Glover (Cary)
April 23	Erin Wynia (N.C. League of Municipalities)
April 27	Tyler Mulligan (SOG)
May 1	Rick Kline
May 7	Tom Carroll (Vulcan Materials)
May 13	Randy Mundt (DEM)
June 17	Ralph Karpinos (Chapel Hill)
Dec. 15	Chris Noles (DOI)

2016

Feb. 1	Robin Bloss (Eastern Carolina Council of Governments)
March 18	Mike Carpenter (NCHBA)
April 1	Chris Murphy (Winston-Salem)
April 21	Mike Carpenter (NCHBA)
May 12	Randy Mundt (DEM)
June 17	Ben Hitchings (Chapel Hill)
Aug. 5	Erin Wynia (N.C. League of Municipalities)
Aug. 7	Dan McLawhorn (Raleigh)
Sept. 6	Catherine Hofmann (Asheville)
Sept. 6	Mark Matheny (Asheville)
Sept. 29	Brad Schuler (New Hanover County)
Oct. 11	Ralph Karpinos (Chapel Hill)
Nov. 3	Lisa Glover (Cary)
Nov. 9	Catherine Hofmann (Asheville)
Nov. 17	Government and public lawyers section, NCBA (city attorneys from Apex, Asheville, Concord, Davidson, Durham, Greensboro, Greenville, Hickory, Holly Springs, Jacksonville, Monroe, Raleigh, Sanford, Wilmington, and Winston-Salem, and N.C. League of Municipalities)
Nov. 28	Ralph Karpinos (Chapel Hill)
Nov. 29	Terri Jones, Jennifer Schneier (Greensboro)
Nov. 29	Brad Williams (Raleigh)
Nov. 30	Lisa Glover (Cary)
Nov. 30	Randy Mundt (DEM)
Dec. 13	Ralph Karpinos (Chapel Hill)
Dec. 14	Legislative staff

Date	Party/Parties Submitting Comments
2017	
Feb. 14	Marlene Sanford (TREBIC)
Feb. 16	Jennifer Schneier (Greensboro)
March 2	Craig Justus, Mike Carpenter (NCHBA)
March 22	Andy Petesch (Raleigh)
March 27	Craig Justus (NCHBA)
April 24	Frank Gray (Manufactured and Modular Home Association)
May 5	Randy Mundt (DEM)
May 23	Craig Justus, Mike Carpenter (NCHBA)
June 6	Henry Jones (Raleigh)
June 13	Bill Bailey
June 16	Randy Mundt (DEM)
July 28	Susan Patterson (Sanford)
Oct. 27	Ken Bowers (Raleigh)
2018	
March 21	Fred Johnson (Concord)
March 21	Randy Mundt (DEM)
April 18	Craig Justus (NCHBA)
April 27	Craig Justus, Mike Carpenter (NCHBA)
April 27	Eric Braun
May 21	Randy Mundt (DEM)
Oct. 25	Amy Scotten (Randolph County)
2019	
Jan.29	Randy Mundt (DEM)
Jan. 31	Cady Thomas, Seth Palmer (N.C. Realtors Association)
Feb. 1	Michael Lee
Feb. 8	Thomas Powers, Chad Essick, Al Beneshoff (ZPLU)
Feb. 11	Eli Johnson (Pitt County, Land Records Task Force)
Feb. 28	Mike Carpenter (NCHBA)
March 13	Erin Wynia (N.C. League of Municipalities), Mike Carpenter (NCHBA)
April 18	Legislative staff

Appendix E. Annotated Text of Chapter 160D

Chapter 160D of the North Carolina General Statutes (hereinafter G.S.) was created by Part II of S.L. 2019-111. Part II of the law, which creates Chapter 160D and repeals the statutes incorporated into the new chapter, is entitled "PROVISIONS TO REORGANIZE, CONSOLIDATE, MODERNIZE, AND CLARIFY STATUTES REGARDING LOCAL PLANNING AND DEVELOPMENT REGULATION." Part II of the act becomes effective January 1, 2021.

This annotated edition of Chapter 160D shows how the new statute relates to prior statutes. Changes to the prior statutes are shown as follows: strikethroughs are used to represent deletions and underlining is used for additions. Pre-existing language that is relocated from prior statutes to Chapter 160D without amendment is shown as plain text.

Annotations similar to the ones presented in this appendix were prepared and circulated for each draft of the bill as it was discussed from 2014 to 2019. The annotations for the forty-two previous editions of the bill that were distributed prior to adoption were approved by the drafting committee of the North Carolina Bar Association's Zoning, Planning, and Land Use Section. Those annotations have been supplemented for this publication with more details and additional footnotes.

The footnotes explain the rationale for most of the amendments to existing statutes. They also indicate changes to the prior statutes made by other legislation enacted in the 2015 to 2018 period. Changes to the prior statutes made by other legislation enacted in 2019 have not yet been incorporated into Chapter 160D, but the footnotes indicate where amendments are likely to be made prior to Chapter 160D becoming effective.

As adopted, each section of Chapter 160D used this numbering convention: chapter number-article number-section number. For example, the first statutory section in Article 7 on zoning regulations was G.S. 160D-7-1. When codified, a similar but slightly different numbering convention will be used, adapting the Chapter 160D numbering to the convention used in other chapters of the General Statutes. Instead of a three-part number, there will be a two-part number using this numbering convention: chapter number-section number. However, each section number will start with the relevant article number. For example, the first section in Article 7 on zoning regulations will be G.S. 160D-701, while the first section in Article 10 on development agreements will be G.S. 160D-1001, thus retaining to the extent possible the clarification to the law's organizational structure. The section numbers as codified are shown in brackets in this annotated bill.

When codified, the revised numbering will be as follows:
- Article 1: 160D-101 through -111
- Article 2: 160D-201 through -204
- Article 3: 160D-301 through -310
- Article 4: 160D-401 through -406
- Article 5: 160D-501 through -503
- Article 6: 160D-601 through -605

- Article 7: 160D-701 through -706
- Article 8: 160D-801 through -808
- Article 9
  - Part 1: 160D-901 through -916
  - Part 2: 160D-920 through -926
  - Part 3: 160D-930 through -938
  - Part 4: 160D-940 through -951
  - Part 5: 160D-960 through -963
- Article 10: 160D-1001 through -1012
- Article 11: 160D-1101 through -1129
- Article 12: 160D-1201 through -1212
- Article 13
  - Part 1: 160D-1301 through -1307
  - Part 2: 160D-1311 through -1316
  - Part 3: 160D-1320
- Article 14: 160D-1401 through -1405

Legislative Findings

SECTION 2.1.(a) The General Assembly finds that a coherent organization of the statutes that authorize local government planning and development regulation is needed to make the statutes simpler to find, easier to follow, and more uniform for all local governments.[1]

SECTION 2.1.(b) The General Assembly finds that the parallel system of separate city and county statutes regarding planning and development regulation has led to redundancy and unintended differences in the wording of planning and development regulation statutes on the same subject.

SECTION 2.1.(c) The General Assembly finds that numerous specialized statutes affecting local planning and development regulation have been added in disparate Chapters of the General Statutes over past decades, and that antiquated and confusing language exists in the planning and development regulation statutes.

SECTION 2.1.(d) The General Assembly finds that, other than collecting some of these statutes into Article 19 of Chapter 160A in 1971 and Article 18 of Chapter 153A in 1973, no comprehensive reorganization of North Carolina's planning and development regulation statutes has been undertaken.

SECTION 2.1.(e) The intent of the General Assembly by enactment of Part II of this act is to collect and organize existing statutes regarding local planning and development into a single Chapter of the General Statutes and to consolidate the statutes affecting cities and counties.

SECTION 2.1.(f) The intent of the General Assembly by enactment of Part II of this act is to neither eliminate, diminish, enlarge, nor expand the authority of local governments to exact land, construction, or money as part of the development approval process or otherwise materially alter the scope of local authority to regulate development and any modifications from earlier versions of Part II of this bill should not be interpreted to affect the scope of local government authority.

---

1. As introduced, Section 2.1 was a series of WHEREAS clauses. Prior to adoption, these introductory clauses were converted to a numbered series of legislative findings and statements of intent, without substantive change in the content of the clauses. The bill section numbers throughout this annotated edition of G.S. Chapter 160D have also been modified to conform to the section numbers in S.L. 2019-111.

Chapter 160D

SECTION 2.4. Chapter 160D of the General Statutes is created to read:[2]

"Chapter 160D[3]

Local Planning and Development Regulation

<u>ARTICLE 1. GENERAL PROVISIONS</u>

§ 160D-1-1. Application.[4] [160D-101]

<u>(a) The provisions of this Article shall apply to all development regulations and programs adopted pursuant to this Chapter or applicable or related local acts.[5] To the extent there are contrary provisions in local charters or acts, G.S. 160D-1-11 is applicable unless this Chapter expressly provides otherwise. The provisions of this Article also apply to any other local ordinance that substantially affects land use and development.[6]</u>

<u>(b) The provisions of this Article are supplemental to specific provisions included in other Articles of this Chapter. To the extent there are conflicts between the provisions of this Article and the provisions of other Articles of this Chapter, the more specific provisions shall control.</u>

<u>(c) Local governments may also apply any of the definitions and procedures authorized by this Chapter to any ordinance that does not substantially affect land use and development adopted under the general police power of cities and counties, Article 8 of Chapter 160A and Article 6 of Chapter 153A respectively, and may employ any organizational structure, board, commission, or staffing arrangement authorized by this Chapter to any or all aspects of those ordinances.[7]</u>

<u>(d) This Chapter does not expand, diminish, or alter the scope of authority for planning and development regulation authorized by other Chapters of the General Statutes.[8]</u>

---

2. For ease in comparing G.S. Chapter 160D to previous law, prior statutory language is shown with additions underlined and with deletions indicated by strikethroughs.

3. The prior law on local government planning and development regulation set out primarily in G.S. Chapter 153A (counties) and Chapter 160A (cities) are now merged into a single Chapter 160D that applies to both counties and cities. Where there are intentional policy differences between the city and county statutes, such as the bona fide farming exemption from county zoning, those differences are retained and incorporated into Chapter 160D. Otherwise, the city and county provisions are merged to secure greater uniformity and simplicity.

4. This is a new section.

5. See G.S. 160D-10 for retained language from G.S. 160A-366 on validation of prior city ordinances. Also note that G.S. 160D-1-12 retains language from current 160A-3 and 153A-3 regarding current law relating to the relation of general statutes to existing local acts. Further, G.S. 160D-1-14 does not require re-adoption of existing local ordinances. Current language in G.S. 160A-391 regarding local acts and city charters is repealed as redundant (see deletion at G.S. 160D-7-7).

6. Consistent with current case law, regulations substantially affecting land use must comply with the procedural requirements for land use ordinances. While some development regulations could also be authorized under a local government unit's general police power, to establish consistent procedures for adoption, amendment, repeal, administration, and enforcement of development regulations, the procedures set by G.S. Chapter 160D for development regulations should be consistently applied to all such ordinances.

7. This subsection allows for the use of G.S. Chapter 160D procedural aspects with local government ordinances adopted pursuant to other statutory authority. Current law contains this same provision for unified development ordinances, now in 160D-1-3. This subsection extends the same options to general-police-power ordinances while not enlarging or constricting the scope of authority granted to cities or counties.

8. The scope of authority provided by one regulatory authorization does not implicitly alter the scope of authority provided elsewhere in the statutes.

§ 160D-1-2. Definitions.[9] [160D-102]

Unless otherwise specifically provided, or unless otherwise clearly required by the context, the words and phrases defined in this section shall have the meaning indicated when used in this Chapter.

(1) Administrative decision. - Decisions made in the implementation, administration, or enforcement of development regulations that involves the determination of facts and the application of objective standards set forth in this Chapter or local government development regulations. These are sometimes referred to as "ministerial" decisions or "administrative determinations."

(2) Administrative hearing[10] - A proceeding to gather facts needed to make an administrative decision.

(3) Bona fide farm purposes. - Agricultural activities as set forth in G.S. 160D-9-3.

(4) Charter. - As defined in G.S. 160A-1(2).[11]

(5) City.[12] – As defined in G.S. 160A-1(2).[13]

(6) Comprehensive plan.[14] – The comprehensive plan, land-use plan, small area plans, neighborhood plans, transportation plan, capital improvement plan, and any other plans regarding land use and development that have been officially adopted by the governing board.

(7) Conditional zoning.[15] - A legislative zoning map amendment with site-specific conditions incorporated into the zoning map amendment.

---

9. This is a new section. It consolidates definitions used in Chapter 160D, while leaving definitions specific or particular to individual articles in those articles.

10. Evidentiary hearings are required for quasi-judicial decisions and legislative hearings for legislative decisions. In most instances, no hearings are required for administrative decisions. However, some articles (housing code administration particularly) allow or require staff members to hold a hearing to gather facts, or allow affected persons to present information, prior to making any administrative decision.

11. G.S.160A-1(1) provides that the term "charter" means "the entire body of local acts currently in force applicable to a particular city, including articles of incorporation issued to a city by an administrative agency of the State, and any amendments thereto adopted pursuant to 1917 Public Laws, Chapter 136, Subchapter 16, Part VIII, sections 1 and 2, or Article 5, Part 4, of . . . Chapter [160A]."

12. This subsection was relocated from G.S. 160A-385.1(b). G.S. 160A-442 was deleted as redundant.

13. G.S. 160A-1(2) defines the term "city" as "a municipal corporation organized under the laws of this State for the better government of the people within its jurisdiction and having the powers, duties, privileges, and immunities conferred by law on cities, towns, and villages. The term 'city' does not include counties or municipal corporations organized for a special purpose. 'City' is interchangeable with the terms 'town' and 'village,' is used throughout this Chapter in preference to those terms, and shall mean any city as defined in this subdivision without regard to the terminology employed in charters, local acts, other portions of the General Statutes, or local customary usage. The terms 'city' or 'incorporated municipality' do not include a municipal corporation that, without regard to its date of incorporation, would be disqualified from receiving gasoline tax allocations by G.S. 136-41.2(a), except that the end of status as a city under this sentence shall not affect the levy or collection of any tax or assessment, or any criminal or civil liability, and shall not serve to escheat any property until five years after the end of such status as a city, or until September 1, 1991, whichever comes later."

14. This subsection was relocated from G.S. 160A-400.21 and 153A-349.2. Also, S.L. 2017-10 had added a sentence including a unified development ordinance within the definition of a "comprehensive plan." Since a unified development ordinance is a collection of binding regulations rather than an advisory plan, this phrase has been deleted from the definition of "comprehensive plan" in Chapter 160D in order to avoid potential confusion between a regulation that has binding effect and a plan that is only advisory in nature. The process for adopting a plan is set forth in G.S. 160D-5-1(c).

15. G.S. 160D-7-3 continues to authorize purely legislative conditional zoning, as is the case with the current statutes, but it eliminates the hybrid legislative/quasi-judicial conditional-use-district and special-use-district forms of zoning so that all rezonings are exclusively legislative. The concepts of special-use-district and conditional-use-district zoning were incorporated into the zoning statutes in the 1980s as work-arounds to avoid contract zoning when individualized site-specific conditions were deemed to be needed. The conditional-use-district concept requires a concurrent legislative rezoning and quasi-judicial conditional-use permit. Subsequent case law and statutory amendment now allow purely legislative conditional zoning. The former practice of concurrent consideration of a legislative rezoning to a conditional-use district and a quasi-judicial conditional-use permit is legally complicated and has been a source of

(8) County.[16] - Any one of the counties listed in G.S. 153A-10.
(9) <u>Decision-making board. - A governing board, planning board, board of adjustment, historic district board, or other board assigned to make quasi-judicial decisions under this Chapter.</u>
(10) <u>Determination. - A written, final and binding order, requirement, or determination regarding an administrative decision.</u>
(11) Developer.[17] - A person, including a governmental agency or redevelopment authority, who ~~intends to~~ undertake<u>s</u> any development and who ~~has a legal or equitable interest in~~ <u>is the landowner of</u> the property to be developed <u>or who has been authorized by the landowner to undertake development on that property.</u>
(12) Development.[18] - Unless the context clearly indicates otherwise,[19] the term means:
  (a) The construction, erection, alteration, enlargement, renovation, substantial[20] repair, movement to another site, or demolition of any structure;
  (b) excavation, grading, filling, clearing, or alteration of land;
  (c) the subdivision of land as defined in G.S. 160D-8-2; or
  (d) the initiation or substantial change in the use of land or the intensity of use of land. <u>This definition does not alter the scope of regulatory authority granted by the Articles of this Chapter.</u>
(13) <u>Development approval.[21] - An administrative or quasi-judicial approval made pursuant to this Chapter that is written and that is required prior to commencing development or undertaking a specific activity, project or development proposal. Development approvals include, but are not limited to, zoning permits, site plan approvals,[22] special use permits, variances, and certificates of appropriateness. The term also includes all other regulatory approvals required by regulations adopted pursuant to his Chapter, including plat approvals, permits issued, development agreements[23] entered into, and building permits issued.[24]</u>

---

considerable confusion for local governments, landowners, and neighbors. The revised statutes allow for the use of the now-legal and more widely used conditional zoning (as well as for the continued use of special-use permits outside the context of a hybrid rezoning). As it is no longer needed, the combined rezoning and quasi-judicial process is eliminated.

16. This subsection applies the same definition as is referenced in G.S. 153A-1(3).

17. This subsection has been relocated from G.S. 160A-400.21 and 153A-349.2.

18. The definition of "development" set out in this subsection has been adapted from the definitions of this term found in G.S. 160A-400.9 (historic preservation), 160A-400.21 (definitions), 153A-349.2 (development agreements), and 113A-105(5) (Coastal Area Management Act).

19. This language clarifies that this subsection's general definition of "development" does not override more-specific provisions located elsewhere in Chapter 160D, such as the provisions defining development subject to a certificate of appropriateness (160D-9-47), subject to a development agreement (160D-10-2), or subject to a building permit (160D-11-8).

20. Since application of the term "substantial" (and similar terms such as "material") is a fact-specific inquiry that will vary with the exact context involved, rather than mandate a statewide definition of the term for this subsection, the usual and ordinary definition of these terms apply.

21. Early drafts of Chapter 160D had incorporated the definition of "permit" into the definition of "development approval." The final version of this subsection uses a single term to provide greater clarity and simplicity. A "development approval" does not include a legislative decision, such as a rezoning, or an advisory action, such as a letter confirming the existing zoning or a non-binding staff opinion as to how an ordinance might be interpreted.

22. A site plan may also be approved as part of a conditional zoning. If it is incorporated as a condition in conditional zoning, it is part of that legislative decision. If it is required and approved as part of an administrative or quasi-judicial decision, it is a development approval.

23. Since the decision to enter into a development agreement and the terms of the agreement are discretionary decisions by a governing board, following a legislative hearing, these decisions are more accurately characterized as legislative decisions rather than administrative or quasi-judicial decisions. The definition of "legislative decision" in this section includes a decision to approve, amend, or rescind a development agreement. Therefore, it is likely that development agreements will be removed from this definition in the future.

24. The building code applied in Article 11 of G.S. Chapter 160D is the uniform State Building Code adopted by the state, not an ordinance adopted by a local government. This sentence includes within local

(14) Development regulation[25] - A unified development ordinance, zoning regulation, subdivision regulation, erosion and sedimentation control regulation, floodplain or flood damage prevention regulation, mountain ridge protection regulation, stormwater control regulation, wireless telecommunication facility regulation, historic preservation or landmark regulation, housing code, State Building Code enforcement, or any other regulation adopted pursuant to this Chapter, or a local act or charter that regulates land use or development.[26]

(15) Dwelling.[27] - Any building, structure, manufactured home or mobile home, or part thereof, used and occupied for human habitation or intended to be so used, and includes any outhouses and appurtenances belonging thereto or usually enjoyed therewith, except that for purposes of Article 12 it does not include any manufactured home, mobile home, or recreational vehicle, which is if used solely for a seasonal vacation purpose.

(16) Evidentiary hearing. - A hearing to gather competent, material, and substantial evidence in order to make findings for a quasi-judicial decision required by a development regulation adopted under this Chapter.

(17) Governing board.[28] - The city council or board of county commissioners. The term is interchangeable with the terms "board of aldermen" and "boards of commissioners" and shall mean any governing board without regard to the terminology employed in charters, local acts, other portions of the General Statutes, or local customary usage.

(18) Landowner[29] or owner. - The holder of the title in fee simple.[30] Absent evidence to the contrary, a local government may rely on the county tax records to determine who is a landowner.[31] The landowner may allow authorize a person holding a valid option, lease, or contract to purchase to act as his or her agent or representative for the purpose of making applications for development approvals. for purposes of submitting a proposed site-specific development plan or a phased development plan under this section, in the manner allowed by ordinance.[32]

(19) Legislative decision. - The adoption, amendment, or repeal of a regulation[33] under this Chapter or an applicable local act. It also includes the decision to approve, amend, or rescind a development agreement consistent with the provisions of Article 10 of this Chapter.

"development approvals" the building permits issued by local governments as mandated by Article 11, even though they are not issued pursuant to an ordinance adopted by a local government.

25. The definition of "development regulation" set out in this subsection has been adapted from G.S. 160A-400.21 and 153A-349.2. It has been updated to reflect the scope of Chapter 160D.

26. The listed regulations are local ordinances previously authorized by Article 19 of G.S. Chapter 160A or Article 18 of Chapter 153A.

27. This subsection has been relocated from G.S. 160A-442. That section of Chapter 160A is also applicable to counties.

28. The definition of "governing board" set out in this subsection has been adapted from G.S. 160A-1(3). For improved consistency and clarity, this term replaces the term "governing body" that was used in some places under former law.

29. The definition of "landowner" set out in this subsection has been adapted from G.S. 160A-385.1(b) and 153A-344.1(b).

30. G.S. 160D-4-3 allows applications for development approval to be submitted by the landowner, lessees, persons holding options to purchase or lease, authorized agents of these entities, and easement holders seeking approvals authorized by their easements.

31. This language has been relocated from G.S. 160A-385(a)(2), the former provision on qualifying protest petitions.

32. The deleted language is applicable only to site-specific vesting plans, so since this definition has broader applicability, it is omitted here. In several provisions within Chapter 160D, specific direction is provided as to how a local government is to identify a "landowner." An example is to use county tax records to identify a landowner so that the landowner can receive notices of proposed rezonings (G.S. 160D-6-2).

33. The term "regulation" is used consistently throughout Chapter 160D to refer to zoning ordinances (which includes a zoning map), subdivision ordinances, housing codes, and the other development regulations, ordinances, and codes authorized by the Chapter. Article 6 of Chapter 160D specifies the process that must be followed to adopt, amend, or repeal any development regulation. Regulations are distinguished from

(20) Legislative hearing.[34] - A hearing to solicit public comment on a proposed legislative decision.

(21) Local act.[35] – As defined in G.S. 160A-1(5).[36]

(22) Local government. - A city or county.

(23) Manufactured home[37] or mobile home. - A structure as defined in G.S. 143-145(7).

(24) Person.[38] - An individual, partnership, firm, association, joint venture, public or private corporation, trust, estate, commission, board, public or private institution, utility, cooperative, interstate body, the State of North Carolina and its agencies and political subdivisions, or other legal entity.

(25) Planning and development regulation jurisdiction. - The geographic area defined in Part 2 of this Chapter within which a city or county may undertake planning and apply the development regulations authorized by this Chapter.

(26) Planning board.[39] - Any ~~planning~~ board or commission established pursuant to G.S. 160D-3-1.

(27) Property.[40] - All real property subject to land-use regulation by a local government and includes any improvements or structures customarily regarded as a part of real property.

(28) Quasi-judicial decision.[41] - A decision involving the finding of facts regarding a specific application of ~~an ordinance~~ development regulation and that requires the exercise of discretion when applying the standards of the ~~ordinance~~ regulation. Quasi-judicial decisions include but are not limited to decisions involving variances, special ~~and conditional~~ use permits, certificates of appropriateness,[42] and appeals of administrative determinations. Decisions on the approval of subdivision plats and site plans are quasi-judicial in nature if the ~~ordinance~~ regulation authorizes a decision-making board to approve or deny the ~~site plan~~ application based not only upon whether the application complies with the specific requirements set forth in the ~~ordinance,~~ regulation, but also on whether the application complies with one or more generally stated standards requiring a discretionary decision on the findings ~~of fact~~ to be made by the decision-making board.

(29) Site plan.[43] - A scaled drawing and supporting text showing the relationship between lot lines and the existing or proposed uses, buildings, or structures on the lot. The site plan may include, but is not limited to, site-specific details such as building areas, building height and floor area, setbacks from lot lines and street rights–of-way, intensities, densities, utility lines and locations, parking, access points, roads, and stormwater control facilities, that are depicted to show

---

any orders issued in an individual case, such as an order to repair a dilapidated house, which must also be adopted by ordinance.

34. Previously, these were often referred to as "public hearings" or, simply, as "hearings." The more specific language is used to clarify when an evidentiary hearing is required and when a legislative hearing is required.

35. The definition of "local act" in this subsection has been borrowed from G.S. 160A-1(5), which provides that the term "means an act of the General Assembly applying to one or more specific cities by name, or to all cities within one or more specifically named counties. 'Local act' is interchangeable with the terms 'special act,' 'public-local act,' and 'private act,' is used throughout this Chapter in preference to those terms, and shall mean a local act as defined in this subdivision without regard to the terminology employed in charters, local acts, or other portions of the General Statutes."

36. As enacted, this cross-reference was mistakenly made to G.S. 160A-1(2), rather than to 160A-1(5). This typographical error is to be corrected in 2020.

37. This subsection has been relocated from G.S. 160A-442.

38. This subsection has been relocated from G.S. 160A-400.21 and 153A-349.2. The more contemporary definition of "person" from G.S. 113A-206(1), the Mountain Ridge Protection Act, is substituted here.

39. This subsection has been relocated from G.S. 160A-400.21 and 153A-349.2.

40. This subsection has been relocated from G.S. 160A-400.21 and 153A-349.2. A similar definition of "property" found in G.S. 160A-385.1 and 153A-344.1 has been deleted as redundant.

41. This subsection has been relocated from G.S. 160A-393(a). That section of Chapter 160A is also applicable to counties.

42. G.S. 160D-9-47 allows decisions regarding certificates of appropriateness for defined minor work to be designated as administrative decisions.

43. G.S. 160A-385.1 and 153A-344.1 (G.S. 160D-1-8(c)(3) below) defined "site specific development plans" for vested rights purposes. This term was also previously defined in local legislation for Durham (S.L. 1973-400) and Raleigh (S.L. 1985-498).

compliance with all legally required development regulations that are applicable to the project and the site plan review. A site plan approval based solely upon application of objective standards is an administrative decision and a site plan approval based in whole or in part upon the application of standards involving judgment and discretion is a quasi-judicial decision. A site plan may also be approved as part of a conditional zoning decision.

(30) Special use permit.[44] - A permit issued to authorize development or land uses in a particular zoning district upon presentation of competent, material, and substantial evidence establishing compliance with one or more general standards requiring that judgment and discretion be exercised as well as compliance with specific standards. This definition includes permits previously referred to as "conditional use permits" or "special exceptions."

(31) Subdivision. - The division of land for the purpose of sale or development as specified in G.S. 160D-8-2.

(32) Subdivision regulation. - A subdivision regulation authorized by Article 8 of this Chapter.

(33) Vested right.[45] - The right to undertake and complete the development and use of property under the terms and conditions of an approval secured as specified in G.S. 160D-1-8 or under common law.[46] ~~approved site specific development plan or an approved phased development plan.~~

(34) Zoning map amendment or rezoning. - An amendment to a zoning regulation to change the zoning district that is applied to a specified property or properties. It does not include the initial adoption of a zoning map by a local government or the repeal of a zoning map and readoption of a new zoning map for the entire planning and development regulation jurisdiction. It does not include updating the zoning map to incorporate amendments to the names of zoning districts made by zoning text amendments where there are no changes in the boundaries of the zoning district or land uses permitted in the district. It does include the initial application of zoning when land is added to the territorial jurisdiction of a local government that has previously adopted zoning regulations. It does include the application of an overlay zoning district or a conditional zoning district.

(35) Zoning regulation. - A zoning regulation authorized by Article 7 of this Chapter.

§ 160D-1-3. Unified development ordinance.[47] [160D-103]

A ~~city~~ local government may elect to combine any of the ~~ordinances~~ regulations authorized by this ~~Article~~ Chapter into a unified ordinance. Unless expressly provided otherwise, a ~~city~~ local government may apply any of the definitions and procedures authorized by law to any or all aspects of the unified ordinance and may employ any organizational structure, board, commission, or staffing arrangement authorized by law to any or all aspects of the ordinance. Inclusion of a regulation authorized by this Chapter or local act in a unified development ordinance does not expand, diminish, or alter the scope of authority for those regulations.[48]

---

44. Simplification. The existing statutes use "special use permit," "conditional use permit," and "special exception" as synonyms. The use of multiple terms in different jurisdictions–and sometimes within the same ordinance–is a source of confusion for the public and for boards and administrators making permit decisions. Use of the term "conditional use permit" also confuses these kinds of permits with legislative conditional zoning. For clarity, only one term—"special use permits"—is used for these quasi-judicial permits, and the term "conditional" is confined to legislative rather than quasi-judicial decisions. Local development regulations may still assign some special-use permits to one board and others to a different board, as this change is one of terminology only. Section 2.9(b) of S.L. 2019-111 provides that local ordinances using different terminology are deemed amended to reflect the new terminology.

45. This subsection has been relocated from G.S. 160A-385.1 and 153A-344.1.

46. This language clarifies that the creation of a statutory vested right does not replace or eliminate common law vesting.

47. This section has been relocated from G.S. 160A-363(d) and 153A-322(d).

48. The merger of ordinances authorized by individual articles of Chapter 160D into a single unified development ordinance does not alter the scope of authority set by those individual articles.

§ 160D-1-4. Development approvals run with the land.[49] [160D-104]

Unless provided otherwise by law, all rights, privileges, benefits, burdens, and obligations created by development approvals made pursuant to this Chapter attach to and run with the land.

§ 160D-1-5. Maps. [160D-105]

(a) *Zoning map.*[50] Zoning district boundaries adopted pursuant to this Chapter shall be drawn on a map that is adopted or incorporated within a duly adopted development regulation. Zoning district maps that are so adopted shall be maintained for public inspection in the office of the local government clerk or such other office as specified in the development regulation. The maps may be in paper or a digital format approved by the local government.

(b) *Incorporation by reference.*[51] Development regulations adopted pursuant to this Chapter may reference or incorporate by reference flood insurance rate maps, watershed boundary maps, or other maps officially adopted or promulgated by state and federal agencies. For these maps, a regulation text or zoning map may reference a specific officially adopted map or may incorporate by reference the most recent officially adopted version of such maps.[52] When zoning district boundaries are based on these maps, the regulation may provide that the zoning district boundaries are automatically amended to remain consistent with changes in the officially promulgated state or federal maps, provided a copy of the currently effective version of any incorporated map shall be maintained for public inspection as provided in subsection (a) of this section.[53]

---

49. This is a new section. It confirms that permits and development approvals are not personal rights that may be transferred to other sites but are, instead, property rights tied to a specific parcel. G.S. 153A-344.1(f)(1) and 160A-385.1(f) (recodified as G.S. 160D-1-8(g)(1)) previously made this rule explicit for vested rights established by site-specific and phased-development plans, but otherwise it was previously only implied.

50. This is a new section. It provides that the official copy of the zoning map, and any other map incorporated within a development ordinance, is to be maintained by the local government clerk. It reflects current law in G.S. 153A-19 relative to the county clerk maintaining township boundary maps and 160A-22 regarding city boundary maps. Authority is provided for maps to be in digital or paper format. As is provided by G.S. 160A-22 for city boundary maps, copies of such maps produced by the local government clerk are admissible in evidence in judicial proceedings.

51. This subsection authorizes the incorporation by reference of flood-insurance rate maps, watershed boundary maps, and other maps officially adopted by state and federal agencies, including updates to those maps that are subsequently officially adopted by state and federal agencies, into development regulations adopted pursuant to Chapter 160D. Such automatic incorporation assures that local regulations accurately reflect the current applicable maps approved by state and federal agencies. This is consistent with G.S. 153A-47 and 160A-76, which allow incorporation by reference into local ordinances "any published technical code or any standards or regulation promulgated by any public agency."

52. This provision clarifies that maps officially adopted by state or federal agencies, including approved updates to those maps, can be incorporated by reference into local development regulations. G.S. 143-215.52 and -215.56 mandate the use of base floodplain maps that are either prepared by the National Flood Insurance Program (see 44 C.F.R. § 60.3) or approved by the state. Local government flood regulations must use state- and federally approved flood-hazard delineations without amendment. This provision allows (but does not require) updated flood-hazard delineations to be automatically incorporated into local ordinances, preventing inadvertent use of outdated and inaccurate maps or zoning-district delineations. It also avoids the time and expense of local hearings and mailed notices of zoning map amendments to incorporate new flood-hazard maps that must be used without further amendment. When flood-hazard studies that are the foundation of Flood Insurance Rate Maps (FIRMs) are updated, the federal government publishes notice—twice in local newspapers as well as in the Federal Register—that the preliminary flood-insurance rate maps are available for a ninety-day review-and-appeal period. After any appeals are addressed, the federal government issues a Letter of Final Determination; the date on which the letter is issued serves as the effective date of the updated FIRM. Local governments must make any necessary amendments to their local flood-hazard ordinances within six months of the date of the Letter of Final Determination. Incorporation of this possibility of automatic updates facilitates this mandatory compliance.

53. This language is consistent with the requirement in G.S. 160A-76 and 153A-47 that copies of incorporated technical codes and standards be maintained in the clerk's office; with provisions in 160A-78 stating

(c) *Copies.* Copies of the zoning district map reproduced by any method of reproduction that gives legible and permanent copies, when certified by the local government clerk in accordance with G.S. 160A-79 or 153A-50, shall be admissible in evidence and shall have the same force and effect as would the original map.[54]

§ 160D-1-6. Refund of illegal fees.[55] [160D-106]

If ~~the city~~ a local government is found to have illegally ~~exacted~~ imposed a tax, fee, or monetary contribution for development or a development approval ~~permit~~ not specifically authorized by law, the ~~city~~ local government shall return the tax, fee, or monetary contribution plus interest of six percent (6%) per annum to the person who made the payment or as directed by a court if the person making the payment is no longer in existence.[56]

§ 160D-1-7. Moratoria.[57] [160D-107]

(a) Authority. As provided in this ~~subsection~~, ~~cities and counties~~ local governments may adopt temporary moratoria on any ~~city or county~~ development approval required by law,[58] except for the purpose of developing and adopting new or amended plans or ~~ordinances as to~~ development regulations governing residential uses. The duration of any moratorium shall be reasonable in light of the specific conditions that warrant imposition of the moratorium and may not exceed the period of time necessary to correct, modify, or resolve such conditions.

(b) Hearing required. Except in cases of imminent and substantial threat to public health or safety, before adopting ~~an ordinance~~ a development regulation imposing a development moratorium with a duration of 60 days or any shorter period, the governing board shall hold a ~~public~~ legislative[59] hearing and shall publish a notice of the hearing in a newspaper having general circulation in the area not less than seven days before the date set for the hearing. A development moratorium with a duration of 61 days or longer, and any extension of a moratorium so that the total duration is 61 days or longer, is subject to the notice and hearing requirements of G.S. 160D-6-1.[60]

(c) Exempt projects. Absent an imminent threat to public health or safety, a development moratorium adopted pursuant to this section shall not apply to any project for which a valid building permit issued pursuant to G.S. 160D-11-8[61] is outstanding, to any project for which a ~~conditional use permit application or~~[62] special use permit application has been accepted as complete,[63] to development set forth in a site-specific or phased ~~development~~ vesting plan approved pursuant to G.S. 160D-1-8, to development for which substantial expenditures have already been made in good faith reliance on a prior valid ~~administrative or quasi-judicial permit or~~ development approval, or to preliminary or final subdivision plats that have been accepted for review by the ~~city~~ local government prior to the call for ~~public~~[64] a hearing to adopt the moratorium. Any preliminary subdivision plat accepted for review by the ~~city~~ local government prior to the call for ~~public~~ a hearing, if subsequently approved, shall be allowed to proceed to final plat approval without being subject

---

that current copies of codes of ordinances and rate schedules are to be maintained by the clerk's office; and with 160A-78 and 153A-49, which mandate that the ordinance book be maintained in the clerk's office.

54. This subsection allows for the admission of certified zoning maps as evidence (1) in quasi-judicial proceedings before boards of adjustment and (2) in court proceedings on judicial review.

55. This section has been relocated from G.S. 160A-363(e) and 153A-324(b).

56. This language clarifies the recipient of the refund.

57. This section has been relocated from G.S. 160A-381(e) and 153A-340(h).

58. S.L. 2017-102 corrects a typographical error in the county version of this provision, G.S. 153A-340(h).

59. This language clarifies the type of hearing required to be held.

60. This is an updated cross-reference (formerly G.S. 160A-364 and 153A-323).

61. This is an updated cross-reference (formerly G.S. 160A-417 and 153A-357).

62. Simplification.

63. This language clarifies that an application has to be complete to trigger an exemption.

64. This language has been deleted as surplusage.

to the moratorium. Notwithstanding the foregoing, if a complete application for a development approval has been submitted prior to the effective date of a moratorium, G.S. 160D-1-8(b) shall be applicable when permit processing resumes.[65]

(d) Required statements. Any ~~ordinance~~ development regulation establishing a development moratorium must ~~expressly~~ include at the time of adoption each of the following:

(1) A ~~clear~~[66] statement of the problems or conditions necessitating the moratorium and what courses of action, alternative to a moratorium, were considered by the ~~city~~ local government and why those alternative courses of action were not deemed adequate.

(2) A ~~clear~~[67] statement of the development approvals subject to the moratorium and how a moratorium on those approvals will address the problems or conditions leading to imposition of the moratorium.

(3) ~~An express~~[68] date for termination of the moratorium and a statement setting forth why that duration is reasonably necessary to address the problems or conditions leading to imposition of the moratorium.

(4) A ~~clear~~[69] statement of the actions, and the schedule for those actions, proposed to be taken by the ~~city~~ local government during the duration of the moratorium to address the problems or conditions leading to imposition of the moratorium.

(e) Limit on renewal or extension. No moratorium may be subsequently renewed or extended for any additional period unless the ~~city~~ local government shall have taken all reasonable and feasible steps proposed to be taken ~~by the city~~ in its ordinance establishing the moratorium to address the problems or conditions leading to imposition of the moratorium and unless new facts and conditions warrant an extension. Any ordinance renewing or extending a development moratorium must ~~expressly~~[70] include, at the time of adoption, the findings set forth in subdivisions (1) through (4) of this subsection, including what new facts or conditions warrant the extension.

(f) Expedited judicial review. Any person aggrieved by the imposition of a moratorium on development approvals required by law may apply to ~~the appropriate division of~~ the General Court of Justice for an order enjoining the enforcement of the moratorium~~, and the court shall have jurisdiction to issue that order.~~[71] Actions brought pursuant to this section shall be ~~set down~~ scheduled for expedited ~~immediate~~ hearing, and subsequent proceedings in those actions shall be accorded priority by the trial and appellate courts. In ~~any~~ such actions, the ~~city~~ local government shall have the burden of showing compliance with the procedural requirements of this subsection.

§ 160D-1-8. Vested rights and permit choice. [160D-108]

(a) *Findings*. ~~Furthermore,~~ The General Assembly recognizes that ~~city~~ local government approval of ~~land-use~~ development typically follows significant ~~landowner~~ investment in site evaluation, planning, development costs, consultant fees, and related expenses. The General Assembly finds ~~and declares~~ that it is necessary and desirable~~, as a matter of public policy,~~[72] to provide for the establishment of certain vested rights in order to ensure reasonable certainty, stability, and fairness in the ~~land-use planning~~ development regulation process, secure the reasonable expectations of landowners, and foster cooperation between the public and private sectors in ~~the area~~ of land-use planning and development regulation.

~~The ability of a landowner to obtain a vested right after city approval of a site specific development plan, a phased development plan, will preserve the prerogatives and authority of local elected officials with~~

---

65. This language clarifies that a moratorium does not override the "permit choice" rule of G.S. 160D-1-8(b).

66. This language has been deleted as superfluous.

67. This language has been deleted as superfluous.

68. This language has been deleted as superfluous.

69. This language has been deleted as superfluous.

70. This language has been deleted as superfluous.

71. This language has been deleted as surplusage.

72. This language has been deleted as surplusage.

respect to land-use matters. There will be ample opportunities for public participation and the public interest will be served.[73] These provisions will strike an appropriate balance between private expectations and the public interest. , while scrupulously protecting the public health, safety, and welfare.

(b) *Permit choice.*[74] (1) If a permit applicant submits a permit for any type of development an application made in accordance with local regulation is submitted for a development approval required pursuant to this Chapter and a rule or ordinance development regulation changes between the time the permit application was submitted and a permit decision is made, the permit applicant may choose which version of the rule or ordinance development regulation will apply to the permit application. If the development permit applicant chooses the version of the rule or ordinance applicable at the time of the permit application, the development permit applicant shall not be required to await the outcome of the amendment to the rule, map, or ordinance prior to acting on the development permit. (2) This section applies to all development permits approvals issued by the State and by local governments.[75] The duration of vested rights created by development approvals are as set forth in subsection (d) of this section.

(c) *Process to claim vested right.*[76] A person claiming a statutory or common law vested right may submit information to substantiate that claim to the zoning administrator or other officer designated by a development regulation, who shall make an initial determination as to the existence of the vested right.[77] The zoning administrator's or officer's determination may be appealed under G.S. 160D-4-5. On appeal the existence of a vested right shall be reviewed de novo.[78] In lieu of seeking such a determination, a person claiming a vested right may bring an original civil action as provided by G.S. 160D-4-5(c).

(d) *Types and duration of statutory vested rights.*[79] Except as provided by this section and subject to subsection (b) of this section,[80] amendments in local development regulations shall not be applicable or enforceable with regard to development that has been permitted or approved pursuant to this Chapter so long as one of the approvals listed in this subsection remains valid and unexpired. Each type of vested right listed below is defined by and is subject to the limitations provided in this section and the cited statutes. Vested rights established under this section are not mutually exclusive. The establishment of a vested right under one subsection does not preclude vesting under one or more other subsections or by common law principles.[81]

---

73. This language has been deleted as surplusage.

74. This subsection has been relocated from G.S. 160A-360.1 and 153A-320.1 and modified to incorporate terms that are defined within Chapter 160D. Subsection numbering has been deleted for improved clarity and reduction of clutter. This subsection is consistent with the same rule set forth in G.S. 143-755. Amendments to this subsection made by Part I of S.L. 2019-111 are to be incorporated in 2020.

75. This language reflects an amendment made by section 5 of S.L. 2015-246.

76. This subsection specifies the administrative process to be followed when a vested right is claimed. It provides that the person claiming either a statutory or common law vested right must gather the appropriate supporting information and submit it to the zoning administrator for a determination. That determination, as in other final, binding decisions of the zoning administrator, can be appealed to the board of adjustment and, thereafter, on to superior court. This process allows for an expeditious staff-level resolution of a vested rights claim while preserving the right to board of adjustment and court review if the staff determination is disputed. It also efficiently establishes a factual record regarding the foundation of the vested right being claimed.

77. This subsection establishes a clear and uniform process for determining the existence of a statutory or common law vested right.

78. This language explicitly provides that the board of adjustment and reviewing courts consider as a question of law the existence of a common law vested right. This subsection modifies G.S. 160D-14-1(j) to allow a court to accept additional evidence if the record is not adequate to determine the issue.

79. This subsection reorganizes provisions of G.S. 160A-385(b) and 153A-344(b) in order to consolidate vested-rights provisions into a single section. Amendments to this subsection made by Part I of S.L. 2019-111 are to be incorporated in 2020.

80. This language clarifies that the "permit choice rule" is applicable.

81. This language explicitly acknowledges the interrelationship of various methods of securing vested rights.

(1) *Six months -- Building permits.* Pursuant to G.S. 160D-11-9, a building permit expires six months after issuance unless work under the permit has commenced. Building permits also expire if work is discontinued for a period of 12 months after work has commenced.

(2) *One year -- Other local development approvals.*[82] Pursuant to G.S. 160D-4-3(c), unless otherwise specified by this section, statute, or local ordinance,[83] all other local development approvals expire one year after issuance unless work has substantially commenced.[84] Expiration of a local development approval does not affect the duration of a vested right established as a site specific vesting plan, a multiphase development plan, a development agreement, or vested rights established under common law.[85]

(3) *Two to five years -- Site specific vesting plans.*[86]

   (a) Duration. A vested right ~~which has been vested~~ for a site specific vesting plan ~~as provided for in this section~~ shall remain vested for a period of two years. This vesting shall not be extended by any amendments or modifications to a site specific ~~development~~ vesting plan unless expressly provided by the ~~city~~ local government. ~~Notwithstanding the provisions of subsection (d)(1), a city~~ A local government may provide that rights regarding a site specific vesting plan shall be vested for a period exceeding two years, but not exceeding five years, ~~where~~ if warranted by ~~in light of all relevant circumstances, including, but not limited to,~~[87] the size and phasing of development, the level of investment, the need for the development, economic cycles, and market conditions or other considerations. ~~These~~ This determinations shall be in the ~~sound~~[88] discretion of the ~~city~~ local government and shall be made following the process specified by subsection (c) below for the particular form of a site specific vesting plan involved. ~~Such vested right shall confer upon the landowner the right to undertake and complete the development and use of said the property under the terms and conditions of the site specific development plan or the phased development vesting plan including any applicable amendments. thereto~~[89]

   (b) Relation to building permits. A right ~~which has been~~ vested as provided in this subsection shall terminate at the end of the applicable vesting period with respect to buildings and

---

82. This provision is to be reconciled in 2020 with provisions in Part I of S.L. 2019-111 setting twenty-four--month vesting periods for life-of-development approvals, discontinuances of work, and discontinuances of nonconforming uses.

83. The statutes set specific time durations for some development approvals. For example, building permits expire in six months if work is not commenced, and site-specific development plans have a minimum two-year life. Local ordinances also sometimes have specific durations for approvals, such as a provision that a site plan or special-use permit expires if work does not commence in two years. Where the statutes set a time period or a local ordinance does so, those periods are preserved by this subsection. However, if neither state statute nor local ordinance specifies the duration of a development approval, this subsection sets a default duration of one year unless work commences. A common law vested right also is established if substantial expenditures of time, effort, or money are made in good faith reliance on a valid approval prior to its expiration.

84. Determining what constitutes a "substantial" commencement of work is a fact-specific inquiry that will vary with the local context. Rather than mandate a statewide uniform definition, the usual and ordinary definitions of the phrase apply. To the extent there is a dispute about a particular application of the term, there is a considerable body of case law on common law vested rights that would be applicable to determine what constitutes "substantial commencement of work" pursuant to a valid development approval.

85. This language clarifies that if a vested right is established by a site-specific vesting plan, a multi-phase vesting plan, or a development agreement, expiration of a vested right established under this subsection does not affect the duration of the vested right established by other means.

86. This subsection has been relocated from G.S. 160A-385.1 and 153A-344.1. It preserves the minimum two-year vested right in a "site specific development plan" as established in the 1990 legislation creating this right.

87. Simplification. If the applicant and local government agree that a vested right beyond five years is needed, a development agreement may be used.

88. This language has been deleted as surplusage.

89. This language has been deleted as surplusage.

uses for which no valid building permit applications have been filed. Upon issuance of a building permit, the provisions of G.S.160D-11-9 and G.S. 160D-11-13 shall apply, except that ~~a~~ the permit shall not expire or be revoked because of the running of time while a vested right under this subsection exists. ~~is outstanding.~~

(c) Requirements for site specific vesting plans.[90] For the purposes of this section a "site-specific ~~development~~ vesting plan" means a plan ~~which has been~~ submitted ~~to a city~~ a local government ~~by a landowner pursuant to this section~~ describing with reasonable certainty the type and intensity of use for a specific parcel or parcels of property. ~~Such~~ The plan may be in the form of, but not be limited to, any of the following plans or approvals: A planned unit development plan, a subdivision plat, a site plan, a preliminary or general development plan, a ~~conditional or~~ special use permit, ~~a conditional or special use district zoning plan,~~ a conditional zoning, or any other ~~land-use approval designation~~ development approval as may be used by a local government. ~~utilized by a city.~~ Unless otherwise expressly provided by the ~~city~~ local government, ~~such a~~ the plan shall include the approximate boundaries of the site; significant topographical and other natural features effecting development of the site; the approximate location on the site of the proposed buildings, structures, and other improvements; the approximate dimensions, including height, of the proposed buildings and other structures; and the approximate location of all existing and proposed infrastructure on the site, including water, sewer, roads, and pedestrian walkways. What constitutes a site specific ~~development~~ vesting plan ~~under this section that would trigger a vested right~~ shall be ~~finally determined by the city~~ local government pursuant to an ordinance, defined by the relevant development regulation[91] and the ~~document~~ development approval that triggers ~~such~~ vesting shall be so identified.[92] ~~at the time of its approval. However, at~~ At a minimum, the ~~ordinance to be adopted by the city~~ regulation shall designate a vesting point earlier than the issuance of a building permit. In the event a ~~city~~ local government fails to adopt ~~an ordinance~~ a regulation setting forth what constitutes a site specific ~~development~~ vesting plan, any development approval shall be considered to be a site specific vesting plan. ~~triggering a vested right,~~ A variance shall not constitute a "site specific ~~development~~ vesting plan," and approval of a site specific ~~development~~ vesting plan with the condition that a variance be obtained shall not confer a vested right unless and until the necessary variance is obtained. ~~Neither~~ If a sketch plan ~~nor~~ or any other document ~~which~~ fails to describe with reasonable certainty the type and intensity of use for a specified parcel or parcels of property, it may not constitute a site specific ~~development~~ vesting plan.

(d) *Process for approval and amendment of site specific vesting plans.*[93] ~~A vested right shall be deemed established with respect to any property upon the valid approval of a site specific~~

---

90. This subsection has been relocated from G.S. 160A-385.1(b)(5) and 153A-344.1(b)(5). It changes the nomenclature to use the term "vesting plan" to clarify that this plan creates vested rights, as opposed to the more generic and frequently used term "development plan" or "site plan."

91. Clarification. Virtually all local governments use existing development approvals, such as a preliminary plat, a special-use permit, or a conditional zoning, to approve a site-specific vesting plan. This updated terminology reflects that widespread practice. Local governments, however, retain the right to use an independently designated "site specific vesting plan" distinct from other development approvals in the unusual situation that such is desired.

92. This language clarifies that this identification is not required for each individual approval. Where the ordinance defines a particular approval, such as a preliminary plat, site plan, or special-use permit, as a site-specific vesting plan, then approval of the plat, site plan, or permit in and of itself creates the site-specific vesting without any additional action under this subsection.

93. This subsection has been relocated from G.S. 160A-385.1(c) and 153A-344.1(c). To improve clarity, throughout this subsection the term "site specific development plan" has been modified to read "site specific vesting plan." This helps distinguish this vesting tool from the more generic "site plan" used in other development regulations. The intent behind the modification is to clearly note when the plan is submitted and approved to secure vested rights and to distinguish this subsection from others that use the more generic terms "site plan" or "development plan," often in contexts other than to establish an extended vested right.

~~development plan or a phased development plan.~~[94] ~~following notice and public hearing by the city with jurisdiction over the property,~~ If a site specific vesting plan is based on an approval required by a local development regulation, the local government shall provide whatever notice and hearing is required for that underlying approval. If the duration of the underlying approval is less than two years, that shall not affect the duration of the site specific vesting established by this subsection. If the site specific vesting plan is not based on such an approval, a legislative hearing with notice as required by G.S. 160D-6-2 shall be held.[95] A ~~city~~ local government may approve a site specific ~~development plan or a phased development~~ vesting plan upon such terms and conditions as may reasonably be necessary to protect the public health, safety, and welfare. Such conditional approval shall result in a vested right, although failure to abide by such terms and conditions will result in a forfeiture of vested rights. A ~~city~~ local government shall not require a landowner to waive ~~his~~ vested rights as a condition of developmental approval. A site specific ~~development plan or a phased development~~ vesting plan shall be deemed approved upon the effective date of the ~~city's~~ local government's ~~action or ordinance relating to~~ decision approving[96] the plan or such other date as determined by the governing board upon approval. ~~thereto.~~ An approved site specific vesting plan and its conditions may be amended with the approval of the owner and the local government as follows: Any substantial modification must be reviewed and approved in the same manner as the original approval;[97] minor modifications may be approved by staff, if such are defined and authorized by local regulation.

~~(2) "Phased development plan"~~[98] ~~means a plan which has been submitted to a city by a landowner or developer for phased development which shows the type and intensity of use for a specific parcel or parcels with a lesser degree of certainty than the plan determined by the city to be a site specific development plan.~~

~~Notwithstanding the provisions of (d)(1) and (d)(2), the city may provide by ordinance that approval by a city of a phased development plan shall vest the zoning classification or classifications so approved for a period not to exceed five years. The document that triggers such vesting shall be so identified at the time of its approval. The city still may require the landowner to submit a site specific development for approval by the city with respect to each phase or phases in order to obtain final approval to develop within the restrictions of the vested zoning classification or classifications. Nothing in this section shall be construed to require a city to adopt an ordinance providing for vesting of rights upon approval of a phased development plan. A right which has been vested as provided in this section shall terminate at the end of the applicable vesting period with respect to buildings and uses for which no valid building permit applications have been filed.~~

---

94. This language has been deleted as surplusage.

95. Simplification. In most local governments, a site-specific vesting plan is defined as approval of a special-use permit, site plan, subdivision plat, or other existing local approval. Where that is the case, the language in this subsection allows the local government to follow whatever administrative or quasi-judicial process is required for that approval without the necessity of separate notice and hearing regarding the vesting plan aspect of the approval. If the vesting plan is an independent approval not based on any other required development approval, a legislative hearing is required, as is the case with current law. This subsection specifies that the same notice as is required for a rezoning be followed for that hearing.

96. Clarification and simplification of terminology.

97. This subsection explicitly authorizes subsequent amendment of approved plans and specifies the process to be followed.

98. This language has been deleted as obsolete. The 1989 legislation creating the site-specific development plan also provided for a more general optional phased development plan for vesting up to five years. Other options now exist that render this option superfluous. The multi-phase development vested right created in 2016 automatically provides for a seven-year vesting for larger multi-phase projects. The development agreement option, created in 2005, was amended in 2014 to allow any size development to be the subject of a development agreement, with a reasonable vesting duration as agreed upon by the parties. Also, the site-specific development plan can be extended from two to five years if the parties deem it appropriate,

(4) *Seven years -- Multi-phase developments*.[99] A multi-phased development shall be vested for the entire development with the zoning regulations, ~~ordinances~~, subdivision regulations, ~~ordinances,~~ and unified development ordinances ~~then~~ in place at the time a site plan approval is granted for the initial phase of the multi-phased development. ~~A right which has been vested as provided for in this subsection~~ This right shall remain vested for a period of seven years from the time a site plan approval is granted for the initial phase of the multi-phased development. For purposes of this subsection, "multi-phased development" means a development containing 100 acres[100] or more that (i) is submitted for site plan approval for construction to occur in more than one phase and (ii) is subject to a master development plan with committed elements, including a requirement to offer land for public use as a condition of its master development plan approval.

(5) *Indefinite -- Development agreements.* A vested right of reasonable duration may be specified in a development agreement approved under Article 10 of this Chapter.

(e) *Continuing review.* Following approval or conditional approval of a ~~site specific development plan or a phased development plan~~ statutory vested right, ~~nothing in this section shall exempt such a plan from~~ a local government may make subsequent reviews and require approvals by the ~~city~~ local government to ensure compliance with the terms and conditions of the original approval, provided that such reviews and approvals are not inconsistent with ~~said~~ the original approval. ~~Nothing in this section shall prohibit the city~~ The local government ~~from revoking~~ may revoke the original approval for failure to comply with applicable terms and conditions of the original approval or the ~~zoning ordinance~~ applicable local development regulations.[101]

(f) *Exceptions.*

(1) A vested right, once established as provided for by subdivisions (3) or (4) of subsection (d)[102] ~~of in~~ this section, precludes any zoning action by a ~~city~~ local government ~~which~~ that would change, alter, impair, prevent, diminish, or otherwise delay the development or use of the property as set forth in an approved vested right,[103] ~~site specific development plan or an approved phased development plan,~~ except:

a. With the written consent of the affected landowner;

b. Upon findings, ~~by ordinance~~ after notice and ~~a public~~ an evidentiary[104] hearing, that natural or man-made hazards on or in the immediate vicinity of the property, if uncorrected, would pose a serious threat to the public health, and safety, and welfare if the project were to proceed as contemplated in the approved vested right; ~~site specific development plan or the phased development plan;~~

c. To the extent that the affected landowner receives compensation for all costs, expenses, and other losses incurred by the landowner, including, but not limited to, all fees paid in consideration of financing, and all architectural, planning, marketing, legal, and other consultant's fees incurred after approval by the ~~city~~ local government, together with interest as is provided in G.S. 160D-1-6.[105] ~~thereon at the legal~~

---

99. This subsection was added by S.L. 2016-111. It was originally codified at G.S. 153A-344, 153A-344.1, 160A-385, and 160A-385.1.

100. Amendments to this subsection made by Part I of S.L. 2019-111 are to be incorporated in 2020. Under one such amendment to this language, the minimum acreage has been reduced from 100 acres to 25 acres.

101. Additional clarification may be made to coordinate the contents of this subsection with amendments made by Part I of S.L. 2019-111.

102. These provisions were originally applicable to site-specific and phased-development plans. That applicability is continued with this provision.

103. This language provides uniformity and consistency by clarifying that the enumerated exceptions to vested rights apply to all statutory vested rights created by this section. Same edit made throughout this subsection.

104. This language specifies the type of hearing required—evidentiary, as this is a quasi-judicial determination. This subdivision deletes a reference to adoption of an ordinance, as this is a determination about a specific previously approved plan, not a policy choice involving approving or revoking a plan.

105. This subdivision provides a uniform rule relative to interest on returned fees.

~~rate until paid.~~ Compensation shall not include any diminution in the value of the property ~~which~~ that is caused by such action;

d. Upon findings, ~~by ordinance~~ after notice and ~~a~~ an evidentiary[106] hearing, that the landowner or his representative intentionally supplied inaccurate information or made material misrepresentations ~~which~~ that made a difference in the approval by the ~~city~~ local government of the vested right; ~~site specific development plan or the phased development plan~~; or

e. Upon the enactment or promulgation of a State or federal law or regulation ~~which~~ that precludes development as contemplated in the approved vested right, ~~site specific development plan or the phased development plan~~, in which case the ~~city~~ local government may modify the affected provisions, upon a finding that the change in State or federal law has a fundamental effect on the plan, ~~by ordinance~~ after notice and ~~a~~ an evidentiary[107] hearing.

(2) The establishment of a vested right under subdivisions (3) or (4) of subsection (d)[108] of this section shall not preclude the application of overlay zoning or other development regulation that ~~which~~ imposes additional requirements but does not affect the allowable type or intensity of use, or ordinances or regulations ~~which~~ that are general in nature and are applicable to all property subject to ~~land-use~~ development regulation by a ~~city~~ local government, including, but not limited to, building, fire, plumbing, electrical, and mechanical codes. Otherwise applicable new regulations shall become effective with respect to property ~~which~~ that is subject to a vested right established under this section ~~site specific development plan or a phased development plan~~ upon the expiration or termination of the ~~vesting~~ rights period provided for in this section.

(3) Notwithstanding any provision of this section, the establishment of a vested right under this section shall not preclude, change or impair the authority of a ~~city~~ local government to adopt and enforce ~~zoning ordinance~~ development regulation provisions governing nonconforming situations or uses.

(g) *Miscellaneous provisions.*

(1) A vested right obtained under this section is not a personal right, but shall attach to and run with the applicable property.[109] After approval of a vested right under this section, ~~site specific development plan or a phased development plan~~, all successors to the original landowner shall be entitled to exercise such rights.

(2) Nothing in this section shall preclude judicial determination, based on common law principles or other statutory provisions, that a vested right exists ~~under subsection (b)(1) of this section.~~ in a particular case or that a compensable taking has occurred.[110] Except as expressly provided in this section, nothing in this section shall be construed to alter the existing common law.

(3) ~~In the event a city local government fails to adopt an ordinance setting forth what constitutes a site specific development plan triggering a vested right, a landowner may establish a vested~~

---

106. This language specifies the type of hearing required—evidentiary, as this is a quasi-judicial determination. This subdivision deletes a reference to adoption of an ordinance, as this is a determination about a specific previously approved plan, not a policy choice involving approving or revoking a plan.

107. This language specifies the type of hearing required—evidentiary, as this is a quasi-judicial determination. This subdivision deletes a reference to adoption of an ordinance, as this is a determination about a specific previously approved plan, not a policy choice involving approving or revoking a plan.

108. This provision was originally applicable to site-specific and phased-development plans. That applicability is continued with this provision.

109. Amendments to this subsection made by Part I of S.L. 2019-111 are to be incorporated in 2020. One amendment acknowledges that rights to outdoor advertising permits run with the owner of the permit.

110. Previous versions of this bill deleted much of the language of this subsection given codification of the common-law vested right. Since that codification has been deleted, this language is left intact.

~~right with respect to property upon the approval of a zoning permit, or otherwise may seek appropriate relief from the Superior Court Division of the General Court of Justice.~~[111]

§ 160D-1-9. Conflicts of interest.[112] [160D-109]

(a) *Governing board.* A ~~city council~~ governing board[113] member shall not vote on any ~~zoning map or text amendment~~ legislative decision regarding a development regulation adopted pursuant to this Chapter[114] where the outcome of the matter being considered is reasonably likely to have a direct, substantial, and readily identifiable financial impact on the member. A governing board member shall not vote on any zoning amendment if the landowner of the property subject to a rezoning petition or the applicant for a text amendment is a person with whom the member has a close familial, business, or other associational relationship.[115]

(b) *Appointed boards.*[116] Members of appointed boards ~~providing advice to the city council~~ governing board shall not vote on ~~recommendations regarding~~ any ~~zoning map or text amendment~~ advisory or[117] legislative decision regarding a development regulation adopted pursuant to this Chapter where the outcome of the matter being considered is reasonably likely to have a direct, substantial, and readily identifiable financial impact on the member. An appointed board member shall not vote on any zoning amendment if the landowner of the property subject to a rezoning petition or the applicant for a text amendment is a person with whom the member has a close familial, business, or other associational relationship.[118]

(c) *Administrative staff.*[119] No staff member shall make a final decision on an administrative decision required by this Chapter if the outcome of that decision would have a direct, substantial, and readily identifiable financial impact on the staff member or if the applicant or other person subject to that decision is a person with whom the staff member has a close familial, business, or other associational relationship.[120]

---

111. This subdivision has been deleted as surplusage. A substantively equivalent provision included in the definition of a site-specific vesting plan provides that if a local government fails to define a two-year vesting plan, any local development approval shall be considered to be a site-specific vesting plan.

112. This section has been relocated from G.S. 160A-381(d) and 153A-340(g).

113. This language reflects a stylistic decision to use the more generic "governing board" in place of "city council" throughout this article.

114. This subsection clarifies that a conflict of interest standard applies to legislative decisions for all development regulations, not just zoning ordinances.

115. This is a new provision. In order to promote public confidence in the integrity of the decision-making process, this provision clarifies that a board member may not vote on a rezoning that directly affects someone with whom he or she has a close relationship, even if no direct financial impact would result for the member. This standard was previously applicable to quasi-judicial decisions. While rezoning an individual parcel is legislative in nature, the potential conflict of interest and public perception of a potential conflict warrant extending this restriction to this particular legislative decision.

116. This subsection has been relocated from G.S. 160A-381(d) and 153A-340(g).

117. Clarification. Local legislation for several counties and cities allows advisory planning boards to be delegated the authority to make legislative rezoning decisions. S.L. 2017-19, for example, makes such a delegation to Randolph County and to cities within that county. This amendment makes explicit that the same conflict of interest standards apply to any board making a legislative decision, whether it is appointed or elected.

118. This is a new pew provision. In order to promote public confidence in the integrity of the decision-making process, this provision clarifies that a planning board or other appointed board member may not vote on a recommendation regarding a rezoning directly affecting someone with whom the board/board member has a close relationship, even if no direct financial impact would result for the board/board member. This standard is already applicable to quasi-judicial decisions. While rezoning an individual parcel is legislative in nature, the potential conflict of interest and public perception of a potential conflict warrant extending this restriction to this particular advisory decision.

119. This subsection has been adapted from G.S. 160A-415 and 153A-355. It provides additional clarity and specificity regarding the general provisions in existing statutes (which are retained as the second paragraph of this subsection) that (1) prohibit a staff member from being "financially interested" in any development decision subject to his or her review and (2) prohibit work inconsistent with a staff member's duties or the interest of the local government. While some local government personnel policies and rules of conduct have similar prohibitions, this establishes a baseline uniform state standard of conduct.

120. This is a new provision. In order to promote public confidence in the integrity of the decision-making process, this provision clarifies that a staff member may not make an administrative decision that affects

If a staff member has a conflict of interest under this section, the decision shall be assigned to the supervisor of the staff person or such other staff person as may be designated by the development regulation or other ordinance.

No staff member shall be financially interested or employed by a business that is financially interested in a development subject to regulation under this ~~Article~~ Chapter unless the staff member is the owner of the land or building involved. No staff member or other individual or an employee of a company contracting with a ~~city~~ local government to provide staff support shall engage in any work that is inconsistent with his or her duties or with the interest of the ~~city~~ local government, as determined by the ~~city~~ local government.

(d) *Quasi-judicial decisions*.[121] A member of any board exercising quasi-judicial functions pursuant to this ~~Article~~ Chapter shall not participate in or vote on any quasi-judicial matter in a manner that would violate affected persons' constitutional rights to an impartial decision maker. Impermissible violations of due process include, but are not limited to, a member having a fixed opinion prior to hearing the matter that is not susceptible to change, undisclosed ex parte communications, a close familial, business, or other associational relationship with an affected person, or a financial interest in the outcome of the matter.

(e) *Resolution of Objection*.[122] If an objection is raised to a board member's participation at or prior to the hearing or vote on that matter[123] and that member does not recuse himself or herself, the remaining members of the board shall by majority vote rule on the objection.

(f) *Familial relationship.* For purposes of this section, a close familial relationship means a spouse, parent, child, brother, sister, grandparent, or grandchild. The term includes the step, half, and in-law relationships.[124]

~~§ 160D1-10. Validation of certain city ordinances.~~[125]

~~Any city ordinance regularly adopted before January 1, 1972, under authority of general laws revised and reenacted in Chapter 160A, Article 19, or under authority of any city charter or local act concerning the same subject matter, is validated with respect to its application within the corporate limits of the city and as to its application within the extraterritorial jurisdiction of the city. Such an ordinance, and any city ordinance adopted since January 1, 1972 under authority of general laws revised and reenacted in Chapter 160A, Article 19, are hereby validated, notwithstanding the fact that such ordinances were not recorded pursuant to G.S. 160A360(b) or 160A364 and notwithstanding the fact that the adopting city council did not also adopt an ordinance defining or delineating by specific description the areas within its extraterritorial jurisdiction pursuant to G.S. 160A360; provided that this act shall be deemed to validate ordinances of cities in Mecklenburg County only with respect to their application within the corporate limits of such cities.~~

---

someone with whom he or she has a close relationship, even if no direct financial impact would result for the staff member. While administrative decisions do not require the exercise of discretion, the potential conflict of interest and public perception of a potential conflict warrant extending this restriction to these particular decisions. The standard on impermissible conflicts is taken from the current statutory provision on quasi-judicial conflicts of interests, set forth in subsection (d) of this section. This establishes a uniform and consistent conflict of interest rule for legislative, quasi-judicial, advisory, and administrative decisions.

121. This subsection has been relocated from G.S. 160A-388(e)(2), which is applicable to cities and counties.

122. This is a new provision. It clarifies that the process for resolving objections to a member's participation—a vote by the remainder of the board—applies to legislative and advisory decisions, as well as to quasi-judicial decisions. It provides a uniform process for resolution by the board of objections to a member's participation.

123. Clarification. This subsection addresses the resolution of objections to a member's participation or vote that are raised before board action is taken. As noted in G.S. 160A-393 (recodified as G.S. 160D-14-2(i)), the hearing record may be supplemented on judicial review with new evidence regarding impermissible conflicts.

124. This is a new provision inserted for the purpose of defining a "close" family relationship. A variety of existing statutes define this term. The language in this version is taken from G.S. 115D-25.3.

125. This subsection has been deleted as no longer necessary. It was originally codified as G.S. 160A-366. The original dates set out in the provision were tied to the initial adoption of G.S. Chapter 160A. As this section dealt with preserving prior ordinance provisions regarding geographic jurisdiction for the transition from Chapter 160 to 160A in 1973, a sentence to address that issue for the transition from 160A to 160D is incorporated at the end of 160D-1-13.

§ 160D-1-10. Construction.[126] [160D-110]

(a) G.S. 153A-4 and 160A-4 are applicable to this Chapter.

(b) "Written" or "in writing" is deemed to include electronic documentation.

(c) Unless specified otherwise, in the absence of evidence to the contrary, delivery by first class mail shall be deemed received on the third business day following deposit of the item for mailing with the United States Postal Service and delivery by electronic mail shall be deemed received on the date sent.[127]

§ 160D-1-11. Effect on prior laws.[128] [160D-111]

(a) The enactment of this Chapter shall not require the readoption of any local government ordinance enacted pursuant to laws that were in effect before the effective date of this Chapter,[129] and are restated or revised herein. The provisions of this Chapter shall not affect any act heretofore done, any liability incurred, any right accrued or vested, or any suit or prosecution begun or cause of action accrued as of the effective date of this Chapter. The enactment of this Chapter shall not be deemed to amend the geographic area within which local government development regulations adopted prior to January 1, 2019 are effective.[130]

(b) G.S. 153A-3 and 160A-3 are applicable to this Chapter.[131] Nothing in this Chapter repeals or amends a charter or local act in effect as of the effective date of this Chapter[132] unless this Chapter or a subsequent enactment of the General Assembly clearly shows a legislative intent to repeal or supersede that charter or local act.

---

126. The provisions in this section are currently applicable to city and county development regulations. This section provides that the general rules of construction as set out in Article 18 of G.S. Chapter 153A and Article 19 of G.S. Chapter 160 remain applicable to these relocated statutory provisions. This preserves the legal status quo relative to the interpretation of the scope of planning and development regulation powers.

127. Each individual requirement in G.S. Chapter 160D for mailed or emailed notice specifies the party to whom the notice must be provided. This provision deals with calculating the timing of receipt of the notice.

128. This provision is comparable G.S. 160A-2 and 153A-2.

129. The effective date of Chapter 160D is January 1, 2021. This date is a carryover from earlier versions of the chapter that were not enacted; the lack of an updated date has little if any practical effect. The date may be updated in 2020. The law as codified will substitute "January 1, 2021" for "the effective date of this Chapter" throughout this section.

130. This sentence functionally replaces G.S. 160A-366, a transition provision preserving geographic boundaries for planning- and development-regulation jurisdiction enacted under general law, charters, or local legislation prior to the effective date of Chapter 160D.

131. This is an updated provision comparable to savings provisions for local acts in G.S. 160A-3 and 153A-3. These statutes provide:

(a) When a procedure that purports to prescribe all acts necessary for the performance or execution of any power, duty, function, privilege, or immunity is provided by both a general law and a city charter or local act, the two procedures may be used as alternatives, and a city may elect to follow either one.

(b) When a procedure for the performance or execution of any power, duty, function, privilege, or immunity is provided by both a general law and a city charter or local act, but the charter or local act procedure does not purport to contain all acts necessary to carry the power, duty, function, privilege, or immunity into execution, the charter or local act procedure shall be supplemented by the general law procedure; but in case of conflict or inconsistency between the two procedures, the charter or local act procedure shall control.

(c) When a power, duty, function, privilege, or immunity is conferred on cities local governments by a general law, and a charter enacted earlier than the general law omits or expressly denies or limits the same power, duty, function, privilege or immunity, the general laws shall supersede the charter or local act.

(d) Except as provided in this section, nothing in this Chapter repeals or amends a charter or local act in effect as of January 1, 1974 or any portion of such an act, unless this Chapter or a subsequent enactment of the General Assembly clearly shows a legislative intent to repeal or supersede that charter or local act.

132. The effective date of G.S. Chapter 160D is January 1, 2021, providing ample time between adoption and effective date for the updating of local development regulations. The codified version of Chapter 160D may substitute this date for the phrase "the effective date of this Chapter" throughout the law.

(c) Whenever a reference is made in another section of the General Statutes or any local act, or any local government ordinance, resolution, or order, to a portion of Article 19 of Chapter 160A or Article 18 of Chapter 153A of the General Statutes that is repealed or superseded by this Chapter, the reference shall be deemed amended to refer to that portion of this Chapter that most nearly corresponds to the repealed or superseded portion of Article 19 of Chapter 160A or Article 18 of Chapter 153A.[133]

ARTICLE 2. PLANNING AND DEVELOPMENT REGULATION JURISDICTION

§ 160D-2-1. Planning and development regulation jurisdiction. [160D-201]

(a) Municipalities. All of the powers granted by this ~~Article~~ Chapter may be exercised by any city within its corporate limits [134] and within any extraterritorial area established pursuant to G.S. 160D-2.

(b) Counties. All ~~Each~~ of the powers granted ~~to counties~~ by this ~~Article~~ Chapter ~~and by Article 19 of Chapter 160A of the General Statutes~~ may be exercised by any county throughout the county except in areas subject to municipal planning and development regulation jurisdiction.[135] ~~as otherwise provided I G.S. 160A-360~~.

§ 160D-2-2. Municipal extraterritorial jurisdiction.[136] [160D-202]

(a) Geographic scope. ~~In addition, a~~ Any city may exercise ~~these~~ the powers granted to cities under this Chapter within a defined area extending not more than one mile beyond its contiguous corporate limits. ~~With the approval of the board or boards of county commissioners with jurisdiction over the area,~~[137] In addition and subject to subsection (c), a city of 10,000 or more population but less than 25,000 may exercise these powers over an area extending not more than two miles beyond its limits and a city of 25,000 or more population may exercise these powers over an area extending not more than three miles beyond its limits. In determining the population of a city for the purposes of this ~~Article~~ Chapter, the city council and the board of county commissioners may use the most recent annual estimate of population as certified by

---

133. This subsection was relocated and updated from G.S. 160A-5. See Appendixes B and C for depictions of where sections previously located in Chapters 153A and 160A are located within the proposed Chapter 160D. While it is anticipated that local ordinances will be amended to become consistent with this Act, to provide uniformity and a transition as may be needed, Section 2.9 of S.L. 2019-111 modifies inconsistent provisions in local ordinances to be consistent with Chapter 160D.

134. This language has been relocated from G.S. 160A-360(a).

135. This language has been relocated from G.S. 153A-320 and edited for parallel construction with the preceding subsection on municipal jurisdiction. G.S. 153A-342(d) previously allowed a county to zone less than its entire jurisdiction but required each zoned area to have at least 640 acres, at least 10 parcels, and at least 10 separate landowners. This provision does not have that limit on county discretion, which provides additional flexibility to counties with partial-county zoning coverage (an increasingly small number of counties, as most counties have either county-wide zoning (69 counties) or no county zoning (19 counties). While formerly common, only 12 counties had partial-county zoning as of January 2019.

136. This section has been relocated from G.S. 160A-360(b) to 160A-360(l). As with current law, (1) local-act modifications of city municipal extraterritorial jurisdiction (ETJ) are not affected by this revision to the General Statutes and (2) this provision only makes the powers granted in Article 19 of Chapter 160A, the planning and development regulation provisions, applicable in the municipal ETJ. As Chapter 160D does not include the general-police-power authorization of G.S. 160A-174, this law retains the current statutory scheme of limiting application of that power to the municipalities' corporate limits and not in the ETJ. Several land use–related powers previously located in Article 8 of Chapter 160A have been relocated to Article 9 of Chapter 160D, and some provide the only exceptions to this general rule regarding regulation in ETJ areas. These include regulation of adult businesses (160D-9-2), outdoor advertising (160D-9-11), solar collectors 160D-9-13), and driveway connections (160D-9-15). Also included in this relocation is regulation of the location of family care homes (160D-9-6).

137. Provisions on county approval of city jurisdiction are consolidated in subsection (b) of this section.

the Secretary of the North Carolina Department of Administration. Pursuant to G.S. 160A-58.4, extraterrito-rial municipal planning and development regulation may be extended only from the primary corporate boundary of a city and not from the boundary of satellite areas of the city.[138]

(b) Authority in the extraterritorial area. ~~No~~ A city may not exercise ~~extraterritorially~~ any power con-ferred by this ~~Article~~ Chapter in its extraterritorial jurisdiction that it is not exercising within its corporate limits.[139] A city may exercise in its extraterritorial area all powers conferred by this Chapter that it is exercising within its corporate limits. If a city fails to extend a particular type of development regulation to the extraterritorial area, the county may elect to exercise that particular type of regulation in the extraterritorial area.[140]

(c) County approval of city jurisdiction.[141] No city may ~~hereafter~~ extend its extraterritorial powers ~~under this Article~~ into any area for which the county ~~at that time~~ has adopted and is enforcing ~~a~~ county zon-ing and subdivision regulations.[142] ~~ordinances, and subdivision regulations and within which it is enforcing the State Building Code~~. However, the city may do so where the county is not exercising ~~all three~~ both of these powers, or when the city and the county have agreed upon the area within which each will exercise the powers conferred by this ~~Article~~ Chapter. No city may extend its extraterritorial powers beyond one mile from its corporate limits without the approval of the board or boards of county commissioners with jurisdiction over the area.[143]

(d)~~(a1)~~ Notice of proposed jurisdiction change. Any municipality ~~planning~~ proposing to exercise extra-territorial jurisdiction under this ~~Article~~ Chapter shall notify the owners of all parcels of land proposed for addition to the area of extraterritorial jurisdiction, as shown on the county tax records. The notice shall be sent by first-class mail to the last addresses listed for affected property owners in the county tax records. The notice shall inform the landowner of the effect of the extension of extraterritorial jurisdiction, of the landowner's right to participate in a ~~public~~ legislative[144] hearing prior to adoption of any ordinance extending the area of extraterritorial jurisdiction, as provided in G.S. 160D-6-1, and the right of all residents of the area to apply to the board of county commissioners to serve as a representative on the planning board and the board of adjustment, as provided in G.S. 160D-3-3. The notice shall be mailed at least 30 days prior to the date of ~~four weeks prior to~~ the ~~public~~ hearing.[145] The person or persons mailing the notices shall certify to the city council that the notices were sent by first-class mail, and the certificate shall be deemed conclusive in the absence of fraud.

---

138. This language reiterates in this section the current law that municipal extraterritorial areas can only be extended from a city's primary, contiguous boundaries and may not be applied to satellite areas.

139. Simplification.

140. This subsection does not require a city to exercise powers in the ETJ that are not exercised within the city. It addresses situations where the city extends some but not all of its development regulation to the ETJ area. Under prior law, once an ETJ has been established, the county loses jurisdiction for all development regulations, thereby creating the possible anomaly of a city and county both having a particular development regulation but neither applying it within an ETJ if the city does not extend that particular ordinance to the ETJ. The city and county can agree to allow the county to continue to exercise those powers in the ETJ, but absent such an agreement, the county is authorized but not required to exercise that regulation in the ETJ.

141. This language has been relocated from G.S. 160A-360(e).

142. A deleted provision regarding the State Building Code is surplusage, since all counties are now required to enforce the building code within their jurisdictions. When the statute authorizing municipal extraterritorial jurisdiction was enacted in 1959, counties were not required to enforce the building code.

143. This language has been relocated from subsection (a) of this section.

144. This language clarifies the type of hearing to be held.

145. This subsection retains extended notice of hearing on extensions of ETJ boundaries but changes the notice mailing period from "four weeks" to "30 days" to be more precise. The requirement for mailed notice of hearings on zoning-map amendments in G.S. 160D-6-2 is also amended to allow the initial notice of a rezoning hearing (which otherwise must be made in the 10 to 25 day period prior to the hearing) to be included within this notice of the ETJ boundary-ordinance hearing, allowing for the possibility of a single hearing on both the ETJ-boundary-ordinance amendment and the rezoning of the area.

(e)(b) Boundaries. Any council wishing to exercise exercising extraterritorial jurisdiction under this Article Chapter shall adopt, and may amend from time to time,[146] an ordinance specifying the areas to be included based upon existing or projected urban development and areas of critical concern to the city, as evidenced by officially adopted plans for its development. The boundaries of the city's extraterritorial jurisdiction shall be the same A single jurisdictional boundary shall be applicable[147] for all powers conferred in this Article Chapter.[148] Boundaries shall be defined, to the extent feasible, in terms of geographical features identifiable on the ground. Boundaries may follow parcel ownership boundaries. A council may, in its discretion, exclude from its extraterritorial jurisdiction areas lying in another county, areas separated from the city by barriers to urban growth, or areas whose projected development will have minimal impact on the city. The boundaries specified in the ordinance shall at all times be drawn on a map, set forth in a written description, or shown by a combination of these techniques. This delineation shall be maintained in the manner provided in G.S. 160A22 for the delineation of the corporate limits, and shall be recorded in the office of the register of deeds of each county in which any portion of the area lies.

(c) Where the extraterritorial jurisdiction of two or more cities overlaps, the jurisdictional boundary between them shall be a line connecting the midway points of the overlapping area unless the city councils agree to another boundary line within the overlapping area based upon existing or projected patterns of development.

(f)(d) County authority within city jurisdiction. If a city fails to adopt an ordinance specifying the boundaries of its extraterritorial jurisdiction, the county of which it is a part shall be authorized to exercise the powers granted by this Article in any area beyond the city's corporate limits.[149] The county may also, on request of the city council, exercise any or all of these powers in any or all areas lying within the city's corporate limits or within the city's specified area of extraterritorial jurisdiction.

(e)[150] No city may hereafter extend its extraterritorial powers under this Article into any area for which the county at that time has adopted and is enforcing a zoning ordinance and subdivision regulations and within which it is enforcing the State Building Code. However, the city may do so where the county is not exercising all three both of these powers, or when the city and the county have agreed upon the area within which each will exercise the powers conferred by this Article.

(g) Transfer of jurisdiction. When a city annexes, or a new city is incorporated in, or a city extends its jurisdiction to include, an area that is currently being regulated by the county, the county development regulations and powers of enforcement shall remain in effect until (i) the city has adopted such development regulations, or (ii) a period of 60 days has elapsed following the annexation, extension or incorporation, whichever is sooner. During this period Prior to the transfer of jurisdiction the city may hold hearings and take any other measures consistent with G.S. 160D-2-4 that may be required in order to adopt and apply its development regulations for the area at the same time it assumes jurisdiction.[151]

(f1)(h) Relinquishment of jurisdiction. When a city relinquishes jurisdiction over an area that it is regulating under this Article Chapter to a county, the city development regulations and powers of enforcement shall remain in effect until (i) the county has adopted this such development regulation or (ii) a period of 60 days[152] has elapsed following the action by which the city relinquished jurisdiction, whichever is sooner.

---

146. This language has been deleted as surplusage. The power to amend is included within the power to adopt.

147. Simplification.

148. This sentence has been relocated within the section to include all provisions related to the boundary lines in a single subsection.

149. This language has been deleted as surplusage. Addressed by G.S. 160D-2-2.

150. This subsection has been relocated to subsection (b) of this section.

151. This language clarifies that the receiving jurisdiction's regulations can be adopted and take effect concurrently upon assumption of jurisdiction.

152. G.S. 160D-2-4, on pending jurisdiction, allows a local government anticipating receipt of jurisdiction to accept applications, hold hearings, and take other actions to allow application of its development regulations concurrently with receipt of jurisdiction.

~~During this period~~ Prior to the transfer of jurisdiction the county may hold hearings and take other measures consistent with G.S. 160D-2-4 that may be required in order to adopt and apply its development regulations for the area at the same time it assumes jurisdiction.[153]

(h) Process for local government approval. When a local government is granted powers by this section subject to the request, approval, or agreement of another local government, the request, approval, or agreement shall be evidenced by a formally adopted resolution of ~~that government's legislative body~~ the governing board of the local government. Any such request, approval, or agreement can be rescinded upon two years' written notice to the other ~~legislative bodies~~ governing boards concerned by repealing the resolution. The resolution may be modified at any time by mutual agreement of the ~~legislative bodies~~ governing boards concerned.

(i) Local acts. Nothing in this section shall repeal, modify, or amend any local act ~~which~~ that defines the boundaries of a city's extraterritorial jurisdiction by metes and bounds or courses and distances.

(j) Effect on vested rights. Whenever a city or county, pursuant to this section, acquires jurisdiction over a territory that theretofore has been subject to the jurisdiction of another local government, any person who has acquired vested rights ~~under a permit, certificate, or other evidence of compliance issued by the local government~~ in the[154] surrendering jurisdiction may exercise those rights as if no change of jurisdiction had occurred. The city or county acquiring jurisdiction may take any action regarding such a development approval, ~~permit,~~ certificate, or other evidence of compliance that could have been taken by the local government surrendering jurisdiction pursuant to its ~~ordinances and~~ development regulations. Except as provided in this subsection, any building, structure, or other land use in a territory over which a city or county has acquired jurisdiction is subject to the ~~ordinances and~~ development regulations of the city or county.

~~(j) Repealed by Session Laws 1973, c. 669, s. 1.~~

~~(k) Agricultural lands and buildings.~~[155] ~~As used in this subsection, "bona fide farm purposes" is as described in G.S. 153A340 As used in this subsection, "property" means a single tract of property or an identifiable portion of a single tract. Property that is located in the geographic area of a municipality's extraterritorial jurisdiction and that is used for bona fide farm purposes is exempt from exercise of a municipality's extraterritorial jurisdiction under this Article. Property that is located in the geographic area of a municipality's extraterritorial jurisdiction and that ceases to be used for bona fide farm purposes it shall become subject to exercise of the municipality's extraterritorial jurisdiction under this Article.~~

~~(l)~~[156]~~A municipality may provide in its zoning ordinance that an accessory building of a "bona fide farm" as defined by G.S. 153A-340(b) has the same exemption from the building code as it would have under county zoning as provided by Part 3 of Article 18 of Chapter 153A of the General Statutes.~~

~~This subsection applies only to the City of Raleigh and the Towns of Apex, Cary, FuquayVarina, Garner, Holly Springs, Knightdale, Morrisville, Rolesville, Wake Forest, Wendell, and Zebulon.~~

§ 160D-2-3. Split jurisdiction.[157] [160D-203]

If a parcel of land lies within the planning and development regulation jurisdiction of more than one local government, for the purposes of this Chapter the local governments may by mutual agreement pursuant to Article 20 of Chapter 160A and with the written consent of the landowner assign exclusive planning and development regulation jurisdiction under this Chapter for the entire parcel to any one of those local governments. Such a mutual agreement shall only be applicable to development regulations and shall not

---

153. This language clarifies that the receiving jurisdiction's regulations can be adopted and take effect concurrently upon assumption of jurisdiction.

154. Simplification.

155. This subsection has been relocated to a different section, on agricultural uses and zoning, G.S. 160D-9-3.

156. This subsection has been relocated to different section, on agricultural uses and zoning, G.S. 160D-9-3.

157. This is a new section. It adds authority to provide that, where multiple local governments share jurisdiction on a single parcel of land, they may agree to assign exclusive jurisdiction for the entire parcel to one unit of government.

affect taxation or other non-regulatory matters. The mutual agreement shall be evidenced by a resolution formally adopted by each governing board and recorded with the register of deeds in the county where the property is located within 14 days of the adoption of the last required resolution.[158]

§ 160D-2-4. Pending jurisdiction.[159] [160D-204]

After consideration of a change in local government jurisdiction has been formally proposed, the local government that is potentially receiving jurisdiction may receive and process proposals to adopt development regulations and any application for development approvals that would be required in that local government if the jurisdiction is changed. No final decisions shall be made on any development approval prior to the actual transfer of jurisdiction. Acceptance of jurisdiction, adoption of development regulations, and decisions on development approvals may be made concurrently and may have a common effective date.

ARTICLE 3. BOARDS AND ORGANIZATIONAL ARRANGEMENTS

§ 160D-3-1. Planning boards.[160] [160D-301]

(a) *Composition*. ~~Any city~~ A local government[161] may by ordinance provide for the appointment and compensation of a planning board[162] ~~create~~ or may designate one or more boards or commissions to perform the ~~following~~ duties of a planning board.[163] A planning board ~~or commission~~[164] ~~created or designated~~ established pursuant to this section may include, but shall not be limited to, one or more of the following:

(1) A planning board ~~or commission~~ of any size (with not fewer than three members) or composition deemed appropriate, organized in any manner deemed appropriate;

(2) A joint planning board created by two or more local governments pursuant to Article 20, Part 1, of Chapter 160A.

(b) Duties. A planning board may be assigned[165] the following powers and duties:

(1) ~~Make studies of the area within its jurisdiction and surrounding areas;~~

(2) ~~Determine objectives to be sought in the development of the study area;~~

(3) ~~Prepare and adopt plans for achieving these objectives;~~

(1) Prepare, review, maintain, monitor, and periodically update and recommend to the governing board a comprehensive plan, and such other plans as deemed appropriate, and conduct ongoing related research, data collection, mapping, and analysis;[166]

(2) Facilitate and coordinate citizen engagement and participation in the planning process;[167]

(3) Develop and recommend policies, ordinances, development regulations, administrative procedures, and other means for carrying out plans in a coordinated and efficient manner;

---

158. This subsection applies a recordation requirement similar to that for development agreements to assure that future landowners are provided adequate notice of the mutual agreement on assignment of regulatory jurisdiction.

159. This is a new section. It adds authority to process applications and conduct hearings for proposed development by the potential receiving jurisdiction where there is a pending shift in jurisdiction, provided that no final action may be taken prior to the actual transfer of jurisdiction.

160. This section has been relocated from G.S. 160A-361 and 153A-321.

161. This language updates a reference to local governments to include cities and counties.

162. This language establishes consistent language for the creation of a planning board and a board of adjustment.

163. While the statutory term is "planning board," an individual local government can assign the planning board any name it deems suitable (such as "planning commission," "zoning commission," or the like).

164. Simplification.

165. This language retains full flexibility regarding the range of duties that may be assigned to planning boards. It does not mandate particular duties for all planning boards, other than the mandated review and comment on proposed zoning amendments noted in subdivision (5) of this section.

166. This subdivision consolidates and updates a reference to the plan-making and analysis functions of a planning board. Original provisions on planning board roles dated to 1919.

167. This subdivision incorporates a reference to the role many planning boards play in securing citizen engagement in planning.

(4) Advise the ~~council~~ governing board concerning the ~~use and amendment of means for carrying out~~ implementation of[168] plans, including, but not limited to, review and comment on all zoning text and map amendments as required by G.S. 160D-6-4.

(5) Exercise any functions in the administration and enforcement of various means for carrying out plans that the ~~council~~ governing board may direct;

(6) Provide a preliminary forum for review of quasi-judicial decisions, provided that no part of the forum or recommendation may be used as a basis for the deciding board;[169]

(7) Perform any other related duties that the ~~council~~ governing board may direct.

§ 160D-3-2. Boards of adjustment.[170] [160D-302]

(a) *Composition.* ~~The zoning or unified development ordinance may~~ A local government may by ordinance provide for the appointment and compensation of a board of adjustment consisting of five or more members, each to be appointed for three years. In appointing the original members or in the filling of vacancies caused by the expiration of the terms of existing members, the ~~city council~~ governing board may appoint certain members for less than three years so that the terms of all members shall not expire at the same time. The ~~council~~ governing board may appoint and provide compensation for alternate members to serve on the board in the absence or temporary disqualification of any regular member or to fill a vacancy pending appointment of a member. Alternate members shall be appointed for the same term, at the same time, and in the same manner as regular members. Each alternate member serving on behalf of any regular member has all the powers and duties of a regular member.

(b) *Duties.* The board shall hear and decide all matters upon which it is required to pass under any statute or development regulation adopted under this Chapter.[171] The ordinance may designate a planning board or governing board to perform any of the duties of a board of adjustment in addition to its other duties and may create and designate specialized boards to hear technical appeals. If any board other than the board of adjustment is assigned decision-making authority for any quasi-judicial matter, that board shall comply with all of the procedures and the process applicable to a board of adjustment in making quasi-judicial decisions.[172]

---

168. Simplification.

169. The practice of submitting a pending quasi-judicial decision to a separate board for an advisory review is common. A 2005 UNC School of Government (SOG) survey indicated that more than 71 percent of responding municipalities and 52 percent of responding counties submitted pending special-use permits to a planning board for an advisory review. A number of reviewers of this proposal suggested prohibiting the practice of advisory reviews of quasi-judicial decisions, and there was substantial support for that position by many attorneys. However, there was not consensus to prohibit the practice, so this amendment recognizes that practice but clarifies that the decision (1) must be based on competent evidence presented at the evidentiary hearing and (2) may not be based on these informal advisory reviews.

170. This section has been relocated from G.S. 160A-388(a), also applicable to counties as provided by G.S. 153A-345.1.

171. This subsection has been relocated from G.S. 160A-388(a1).

172. This language reiterates for clarity the current requirement that any board making quasi-judicial decisions is subject to the same procedures and limitations applicable to boards of adjustment making similar decisions. The same clarification appears in the statute on appeals, G.S. 160D-4-6, and in the provision on variances and special-use permits, G.S. 160D-7-5. Some commentators suggested prohibiting assignment of any quasi-judicial decision to a governing board, as these boards are more accustomed to making legislative decisions. However, the 2005 SOG surveys indicate that some 70 percent of North Carolina cities and counties currently assign at least some special-use permits to a governing board (and others send some to planning boards). Given the widespread choice of local governments to assign some quasi-judicial decisions to the governing board, it was deemed appropriate to retain this option in Chapter 160D.

§ 160D-3-3. Historic Preservation Commission.[173] [160D-303]

(a) *Composition.* Before it may designate one or more landmarks or historic districts <u>pursuant to Article 9, Part 4 of this Chapter</u>, ~~a municipality~~ <u>the governing board</u>[174] shall establish ~~or designate~~ a historic preservation commission<u>.</u> The ~~municipal~~ governing board shall determine the number of the members of the commission, which shall be at least three, and the length of their terms, which shall be no greater than four years. A majority of the members of such a commission shall have demonstrated special interest, experience, or education in history, architecture, archaeology, or related fields. All the members shall reside within the ~~territorial~~ <u>planning and development</u>[175] regulation jurisdiction of the ~~municipality~~ <u>local government</u> as established pursuant to ~~G.S. 160A-360~~ <u>this Chapter</u>. The commission may appoint advisory bodies and committees as appropriate. Members of the commission may be reimbursed for actual expenses incidental to the performance of their duties within the limits of any funds available to the commission, but shall serve without pay unless otherwise provided in the ordinance establishing the commission.[176]

(b) *Alternate forms.* In lieu of establishing a historic preservation commission, a ~~municipality~~ <u>local government</u> may designate as its historic preservation commission, (i) a separate historic districts commission or a separate historic landmarks commission established pursuant to this <u>Chapter</u> ~~Part~~ to deal only with historic districts or landmarks respectively, (ii) a planning board established pursuant to this ~~Article~~ <u>Chapter</u>, or (iii) a community appearance commission established pursuant to ~~Part 7 of~~ this ~~Article~~ <u>Chapter</u>. In order for a commission or board other than the preservation commission to be designated, at least three of its members shall have demonstrated special interest, experience, or education in history, architecture, or related fields. At the discretion of ~~the municipality~~ <u>a local government</u> the ordinance may also provide that the preservation commission may exercise within a historic district any or all of the powers of a planning board or a community appearance commission.

(c) *Joint commissions.* ~~A county and one or more cities in the county~~ <u>Local governments</u> may establish or designate a joint preservation commission. If a joint commission is established or designated, ~~the county and cities~~ it shall have the same composition as specified by this section and the <u>local governments</u> involved shall determine the residence requirements of members of the joint preservation commission.

(d) <u>*Duties.* The historic preservation commission shall have the duties specified in G.S. 160D-9-42.</u>

§ 160D-3-4. Appearance Commission.[177] [160D-304]

(a) *Composition.* Each ~~municipality and county in the State~~ <u>local government</u> may ~~by ordinance~~ create a special commission, to be known as the ~~official~~ appearance commission ~~for the city or county~~. The commission shall consist of not less than seven nor more than 15 members, to be appointed by the governing <u>board</u> ~~body of the municipality or county~~ for such terms, not to exceed four years, as the governing ~~body~~ <u>board</u> may by ordinance provide. All members shall be residents of the ~~municipality's or county's~~ <u>local government's</u> area of planning and ~~zoning~~ <u>development regulation</u> jurisdiction at the time of appointment. Where possible, appointments shall be made in such a manner as to maintain on the commission at all times a majority of members who have had special training or experience in a design field, such as architecture, landscape design, horticulture, city planning, or a ~~closely~~[178] related field. Members of the commission may be reimbursed for actual expenses incidental to the performance of their duties within the limits of any funds available to the commission, but shall serve without pay unless otherwise provided in the ordinance establishing the commission. Membership of the commission is ~~declared to be~~[179] an office that may be held concurrently with any other elective or appointive office pursuant to Article VI, Sec. 9, of the Constitution.

---

173. This section has been relocated from G.S. 160A-400.7. It is also applicable to counties, as provided by G.S. 160A-400.2.

174. This updated language recognizes that counties as well as municipalities may establish historic-preservation commissions. This stylistic change is made throughout this section.

175. Clarification.

176. Clarification. This subsection adds the same language for historic commissions as is currently provided for appearance commissions in the next section.

177. This section has been relocated from G.S. 160A-451, which is applicable to both cities and counties.

178. This language has been deleted as surplusage.

179. This language has been deleted as surplusage.

(b) *Joint commissions.* A county and one or more cities in the county Local governments may establish a joint appearance commission. If a joint commission is established, the county and the city or cities it shall have the same composition as specified by this section and the local governments involved shall determine the residence requirements for members of the joint commission.

(c) *Duties.* The community appearance commission shall have the duties specified in G.S. 160D-9-60.

§ 160D-3-5. Housing Appeals Board.[180] [160D-305]

(a) *Composition.* The governing body board may by ordinance provide for the creation and organization of a housing appeals board. Instead of establishing a housing appeals board, a local government may designate the board of adjustment as its housing appeals board. The housing appeals board, if created, shall consist of five members to serve for three-year staggered terms. It shall have the power to elect its own officers and to fix the times and places for its meetings, to adopt necessary rules of procedure, and to adopt other rules and regulations for the proper discharge of its duties. It shall keep an accurate record of all its proceedings.[181]

(b) *Duties.* The housing appeals board shall have the duties specified in G.S. 160D-12-8. to which a

§ 160D-3-6. Other advisory boards. [160D-306]

A local government may by ordinance establish additional advisory boards as deemed appropriate. The ordinance establishing such boards shall specify the composition and duties of such boards.[182]

§ 160D-3-7. Extraterritorial representation on boards.[183] [160D-307]

(a) *Proportional representation.* When a city elects to exercise extraterritorial zoning or subdivision regulation powers under this Chapter G.S. 160A360, it shall in the ordinance creating or designating its planning board provide a means of proportional representation[184] based on population for residents of the extraterritorial area to be regulated. The population estimates for this calculation shall be updated no less frequently than after each decennial census. Representation shall be provided by appointing at least one resident of the entire extraterritorial zoning and subdivision regulation planning and development regulation area to the planning board, board of adjustment, appearance commission,[185] and the historic preservation commission if there are historic districts or designated landmarks in the extraterritorial area.[186] that makes recommendations or grants relief in these matters. For purposes of this section, an additional member must be appointed to the planning board or board of adjustment to achieve proportional representation only when the population of the entire extraterritorial zoning and subdivision area constitutes a full fraction of the municipality's population divided by the total membership of the planning board or board of adjustment.[187]

---

180. This section has been relocated from G.S. 160A-446. It is also applicable to counties pursuant to G.S. 160A-442(1).

181. This language has been deleted as redundant of provisions in G.S. 160D-3-8.

182. Local governments currently have the authority to appoint additional advisory boards. G.S. 160A-361(a) and 153A-321 allow for the designation of "one or more boards or commissions" to perform the duties of a planning board.

183. This section has been relocated from G.S. 160A-362.

184. Rather than attempt to include a complicated formula in the statute, each local government is allowed to follow the ordinary, common definition of "proportional" in meeting this requirement. Since ETJ boundaries are not based on existing governmental boundaries or census tracts, each local government must make reasonable population estimates for the ETJ area and compare them to concurrent estimates of the population within the corporate boundaries.

185. The appearance-commission statute (previously G.S. 160A-451, now G.S. 160D-3-5) already provides that members reside within the planning and development regulation jurisdiction rather than within corporate limits, so this is a conforming clarification.

186. This language provides for consistent treatment of all boards with regulatory authority in the extraterritorial area.

187. Simplification. This change eliminates redundant language and a complicated formula, while retaining the requirement for proportional representation on both the planning board and board of adjustment.

(b) *Appointment.* Membership of joint municipal-county planning agencies or boards of adjustment may be appointed as agreed by counties and municipalities. ~~Any advisory board established prior to July 1, 1983, to provide the required extraterritorial representation shall constitute compliance with this section until the board is abolished by ordinance of the city.~~[188] The extraterritorial representatives on ~~the planning board and the board of adjustment~~ a city advisory board authorized by this Article shall be appointed by the board of county commissioners with jurisdiction over the area. ~~When selecting a new representative to the planning board or to the board of adjustment as a result of an extension of the extraterritorial jurisdiction, the board of county commissioners shall hold a public hearing on the selection. A notice of the hearing shall be given once a week for two successive calendar weeks in a newspaper having general circulation in the area. The board of county commissioners shall select appointees only from those who apply at or before the public hearing.~~[189] The county shall make the appointments within ~~45~~ 90 days[190] following the ~~public~~ hearing.[191] Once a city provides proportional representation, no power available to a city under ~~G.S. 160A-360~~ this Chapter shall be ineffective in its extraterritorial area solely because county appointments have not yet been made. If there is an insufficient number of qualified residents of the extraterritorial area to meet membership requirements, the board of county commissioners may appoint as many other residents of the county as necessary to make up the requisite number. When the extraterritorial area extends into two or more counties, each board of county commissioners concerned shall appoint representatives from its portion of the area, as specified in the ordinance. If a board of county commissioners fails to make these appointments within 90 days after receiving a resolution from the city council requesting that they be made, the city council may make them.

(c) *Voting rights.* If the ordinance so provides, the outside representatives may have equal rights, privileges, and duties with the other members of the board to which they are appointed, regardless of whether the matters at issue arise within the city or within the extraterritorial area; otherwise they shall function only with respect to matters within the extraterritorial area.

§ 160D-3-8. Rules of procedure. [160D-308]

Rules of procedure that are consistent with the provisions of this Chapter may be adopted by the governing board for any or all boards created under this Article.[192] In the absence of action by the governing board, each board created under this Article is authorized to adopt its own rules of procedure that are consistent with the provisions of this Chapter. A copy of any adopted rules of procedure shall be maintained by the local government clerk or such other official as designated by ordinance and posted on the local government web site if one exists.[193] Each board shall keep minutes of its proceedings.

§ 160D-3-9. Oath of office.[194] [160D-309]

All members appointed to boards under this Article shall, before entering their duties, qualify by taking an oath of office as required by G.S. 153A-26 and 160A-61.

---

188. This language has been deleted as obsolete.

189. This language has been deleted as obsolete. Each county is authorized to set the process it will follow in making appointments to boards. Having a special hearing requirement for ETJ appointments has proven confusing in practice.

190. This subsection has been amended for consistency with a provision later in this section allowing a city council to make appointments if no action is taken by a county board in ninety days. Since the requirement of a public hearing on the appointments is deleted by this section, the phrase regarding hearings in this sentence will likely be deleted in technical updates to this section.

191. This language is likely to be amended in 2020, as the hearing it references is no longer mandated. The time limit is likely to run from the date of receipt of a request for appointments.

192. This language clarifies that binding rules of procedure may be set for each appointed board, but this is not mandatory. If rules are set by local act or charter, those would remain binding.

193. This language explicitly authorizes the common practice of having rules of procedure for these boards and establishes a uniform and consistent location for maintaining a copy of the rules, making them readily available and easy to find.

194. This section makes uniform the common practice of having all appointed board members take an oath of office. For consistency and ease of application, it applies to all boards rather than only to boards with

§ 160D-3-10. Appointments to boards.[195] [160D-3101]

Unless specified otherwise by statute or local ordinance, all appointments to boards authorized by this Chapter shall be made by the governing board of the local government. The governing board may establish reasonable procedures to solicit, review, and make appointments.

ARTICLE 4. ADMINISTRATION, ENFORCEMENT, AND APPEALS[196]

§ 160D-4-1. Application. [160D-401]

(a) The provisions of this Article shall apply to all development regulations adopted pursuant to this Chapter. Local governments may apply any of the definitions and procedures authorized by this Article to any ordinance adopted under the general police power of cities and counties, Article 8 of Chapter 160A and Article 6 of Chapter 153A respectively, and may employ any organizational structure, board, commission, or staffing arrangement authorized by this Article to any or all aspects of those ordinances.[197] The provisions of this Article also apply to any other local ordinance that substantially affects land use and development.[198]

(b) The provisions of this Article are supplemental to specific provisions included in other Articles of this Chapter. To the extent there is a conflict between the provisions of this Article and other Articles, the more specific provision shall control.[199] This Article does not expand, diminish, or alter the scope of authority for development regulations authorized by this Chapter.[200]

§ 160D-4-2. Administrative staff. [160D-402]

(a) Authorization. Local governments may appoint administrators, inspectors, enforcement officers, planners, technicians, and other staff to develop, administer and enforce development regulations authorized by this Chapter.

(b) Duties.[201] Duties assigned to staff may include, but are not limited to, the receipt drafting and implementing plans and development regulations to be adopted pursuant to this Chapter; determining whether applications for development approvals are complete; receipt and processing of applications for permits development approvals; providing notices of applications and hearings; and making permit decisions and determinations regarding development regulation implementation; determining whether applications for development approvals meet applicable standards as established by law and local ordinance; the making of any necessary conducting inspections; issuance or denial of issuing or denying certificates of compliance or occupancy; enforcing development regulations, including issuance of issuing notices of

---

decision-making authority.

195. Clarification. This section makes explicit the requirement that appointments be made by the city council or county board of commissioners unless an applicable local ordinance provides otherwise.

196. Many of these administrative provisions are adapted from the building code Parts in G.S. Chapters 160A and 153A. Under prior law, most of these provisions were applicable to all development regulations, not just the building code. Those provisions that are only applicable or relevant to the building code remain in Article 11 of Chapter 160D.

197. Prior law has this same provision for unified development ordinances (now in G.S. 160D-1-3). This language extends the same options to general-police-power ordinances while not enlarging or constricting the scope of authority granted to cities or counties.

198. As with the same provision included in G.S. 160D-1-1(a), this language confirms that if a local ordinance substantially affects land use and development, whether explicitly adopted pursuant to the authority of Chapter 160D or not, these provisions are applicable.

199. As with the same provision included in G.S. 160D-1-1(b), this language confirms that if an individual article has more detailed administrative provisions, such as the mandatory qualifications for building inspectors in G.S. 160D-11-3, those more-specific provisions control over the general provisions of this article.

200. This language reiterates a provision in G.S. 160D-1-1(d).

201. This subsection has been adapted from G.S. 160A-411 and -412, and G.S. 153A-351 and -352. Provisions specific to building-code administration are in G.S. 160D-11-2. Some of the procedures that are optional in Chapter 160D Article 4 are mandatory with respect to building-code administration in Article 11. G.S. 160D-11-3 continues to require that inspections regarding the State Building Code must still be performed by qualified building inspectors.

violation, ~~and~~ orders to correct violations, <u>and</u> ~~the~~ <u>recommending</u> bringing ~~of~~ judicial actions against actual or threatened violations; ~~the~~ keeping ~~of~~ adequate records; and any other actions that may be required in order adequately to enforce the laws <u>and development regulations under their jurisdiction. A development regulation may require that designated staff members take an oath of office.</u>[202] The ~~city~~ <u>local government</u> shall have the authority to enact ~~reasonable and appropriate~~[203] ordinances, procedures, and fee schedules relating to the administration and the enforcement of this ~~Article~~ <u>Chapter</u>.[204] <u>The administrative and enforcement provisions related to building permits set forth in Article 11 shall be followed for those permits.</u>

(c) <u>Alternative staff arrangements.</u>[205] A ~~city~~ <u>local government</u> may enter into contracts with another city, county, or combination thereof under which the parties agree to create a joint staff for the enforcement of State and local laws specified in the agreement. The governing boards of the contracting parties may make any necessary appropriations for this purpose.

In lieu of joint staff, a ~~city council~~ <u>governing board</u> may designate staff from any other city or county to serve as a member of its staff with the approval of the governing ~~body~~ <u>board</u> of the other city or county. A staff member, if designated from another city or county under this section, shall, while exercising the duties of the position, be considered <u>an</u> ~~municipal employee~~ <u>agent</u>[206] <u>of the local government exercising those duties.</u> The <u>governing board of one local government</u> ~~city~~ may request the <u>governing board of a second local government</u> ~~board of county commissioners of the county in which the city is located~~ to direct one or more <u>of the second local government's</u> ~~county~~ staff members to exercise their powers within part or all of the <u>first local government's</u> ~~city's~~ jurisdiction, and they shall thereupon be empowered to do so until the <u>first local government</u> ~~city~~ officially withdraws its request in the manner provided in G.S. <u>160D-2-2.</u>

A ~~city~~ <u>local government</u> may contract with an individual, company, council of governments, regional planning agency, metropolitan planning organization, or rural planning agency to designate an individual who is not a city or county employee to<u> work under the supervision of the local government</u> to exercise the functions authorized by this section. The ~~city~~ <u>local government</u> shall have the same potential liability, if any, for inspections conducted by an individual who is not an employee of the ~~city~~ <u>local government</u> as it does for an individual who is an employee of the ~~city~~ <u>local government</u>. The company or individual with whom the ~~city~~ <u>local government</u> contracts shall have errors and omissions and other insurance coverage acceptable to the ~~city~~ <u>local government</u>.

(d) <u>Financial support.</u>[207] The ~~city~~ <u>local government</u> may appropriate for the support of the staff any funds that it deems necessary. ~~It may provide for paying staff fixed salaries or it may reimburse them for their services by paying over part or all of any fees collected.~~[208] It shall have power to fix reasonable fees <u>for support, administration, and implementation of programs authorized by this Chapter</u> ~~for issuance of permits, inspections, and other services of the staff.~~ <u>and all such fees shall be used for no other purposes.</u>[209] When an inspection, for which the permit holder has paid a fee to the ~~city~~ <u>local government</u>, is performed by a marketplace pool Code-enforcement official upon request of the Insurance Commissioner under G.S. 143-151.12(9)a., the ~~city~~ <u>local government</u> shall promptly return to the permit holder the fee collected by

---

202. This language recognizes that many local governments require any staff member who is considered a "public official" rather than a "public employee" to take an oath of office. Generally, this means any staff member whose position is defined by statute, as is done here, and who exercises discretion rather than performs only ministerial duties.

203. This language has been deleted as surplusage.

204. Also see G.S. 160D-8-5 for a more-specific provision regarding subdivision fees (formerly G.S. 160A-4.1 and 153A-102.1).

205. This subsection has been adapted from G.S. 160A-413 and 153A-353.

206. This change clarifies language to avoid unintended implications for broader human resource issues.

207. This subsection has been adapted from G.S. 160A-414 and 153A-354.

208. Deleted as surplusage (unnecessary detail about how local governments finance permit administration).

209. This language incorporates an amendment made by S.L. 2015-145. The language is generalized to be applicable to all development permits, not just building-code enforcement.

the ~~city~~ local government for such inspection. This applies to the following inspections: plumbing, electrical systems, general building restrictions and regulations, heating and air-conditioning, and the general construction of buildings.[210]

§ 160D-4-3. Administrative development approvals and determinations. [160D-403]

(a) Development approvals.[211] To the extent consistent with the scope of regulatory authority granted by the Articles of this Chapter,[212] no person shall commence or proceed with development[213] without first securing any required ~~permits or~~ development approvals from the ~~city~~ local government with jurisdiction over the site of the development. ~~work.~~ A ~~permit~~ development approval shall be in writing and ~~shall~~ may[214] contain a provision that the development ~~work done~~ shall comply with all applicable State and local laws. A local government may issue development approvals in print or electronic form. Any development approval issued exclusively in electronic form shall be protected from further editing once issued. Applications for development approvals may be made by the landowner, a lessee or person holding an option or contract to purchase or lease land, or an authorized agent of the landowner.[215] An easement holder may also apply for development approval for such development as is authorized by the easement.[216]

(b) Determinations and Notice of Determinations.[217] – A development regulation enacted under the authority of this Chapter may designate the staff member or members charged with making determinations under the development regulation.

The officer making the determination shall give written notice to the owner of the property that is the subject of the determination and to the party who sought the determination if different from the owner. The written notice shall be delivered by personal delivery, electronic mail, or by first-class mail. The notice shall be delivered to the last address listed for the owner of the affected property on the county tax abstract and to the address provided in the application or request for a determination if the party seeking the determination is different from the owner.[218]

It shall be conclusively presumed that all persons with standing to appeal have constructive notice of the determination from the date a sign providing notice that a determination has been made is prominently posted on the property that is the subject of the determination, provided the sign remains on the property for at least 10 days. The sign shall contain the words "Zoning Decision" or "Subdivision Decision" or similar language for other determinations in letters at least six inches high and shall identify the means to contact a local government staff member for information about the determination. Posting of signs is not the only form of constructive notice. Any such posting shall be the responsibility of the landowner, applicant, or

---

210. This sentence has been added by S.L. 2018-29.

211. This subsection has been adapted from G.S. 160A-417 and 153A-357. The comparable, more-detailed provision for building permits is G.S. 160D-11-8. The more-detailed requirements of that section apply to all building permits.

212. This language clarifies that these administrative provisions do not enlarge, contract, or alter the scope of the regulatory authority grant for zoning, subdivision, and other development regulations. Note that these provisions are only applicable to "required permits" and that permits can only be required where authorized by statute.

213. This addition reflects a broader application of Article 4 of Chapter 160D to zoning and other development regulations, not just to construction regulated under the building code.

214. This remains a mandatory provision for building permits in G.S. 160D-11-8, as is the case in prior law.

215. This language clarifies who is authorized to make application for a development approval.

216. While an application for development is usually made by the owner of the fee interest in the affected property, an easement holder may directly make an application for development that is authorized by the terms of the easement.

217. This subsection has been relocated from G.S. 160A-388(b1) (also applicable to counties). For clarity, the term "determination" is consistently used in place of the term "decision." Appeals of determinations, and the time period for taking them, are addressed in G.S. 160D-4-5.

218. This language clarifies who must be provided with notice of a determination made under a development regulation.

person who sought the determination. Verification of the posting shall be provided to the staff member responsible for the determination. Absent an ordinance provision to the contrary, posting of signs shall not be required.

(c) Duration of development approval.[219] Unless a different period is specified by this Chapter or other specific applicable law[220] or a different period is provided[221] by a quasi-judicial development approval, a development agreement, or a local ordinance, a ~~permit~~ development approval issued pursuant to this ~~Article~~ Chapter shall expire ~~six months~~ one year after the date of issuance if the work authorized by the ~~permit~~ development approval has not been substantially commenced.[222] Local development regulations may provide for development approvals of shorter duration for temporary land uses, special events, temporary signs, and similar development. Unless provided otherwise by this Chapter or other specific applicable law or a longer period is provided by local ordinance, if after commencement the work or activity is discontinued for a period of 12 months after commencement, the ~~permit~~ development approval ~~therefor~~ shall immediately expire. The time periods set out in this subsection shall be tolled during the pendency of any appeal.[223] No work or activity authorized by any ~~permit~~ development approval that has expired shall thereafter be performed until a new ~~permit~~ development approval has been secured.[224] This subsection shall not limit any vested rights secured by G.S. 160D-1-8.[225]

(d) Changes.[226] After a ~~permit~~ development approval has been issued, no deviations from the terms of the application, ~~plans and specifications,~~[227] or the ~~permit~~ development approval shall be made until ~~specific~~ written approval of proposed changes or deviations has been obtained. A ~~city~~ local government may define by ordinance minor modifications[228] to ~~permits~~ development approvals that can be exempted or administratively approved. The local government shall follow the same development review and approval process required for issuance of the development approval in the review and approval of any major modification of that approval.[229]

---

219. This subsection has been adapted from G.S. 160A-418 and 153A-358. The current statute, with its six-month permit duration, is applicable only to building permits. This provision is applicable only in those instances where neither the statute nor the local ordinance sets a duration for a development approval. The provision applies to permits and other development approvals but is not applicable to enforcement orders.

220. Where a shorter period is provided elsewhere in Chapter 160D, such as the six-month expiration period for building permits set out in G.S. 160D-11-8, that shorter period is still applicable. Where a longer period is provided by statute, such as with two years allotted for site-specific vesting plans or development agreements, that longer period is still applicable.

221. While a one-year permit-expiration period is the statutory default, a local ordinance may provide for longer permit periods for various permits and development approvals.

222. The permit-expiration period does not apply to legislative decisions, such as rezonings or conditional zonings. Determining what constitutes a "substantial" commencement of work is a fact-specific inquiry that will vary with the local context. Rather than mandate a statewide uniform definition, the usual and ordinary definitions of the phrase apply. To the extent that there is a dispute about a particular application of terms, standard case law on interpretation of similar terms that have long been used in zoning (such as with limits on nonconformities) can be applied.

223. This language clarifies that if an appeal contesting the validity of a development approval has been made, the time period setting the life of the approval does not run while the appeal is pending.

224. As provided in common law and under G.S. 160D-1-8(b), a vested right pursuant to a local development permit expires when the development permit expires, unless vesting has been established by some other means (such as by making substantial expenditures in reliance on the permit).

225. This language clarifies that the duration of a local development approval does not shorten or alter any statutory vested rights.

226. This subsection has been adapted from G.S. 160A- 419 and 153A-359.

227. This language has been deleted as superfluous.

228. Rather than include a statutory definition of "minor modifications" that may not fit all local government settings, each local government is left the flexibility to adopt reasonable regulations defining that phrase.

229. This language clarifies the process to be followed for substantial permit modifications. Rather than include a statutory definition of "substantial or major modifications" that may not fit all local government settings, each local government is given the flexibility to adopt reasonable regulations defining that phrase.

(e) Inspections.[230] ~~Local~~ Administrative staff may[231] inspect work undertaken pursuant to a ~~permit~~ development approval to assure that the work is being done ~~to the provisions of any~~ in accordance with applicable State and local laws and of the terms of the ~~permit~~ approval. In exercising this power, staff ~~shall have a right~~ are authorized to enter ~~on~~ any premises within the jurisdiction of the ~~city~~ local government at all reasonable hours for the purposes of inspection or other enforcement action, upon presentation of proper credentials, provided the appropriate consent has been given for inspection of areas not open to the public or that an appropriate inspection warrant has been secured.[232]

(f) Revocation of development approvals.[233] In addition to initiation of enforcement actions under G.S. 160D-4-4, development approvals may be revoked ~~Staff may revoke any permit~~ by the local government issuing the ~~permit~~ development approval by notifying the ~~permit~~ holder in writing stating the reason for the revocation.[234] The local government shall follow the same development review and approval process required for issuance of the development approval, including any required notice or hearing, in the review and approval of any revocation of that approval.[235] ~~Permits~~ Development approvals shall be revoked for any substantial departure from the approved application, plans, or specifications; for refusal or failure to comply with the requirements of any applicable ~~State or~~ local ~~laws~~ development regulation or any State law delegated to the local government for enforcement purposes in lieu of the State;[236] or for false statements or misrepresentations made in securing the ~~permit~~ approval. Any ~~permit~~ development approval mistakenly issued in violation of an applicable State or local law may also be revoked. The revocation of a ~~permit~~ development approval by ~~the staff~~ a staff member ~~A permit revocation~~ may be appealed ~~to the board of adjustment~~ pursuant to G.S. 160D-4-5. ~~No further work shall take place pursuant to a revoked permit order pending a ruling on the appeal.~~ If an appeal is filed regarding a development regulation adopted by a local government pursuant to this Chapter, the provisions of G.S. 160D-4-5(e) regarding stays shall be applicable.[237]

(g) Certificate of occupancy.[238] A local government may, upon completion of work or activity undertaken pursuant to a development approval, make final inspections and issue a certificate of compliance or occupancy if staff finds that the completed work complies with all applicable State and local laws and with the terms of the permit approval. No building, structure, or use of land that is subject to a building permit required by Article 11 shall be occupied or used until a certificate of occupancy or temporary certificate pursuant to G.S. 160D-11-14 has been issued.

(h) Optional communication requirements. A regulation adopted pursuant to this Chapter may require notice and/or informational meetings as part of the administrative decision-making process.[239]

---

230. This subsection has been adapted from G.S. 160A-420 and 153A-360.

231. Inspections are mandatory for building permits, as required by G.S. 160D-11-11. Greater flexibility is provided for other local development regulations.

232. This subsection confirms the constitutional mandates that consent must be secured for searches and inspections and that, absent such consent, an administrative inspection warrant must be secured. The subsection avoids the unintended inference in current law that a statute can authorize searches beyond those that are constitutionally permissible.

233. This subsection has been adapted from G.S. 160A-422 and 153A-362.

234. G.S.160D-11-13 preserves the current law on revocation of building permits. Article 10 of Chapter 160D has more-specific provisions regarding breach of development agreements.

235. Staff can issue a notice of violation and a stop-work order as an administrative decision to stop work in the event of a permit violation. This provision clarifies the process to be followed if the permit itself is to be permanently revoked. When an administratively issued permit is revoked, the revocation is made by the same administrative official who issued the permit. If a quasi-judicial permit is revoked, the board issuing the permit is responsible for the revocation.

236. This language clarifies which state or local law violations trigger a permit revocation.

237. This language applies the consistent and uniform rule regarding stays during appeals, adopting the same provisions as previously applied in G.S. 160A-388.

238. This subsection has been adapted from G.S. 160A-423 and 153A-363. A certificate of compliance is mandatory for projects that require a building permit under Article 11 of Chapter 160D (G.S. 160D-11-14) but is optional as a means of verifying compliance for other permits.

239. This provision explicitly allows, but does not mandate, for the provision of notices or for meetings with potentially affected persons in the consideration of administrative decisions.

§ 160D-4-4. Enforcement. [160D-404]

(a) Notices of violation. When staff determines work or activity has been undertaken in violation of a development regulation adopted pursuant to this Chapter or other local development regulation or any State law delegated to the local government for enforcement purposes in lieu of the State or in violation of the terms of a development approval, a written notice of violation may be issued. The notice of violation shall be delivered to the holder of the development approval and to the landowner of the property involved, if the landowner is not the holder of the development approval, by personal delivery, electronic delivery, or first class mail and may be provided by similar means to the occupant of the property or the person undertaking the work or activity. The notice of violation may be posted on the property. The person providing the notice of violation shall certify to the local government that the notice was provided and the certificate shall be deemed conclusive in the absence of fraud.[240] Except as provided by G.S. 160D-11-23, 160D-12-6, or otherwise provided by law, a notice of violation may be appealed to the board of adjustment pursuant to G.S. 160D-4-5.[241]

(b) Stop work orders.[242] Whenever any work or activity subject to regulation pursuant to this ~~Article~~ Chapter or other applicable local development regulation or any State law delegated to the local government for enforcement purposes in lieu of the State is undertaken in substantial violation of any State or local law, or in a manner that endangers life or property, staff may order the specific part of the work or activity that is in violation or presents such a hazard to be immediately stopped. The order shall be in writing, directed to the person doing the work or activity, and shall state the specific work or activity to be stopped, the ~~specific~~ reasons therefor, and the conditions under which the work or activity may be resumed. A copy of the order shall be delivered to the holder of the development approval and to the owner of the property involved (if that person is not the holder of the development approval) by personal delivery, ~~email~~ electronic delivery, or first class mail. The person or persons delivering the stop work order shall certify to the local government that the order was delivered and that certificate shall be deemed conclusive in the absence of fraud. Except as provided by G.S. 160D-11-12 and 160D-12-8, a stop work order may be appealed ~~to the board of adjustment~~ pursuant to G.S. 160D-4-5. No further work or activity shall take place in violation of a stop work order pending a ruling on the appeal. Violation of a stop work order shall constitute a Class 1 misdemeanor.[243]

(c) Remedies.[244]

(1) Subject to the provisions of the development regulation, ~~ordinance,~~ any development regulation ~~ordinance~~ adopted pursuant to authority conferred by this ~~Article~~ Chapter ~~or to Chapter 157A~~[245] may be enforced by any remedy provided by G.S. 160A-175 or G.S. 153A-123. If a building or structure is erected, constructed, reconstructed, altered, repaired, converted, or maintained, or any building, structure or land is used or developed in violation of this ~~Part~~ Chapter or of any development regulation ~~ordinance~~ or other regulation made under authority ~~conferred thereby~~ of this Chapter, the ~~city~~ local government, in addition to other remedies, may institute any appropriate action or proceedings to prevent the unlawful erection, construction, reconstruction, alteration, repair, conversion, maintenance,

---

240. This certification provides documentation for local government files as to the content and timing of the notice of violation. It is similar to the certification that mailed notice of rezoning hearings has been made, a certification that has long been included in G.S. 160A-384 and 153A-343 (now G.S. 160D-6-2(a)).

241. The cited provisions have specialized appeal routes for building permits where the State Building Code is involved and for housing code enforcement. G.S. 160D-4-5(b) allows direct appeal to the courts where the scope of authority or constitutional claims are at issue.

242. This subsection has been adapted from G.S. 160A-421 and 153A-361. It amends a county provision to conform to a municipal provision (a county statute previously applied to stop-work orders for violations of any "local building law or local building ordinance or regulation"). As with current law, appeals of both municipal and county stop-work orders related to State Building Code violations are made to the Commissioner of Insurance, as set out in G.S. 160D-11-12.

243. This subsection has been relocated from G.S. 160A-421(d).

244. This subsection has been relocated from G.S. 160A-365 and 153A-324.

245. This change deletes an obsolete cross-reference in a prior county statute.

use, or development; to restrain, correct or abate the violation; to prevent occupancy of the building, structure or land; or to prevent any illegal act, conduct, business or use in or about the premises.[246]

(2)[247] When ~~any~~ a development regulation.~~ordinance~~ adopted pursuant to authority conferred by this ~~Article~~ Chapter is to be applied or enforced in any area outside the ~~territorial~~ planning and development regulation jurisdiction of ~~the~~ a city as ~~described~~ set forth in ~~G.S. 160A-360(a)~~ Article 2 of this Chapter, the city and the property owner shall certify that the application or enforcement of the city development regulation ~~ordinance~~ is not under coercion or otherwise based on representation by the city that the city's development approval ~~of any land use planning~~ would be withheld ~~from the property owner~~ without the application or enforcement of the city development regulation ~~ordinance~~ outside the ~~territorial~~ jurisdiction of the city. The certification may be evidenced by a signed statement of the parties on any development approval. ~~approved plat recorded in accordance with this Article~~ Chapter.

(3) In case any building, structure, site, area or object designated as a historic landmark or located within a historic district designated pursuant to this ~~Part~~ Chapter is about to be demolished whether as the result of deliberate neglect or otherwise, materially altered, remodeled, removed or destroyed, except in compliance with the development regulation ~~ordinance~~ or other provisions of this ~~Part~~ Chapter, the ~~city or county~~ local government, the historic preservation commission, or other party aggrieved by such action may institute any appropriate action or proceedings to prevent such unlawful demolition, destruction, material alteration, remodeling or removal, to restrain, correct or abate such violation, or to prevent any illegal act or conduct with respect to such building, structure, site, area or object.[248] Such remedies shall be in addition to any others authorized by this Chapter for violation of an ~~municipal~~ ordinance.

§ 160D-4-5. Appeals of administrative decisions.[249] [160D-405]

(a) *Appeals.* Except as provided in subsection (c), appeals of decisions made by the staff under this Chapter shall be made to the board of adjustment unless a different board is provided or authorized otherwise by statute or an ordinance adopted pursuant to this Chapter.[250] If this function of the board of adjustment is assigned to any other board pursuant to G.S. 160D-3-2(b), that board shall comply with all of the procedures and processes applicable to a board of adjustment hearing appeals.[251] Appeal of a decision made pursuant to an erosion and sedimentation control regulation, a stormwater control regulation, or a provision of the housing code shall not be made to the board of adjustment unless required by a local government ordinance or code provision. ~~As used in this section, the term "decision" includes any final and binding order, requirement, or determination.~~

---

246. This subdivision has been relocated from G.S. 160A-389.

247. This provision has been added by S.L. 2015-246, § 3. It has been edited for clarity.

248. This language has been relocated from G.S. 160A-400.11 (also applicable to counties).

249. Most of this section has been relocated from the section on appeals in the current zoning enabling statute, G.S. 160A-388(b1), which is also applicable to counties. It is generalized to establish uniform times and procedures for all administrative appeals (with any needed variation provided by specific provisions in other articles).

250. As with current law, G.S. 160D-3-2(b) allows a local development ordinance to create and designate specialized boards to hear technical appeals. Appeals for building permits are addressed in G.S. 160D-11-23.

251. This language reiterates for clarity the current requirement that any board making quasi-judicial decisions is subject to the same procedures and limitations applicable to boards of adjustment making similar decisions. Stylistic changes to reflect this clarification have been made throughout the section, replacing references to the "board of adjustment" with references to the "board."

(b) *Standing.* [252] Any person who has standing under G.S. 160D-14-2(d) or the ~~city~~ local government may appeal an administrative decision to the board. ~~of adjustment.~~ An appeal is taken by filing a notice of appeal with the ~~city~~ local government clerk or such other local government official as designated by ordinance. The notice of appeal shall state the grounds for the appeal.

(c) *Judicial challenge.* A person with standing may bring a separate and original civil action to challenge the ~~validity or~~ constitutionality of an ordinance or development regulation or that it is ultra vires, preempted, or otherwise in excess of statutory authority without filing an appeal under subsection (a).[253]

(d) *Time to appeal.* The owner or other party shall have 30 days from receipt of the written notice of the determination within which to file an appeal. Any other person with standing to appeal shall have 30 days from receipt from any source of actual or constructive notice of the ~~decision~~ determination within which to file an appeal. In the absence of evidence to the contrary, notice pursuant to G.S. 160D-4-3(b) given by first class mail shall be deemed received on the third business day following deposit of the notice for mailing with the United States Postal Service.

(e) *Record of decision.* The official who made the decision shall transmit to the board all documents and exhibits constituting the record upon which the ~~action~~ decision appealed from is taken. The official shall also provide a copy of the record to the appellant and to the owner of the property that is the subject of the appeal if the appellant is not the owner.

(f) *Stays.* An appeal of a notice of violation or other enforcement order stays enforcement of the action appealed from and accrual of any fines assessed[254] unless the official who made the decision certifies to the board ~~of adjustment~~ after notice of appeal has been filed that because of the facts stated in an affidavit, a stay would cause imminent peril to life or property or because the violation is transitory in nature, a stay would seriously interfere with enforcement of the development regulation. ~~ordinance.~~ In that case, enforcement proceedings shall not be stayed except by a restraining order, which may be granted by a court. If enforcement proceedings are not stayed, the appellant may file with the official a request for an expedited hearing of the appeal, and the board ~~of adjustment~~ shall meet to hear the appeal within 15 days after such a request is filed.[255] Notwithstanding the foregoing, appeals of decisions granting a ~~permit~~ development approval or otherwise affirming that a proposed use of property is consistent with the development regulation ~~ordinance~~ shall not stay the further review of an application for ~~permits or permissions~~ development approvals to use such property; in these situations the appellant or local government may request and the board may grant a stay of a final decision of ~~permit~~ development approval applications, including ~~or~~ building permits affected by the issue being appealed.

(g) *Alternative dispute resolution.* The parties to an appeal that has been made under this ~~subsection~~ section may agree to mediation or other forms of alternative dispute resolution. The development regulation ~~ordinance~~ may set standards and procedures to facilitate and manage such voluntary alternative dispute resolution.

---

252. This subsection and the immediately following one have been relocated from G.S. 160A-388(b1).

253. G.S. 160D-14-1 provides for declaratory judgment actions to challenge the validity or constitutionality of ordinances. G.S. 160D-14-4 provides for other civil actions. G.S. 160D-14-2 provides for reviews of quasi-judicial decisions in the nature of certiorari. An amendment to this subsection made by Part I of S.L. 2019-111, which addresses appeal of enforcement actions that contest interpretation of the ordinance, is to be incorporated in 2020.

254. Clarification. This language explicitly provides that fines, along with other enforcement actions, do not accrue while an enforcement action is stayed during the appeal of a notice of violation. An amendment to this subsection made by Part I of S.L. 2019-111, which addresses stays during the pendency of both the quasi-judicial appeal and a judicial appeal, is to be incorporated in 2020.

255. The fifteen-day time period for a board of adjustment hearing, a feature of current law, applies in those rare instances where an appeal of a stop-work order has been made but enforcement has not been stayed because the zoning administrator has certified that there is an imminent danger to public health or safety or that the violation is transitory in nature and the appellant has requested an expedited hearing.

§ 160D-4-6. Quasi-judicial procedure.[256] [160D-406]

(a) *Process required.* Boards shall follow quasi-judicial procedures in determining appeals of adminis-trative decisions, special use permits, certificates of appropriateness,[257] variances, or any other quasi-judicial decision.[258] ~~The board of adjustment shall follow quasi-judicial procedures when deciding appeals and requests for variances and special and conditional use permits.~~[259]

(b) *Notice of Hearing.* Notice of evidentiary[260] hearings conducted pursuant to this ~~section~~ Chapter shall be mailed to the person or entity whose appeal, application, or request is the subject of the hearing; to the owner of the property that is the subject of the hearing if the owner did not initiate the hearing; to the owners of all parcels of land abutting the parcel of land that is the subject of the hearing; and to any other persons entitled to receive notice as provided by the local development regulation. ~~zoning or unified development ordinance.~~ In the absence of evidence to the contrary, the ~~city~~ local government may rely on the county tax listing to determine owners of property entitled to mailed notice. The notice must be deposited in the mail at least 10 days, but not more than 25 days, prior to the date of the hearing. Within that same time period, the ~~city~~ local government shall also prominently post a notice of the hearing on the site that is the subject of the hearing or on an adjacent street or highway right-of-way.

The board may continue an evidentiary hearing that has been convened without further advertise-ment. If an evidentiary hearing is set for a given date and a quorum of the board is not then present, the hearing shall be continued until the next regular board meeting without further advertisement.[261]

(c) *Administrative materials.*[262] The administrator or staff to the board shall transmit to the board all applications, reports, and written materials[263] relevant to the matter being considered. The administrative materials may be distributed to the members of the board prior to the hearing if at the same time they are distributed to the board a copy is also provided to the appellant or applicant and to the landowner if that person is not the appellant or applicant. The administrative materials shall become a part of the hearing record. The administrative materials may be provided in written or electronic form. Objections to inclusion or exclusion of administrative materials may be made before or during the hearing. Rulings on unresolved objections shall be made by the board at the hearing.

---

256. Most of this section has been relocated from the section on appeals in the current zoning enabling statute, G.S. 160A-388.

257. G.S. 160D-9-47 allows certain minor work defined by ordinance to be addressed as an administrative decision.

258. The subsection lists the common and usual quasi-judicial decisions made under local development regulations. Occasionally, local regulations add discretionary standards for other types of approvals, such as subdivision plats or site plans. To the extent that is done, they are "other quasi-judicial decisions" covered by this subsection.

259. Simplification and stylistic modernization.

260. This language clarifies the type of hearing required.

261. This language clarifies that the provisions of G.S. 160A-81 and 153A-52, which govern continuances of legislative hearings by governing boards, also apply to continuation of evidentiary hearings.

262. This subsection explicitly provides that applications, staff reports, and other relevant administrative materials shall be provided to the board, as is specified in G.S. 160A-388(b1)(5) for appeals. The subsection allows, but does not require, materials to be submitted to the board prior to the hearing. It requires that copies be provided to all parties at the same time the material is distributed to the board. This incorporates the standard practice of allowing distribution of hearing packets to board members prior to the hearing to allow the board to review written materials in advance of the hearing, while assuring fairness by requiring that the materials be contemporaneously distributed to all parties.

263. Reference to "analysis," "staff recommendations," and "comments" have been deleted and replaced by the more-generic term "written materials." Many local governments do not make staff recommendations on quasi-judicial matters, so language was deleted to avoid an implication that these are mandatory.

(d) *Presentation of evidence.* The applicant, the local government, and any person who would have standing to appeal the decision under G.S. 160D-14-2(d) shall have the right to participate as a party at the evidentiary hearing.[264] Other witnesses may present competent, material, and substantial evidence that is not repetitive as allowed by the board.

Objections regarding jurisdictional and evidentiary issues, including but not limited to, the timeliness of an appeal or the standing of a party, may be made to the board.[265] The board chair shall rule on any objections and the chair's rulings may be appealed to the full board. These rulings are also subject to judicial review pursuant to G.S. 160D-14-2. Objections based on jurisdictional issues may be raised for the first time on judicial review.

(e) *Appearance of official, new issues.* The official who made the decision ~~or prepared the staff analysis included in the administrative record,~~[266] or the person currently occupying that position if the decision-maker is no longer employed by the local government,[267] shall be present at the evidentiary hearing as a witness. The appellant shall not be limited at the hearing to matters stated in ~~the~~ a notice of appeal. If any party or the ~~city~~ local government would be unduly prejudiced by the presentation of matters not presented in the notice of appeal, the board shall continue the hearing.

(f) *Oaths.* The chair of the board or any member acting as chair and the clerk to the board are authorized to administer oaths to witnesses in any matter coming before the board. Any person who, while under oath during a proceeding before the ~~board of adjustment~~ board determining a quasi-judicial matter,[268] willfully swears falsely is guilty of a Class 1 misdemeanor.

(g) *Subpoenas.* The board making a quasi-judicial decision under this Chapter ~~of adjustment~~[269] through the chair, or in the chair's absence anyone acting as chair, may subpoena witnesses and compel the production of evidence. To request issuance of a subpoena, the applicant, the local government, and any person[270] ~~persons~~ with standing under G.S. 160D-14-2(d) may make a written request to the chair explaining why it is necessary for certain witnesses or evidence to be compelled. The chair shall issue requested subpoenas he or she determines to be relevant, reasonable in nature and scope, and not oppressive. The chair shall rule on any motion to quash or modify a subpoena. Decisions regarding subpoenas made by the chair may be immediately[271] appealed to the full board ~~of adjustment~~. If a person fails or refuses to obey a subpoena issued pursuant to this subsection, the board ~~of adjustment~~ or the party seeking the subpoena may apply to the General Court of Justice for an order requiring that its subpoena be obeyed, and the court shall have jurisdiction to issue these orders after notice to all proper parties.

---

264. Case law has established that the rights of a party include the right to present evidence, cross-examine witnesses, inspect documents, offer rebuttal evidence, and otherwise participate as a party in a hearing. Humble Oil & Ref. Co. v. Bd. of Aldermen, 284 N.C. 458, 470, 202 S.E.2d 129, 137 (1974). Many boards allow persons without standing to present relevant evidence to the board, particularly if there is no objection to this by a party. Other boards only allow parties to submit evidence.

265. This language clarifies that the board, rather than administrative staff, must make rulings on standing, timeliness, and similar jurisdictional issues. These board rulings are subject to judicial review, where a de novo review is made.

266. This change clarifies that not all staff members involved in staff review are required to attend the hearing; only the official responsible for the decision is required to attend. Parties may subpoena witness as needed.

267. This subsection adds a provision regarding instances where the decision-maker is no longer reasonably available to testify about the decision.

268. This language recognizes that boards other than the board of adjustment may be assigned quasi-judicial decision-making authority.

269. This language reflects the fact that these decisions may be assigned to other boards. The same edit has been made throughout this subsection.

270. Clarification. This subsection adopts parallel language from subsection (d) of this section so that the same terminology is used to refer to individuals entitled to present evidence at quasi-judicial hearings and those authorized to seek subpoenas to compel the production of evidence.

271. This language allows for resolution of contested subpoenas prior to hearings, preventing undue delay.

(h) *Appeals in nature of certiorari*.[272] When hearing an appeal pursuant to ~~G.S. 160A-400.9(e)~~ G.S. 160D-9-47(e) or any other appeal[273] in the nature of certiorari, the hearing shall be based on the record below and the scope of review shall be as provided in G.S. 160D-14-2(k).

(i) *Voting*. The concurring vote of four-fifths of the board[274] shall be necessary to grant a variance. A majority of the members shall be required to decide any other quasi-judicial matter or to determine an appeal made in the nature of certiorari. For the purposes of this subsection, vacant positions on the board and members who are disqualified from voting on a quasi-judicial matter under G.S. 160D-1-9(d) shall not be considered members of the board for calculation of the requisite majority if there are no qualified alternates available to take the place of such members.

(j) ~~*Quasi-Judicial* Decisions *and Judicial Review*.~~ ~~(1)~~ The board shall determine contested facts and make its decision within a reasonable time.[275] When hearing an appeal, the board ~~of adjustment~~ may reverse or affirm, wholly or partly, or may modify the decision appealed from and shall make any order, requirement, decision, or determination that ought to be made. The board shall have all the powers of the official who made the decision. Every quasi-judicial decision shall be based upon competent, material, and substantial evidence in the record. Each quasi-judicial decision shall be reduced to writing, reflect the board's determination of contested facts and their application to the applicable standards and be approved by the board and signed by the chair or other duly authorized member of the board. A quasi-judicial decision is effective upon filing the written decision with the clerk to the board or such other office or official as the development regulation ~~ordinance~~ specifies. The decision of the board shall be delivered within a reasonable time by personal delivery, electronic mail, or by first-class mail to the applicant, ~~property~~ landowner, and to any person who has submitted a written request for a copy prior to the date the decision becomes effective.[276] The person required to provide notice shall certify to the local government that proper notice has been made and the certificate shall be deemed conclusive in the absence of fraud. ~~Subject to the provisions of subdivision (e) of this subsection, the board of adjustment shall hear and decide the appeal within a reasonable time.~~[277]

(k) *Judicial Review*. ~~(2)~~ Every quasi-judicial decision shall be subject to review by the superior court by proceedings in the nature of certiorari pursuant to G.S. ~~160A-393~~ 160D-14-2. Appeals shall be filed within the times specified in G.S. 160D-14-5(d). ~~A petition for review shall be filed with the clerk of superior court by the later of 30 days after the decision is effective or after a written copy thereof is given in accordance with subdivision (1) of this subsection. When first-class mail is used to deliver notice, three days shall be added to the time to file the petition.~~[278]

---

272. An earlier draft of this bill deleted appeals of historic-district-commission decisions on certificates of appropriateness to the board of adjustment. As consensus was not reached on that amendment, this subsection has been retained.

273. This subsection deletes specific reference to the appeal of a historic-district-commission decision to the board of adjustment, given the proposed amendment of that statute to provide a uniform appeal of quasi-judicial decisions directly to superior court.

274. No change has been made to the provision in in the prior statute that a simple majority and a four-fifths majority are both counted based on the membership of the entire board, as clarified in 2005 to exclude from the computation only vacant seats and those ineligible to vote for constitutional due process reasons.

275. When this provision was amended by the General Assembly in 2013, there was discussion of adding a specific time period for making a decision. Given the variety of settings across the state, it was deemed best to leave this as a "reasonable" time requirement; this draft does not revisit that decision.

276. As with the board decision, the delivery of the decision must be made within a reasonable time.

277. This language has been deleted as redundant (see the first sentence of this subsection).

278. This language has been relocated to Article 14 of Chapter 160D, on judicial review.

ARTICLE 5. PLANNING

§ 160D-5-1. Plans. [160D-501]

(a) *Preparation of plans and studies.* As a condition of adopting and applying zoning regulations under this Chapter,[279] a local government shall adopt and reasonably maintain[280] a comprehensive plan[281] that sets forth goals, policies, and programs intended to guide the present and future physical, social, and economic development of the jurisdiction.

A comprehensive plan is intended to guide coordinated, efficient, and orderly development within the planning and development regulation jurisdiction based on an analysis of present and future needs. Planning analysis may address inventories of existing conditions and assess future trends regarding demographics, economic, environmental, and cultural factors. The planning process shall include opportunities for citizen engagement in plan preparation and adoption.

In addition to a comprehensive plan, a local government may prepare and adopt such other plans as deemed appropriate. This may include, but is not limited to, land use plans, small area plans, neighborhood plans, hazard mitigation plans, transportation plans, housing plans, and recreation and open space plans.[282] If adopted pursuant to the process set forth in this section, such plans shall be considered in review of proposed zoning amendments.

(b) *Contents.*[283] A comprehensive plan may, among other topics, address any of the following as determined by the local government:

---

279. This is a new section. Section 2.9(c) of S.L. 2019-111 allows a grace period until July 1, 2022, for local governments to prepare and adopt a plan in order to retain zoning authority. A 2008 UNC School of Government survey indicated that more than 75 percent of responding cities with populations above 10,000 had adopted a comprehensive plan, as did more than half the responding counties.

Since 1923, the zoning enabling statute has required that regulation be "in accordance with a comprehensive plan." Since 2006, an analysis of plan consistency has been required for any proposed zoning amendment. Early case law required that zoning be based on a comprehensive consideration of the entire jurisdiction rather than be focused on the idea of having a plan. Shuford v. Town of Waynesville, 214 N.C. 135 (1938). This section clarifies that some analysis and planning must serve as the foundation for development regulations by mandating that a plan be prepared and maintained in order to adopt and enforce development regulations. Given the significant impact local development regulations can have on private property rights and community interests, at least some modest effort to prepare and adopt a plan is warranted. Other states require preparation of at least the land-use element of a comprehensive plan in order to enact zoning. *See, e.g.,* S.C. CODE ANN. § 6-29-720(A). This section leaves the scope and content of plans that are prepared to the good judgment of local elected officials, in recognition of the wide variety of North Carolina local government needs and capacities, but removes the option of having no plan at all.

280. The time frame that is reasonable for updating and refining plans varies significantly depending on the varying conditions applicable to the more than 500 different North Carolina local governments with zoning ordinances. The rate of growth and change; the population; and the physical, economic, and social conditions of each local government are too varied for a uniform period to be "reasonable" under all circumstances. Therefore, the schedule for updates is left to the good judgment of each jurisdiction, provided officials act in a reasonable fashion under the particular circumstances.

281. Given the broad definition of "comprehensive plan" in Section 160D-1-2, local governments have considerable flexibility in determining the type and nature of planning that is appropriate for their jurisdiction. For example, a small town or rural county with little growth or change could prepare a very simple, quick, and inexpensive plan, while a large city with substantial growth pressures may determine that a more-detailed planning effort is warranted.

282. This language recognizes, but does not require, other commonly used types of local government plans. It is consistent with provisions in current law and with provisions in S.L. 2017-10 that are codified in that law as G.S. 160A-383(e) and 153A-341(e), that require consideration of all officially adopted plans that are applicable when reviewing proposed zoning amendments.

283. Rather than mandate a particular set of planning requirements to be applied by all jurisdictions, flexibility has been left to each local government to determine the appropriate scope of its planning efforts.

(1)   Issues and opportunities facing the local government, including consideration of trends, the values expressed by citizens, community vision, and guiding principles for growth, and development;

(2)   The pattern of desired growth and development and civic design, including the location, distribution, and characteristics of future land uses, urban form, utilities, and transportation networks;

(3)   Employment opportunities, economic development, and community development;

(4)   Acceptable levels of public services and infrastructure to support development, including water, waste disposal, utilities, emergency services, transportation, education, recreation, community facilities, and other public services, including plans and policies for provision of and financing for public infrastructure;

(5)   Housing with a range of types and affordability to accommodate persons and households of all types and income levels;

(6)   Recreation and open spaces;

(7)   Mitigation of natural hazards such as flooding, winds, wildfires, and unstable lands;

(8)   Protection of the environment and natural resources, including agricultural resources, mineral resources, and water and air quality;

(9)   Protection of significant architectural, scenic, cultural, historical, or archaeological resources; and

(10) Analysis and evaluation of implementation measures, including regulations, public investments, and educational programs.

(c) *Adoption and effect of plans.* Plans shall be adopted by the governing board with the advice and consultation of the planning board. Adoption and amendment of a comprehensive plan is a legislative decision and shall follow the process mandated for zoning text amendments set by G.S. 160D-6-1.[284] Plans adopted under this Chapter may be undertaken and adopted as part of or in conjunction with plans required under other statutes, including but not limited to the plans required by G.S. 113A-110.[285] Plans adopted under this Chapter shall be advisory in nature without independent regulatory effect. Plans adopted under this Chapter do not expand, diminish, or alter the scope of authority for development regulations adopted under this Chapter.[286] Plans adopted under this section shall be considered by the planning board and governing board when considering proposed amendments to zoning regulations as required by G.S. 160D-6-4 and 160D-6-5.

If a plan is deemed amended by G.S. 160D-6-5 by virtue of adoption of a zoning amendment that is inconsistent with the plan, that amendment shall be noted in the plan. However, if the plan is one that requires review and approval subject to G.S. 113A-110, the plan amendment shall not be effective until that review and approval is completed.

§ 160D-5-2. Grants, contracts, and technical assistance. [287] [160D-502]

(a) *Grants and services.* A ~~city or its designated planning board~~ local government[288] may accept, receive, and disburse in furtherance of its functions any funds, grants, and services made available by the federal government and its agencies, the State government and its agencies, any local government and its agencies, and any private and civic sources. ~~Any city, or its designated planning board with the concurrence~~

---

284. This language sets out the requirement that before the governing board can adopt a comprehensive plan, there must be a public hearing with published notice and planning board referral. This provision does not affect the validity of plans adopted prior to the effective date of this act, as provided in Section 2.9(a) of S.L. 2019-111.

285. Where other statutes and regulations set minimum planning requirements, such as with the Coastal Area Management Act, those requirements are still applicable and are not reduced by the flexibility provided in this article of Chapter 160D.

286. This subsection clarifies that the fact that a particular topic is addressed in a plan does not change the scope of authority of regulations that may be adopted relative to that topic.

287. This section has been relocated from G.S. 160A-363(c) to (e) and 153A-322.

288. Simplification.

of the council, local government[289] may enter into and carry out contracts with the State and federal governments or any agencies thereof under which financial or other planning assistance is made available to the city local government and may agree to and comply with any reasonable conditions that are imposed upon such assistance.

(b) *Contracts*. Any city, or its designated planning board with the concurrence of the council, local government may enter into and carry out contracts with any other city, county, or regional council, or planning agency, or private consultant under which it agrees to furnish technical planning assistance to the other local government or planning agency. Any city, or its designated planning board with the concurrence of its council, local government may enter into and carry out contracts with any other city, county, or regional council or planning agency under which it agrees to pay the other local government or planning board for technical planning assistance.

(c) *Appropriations, compensation, and financing*. Any city council local government is authorized to make any appropriations that may be necessary to carry out any activities or contracts authorized by this Article or to support, and compensate members of a any planning board that it may create pursuant to this Article Chapter, and to levy taxes for these purposes as a necessary expense.

§ 160D-5-3. Coordination of planning. [160D-503]

A local government may undertake any of the planning activities authorized by this Article in coordination with other local governments, state agencies, or regional agencies created under Article 19 of Chapter 153A or Article 20 of Chapter 160A.[290]

ARTICLE 6. PROCESS FOR ADOPTION OF DEVELOPMENT REGULATIONS

§ 160D-6-1. Procedure for adopting, amending, or repealing development regulations.[291] [160D-601]

(a) *Hearing with published notice*. Before adopting, amending, or repealing any ordinance or development regulation authorized by this Article Chapter, the city council governing board shall hold a public legislative[292] hearing. on it. A notice of the public hearing shall be given once a week for two successive calendar weeks in a newspaper having general circulation in the area.[293] The notice shall be published the first time not less than 10 days nor more than 25 days before the date fixed scheduled for the hearing. In computing such period, the day of publication is not to be included but the day of the hearing shall be included.

(b) *Notice to military bases*. If the adoption or modification of the ordinance would result in changes to the zoning map or would change or affect the permitted uses of land located five miles or less from the perimeter boundary of a military base, the governing body of the local government shall provide written notice of the proposed changes by certified mail, return receipt requested, to the commander of the military base not less than 10 days nor more than 25 days before the date fixed for the public[294] hearing. If the

---

289. Simplification; removes redundant language.

290. This language clarifies and explicitly authorizes coordinated planning.

291. This section has been relocated from G.S. 160A-364 and 153A-323. Amendments to this section made by Part I of S.L. 2019-111 are to be incorporated in 2020. One amendment limits initiation of down-zoning petitions to the landowner and the local government.

292. This subsection continues the mandate set out in prior law (Article 18 of G.S. Chapter 153A and Article 19 of Chapter 160A) that notice must be provided, and a hearing held, for adoption of all local development regulations. It clarifies the type of public hearing to be held. (The term "legislative hearing" is defined in Article 1 of Chapter 160D.) The existing additional notice requirements for zoning-map amendments are in the immediately following section of Chapter 160D. Earlier drafts of the bill included provisions explicitly addressing (1) optional provisions for reversion of conditional rezonings if development did not proceed on property and (2) the process for review of landowner and third-party rezoning proposals. As consensus was not reached on those provisions, they were deleted.

293. Several local governments are authorized by local act to substitute electronic publication for newspaper publication. Those special authorizations are not affected by this act, given G.S. 160D-1-11(d).

294. This language has been deleted as surplusage.

military provides comments or analysis regarding the compatibility of the proposed ~~ordinance~~ development regulation or amendment with military operations at the base, the governing ~~body~~ board of the local government shall take the comments and analysis into consideration before making a final determination on the ordinance.

(c) A development regulation adopted pursuant to this Chapter shall be adopted by ordinance.[295]

§ 160D-6-2. Notice of hearing on proposed zoning map amendments.[296] [160D-602]

(a) *Mailed notice.* An ~~The city council~~ ordinance shall provide for the manner in which zoning regulations ~~and restrictions~~ and the boundaries of zoning districts shall be determined, established and enforced, and from time to time amended, supplemented or changed, in accordance with the provisions of this ~~Article~~ Chapter. ~~The procedures adopted pursuant to this section shall provide that whenever there is an amendment, the~~[297] The owner of ~~that parcel~~ affected parcels of land ~~as shown on the county tax listing~~,[298] and the owners of all parcels of land abutting that parcel of land ~~as shown on the county tax listing~~, shall be mailed a notice of ~~a public~~ the hearing on a proposed zoning map amendment by first class mail at the last addresses listed for such owners on the county tax abstracts. For the purpose of this section, properties are "abutting" even if separated by a street, railroad, or other transportation corridor.[299] This notice must be deposited in the mail at least 10 but not more than 25 days prior to the date of the ~~public~~[300] hearing. If the zoning map amendment is being proposed in conjunction with an expansion of municipal extraterritorial planning and development regulation jurisdiction under G.S. 160D-2-2, a single hearing on the zoning map amendment and the boundary amendment may be held. In this instance the initial notice of the zoning map amendment hearing may be combined with the boundary hearing notice and the combined hearing notice mailed at least 30 days prior to the hearing.

(b) *Option to mailed notice for large-scale zoning map amendments.* The first class mail notice required under subsection (a) of this section shall not be required if the zoning map amendment ~~directly affects~~ proposes to change the zoning designation[301] of more than 50 properties, owned by ~~a total of~~ at least 50 different property owners, and the ~~city~~ local government elects to use the expanded published notice provided for in this subsection. In this instance, a ~~city~~ local government may elect to ~~either~~ make the mailed notice provided for in subsection (a) of this section, or ~~may~~ as an alternative, elect to publish notice of the hearing as required by G.S. ~~160A-364~~ 160D-6-1,[302] ~~but~~ provided that each advertisement shall not be less than one-half of a newspaper page in size. The advertisement shall only be effective for property owners who reside in the area of general circulation of the newspaper ~~which~~ that publishes the notice. Property owners who reside outside of the newspaper circulation area, according to the address listed on the most recent property tax listing for the affected property, shall be notified according to the provisions of subsection (a) of this section.

(b1)[303] ~~This subsection applies only to an application to request a zoning map amendment where the application is not made by the landowner of the parcel of land to which the amendment would apply. This subsection does not apply to a city-initiated zoning map amendment.~~

---

295. This subsection confirms current law and practice. As the term "regulation" is used throughout Chapter 160D to refer to various types of local development regulations, this clarification assures that the actual adoption and amendment of the regulations is made by ordinance.

296. This section has been relocated from G.S. 160A-384 and 153A-343 and has been retitled.

297. This subsection has been edited for clarity and to remove archaic language.

298. This language is redundant, given the definition of "landowner" in Article 1 of Chapter 160D, which includes reference to county tax maps to identify an owner.

299. This language clarifies that even if properties do not touch because they are separated by a transportation right of way that is owned in fee rather than as an easement, notice is required to properties immediately across that right of way.

300. This language has been deleted as surplusage.

301. Clarification.

302. This language updates a cross-reference.

303. The provision on actual notice to an owner with third-party rezonings has been relocated to subsection (d) of this section.

(c) *Posted notice.* When a zoning map amendment is proposed, the ~~city~~ local government shall prominently post a notice of the ~~public~~[304] hearing on the site proposed for ~~rezoning~~ the amendment or on an adjacent public street or highway right-of-way. The notice shall be posted within the same time period specified for mailed notices of the hearing.[305] When multiple parcels are included within a proposed zoning map amendment, a posting on each individual parcel is not required, but the ~~city~~ local government shall post sufficient notices to provide reasonable notice to interested persons.

(d) *Actual notice.*[306] Except for a ~~city-initiated~~ government-initiated zoning map amendment, when an application is filed to request a zoning map amendment and that application is not made by the ~~owner of the parcel of land to which the amendment would apply,~~ landowner or authorized agent, the applicant shall certify to the ~~city council~~ local government that the owner of the parcel of land as shown on the county tax listing has received actual notice of the proposed amendment and a copy of the notice of the ~~public~~[307] hearing. Actual notice ~~of the proposed amendment and a copy of the notice of public~~[308] ~~hearing required under subsection (a) of this section~~ shall be provided in any manner permitted under G.S. 1A-1, Rule 4(j). If notice cannot with due diligence be achieved by personal delivery, ~~registered or~~ certified mail, or by a designated delivery service authorized pursuant to 26 U.S.C. § 7502(f)(2), notice may be given by publication consistent with G.S. 1A-1, Rule 4(j1). The person or persons required to provide notice shall certify to the ~~city council~~ local government that ~~proper~~ actual notice has been provided ~~in fact~~, and such certificate shall be deemed conclusive in the absence of fraud.

(e) Optional communication requirements. When a zoning map amendment is proposed, a zoning regulation may require communication by the person proposing the map amendment to neighboring property owners and residents and may require the person proposing the zoning map amendment to report on any communication with neighboring property owners and residents.[309]

§ 160D-6-3. Citizen comments.[310] [160D-603]

Subject to the limitations in this Chapter, zoning regulations ~~ordinances~~ may from time to time be amended, supplemented, changed, modified or repealed. If any resident or property owner in the ~~city~~ local government submits a written statement regarding a proposed amendment, modification, or repeal to a zoning regulation (including a text or map amendment) ~~ordinance~~ to the clerk to the board at least two business days prior to the proposed vote on such change, the clerk to the board shall deliver such written statement to the ~~city council~~ governing board.[311] If the proposed change is the subject of a quasi-judicial proceeding under G.S.~~160A-388~~ 160D-7-5 or any other statute, the clerk shall provide only the names and addresses of the individuals providing written comment, and the provision of such names and addresses to all members of the board shall not disqualify any member of the board from voting.

---

304. This is a stylistic amendment to provide consistent reference to hearings.

305. To provide consistency with the parallel provisions for mailed and posted notices of hearings on quasi-judicial evidentiary hearings that are found in current law (G.S. 160D-4-6(b)), the time period for posting notice of the hearing is specified.

306. Amendments made by Part I of S.L. 2019-111 to reconcile this subsection are to be incorporated in 2020. Amendments prohibit initiation of down-zoning petitions by persons other than landowners or local governments; this prohibition was, in large part, the basis for the original adoption of this subsection.

307. This is a stylistic amendment.

308. This language has been deleted as surplusage.

309. This is a common requirement in many zoning ordinances that allow conditional zoning. Some ordinances require mailed notices to neighbors, while others require an informal neighborhood meeting prior to submission of some rezoning petitions. The statute explicitly allows for, but does not mandate, zoning regulations to require "communication" with the neighbors, which may take the form of a notice or a neighborhood meeting, as part of the rezoning-application process.

310. Provisions in this subsection have been relocated from G.S. 160A-385(a) and 160A-386 and have been retitled. The subsection incorporates provisions of S.L. 2015-160, which replaced the municipal protest petition with these provisions on citizen comments on proposed amendments.

311. As this provision applies to cities and counties, it replaces references to "city council" with references to "governing board."

§ 160D-6-4. Planning board review and comment.[312] [160D-604]

(a) *Initial zoning.* In order to ~~initially~~[313] exercise ~~the~~ zoning powers conferred by this ~~Part~~ Article 7 of this Chapter for the first time, a ~~city council~~ local government shall create or designate a planning board under the provisions of this Article or of a special act of the General Assembly. The planning board shall prepare or shall review and comment upon a proposed zoning regulation ~~ordinance~~, including ~~both~~ the full text of such regulation ~~ordinance~~ and maps showing proposed district boundaries. The planning board may hold public meetings and legislative hearings[314] in the course of preparing the regulation. ~~ordinance.~~ Upon completion, the planning board shall make a written recommendation regarding adoption of the regulation ~~ordinance~~ to the governing board ~~city council~~. The governing board ~~city council~~ shall not hold its required ~~public~~ legislative hearing or take action until it has received a recommendation regarding the regulation ~~ordinance~~ from the planning board. Following its required ~~public~~[315] hearing, the governing board ~~city council~~ may refer the regulation ~~ordinance~~ back to the planning board for any further recommendations that the board may wish to make prior to final action by the governing board ~~city council~~ in adopting, modifying and adopting, or rejecting the regulation ~~ordinance~~.

(b) *Zoning amendments.* Subsequent to initial adoption of a zoning regulation, ~~ordinance,~~ all proposed amendments to the zoning regulation ~~ordinance~~ or zoning map shall be submitted to the planning board for review and comment. If no written report is received from the planning board within 30 days of referral of the amendment to that board, the governing board may ~~proceed in its consideration of~~ act on[316] the amendment without the planning board report. The governing board is not bound by the recommendations, if any, of the planning board.

(c) *Review of other ordinances and actions.*[317] Any development regulation other than a zoning regulation that is proposed to be adopted pursuant to this Chapter may be referred to the planning board for review and comment. Any development regulation other than a zoning regulation may provide that future proposed amendments of that ordinance be submitted to the planning board for review and comment. Any other action proposed to be taken pursuant to this Chapter may be referred to the planning board for review and comment.

(d) *Plan consistency.*[318] When conducting a review of proposed zoning text or map amendments pursuant to this section, ~~Prior to consideration by the governing board of the proposed zoning amendment,~~[319] the planning board shall advise and comment on whether the proposed action ~~amendment~~ is consistent with any comprehensive plan that has been adopted and any other officially adopted plan that is applicable.[320] The planning board shall provide a written recommendation to the governing board that addresses plan consistency and other matters as deemed appropriate by the planning board, but a comment by the planning board that a proposed amendment is inconsistent with the comprehensive plan shall not preclude consideration or approval of the proposed amendment by the governing board. If a zoning map amendment qualifies as a "large-scale rezoning" under G.S. 160D-6-2(b), the planning board statement describing

---

312. This section has been relocated from G.S. 160A-387 and 153A-344.

313. Since planning-board recommendations are required for all zoning amendments (or for repeal of the ordinance), the board must continue in existence as long as the local government exercises zoning authority.

314. This language clarifies that public meetings, as well as hearings, may be held and specifies the type of hearing that is held by the planning board, if any are conducted.

315. This language has been deleted as surplusage.

316. This subsection clarifies that the governing board hearing may be scheduled and that action —other than an actual vote by the governing board—may be taken during the thirty-day period allowed for planning-board action.

317. As under current law, amendments to a zoning ordinance or zoning regulations within a unified development ordinance must be referred to the planning board for review and comment. This subsection clarifies that proposed action on other development regulations may also be referred to the planning board for review, but this is not mandated and is at the option of each local government.

318. This subsection has been relocated from G.S. 160A-383(c) and 153A-341(c).

319. The deleted language was added to the statute by S.L. 2017-10. This subsection has been edited for clarity and for consistency in style and terminology.

320. This phrase, deleted by S.L. 2017-10, has been reinserted for clarity.

plan consistency may address the overall rezoning and describe how the analysis and polices in the relevant adopted plans were considered in the recommendation made. ~~As used in this section, "comprehensive plan" includes a unified development ordinance and any other officially adopted plan that is applicable.~~[321]

(e) *Separate board required.* Notwithstanding the authority to assign duties of the planning board to the governing board as provided by this Chapter, the review and comment required by this section shall not be assigned to the governing board and must be performed by a separate board.[322]

160D-6-5. Governing board statement. [160D-605]

(a) *Plan consistency.*[323] ~~Prior to~~ When adopting or rejecting any zoning text or map amendment,[324] the governing board shall ~~also~~ approve a brief[325]statement describing whether its action is consistent or inconsistent with an adopted comprehensive plan. The requirement for a plan consistency statement may also be met by a clear indication in the minutes of the governing board that at the time of action on the amendment the governing board was aware of and considered the planning board's recommendations and any relevant portions of an adopted comprehensive plan. ~~and any other officially applicable adopted plan that is applicable, and briefly explaining why the board considers the action taken to be reasonable and in the public interest. That~~ If the amendment is adopted and the action was deemed inconsistent with the adopted plan, the zoning amendment shall have the effect of also amending any future land use map in the approved plan and no additional request or application for a plan amendment shall be required. ~~In such instances, the statement shall also explain the change in conditions the governing board took into account in making the zoning amendment to meet the development needs of the community.~~[326] A plan amendment and a zoning amendment may be considered concurrently. The plan consistency statement is not subject to judicial review. If a zoning map amendment qualifies as a "large-scale rezoning" under G.S. 160D-6-2(b), the governing board statement describing plan consistency may address the overall rezoning and describe how the analysis and polices in the relevant adopted plans were considered in the action taken.

---

321. "Comprehensive plan" defined in G.S. 160D-1-2. The deleted sentence was added to the statute by S.L. 2017-10. Since the unified development ordinance is a collection of binding regulations rather than an advisory plan, this phrase has been deleted from the definition of "comprehensive plan" in order to avoid potential confusion between a regulation that has binding effect and a plan that is only advisory in nature.

322. While any other functions of a planning board may be assigned to other boards, including the governing board, this subsection clarifies that the mandatory recommendations to the governing board regarding proposed ordinance amendments must be provided by a board other than the governing board itself.

323. This subsection has been relocated from G.S. 160A-383 and 153A-341.

324. This subsection clarifies that the governing board statement needs to be "approved' by the governing board and that it is not necessary to "adopt" the statement as a separate motion. The city and county statutory provisions were identical when adopted in 2005, but the city provision was amended to make this clarification in 2006 (though the municipal amendment was again amended in 2017). The language in this subsection reverts to the formulation of "when adopting," as opposed to "prior to adopting," to avoid confusion about the necessity for separate motions to approve a statement and then adopt the amendment.

325. This language has been added for parallel construction in the first two subsections of this section.

326. This revision retains the requirement that the board must approve a statement of whether the action is consistent or inconsistent with an adopted comprehensive plan. The plan is deemed amended if the action is inconsistent. The revision deletes the sentence regarding the explanation of changed circumstances in such instances, as that is only one of multiple reasons the governing board may decide to take action inconsistent with a prior plan. It incorporates the substance of this concept into the statement of reasonableness required by the immediately following subsection. The revision simplifies this provision by deleting the requirement that one of three mandated forms had to be used for the plan consistency statement. It also adds a provision that a formal statement of the governing board is not required if the board's minutes show board awareness and consideration of the plan contents at the time of consideration of the zoning amendment, which is the purpose of the plan consistency statement. The minutes can be an alternative means of showing compliance with the intent of the statute, namely, that adopted plans, while not binding, be considered during the zoning-amendment consideration.

(b) *Statement of reasonableness.* ~~Additional statement of reasonableness for rezonings.~~[327] When adopting or rejecting any petition for a zoning text or map amendment,[328] a brief statement ~~briefly~~ explaining the reasonableness of the proposed rezoning shall be ~~prepared for each petition for a rezoning to~~ a ~~special or conditional use district, or a conditional district, or other small-scale rezoning,~~ approved by the governing board. The statement of reasonableness may consider, among other factors: (i) the size, physical conditions, and other attributes of ~~the tract~~ any area proposed to be rezoned; (ii) the benefits and detriments to the landowners, the neighbors, and the surrounding community; (iii) the relationship between the current actual and permissible development ~~on the tract and adjoining areas~~ and the development ~~that would be~~ permissible under the proposed amendment; ~~and~~ (iv) why the action taken is in the public interest; and (v) any changed conditions warranting the amendment.[329] If a zoning map amendment qualifies as a "large-scale rezoning" under G.S. 160D-6-2(b), the governing board statement on reasonableness may address the overall rezoning.

(c) *Single statement permissible.* The statement of reasonableness and the plan consistency statement required by this section may be approved as a single statement.

ARTICLE 7. ZONING REGULATION

§ 160D-7-1. Purposes ~~in view.~~[330] [160D-701]

~~Zoning regulations shall be made in accordance with a comprehensive plan. When adopting or rejecting any zoning amendment, the governing board shall also approve a statement describing whether its action is consistent with an adopted comprehensive plan and any other officially adopted plan that is applicable, and briefly explaining why the board considers the action taken to be reasonable and in the public interest. That statement is not subject to judicial review.~~[331]

Zoning regulations shall be made in accordance with a comprehensive plan[332] and shall be designed to promote the public health, safety, and general welfare. To that end, the regulations may address, among other things, the following public purposes: to provide adequate light and air; to prevent the overcrowding of land; to avoid undue concentration of population; to lessen congestion in the streets; to secure safety from fire, panic, and dangers; ~~and~~ to facilitate the efficient and adequate provision of transportation, water, sewerage, schools, parks, and other public requirements; and ~~promoting~~ to promote the health, safety, morals, or the general welfare of the community.[333] The regulations shall be made with reasonable consideration,

---

327. This subsection has been relocated from G.S. 160A-382(b) and 153A-342(b). The plan consistency statement continues to be required for all zoning amendments, both text and map amendments. Subsection (b) clarifies that the statement of reasonableness is not required for zoning-text amendments, though a local government can make such a statement if desired. This subsection adds specificity to the statement of reasonableness when a zoning map amendment is proposed.

328. This subsection clarifies when during the zoning-amendment process the statement of reasonableness must be approved. The subsection uses the same language regarding timing as is used in relation to the plan consistency statement in the prior subsection. The subsection simplifies the requirement by applying it to all zoning-map amendments, eliminating the need to determine whether a particular rezoning is spot zoning.

329. This language elaborates on the 2005 codification of the statement of reasonableness required for conditional zoning and spot zoning by specifying the basic factors to be considered by a governing board in making these statements. The factors are adapted from *Chrismon v. Guilford County*, 322 N.C. 611, 628, 370 S.E.2d 579, 589 (1988). The subsection notes that the enumerated factors "may" be considered rather than mandating that all of them must be addressed, as not all of the factors are relevant to every zoning-map amendment. The subsection incorporates a provision from S.L. 2017-10 and simplifies it by incorporating it into the statutory requirement for an explanation of the reasonableness of actions taken.

330. This section has been relocated from G.S. 160A-383 and 153A-341.

331. This provision has been relocated to G.S.160D-6-5.

332. This language has been relocated from the preceding paragraph in this same section.

333. Additional provisions to modernize the statement of purposes by including common purposes of contemporary zoning regulations were included in early bill drafts. Given a lack of consensus as to the implications of deleting language dating to 1923 and inserting modernized language, the potential

among other things, as to the character of the district and its peculiar suitability for particular uses, and with a view to conserving the value of buildings and encouraging the most appropriate use of land throughout ~~such city.~~ the local government's planning and development regulation jurisdiction. The regulations may not include, as a basis for denying a zoning or rezoning request from a school, the level of service of a road facility or facilities abutting the school or proximately located to the school.[334]

§ 160D-7-2. Grant of power.[335] [160D-702]

(a) ~~For the purpose of promoting health, safety, morals, or the general welfare of the community,~~[336] ~~any city~~ A local government[337] may adopt zoning regulations. ~~and development regulation ordinances. These ordinances may be adopted as part of a unified development ordinance or as a separate ordinance.~~[338] A zoning ~~ordinance~~ regulation may regulate and restrict the height, number of stories and size of buildings and other structures; the percentage of lots that may be occupied; the size of yards, courts and other open spaces; the density of population; and the location and use of buildings, structures and land[339] A ~~county~~ local government may regulate ~~the~~ development, including floating homes, over estuarine waters and over lands covered by navigable waters owned by the State pursuant to G.S. 146-12.[340] ~~, within the bounds of that county. For the purpose of this section, the term "structures" shall include floating homes. The ordinance~~ A zoning regulation shall[341] provide density credits or severable development rights for dedicated rights-of-way pursuant to G.S. 136-66.10 or G.S. 136-66.11. Where appropriate a zoning regulation ~~such conditions~~ may include requirements that street and utility rights-of-way be dedicated to the public, ~~and~~ that provision be made of recreational space and facilities, and that performance guarantees be provided, all to the same extent and with the same limitations as provided for in G.S. 160D-8-4.[342]

(b)[343] Any ~~zoning and development~~ regulation ~~ordinance~~ relating to building design elements adopted under this Chapter ~~Part, under Part 2 of this Article, or under any recommendation made under G.S. 160A-452(6)c.~~ may not be applied to any structures subject to regulation under the North Carolina Residential Code for One-and Two-Family Dwellings except under one or more of the following circumstances:

---

amendments were deleted, leaving the provision essentially the same as it is in the current statute, with no changes proposed that would enlarge or constrict the range of purposes of zoning regulation.

334. This sentence was added to the statutes by S.L. 2018-5, § 34.18.

335. This section has been relocated from G.S. 160A-381 and 153A-340. Amendments to this section made by S.L. 2019-174 are to be incorporated in 2020. One amendment restricts regulation of minimum house size.

336. This subsection has been relocated to G.S. 160D-7-1, on purposes of zoning.

337. This language has been amended to provide consistency in the terminology used to refer to cities and counties. This subsection reflects the consolidation of provisions for cities and counties rather than the continuation of separate parallel provisions in Chapters 153A and 160A. This change has been made throughout proposed Chapter 160D.

338. This language has been deleted as redundant, given G.S. 160D-1-3.

339. Drafts of the bill proposed modernizing the list of items that could be regulated. Given a lack of consensus as to the implications of doing so, those potential amendments were deleted, leaving the provision essentially the same as it is in the current statute, with no changes proposed that would enlarge or constrict the scope of zoning regulations.

340. This provision has been relocated from G.S. 153A-340(d) and (e).

341. This provision has been amended by S.L. 2015-246, § 16.

342. This subsection has been relocated from G.S. 160A-381(c) and 153A-340(c1). It clarifies the use of and limits on existing statutory provisions regarding the provision of utilities, recreation, open space, and performance guarantees for commercial, industrial, institutional, and other development that does not involve a residential subdivision. The subsection makes the scope of exaction authority the same for all types of zoning decisions. It explicitly states that zoning regulations may be limited to the same extent as subdivision regulations are under current law. It also provides for uniformity, consistency, and simplification, especially where zoning and subdivision reviews are concurrently conducted and where zoning and subdivision ordinances are integrated into a unified development ordinance. Further simplification may be considered in 2020.

343. This provision regarding building design elements was added by S.L. 2015-86. Edits to this subsection are stylistic and made to provide consistent references to terminology used in Chapter 160D.

(1) The structures are located in an area designated as a local historic district pursuant to <u>Part 4 of Article 9 of this Chapter</u>. ~~Part 3C of Article 19 of Chapter 160A of the General Statutes~~.

(2) The structures are located in an area designated as a historic district on the National Register of Historic Places.

(3) The structures are individually designated as local, State, or national historic landmarks.

(4) The regulations are directly and substantially related to the requirements of applicable safety codes adopted under G.S. 143-138.

(5) Where the regulations are applied to manufactured housing in a manner consistent with G.S. <u>160D-9-7</u> ~~160A-383.1~~ and federal law.

(6) Where the regulations are adopted as a condition of participation in the National Flood Insurance Program.

Regulations prohibited by this subsection may not be applied, directly or indirectly, in any zoning district~~, special use district, conditional use district,~~ or conditional district unless voluntarily consented to by the owners of all the property to which those regulations may be applied as part of and in the course of the process of seeking and obtaining a zoning amendment or a zoning, subdivision, or development approval, nor may any such regulations be applied indirectly as part of a review pursuant to G.S. <u>160D-6-4 or 160D-6-5</u> ~~160A-383~~ of any proposed zoning amendment for consistency with an adopted comprehensive plan or other applicable officially adopted plan.

For the purposes of this subsection, the phrase "building design elements" means exterior building color; type or style of exterior cladding material; style or materials of roof structures or porches; exterior non-structural architectural ornamentation; location or architectural styling of windows and doors, including garage doors; the number and types of rooms; and the interior layout of rooms. The phrase "building design elements" does not include any of the following: (i) the height, bulk, orientation, or location of a structure on a zoning lot; (ii) the use of buffering or screening to minimize visual impacts, to mitigate the impacts of light and noise, or to protect the privacy of neighbors; or (iii) regulations adopted pursuant to this Article governing the permitted uses of land or structures subject to the North Carolina Residential Code for One-and Two-Family Dwellings.

~~(i)~~ Nothing in <u>this</u> subsection ~~(h) of this section~~ shall affect the validity or enforceability of private covenants or other contractual agreements among property owners relating to building design elements.

~~(b) Expired.~~

~~(b1)~~ [344] ~~These regulations may provide that a board of adjustment may determine and vary their application in harmony with their general purpose and intent and in accordance with general or specific rules therein contained, provided no change in permitted uses may be authorized by variance.~~

~~(c)~~ [345] ~~The regulations may also provide that the board of adjustment, the planning board, or the city council may issue special use permits or conditional use permits in the classes of cases or situations and in accordance with the principles, conditions, safeguards, and procedures specified therein and may impose reasonable and appropriate conditions and safeguards upon these permits. When deciding special use permits or conditional use permits, the city council or planning board shall follow quasi-judicial procedures. Notice of hearings on special or conditional use permit applications shall be as provided in G.S. 160A-388(a2). No vote greater than a majority vote shall be required for the city council or planning board to issue such permits. For the purposes of this section, vacant positions on the board and members who are disqualified from voting on a quasi-judicial matter shall not be considered "members of the board" for calculation of the requisite majority. Every such decision of the city council or planning board shall be subject to review of the superior court in the nature of certiorari in accordance with G.S. 160A-388.~~

~~Where appropriate, such conditions may include requirements that street and utility rights-of-way be dedicated to the public and that provision be made of recreational space and facilities.~~ [346]

---

344. This subsection has been deleted as surplusage. The deleted provision is now covered by G.S. 160D-7-5 (formerly G.S. 160A-388).

345. These special-use-permit provisions have been relocated to G.S. 160D-7-5.

346. This subsection has been relocated from G.S. 160A-388(c), which is also applicable to counties. It has been eliminated as redundant, given the impact-mitigation provision located earlier in this section that cross-references G.S. 160D-8-4.

(d)[347] ~~A city council member shall not vote on any zoning map or text amendment where the outcome of the matter being considered is reasonably likely to have a direct, substantial, and readily identifiable financial impact on the member. Members of appointed boards providing advice to the city council shall not vote on recommendations regarding any zoning map or text amendment where the outcome of the matter being considered is reasonably likely to have a direct, substantial, and readily identifiable financial impact on the member.~~

(f)[348] ~~In order to encourage construction that uses sustainable design principles and to improve energy efficiency in buildings, a city may charge reduced building permit fees or provide partial rebates of building permit fees for buildings that are constructed or renovated using design principles that conform to or exceed one or more of the following certifications or ratings:~~

    (1) ~~Leadership in Energy and Environmental Design (LEED) certification or higher rating under certification standards adopted by the U.S. Green Building Council.~~

    (2) ~~A One Globe or higher rating under the Green Globes program standards adopted by the Green Building Initiative.~~

    (3) ~~A certification or rating by another nationally recognized certification or rating system that is equivalent or greater than those listed in subdivisions (1) and (2) of this subsection.~~

(g)[349] ~~A zoning or unified development ordinance may not differentiate in terms of the regulations applicable to fraternities or sororities between those fraternities or sororities that are approved or recognized by a college or university and those that are not.~~

§ 160D-7-3. Zoning districts.[350] [160D-703]

(a) *Types of zoning districts*. ~~For any or all these purposes, the city~~ <u>A local government</u> may divide its territorial jurisdiction into <u>zoning</u> districts of any number, shape, and area ~~that may be~~ deemed best suited to carry out the purposes of this ~~Part~~ <u>Article</u>. ~~and~~ Within those districts it may regulate and restrict the erection, construction, reconstruction, alteration, repair or use of buildings, structures, or land. ~~Such~~ <u>Zoning</u> districts may include, but shall not be limited to:

    1. <u>Conventional</u> ~~or general use~~[351] districts, in which a variety of uses are ~~permissible in accordance with general standards~~ <u>allowed as permitted uses or uses by right and that may also include uses permitted only with a special use permit;</u>

    2. ~~or a conditional use permit and~~ <u>Conditional</u> ~~zoning~~ districts,[352] in which site plans ~~and~~ <u>or</u> individualized development conditions are imposed.

    3. <u>Form-based Districts,[353] or development form controls, that address the physical form, mass, and density of structures, public spaces, and streetscapes;</u>

---

347. This subsection has been relocated to Article 1 of Chapter 160D in order to establish uniform standards on conflicts of interest regarding any legislative decision made pursuant to theChapter.

348. This subsection has been relocated to G.S. 160D-7-4.

349. This subsection has been relocated to G.S. 160D-9-6.

350. This section has been relocated from G.S. 160A-382 and 153A-342.

351. This revision simplifies terminology.

352. This revision simplifies and clarifies zoning law by eliminating the use of districts that have no permitted uses but only uses permitted with a special- or conditional-use permit. This tool was added to the zoning statutes in the 1980s prior to the legalization of purely legislative conditional zoning. At that time, this was a necessary work-around to avoid contract zoning and to allow site-specific conditions to be applied in the context of a rezoning. However, the use of concurrent legislative and quasi-judicial decision-making proved to be legally and practically challenging for local governments and has been a source of considerable confusion for landowners and neighbors, as well as for local governments and the courts. As use of this tool is no longer necessary (given the use of either legislative conditional zoning or quasi-judicial special-use permits), its elimination will simplify the law while not reducing the tools available to address development review.

353. A number of jurisdictions now use form-based zoning codes in combination with, or as a replacement for, traditional conventional zoning districts that are organized around regulation of land uses. Examples include the new Raleigh unified development ordinance and districts along major corridors in Asheville and Chapel Hill. This provision does not expand or contract the scope of zoning powers set forth in G.S. 160D-7-2 but explicitly authorizes use of this emerging zoning tool.

4. Overlay districts, in which ~~additional~~ different[354] requirements are imposed on certain properties within one or more underlying conventional, conditional, or form-based districts; and,~~general or special use or conditional districts and special use districts or conditional use districts, in which uses are permitted only upon the issuance of a special use permit;~~

5. Districts allowed by charter.

(b) _Conditional districts._[355] Property may be placed in a ~~special use district, conditional use district, or~~ conditional district only in response to a petition by ~~the~~ all owners of ~~all~~ the property to be included. Specific conditions ~~applicable to these districts~~ may be proposed by the petitioner or the ~~city~~ local government or its agencies, but only those conditions mutually approved by the ~~city~~ local government and the petitioner may be incorporated into the zoning regulations. ~~or permit requirements.~~ Conditions and site-specific standards imposed in a conditional district shall be limited to those that address the conformance of the development and use of the site to ~~city~~ local government ordinances, ~~and an officially~~ plans adopted pursuant to G.S. 160D-5-1, ~~comprehensive or other plan~~[356] or ~~and those that address~~ the impacts reasonably expected to be generated by the development or use of the site. The zoning regulation may provide that defined minor modifications in conditional district standards that do not involve a change in uses permitted or the density of overall development permitted may be reviewed and approved administratively.[357] Any other modification of the conditions and standards in a conditional district shall follow the same process for approval as are applicable to zoning map amendments.[358] If multiple parcels of land are subject to a conditional zoning, the owners of individual parcels may apply for modification of the conditions so long as the modification would not result in other properties failing to meet the terms of the conditions. Any modifications approved shall only be applicable to those properties whose owners petition for the modification.

~~A statement analyzing the reasonableness of the proposed rezoning shall be prepared for each petition for a rezoning to a special or conditional use district, or a conditional district, or other small-scale rezoning.~~[359]

(c) _Uniformity within districts._ Except as authorized by the foregoing, all regulations shall be uniform for each class or kind of building throughout each district, but the regulations in one district may differ from those in other districts.

(d) _Standards applicable regardless of district._ A zoning regulation or unified development ordinance may also include development standards that apply uniformly jurisdiction-wide rather than being applicable only in particular zoning districts.[360]

---

354. Clarification. Overlay zoning districts typically apply more-restrictive provisions, such as flood damage–reduction provisions in floodplain overlay districts. However, sometimes certain standards are relaxed, as in planned development or mixed-use overlay districts. The additional standards, whether more or less restrictive, must be uniformly applied within the overlay district.

355. Amendments to this subsection made by Part I of S.L. 2019-111 are to be incorporated in 2020. One amendment adds explicit limits on permissible conditions that may be imposed.

356. This language has been deleted as surplusage.

357. This is an optional provision for local governments. If so desired, the ordinance can define minor modifications to conditional districts and allow them to be approved administratively without going through the full zoning-text-amendment process. If a local government does not want to allow this, there is no requirement that it must.

358. This subsection explicitly authorizes modification of conditional districts and requires major modifications to follow the legislative process used to rezone property. If property subject to a conditional zoning has multiple parcels, modification requests can be made by some owners without participation of all owners, but the modifications will only apply to those properties whose owners participated in the petition for modification.

359. This provision has been relocated to G.S. 160D-5-2.

360. This subsection clarifies that while many development standards in a zoning ordinance vary from zoning district to zoning district, it is permissible to have some zoning standards that apply uniformly jurisdictionwide. For example, an ordinance could require a specified setback from a major arterial road or a perineal stream in all zoning districts.

§ 160D-7-4. ~~Local energy efficiency~~ Incentives.[361] [160D-704]

~~Land-Use Development Incentives Counties and municipalities,~~(a) For the purpose of reducing the amount of energy consumption by new development, ~~and thereby promoting the public health, safety, and welfare,~~[362] local governments may adopt ordinances to grant a density bonus, make adjustments to otherwise applicable development requirements, or provide other incentives ~~to a developer or builder~~ within ~~the county or municipality and~~ its ~~extraterritorial~~ planning and development regulation jurisdiction, if the ~~developer or builder~~ person receiving the incentives agrees to construct new development or reconstruct existing development in a manner that the ~~county or municipality~~ local government determines, based on generally recognized standards established for such purposes, makes a significant contribution to the reduction of energy consumption and increased use of sustainable design principles.

(b) In order to encourage construction that uses sustainable design principles and to improve energy efficiency in buildings, a ~~city~~ local government may charge reduced building permit fees or provide partial rebates of building permit fees for buildings that are constructed or renovated using design principles that conform to or exceed one or more of the following certifications or ratings:[363]

(1) Leadership in Energy and Environmental Design (LEED) certification or higher rating under certification standards adopted by the U.S. Green Building Council.

(2) A One Globe or higher rating under the Green Globes program standards adopted by the Green Building Initiative.

(3) A certification or rating by another nationally recognized certification or rating system that is equivalent or greater than those listed in subdivisions (1) and (2) of this subsection.

~~§ 160A-385. Changes.~~[364]

~~§ 160A-385.1/153A-344.1. Vested Rights.~~[365]

§ 160D-7-5. ~~Board of adjustment.~~ Quasi-judicial zoning decisions.[366] [160D-705]

(a) *Provisions of Ordinance.* The zoning or unified development ordinance may provide that the board of adjustment, planning board, or governing board hear and decide quasi-judicial zoning decisions.[367] ~~special and conditional use permits, requests for variances, and of administrative officials charged with enforcement of the ordinance. As used in this section, the term "decision" includes any final and binding order, requirement, or determination.~~[368] The board ~~of adjustment~~ shall follow quasi-judicial procedures as specified in G.S. 160D-4-6 when ~~deciding appeals, requests for variances and special and conditional use permits, and~~ making any ~~other~~ quasi-judicial decision. ~~that may by ordinance be assigned to the board.~~[369] ~~The board shall hear and decide all matters upon which it is required to pass under any statute or ordinance that regulates land use or development.~~[370]

---

361. This provision has been relocated from G.S. 160A-383.4, which is also applicable to counties. Earlier drafts of the bill also included a proposal to expand statewide the provisions for density bonuses for affordable housing. Given a lack of consensus as to the need for such an expansion, those provisions were deleted and current statutes and local legislation on the matter were left unchanged.

362. This language has been deleted as surplusage.

363. This provision has been relocated from G.S. 160A-381(f) and 153A-340(i).

364. G.S. 160A-385(a), regarding protest petitions (now repealed), has been relocated to G.S. 160D-6-3. G.S. 160A-385(b) and 153A-344(b), regarding building permits and vested rights, have been relocated to Article 1 of G.S. Chapter 160D (160D-1-8, regarding vested rights), as these sections affect all development approvals, not just those made under a zoning regulation.

365. All provisions regarding vested rights have been relocated to Article 1 of G.S. Chapter 160D, as those provisions affect all development approvals, not just zoning.

366. This section has been relocated from G.S. 160A-388, which is also applicable to counties. General provisions on quasi-judicial process and appeals that are applicable to development regulations other than zoning have been relocated to G.S. 160D-4-5 and 160D-4-6.

367. The deleted material that follows is surplusage, as it is addressed in later subsections of this section or in the general provisions of G.S. 160D-4-5 and 160D-4-6.

368. This provision has been relocated to G.S. 160D-4-5(a).

369. This language has been deleted as surplusage.

370. This provision has been relocated to G.S. 160D-4-5(a).

(a2)[371] Notice of hearings conducted pursuant to this section shall be mailed to the person or entity whose appeal, application, or request is the subject of the hearing; to the owner of the property that is the subject of the hearing if the owner did not initiate the hearing; to the owners of all parcels of land abutting the parcel of land that is the subject of the hearing; and to any other persons entitled to receive notice as provided by the zoning or unified development ordinance. In the absence of evidence to the contrary, the city may rely on the county tax listing to determine owners of property entitled to mailed notice. The notice must be deposited in the mail at least 10 days, but not more than 25 days, prior to the date of the hearing. Within that same time period, the city shall also prominently post a notice of the hearing on the site that is the subject of the hearing or on an adjacent street or highway right-of-way.

(b) Repealed.

(b) *Appeals*. Except as otherwise provided by this Chapter, the board of adjustment shall hear and decide appeals from administrative decisions of administrative officials charged with regarding administration and enforcement of the zoning regulation or unified development ordinance and may hear appeals arising out of any other ordinance that regulates land use or development. The provisions of G.S. 160D-4-5 and 4-6 are applicable to these appeals.[372] , pursuant to all of the following:

(1) Any person who has standing under G.S. 160A-393(d) or the city may appeal a decision to the board of adjustment. An appeal is taken by filing a notice of appeal with the city clerk. The notice of appeal shall state the grounds for the appeal.

(2) The official who made the decision shall give written notice to the owner of the property that is the subject of the decision and to the party who sought the decision, if different from the owner. The written notice shall be delivered by personal delivery, electronic mail, or by first-class mail.

(3) The owner or other party shall have 30 days from receipt of the written notice within which to file an appeal. Any other person with standing to appeal shall have 30 days from receipt from any source of actual or constructive notice of the decision within which to file an appeal.

(4) It shall be conclusively presumed that all persons with standing to appeal have constructive notice of the decision from the date a sign containing the words "Zoning Decision" or "Subdivision Decision" in letters at least six inches high and identifying the means to contact an official for information about the decision is prominently posted on the property that is the subject of the decision, provided the sign remains on the property for at least 10 days. Posting of signs is not the only form of constructive notice. Any such posting shall be the responsibility of the landowner or applicant. Verification of the posting shall be provided to the official who made the decision. Absent an ordinance provision to the contrary, posting of signs shall not be required.

(5) The official who made the decision shall transmit to the board all documents and exhibits constituting the record upon which the action appealed from is taken. The official shall also provide a copy of the record to the appellant and to the owner of the property that is the subject of the appeal if the appellant is not the owner.

(6) An appeal of a notice of violation or other enforcement order stays enforcement of the action appealed from unless the official who made the decision certifies to the board of adjustment after notice of appeal has been filed that because of the facts stated in an affidavit, a stay would cause imminent peril to life or property or because the violation is transitory in nature, a stay would seriously interfere with enforcement of the ordinance. In that case, enforcement proceedings shall not be stayed except by a restraining order, which may be granted by a court. If enforcement proceedings are not stayed, the appellant may file with the official a request for an expedited hearing of the appeal, and the board of adjustment shall meet to hear the appeal within 15 days after such a request is

---

371. This subsection has been relocated to G.S. 160D-4-6(b).

372. Remaining provisions related to the appeals process have been relocated to G.S. 160D-4-5 and 160D-4-6.

~~filed. Notwithstanding the foregoing, appeals of decisions granting a permit or otherwise affirming that a proposed use of property is consistent with the ordinance shall not stay the further review of an application for permits or permissions to use such property; in these situations the appellant may request and the board may grant a stay of a final decision of permit applications or building permits affected by the issue being appealed.~~

~~(7) Subject to the provisions of subdivision (6) of this subsection, the board of adjustment shall hear and decide the appeal within a reasonable time.~~

~~(8) The official who made the decision shall be present at the hearing as a witness. The appellant shall not be limited at the hearing to matters stated in the notice of appeal. If any party or the city would be unduly prejudiced by the presentation of matters not presented in the notice of appeal, the board shall continue the hearing. The board of adjustment may reverse or affirm, wholly or partly, or may modify the decision appealed from and shall make any order, requirement, decision, or determination that ought to be made. The board shall have all the powers of the official who made the decision.~~

~~(9) When hearing an appeal pursuant to G.S. 160A-400.9(e) or any other appeal in the nature of certiorari, the hearing shall be based on the record below and the scope of review shall be as provided in G.S. 160A-393(k).~~

~~(10) The parties to an appeal that has been made under this subsection may agree to mediation or other forms of alternative dispute resolution. The ordinance may set standards and procedures to facilitate and manage such voluntary alternative dispute resolution.~~

(c) *Special ~~and Conditional~~ Use Permits.*[373] The ~~ordinance~~ regulations may provide[374] that the board of adjustment, planning board, or governing board ~~may issue~~ hear and decide special ~~and conditional~~ use permits in accordance with principles, conditions, safeguards, and procedures specified ~~therein~~ in the regulations. Reasonable and appropriate conditions and safeguards may be imposed upon these permits. Where appropriate, such conditions may include requirements that street and utility rights-of-way be dedicated to the public and that provision be made ~~of~~ for recreational space and facilities.[375] Conditions and safeguards imposed under this subsection shall not include requirements for which the local government does not have authority under statute to regulate nor requirements for which the courts have held to be unenforceable if imposed directly by the local government.[376]

The regulation may provide that defined minor modifications[377] to special use permits that do not involve a change in uses permitted or the density of overall development permitted may be reviewed and approved administratively.[378] Any other modification or revocation of a special use permit shall follow the same process for approval as is applicable to the approval of a special use permit. If multiple parcels of land are subject to a special use permit, the owners of individual parcels may apply for permit modification so long as the modification would not result in other properties failing to meet the terms of the special use

---

373. This subsection has been relocated from G.S. 160A-381(c), 153A-340(c1), and 160A-388 in order to consolidate provisions on special- and conditional-use permits in one location. The provisions have been modestly edited and reordered for improved clarity.

374. This subsection continues current law that allows for, but does not require, the use of special-use permits. The subsection uses a single term ("special use permit") for these quasi-judicial approvals to reduce confusion.

375. This existing provision regarding exactions with special-use permits is consistent with the more-general authorization for exactions as part of zoning regulations in G.S. 160d-7-2(a).

376. This provision was added by S.L. 2015-286, § 1.8. Amendments to this sentence made by Part I of S.L. 2019-111 are to be incorporated in 2020. One amendment adds explicit limits on permissible conditions that may be imposed.

377. This language allows each local government to specifically define "minor" modifications if it elects to use this option.

378. If administrative staff determine that a modification does not qualify as minor, as defined by the ordinance, that determination can be appealed in the same manner as any other determination.

permit or regulations. Any modifications approved shall only be applicable to those properties whose owners apply for the modification.[379] The regulation may require that special uses permits be recorded with the Register of Deeds.[380]

(d) *Variances.* When unnecessary hardships would result from carrying out the strict letter of a zoning regulation, ~~ordinance,~~ the board of adjustment shall vary any of the provisions of the ~~ordinance~~ zoning regulation upon a showing of all of the following:

(1) Unnecessary hardship would result from the strict application of the ~~ordinance~~ regulation. It shall not be necessary to demonstrate that, in the absence of the variance, no reasonable use can be made of the property.

(2) The hardship results from conditions that are peculiar to the property, such as location, size, or topography. Hardships resulting from personal circumstances, as well as hardships resulting from conditions that are common to the neighborhood or the general public, may not be the basis for granting a variance. <u>A variance may be granted when necessary and appropriate to make a reasonable accommodation under the Federal Fair Housing Act for a person with a disability.</u>[381]

(3) The hardship did not result from actions taken by the applicant or the property owner. The act of purchasing property with knowledge that circumstances exist that may justify the granting of a variance shall not be regarded as a self-created hardship.

(4) The requested variance is consistent with the spirit, purpose, and intent of the <u>regulation,</u> ~~ordinance,~~ such that public safety is secured, and substantial justice is achieved.

No change in permitted uses may be authorized by variance. Appropriate conditions may be imposed on any variance, provided that the conditions are reasonably related to the variance. Any other <u>development regulation</u> ~~ordinance~~ that regulates land use or development may provide for variances from the provisions of those ordinances[382] consistent with the provisions of this subsection.

~~(e) *Voting.*~~[383]

~~(1) The concurring vote of four-fifths of the board shall be necessary to grant a variance. A majority of the members shall be required to decide any other quasi-judicial matter or to determine an appeal made in the nature of certiorari. For the purposes of this subsection, vacant positions on the board and members who are disqualified from voting on a quasi-judicial matter shall not be considered members of the board for calculation of the requisite majority if there are no qualified alternates available to take the place of such members.~~

~~(2) A member of any board exercising quasi-judicial functions pursuant to this Article shall not participate in or vote on any quasi-judicial matter in a manner that would violate affected~~

---

379. This provision explicitly authorizes modification of special-use permits and requires major modifications to any permit to follow the quasi-judicial process used to originally decide the permit. If property subject to a special-use permit has multiple parcels, modification requests can be made by some owners without participation of all owners, but the modifications will only apply to those properties whose owners participated in the request for modification.

380. Some local governments required recordation of special- and conditional-use permits to provide notice to subsequent purchasers of the terms and conditions of the permits. This provision expressly authorizes, but does not require, requirements to record these permits.

381. Since a variance runs with the land and is not a personal right of an individual applicant, the personal circumstances of a particular applicant are generally irrelevant. However, the federal Fair Housing Act requires that local governments make reasonable accommodations for persons with disabilities. While some zoning ordinances have specific sections authorizing that flexibility when needed, others rely on the variance power to adjust dimensional standards or otherwise make adjustments to regulations in such situations. This addition clarifies that the variance tool can be used to meet this need; a separate ordinance authorization is not required. Consistent with housing laws, an accommodation is reasonable only if it does not require a fundamental alteration in the nature of the program or regulation. This later provision is consistent with the requirement that use variances are not allowed and with the idea that the spirit, purpose, and intent of the regulation should be observed.

382. Clarification.

383. This subsection has been relocated to G.S. 160D-4-6.

~~persons' constitutional rights to an impartial decision maker. Impermissible violations of due process include, but are not limited to, a member having a fixed opinion prior to hearing the matter that is not susceptible to change, undisclosed ex parte communications, a close familial, business, or other associational relationship with an affected person, or a financial interest in the outcome of the matter. If an objection is raised to a member's participation and that member does not recuse himself or herself, the remaining members shall by majority vote rule on the objection.~~

~~(e1) Recodified as subdivision (e)(2).~~

~~(e2) *Quasi-Judicial Decisions and Judicial Review.*~~ [384]

~~(1) The board shall determine contested facts and make its decision within a reasonable time. Every quasi-judicial decision shall be based upon competent, material, and substantial evidence in the record. Each quasi-judicial decision shall be reduced to writing and reflect the board's determination of contested facts and their application to the applicable standards. The written decision shall be signed by the chair or other duly authorized member of the board. A quasi-judicial decision is effective upon filing the written decision with the clerk to the board or such other office or official as the ordinance specifies. The decision of the board shall be delivered by personal delivery, electronic mail, or by first-class mail to the applicant, property owner, and to any person who has submitted a written request for a copy, prior to the date the decision becomes effective. The person required to provide notice shall certify that proper notice has been made.~~

~~(2)~~ [385] ~~Every quasi-judicial decision shall be subject to review by the superior court by proceedings in the nature of certiorari pursuant to G.S. 160A-393. A petition for review shall be filed with the clerk of superior court by the later of 30 days after the decision is effective or after a written copy thereof is given in accordance with subdivision (1) of this subsection. When first-class mail is used to deliver notice, three days shall be added to the time to file the petition.~~

~~(f) *Oaths.*~~ [386] ~~The chair of the board or any member acting as chair and the clerk to the board are authorized to administer oaths to witnesses in any matter coming before the board. Any person who, while under oath during a proceeding before the board of adjustment board determining a quasi-judicial matter, willfully swears falsely is guilty of a Class 1 misdemeanor.~~

~~(g) *Subpoenas.*~~ [387] ~~The board of adjustment through the chair, or in the chair's absence anyone acting as chair, may subpoena witnesses and compel the production of evidence. To request issuance of a subpoena, persons with standing under G.S. 160A-393(d) may make a written request to the chair explaining why it is necessary for certain witnesses or evidence to be compelled. The chair shall issue requested subpoenas he or she determines to be relevant, reasonable in nature and scope, and not oppressive. The chair shall rule on any motion to quash or modify a subpoena. Decisions regarding subpoenas made by the chair may be appealed to the full board of adjustment. If a person fails or refuses to obey a subpoena issued pursuant to this subsection, the board of adjustment or the party seeking the subpoena may apply to the General Court of Justice for an order requiring that its subpoena be obeyed, and the court shall have jurisdiction to issue these orders after notice to all proper parties.~~

---

384. This subsection has been relocated to G.S. 160D-4-6.

385. This subdivision has been relocated to Article 14 on judicial review, specifically, to G.S. 160D-14-4, to establish a uniform time period within which to seek judicial review for all quasi-judicial decisions made under Chapter 160D.

386. This subsection has been relocated to G.S. 160D-4-6.

387. This subsection has been relocated to G.S. 160D-4-6.

§ 160A-389. Remedies.[388]

If a building or structure is erected, constructed, reconstructed, altered, repaired, converted, or maintained, or any building, structure or land is used in violation of this Part or of any ordinance or other regulation made under authority conferred thereby, the city, in addition to other remedies, may institute any appropriate action or proceedings to prevent the unlawful erection, construction, reconstruction, alteration, repair, conversion, maintenance or use, to restrain, correct or abate the violation, to prevent occupancy of the building, structure or land, or to prevent any illegal act, conduct, business or use in or about the premises.

§ 160D-7-6. Zoning conflicts with other development standards.[389] [160D-706]

(a) When regulations made under authority of this ~~Part~~ Article require a greater width or size of yards or courts, or require a lower height of a building or fewer number of stories, or require a greater percentage of a lot to be left unoccupied, or impose other higher standards than are required in any other statute or local ordinance or regulation, the regulations made under authority of this ~~Part~~ Article shall govern. When the provisions of any other statute or local ordinance or regulation require a greater width or size of yards or courts, or require a lower height of a building or a fewer number of stories, or require a greater percentage of a lot to be left unoccupied, or impose other higher standards than are required by the regulations made under authority of this ~~Part~~ Article, the provisions of that statute or local ordinance or regulation shall govern.

(b)[390] When adopting regulations under this Part, a local government may not use a definition of dwelling unit, bedroom, or sleeping unit that is more expansive than any definition of the same in another statute or in a rule adopted by a State agency.[391]

§ 160D-7-7. Other statutes not repealed.[392]

This Part shall not repeal any zoning act or city or county planning act, local or general, now in force, except those that are repugnant to or inconsistent herewith. This Part shall be construed to be an enlargement of the duties, powers, and authority contained in other laws authorizing the appointment and proper functioning of city planning commissions or zoning commissions by any city or town in the State of North Carolina.

ARTICLE 8. SUBDIVISION REGULATION

§ 160D-8-1. ~~Subdivision regulation~~ Authority.[393] [160D-801]

A ~~city~~ local government may by ordinance regulate the subdivision of land within its ~~territorial~~ planning and development regulation jurisdiction. In addition to final plat approval, the regulation ~~ordinance~~ may include provisions for review and approval of sketch plans and preliminary plats. The regulation ~~ordinance~~ may provide for different review procedures for ~~differing~~ different classes of subdivisions. ~~The ordinance may be adopted as part of a unified development ordinance or as a separate subdivision ordinance.~~[394] Decisions on approval or denial of preliminary or final plats may be made only on the basis of standards explicitly set forth in the subdivision or unified development ordinance.

§ 160D-8-2. ~~Definition~~ Applicability.[395] [160D-802]

(a) For the purpose of this ~~Part~~ Article, ~~"subdivision" means~~ subdivision regulations shall be applicable to all divisions of a tract or parcel of land into two or more lots, building sites, or other divisions when any one or more of those divisions is created for the purpose of sale or building development (whether immediate

---

388. This section has been relocated to G.S. 160D-4-4.
389. This subsection has been relocated from G.S. 160A-390 and 153A-346.
390. This provision was added by S.L. 2015-246, § 18.
391. Amendments to this subsection made by Part I of S.L. 2019-111 are to be incorporated in 2020. One amendment adds limits regarding the definitions of "building" and "dwelling."
392. This section has been relocated from G.S. 160A-391.
393. This section has been relocated from G.S. 160A-371 and 153A-330.
394. This language has been deleted as redundant, given G.S. 160D-1-3.
395. This section has been relocated from G.S. 160A-376 and 153A-335.

or future) and shall include all divisions of land involving the dedication of a new street or a change in existing streets; but the following shall not be included within this definition nor be subject to the regulations authorized by this ~~Part~~ Article:

(1) The combination or recombination of portions of previously subdivided and recorded lots where the total number of lots is not increased and the resultant lots are equal to or exceed the standards of the ~~municipality~~ local government as shown in its subdivision regulations.

(2) The division of land into parcels greater than 10 acres where no street right-of-way dedication is involved.

(3) The public acquisition by purchase of strips of land for the widening or opening of streets or for public transportation system corridors.

(4) The division of a tract in single ownership whose entire area is no greater than two acres into not more than three lots, where no street right-of-way dedication is involved and where the resultant lots are equal to or exceed the standards of the ~~municipality~~ local government, as shown in its subdivision regulations.

(5) The division of a tract into parcels in accordance with the terms of a probated will or in accordance with intestate succession under Chapter 29 of the General Statutes.[396]

(b) A ~~city~~ local government may provide for expedited review of specified classes of subdivisions.

(c)[397] ~~The county~~ A local government may require only a plat for recordation for the division of a tract or parcel of land in single ownership if all of the following criteria are met:

(1) The tract or parcel to be divided is not exempted under subdivision (2) of subsection (a) of this section.

(2) No part of the tract or parcel to be divided has been divided under this subsection in the 10 years prior to division.

(3) The entire area of the tract or parcel to be divided is greater than five acres.

(4) After division, no more than three lots result from the division.

(5) After division, all resultant lots comply with all of the following:

a. Any lot dimension size requirements of the applicable land-use regulations, if any.

b. The use of the lots is in conformity with the applicable zoning requirements, if any.

c. A permanent means of ingress and egress is recorded for each lot.

§ 160D-8-3. ~~Ordinance to contain procedure for plat approval; approval prerequisite to plat recordation; statement by owner.~~ Review process, filing, and recording of subdivision plats.[398] [160D-803]

(a) Any subdivision regulation ~~ordinance~~ adopted pursuant to this ~~Part~~ Article shall contain provisions setting forth the procedures and standards to be followed in granting or denying approval of a subdivision plat prior to its registration.

(b) ~~The~~ A subdivision regulation ~~ordinance~~[399] shall provide that the following agencies be given an opportunity to make recommendations concerning an individual subdivision plat before the plat is approved:

(1) The district highway engineer as to proposed State streets, State highways, and related drainage systems;

(2) The county health director or local public utility, as appropriate, as to proposed water or sewerage systems;

(3) Any other agency or official designated by the governing board. ~~of commissioners.~~

(c) The subdivision regulation ~~ordinance~~ may provide that final decisions on preliminary plats and final plats are to be made by:

(1) The ~~city council~~ governing board,

---

396. This subdivision incorporates a provision added by S.L. 2017-10.

397. This subsection incorporates a provision added by S.L. 2017-10.

398. This section has been relocated from G.S. 160A-373 and 153A-332.

399. This paragraph has been relocated from G.S. 153A-332.

(2) The ~~city council~~ governing board on recommendation of a designated body, or

(3) A designated planning board, technical review committee of local government staff members, or other designated body or staff person.

If the final decision on a subdivision plat is administrative, the decision may be assigned to a staff person or committee comprised entirely of staff persons and notice of the decision shall be as provided by G.S. 160D-4-3(b). If the final decision on a subdivision plat is quasi-judicial, the decision shall be assigned to the governing board, the planning board, the board of adjustment, or other board appointed pursuant to this Chapter, and the procedures set forth in G.S. 160D-4-6 shall apply.

(d) ~~From and~~ After the effective date ~~of~~ that a subdivision regulation ~~ordinance that~~ is adopted, ~~by the city,~~ no subdivision ~~plat of land within the city's~~ within a local government's planning and development regulation jurisdiction shall be filed or recorded until it shall have been submitted to and approved by the ~~council~~ governing board or appropriate ~~agency~~ body, as specified in the subdivision regulation ~~ordinance~~, and until this approval shall have been entered on the face of the plat in writing by an authorized representative of the ~~city~~ local government. The Review Officer, pursuant to G.S. 47-30.2, shall not certify ~~a plat of~~ a subdivision plat ~~of land located within the territorial jurisdiction of a city~~ that has not been approved in accordance with these provisions nor shall the clerk of superior court order or direct the recording of a plat if the recording would be in conflict with this section.[400]

§ 160D-8-4. Contents and requirements of regulation ~~ordinance~~.[401] [160D-804]

(a) *Purposes.* A subdivision ~~control ordinance~~ regulation may provide for the orderly growth and development of the ~~city~~ local government; for the coordination of transportation networks and utilities within proposed subdivisions with existing or planned streets and highways and with other public facilities; ~~for the dedication or reservation of recreation areas serving residents of the immediate neighborhood within the subdivision or, alternatively, for provision of funds to be used to acquire recreation areas serving residents of the development or subdivision or more than one subdivision or development within the immediate area, and rights-of-way or easements for street and utility purposes including the dedication of rights-of-way pursuant to G.S. 136-66.10 or G.S. 136-66.11;~~[402] and for the distribution of population and traffic in a manner that will avoid congestion and overcrowding and will create conditions that substantially promote public health, safety, and the general welfare.

(b) *Plats.* The regulation ~~ordinance~~ may require a plat be prepared, approved, and recorded pursuant to the provisions of the regulation ~~ordinance~~ whenever any subdivision of land takes place. The regulation ~~ordinance~~ may include requirements that plats show sufficient data to determine readily and reproduce accurately on the ground the location, bearing, and length of every street and alley line, lot line, easement boundary line, and other property boundaries, including the radius and other data for curved property lines, to an appropriate accuracy and in conformance with good surveying practice.

(c) *Transportation and utilities.*[403] The regulation may provide for the dedication of ~~and~~ rights-of-way or easements for street and utility purposes, including the dedication of rights-of-way pursuant to G.S. 136-66.10 or G.S. 136-66.11

The regulation ~~ordinance~~ may provide that in lieu of required street construction, a developer ~~may~~[404] be required to provide funds ~~that~~ for city[405] ~~may~~ use for the construction of roads to serve the occupants,

---

400. Simplifies and clarifies language.

401. This section has been relocated from G.S. 160A-372 and 153A-331. Amendments to this section made by S.L. 2019-174 are to be incorporated in 2020. Amendments deal with buried power lines and minimum square footage of structures.

402. This provision has been relocated to later subsections of this section.

403. This subsection consolidates existing provisions relative to transportation and utilities.

404. This revision clarifies that subdivision regulations are not required to provide for fees in lieu of dedication of land or construction of facilities, but that if such provisions are allowed by the ordinance and are elected for use in a particular plat review, they are binding on the local government and the property owner.

405. "City" rather than "local government" is used here since counties have no authority for county streets or roads.

residents, or invitees of the subdivision or development and these funds may be used for roads ~~which~~ that serve more than one subdivision or development within the area. All funds received by the city pursuant to this ~~paragraph~~ subsection shall be used only for development of roads, including design, land acquisition, and construction. However, a city may undertake these activities in conjunction with the Department of Transportation under an agreement between the city and the Department of Transportation. Any formula adopted to determine the amount of funds the developer is to pay in lieu of required street construction shall be based on the trips generated from the subdivision or development. The regulation ~~ordinance~~ may require a combination of partial payment of funds and partial dedication of constructed streets when the governing ~~body~~ board of the city determines that a combination is in the best interests of the citizens of the area to be served.

(d) *Recreation Areas and Open Space.* – The regulation may provide for the dedication or reservation of recreation areas serving residents of the immediate neighborhood within the subdivision or, alternatively, for ~~provision~~ payment of funds to be used to acquire or develop recreation areas serving residents of the development or subdivision or more than one subdivision or development within the immediate area.

~~The ordinance may provide that a developer may provide funds to the city whereby the city may acquire recreational land or areas to serve the development or subdivision, including the purchase of land that may be used to serve more than one subdivision or development within the immediate area.~~ [406] All funds received by ~~the city~~ municipalities pursuant to this subsection shall be used only for the acquisition or development of recreation, park, or open space sites. All funds received by counties pursuant to this subsection shall be used only for the acquisition of recreation, park, or open space sites.[407] Any formula enacted to determine the amount of funds that are to be provided under this subsection shall be based on the value of the development or subdivision for property tax purposes. The ~~ordinance~~ regulation may allow a combination or partial payment of funds and partial dedication of land when the governing ~~body~~ board ~~of the city~~ determines that this combination is in the best interests of the citizens of the area to be served.

(e) *Community service facilities.* The regulation ~~ordinance~~ may provide for the more orderly development of subdivisions by requiring the construction of community service facilities in accordance with ~~municipal~~ local government plans, policies, and standards.

(f) *School sites.*

The regulation ~~ordinance~~ may provide for the reservation of school sites in accordance with ~~comprehensive land use~~ plans approved by the ~~council~~ governing board ~~or the planning board.~~[408] In order for this authorization to become effective, before approving such plans the ~~council~~ governing board ~~or planning board~~ and the board of education with jurisdiction over the area shall jointly determine the ~~specific~~ location and size of any school sites to be reserved. ~~; which information shall appear in the comprehensive land use plan.~~ Whenever a subdivision is submitted for approval ~~which~~ that includes part or all of a school site to be reserved under the plan, the ~~council~~ governing board ~~or planning board~~ shall immediately notify the board of education and the board of education shall promptly decide whether it still wishes the site to be reserved. If the board of education does not wish to reserve the site, it shall so notify the ~~council~~ governing board ~~or planning board~~ and no site shall be reserved. If the board of education does wish to reserve the site, the subdivision or site plan shall not be approved without such reservation. The board of education shall then have 18 months beginning on the date of final approval of the subdivision or site plan within which to acquire the site by purchase or by initiating condemnation proceedings. If the board of education has not purchased or begun proceedings to condemn the site within 18 months, the ~~subdivider~~ landowner may treat the land as freed of the reservation.

---

406. This language has been deleted as redundant, as it repeats the previous sentence. The rest of this subsection notes that these funds can be used for land acquisition for or development of recreation facilities.

407. This provision preserves the current statutory differences in the way cities and counties can use funds received in lieu of park and open-space land dedications. S.L. 2017-102 also corrected a typographical error in this section.

408. This language has been deleted for consistency with G.S. 160D-5-1(c), which requires plan adoption by the governing board.

(g) *Performance guarantees.*[409] To assure compliance with these and other <u>development</u> <u>regulation</u> ~~ordinance~~ requirements, the <u>regulation</u> ~~ordinance~~ may provide for performance guarantees to assure successful completion of required ~~improvements. If a performance guarantee is required, the city local government shall provide a range of options of types of performance guarantees, including, but not limited to, surety bonds or letters of credit, from which the developer person required to give the performance guarantee may choose.~~ <u>improvements at the time the plat is recorded as provided in subsection (b) of this section.</u> For any specific development, the type of performance guarantee ~~from the range specified by the city~~ <u></u> shall be at the election of the ~~developer~~ <u>person required to give the performance guarantee.</u>[410]

For purposes of this section, all of the following shall apply with respect to performance guarantees:

(1) The term "performance guarantee" shall mean any of the following forms of guarantee:
   a. Surety bond issued by any company authorized to do business in this State.
   b. Letter of credit issued by any financial institution licensed to do business in this State.
   c. Other form of guarantee that provides equivalent security to a surety bond or letter of credit.

(2) The performance guarantee shall be returned or released, as appropriate, in a timely manner upon the acknowledgement by the local government that the improvements for which the performance guarantee is being required are complete. If the improvements are not complete and the current performance guarantee is expiring, the performance guarantee shall be extended, or a new performance guarantee issued, for an additional period until such required improvements are complete. A developer shall demonstrate reasonable, good faith progress toward completion of the required improvements that are the subject of the performance guarantee or any extension. The form of any extension shall remain at the election of the developer.

(3) The amount of the performance guarantee shall not exceed one hundred twenty-five percent (125%) of the reasonably estimated cost of completion at the time the performance guarantee is issued. Any extension of the performance guarantee necessary to complete required improvements shall not exceed one hundred twenty-five percent (125%) of the reasonably estimated cost of completion of the remaining incomplete improvements still outstanding at the time the extension is obtained.

(4) The performance guarantee shall only be used for completion of the required improvements and not for repairs or maintenance after completion.

(5) [411] No person shall have or may claim any rights under or to any performance guarantee provided pursuant to this subsection or in the proceeds of any such performance guarantee other than the following:
   a. The local government to whom such performance guarantee is provided.
   b. The developer at whose request or for whose benefit such performance guarantee is given.
   c. The person or entity issuing or providing such performance guarantee at the request of or for the benefit of the developer.

---

409. This subsection has been relocated from G.S. 160A-372(c) and 153A-331(c). Amendments to this subsection made by S.L. 2019-79 are to be incorporated in 2020. Amendments add provisions regarding performance guarantees.

410. This subsection has been updated to reflect amendments made by S.L. 2015-187.

411. Subparagraph (5) was added by S.L. 2017-40.

§ 160D-8-5. Notice of new subdivision fees and fee increases; public comment period.[412] [160D-805]

(a) A ~~city~~ local government shall provide notice to interested parties of the imposition of or increase in fees or charges applicable solely to the construction of development subject to ~~the provisions of Part 2 of Article 19 of this Chapter~~ this Article at least seven days prior to the first meeting where the imposition of or increase in the fees or charges is on the agenda for consideration. The ~~city~~ local government shall employ at least two of the following means of communication in order to provide the notice required by this section:

    (1) Notice of the meeting in a prominent location on a web site managed or maintained by the ~~city~~ local government.

    (2) Notice of the meeting in a prominent physical location, including, but not limited to, any government building, library, or courthouse within the ~~city~~ planning and development regulation jurisdiction of the local government.

    (3) Notice of the meeting by electronic mail or other reasonable means ~~mail~~ to a list of interested parties that is created by the ~~city~~ local government for the purpose of notification as required by this section.

    ~~(4) Notice of the meeting by facsimile to a list of interested parties that is created by the city local government for the purpose of notification as required by this section.~~

~~(a1)~~If a city does not maintain its own web site, it may employ the notice option provided by subdivision (1) of subsection (a) of this section by submitting a request to a county or counties in which the city is located to post such notice in a prominent location on a web site that is maintained by the county or counties. Any city that elects to provide such notice shall make its request to the county or counties at least 15 days prior to the date of the first meeting where the imposition of or increase in the fees or charges is on the agenda for consideration.

(b) During the consideration of the imposition of or increase in fees or charges as provided in subsection (a) of this section, the governing ~~body~~ board of the ~~city~~ local government shall permit a period of public comment.

(c) This section shall not apply if the imposition of or increase in fees or charges is contained in a budget filed in accordance with the requirements of G.S. 159-12.

§ 160D-8-6. Effect of plat approval on dedications.[413] [160D-806]

The approval of a plat shall not be deemed to constitute or effect the acceptance by the ~~city~~ local government or public of the dedication of any street or other ground, public utility line, or other public facility shown on the plat. However, any ~~city council~~ governing board may by resolution accept any dedication made to the public of lands or facilities for streets, parks, public utility lines, or other public purposes, when the lands or facilities are located within its ~~subdivision-regulation~~ planning and development regulation jurisdiction. Acceptance of dedication of lands or facilities located within the ~~subdivision-regulation~~ planning and development regulation jurisdiction but outside the corporate limits of a city shall not place on the city any duty to open, operate, repair, or maintain any street, utility line, or other land or facility, and a city shall in no event be held to answer in any civil action or proceeding for failure to open, repair, or maintain any street located outside its corporate limits. Unless a city, county or other public entity operating a water system shall have agreed to begin operation and maintenance of the water system or water system facilities within one year of the time of issuance of a certificate of occupancy for the first unit of housing in the subdivision, a city or county shall not, as part of its subdivision regulation applied to facilities or land outside the corporate limits of a city, require dedication of water systems or facilities as a condition for subdivision approval.

---

412. This section has been relocated from G.S. 160A-4.1 and 153A-102.1.
413. This section has been relocated from G.S. 160A-374 and 153A-333.

§ 160D-8-7. Penalties for transferring lots in unapproved subdivisions.[414] [160D-807]

(a) If a ~~city~~ local government adopts a subdivision regulation, ~~an ordinance regulating the subdivision of land as authorized herein,~~ any person who, being the owner or agent of the owner of any land located within the planning and development regulation jurisdiction of that ~~city~~ local government, thereafter subdivides his land in violation of the regulation ~~ordinance~~ or transfers or sells land by reference to, exhibition of, or any other use of a plat showing a subdivision of the land before the plat has been properly approved under such regulation ~~ordinance~~ and recorded in the office of the appropriate register of deeds, shall be guilty of a Class 1 misdemeanor. The description by metes and bounds in the instrument of transfer or other document used in the process of selling or transferring land shall not exempt the transaction from this penalty. The ~~city~~ local government may bring an action for injunction of any illegal subdivision, transfer, conveyance, or sale of land, and the court shall, upon appropriate findings, issue an injunction and order requiring the offending party to comply with the subdivision regulation. ~~ordinance.~~ Building permits required pursuant to G.S. 160D-11-8 may be denied for lots that have been illegally subdivided. In addition to other remedies, a ~~city~~ local government may institute any appropriate action or proceedings to prevent the unlawful subdivision of land, to restrain, correct, or abate the violation, or to prevent any illegal act or conduct.

(b) The provisions of this section shall not prohibit any owner or its agent from entering into contracts to sell or lease by reference to an approved preliminary plat for which a final plat has not yet been properly approved under the subdivision regulation ~~ordinance~~ or recorded with the register of deeds, provided the contract does all of the following:

(1) Incorporates as an attachment a copy of the preliminary plat referenced in the contract and obligates the owner to deliver to the buyer a copy of the recorded plat prior to closing and conveyance.

(2) Plainly and conspicuously notifies the prospective buyer or lessee that a final subdivision plat has not been approved or recorded at the time of the contract, that no governmental body will incur any obligation to the prospective buyer or lessee with respect to the approval of the final subdivision plat, that changes between the preliminary and final plats are possible, and that the contract or lease may be terminated without breach by the buyer or lessee if the final recorded plat differs in any material respect from the preliminary plat.

(3) Provides that if the approved and recorded final plat does not differ in any material respect from the plat referred to in the contract, the buyer or lessee may not be required by the seller or lessor to close any earlier than five days after the delivery of a copy of the final recorded plat.

(4) Provides that if the approved and recorded final plat differs in any material respect from the preliminary plat referred to in the contract, the buyer or lessee may not be required by the seller or lessor to close any earlier than 15 days after the delivery of the final recorded plat, during which 15-day period the buyer or lessee may terminate the contract without breach or any further obligation and may receive a refund of all earnest money or prepaid purchase price.

(c) The provisions of this section shall not prohibit any owner or its agent from entering into contracts to sell or lease land by reference to an approved preliminary plat for which a final plat has not been properly approved under the subdivision regulation ~~ordinance~~ or recorded with the register of deeds where the buyer or lessee is any person who has contracted to acquire or lease the land for the purpose of engaging in the business of construction of residential, commercial, or industrial buildings on the land, or for the purpose of resale or lease of the land to persons engaged in that kind of business, provided that no conveyance of that land may occur and no contract to lease it may become effective until after the final plat has been properly approved under the subdivision regulation ~~ordinance~~ and recorded with the register of deeds.

---

414. This section has been relocated from G.S. 160A-375 and 153A-334.

§ 160D-8-8. Appeals of decisions on subdivision plats.[415] [160D-808]

Appeals of subdivision decisions may be made pursuant to G.S. 160D-14-3.

(a) When a subdivision ordinance adopted under this Part provides that the decision whether to approve or deny a preliminary or final subdivision plat is to be made by a city council or a planning board, other than a planning board comprised solely of members of a city planning staff, and the ordinance authorizes the council or planning board to make a quasi-judicial decision in deciding whether to approve the subdivision plat, then that quasi-judicial decision of the council or planning board shall be subject to review by the superior court by proceedings in the nature of certiorari. The provisions of G.S. 160A-381(c), 160A-388(e2) (2), and 160A-393 shall apply to those appeals.

(b) When a subdivision ordinance adopted under this Part provides that a city council, planning board, or staff member is authorized to make only an administrative or ministerial decision in deciding whether to approve a preliminary or final subdivision plat, then any party aggrieved by that administrative or ministerial decision may seek to have the decision reviewed by filing an action in superior court seeking appropriate declaratory or equitable relief. Such an action must be filed within the time frame specified in G.S. 160A-393 381(c) for petitions in the nature of certiorari.

(c) For purposes of this section, an ordinance shall be deemed to authorize a quasi-judicial decision if the city council or planning board is authorized to decide whether to approve or deny the plat based not only upon whether the application complies with the specific requirements set forth in the ordinance, but also on whether the application complies with one or more generally stated standards requiring a discretionary decision to be made by the city council or planning board.

§ 160A-378 to -380/153A-337 to -339. Reserved for future codification purposes.

ARTICLE 9. REGULATION OF PARTICULAR USES AND AREAS

Part 1. Particular Land Uses[416]

§ 160D-9-1. Regulation of particular uses and areas.[417] [160D-901]

A local government may regulate the uses and areas set forth in this Article in zoning regulations pursuant to Article 7 of this Chapter, a unified development ordinance, or in separate development regulations authorized by this Article. This shall not be deemed to expand, diminish, or alter the scope of authority granted pursuant to those Articles. In all instances, the substance of the local government regulation shall be consistent with the provisions in this Article. The provisions of this Chapter apply to any regulation adopted pursuant to this Article that substantially affects land use and development.

§ 160D-9-2. Adult businesses.[418] [160D-902]

(a) The General Assembly finds and determines that sexually oriented businesses can and do cause adverse secondary impacts on neighboring properties. Numerous studies that are relevant to North Carolina have found increases in crime rates and decreases in neighboring property values as a result of the location of sexually oriented businesses in inappropriate locations or from the operation of such businesses in an

---

415. This section has been relocated from G.S. 160A-377 and 153A-336. Provisions regarding judicial review have been relocated to Article 14 of Chapter 160D, on judicial review.

416. When codified, the Revisor of Statutes will reorder G.S. 160D-9-16, regarding bee hives, to G.S. 160D-9-6 in order to maintain the alphabetical order in which the particular uses addressed in this Part are listed.

417. This is a new section. It consolidates provisions regarding regulation of particular land uses into a single statutory part for ease of user access.

418. This section has been relocated from G.S. 160A-181.1, which is also applicable to counties.

inappropriate manner. Reasonable local government regulation of sexually oriented businesses in order to prevent or ameliorate adverse secondary impacts is consistent with the federal constitutional protection afforded to nonobscene but sexually explicit speech.

(b) In addition to State laws on obscenity, indecent exposure, and adult establishments, local government regulation of the location and operation of sexually oriented businesses is necessary to prevent undue adverse secondary impacts that would otherwise result from these businesses.

(c) A ~~city or county~~ local government may regulate sexually oriented businesses through zoning regulations, licensing requirements, or other appropriate local ordinances. The ~~city or county~~ local government may require a fee for the initial license and any annual renewal. Such local regulations may include, but are not limited to:

(1) Restrictions on location of sexually oriented businesses, such as limitation to specified zoning districts and minimum separation from sensitive land uses and other sexually oriented businesses;

(2) Regulations on operation of sexually oriented businesses, such as limits on hours of operation, open booth requirements, limitations on exterior advertising and noise, age of patrons and employees, required separation of patrons and performers, clothing restrictions for masseuses, and clothing restrictions for servers of alcoholic beverages;

(3) Clothing restrictions for entertainers; and

(4) Registration and disclosure requirements for owners and employees with a criminal record other than minor traffic offenses, and restrictions on ownership by or employment of a person with a criminal record that includes offenses reasonably related to the legal operation of sexually oriented businesses.

(d) In order to preserve the status quo while appropriate studies are conducted and the scope of potential regulations is deliberated, ~~city or county~~ local governments may enact moratoria of reasonable duration on either the opening of any new businesses authorized to be regulated under this section or the expansion of any such existing business. Businesses existing at the time of the effective date of regulations adopted under this section may be required to come into compliance with newly adopted regulations within an appropriate and reasonable period of time.

(e) ~~Cities and counties~~ Local governments may enter into cooperative agreements regarding coordinated regulation of sexually oriented businesses, including provision of adequate alternative sites for the location of constitutionally protected speech within an interrelated geographic area.

(f) For the purpose of this section, "sexually oriented businesses" means any businesses or enterprises that ~~have~~ has as one of ~~their~~ its principal business purposes or as a significant portion of ~~their~~ its business an emphasis on matter and conduct depicting, describing, or related to anatomical areas and sexual activities specified in G.S. 14-202.10. Local governments may adopt detailed definitions of these and similar businesses in order to precisely define the scope of any local regulations.

§ 160D-9-3. Agricultural uses.[419] [160D-903]

(a) *Bona fide farming exempt from county zoning.* ~~These~~ County zoning regulations may not affect property used for bona fide farm purposes; provided, however, that this section does not limit zoning regulation ~~under this Part~~ with respect to the use of farm property for nonfarm purposes.[420] Except as provided in G.S. 106-743.4 for farms that are subject to a conservation agreement under G.S. 106-743.2, bona fide farm purposes include the production and activities relating or incidental to the production of crops, grains, fruits, vegetables, ornamental and flowering plants, dairy, livestock, poultry, and all other forms of agriculture, as defined in G.S. 106-581.1. Activities incident to the farm include existing or new residences constructed to the applicable residential building code situated on the farm occupied by the owner, lessee, or operator of the farm and other buildings or structures sheltering or supporting the farm use and operation.[421] For purposes of this ~~subdivision~~ section, "when performed on the farm" in G.S. 106-581.1(6) shall include the

---

419. This section has been relocated from G.S. 153A-340(b) and (j) and 160A-360(k) and (l).
420. This sentence was rewritten by S.L. 2017-108.
421. This sentence was added by S.L. 2017-108.

farm within the jurisdiction of the county and any other farm owned or leased to or from others by the bona fide farm operator, no matter where located. For purposes of this ~~subdivision~~ <u>section</u>, the production of a nonfarm product that the Department of Agriculture and Consumer Services recognizes as a "Goodness Grows in North Carolina" product that is produced on a farm subject to a conservation agreement under G.S. 106-743.2 is a bona fide farm purpose. For purposes of determining whether a property is being used for bona fide farm purposes, any of the following shall constitute sufficient evidence that the property is being used for bona fide farm purposes:

1. A farm sales tax exemption certificate issued by the Department of Revenue.
2. A copy of the property tax listing showing that the property is eligible for participation in the present use value program pursuant to G.S. 105-277.3.
3. A copy of the farm owner's or operator's Schedule F from the owner's or operator's most recent federal income tax return.
4. A forest management plan.[422]

A building or structure that is used for agritourism is a bona fide farm purpose if the building or structure is located on a property that (i) is owned by a person who holds a qualifying farmer sales tax exemption certificate from the Department of Revenue pursuant to G.S. 105-164.13E(a) or (ii) is enrolled in the present-use value program pursuant to G.S. 105-277.3. Failure to maintain the requirements of this subsection for a period of three years after the date the building or structure was originally classified as a bona fide purpose pursuant to this subdivision shall subject the building or structure to applicable zoning and development regulation ordinances adopted by a county pursuant to subsection (a) of this section in effect on the date the property no longer meets the requirements of this subsection. For purposes of this section, "agritourism" means any activity carried out on a farm or ranch that allows members of the general public, for recreational, entertainment, or educational purposes, to view or enjoy rural activities, including farming, ranching, historic, cultural, harvest-your-own activities, or natural activities and attractions. A building or structure used for agritourism includes any building or structure used for public or private events, including, but not limited to, weddings, receptions, meetings, demonstrations of farm activities, meals, and other events that are taking place on the farm because of its farm or rural setting.[423]

(b) *County zoning of residential uses on large lots in agricultural districts.* ~~An ordinance adopted pursuant to this section~~ <u>A county zoning regulation</u> shall not prohibit single-family detached residential uses constructed in accordance with the North Carolina State Building Code on lots greater than 10 acres in size in zoning districts where more than fifty percent (50%) of the land is in use for agricultural or silvicultural purposes, except that this restriction shall not apply to commercial or industrial districts where a broad variety of commercial or industrial uses are permissible. ~~An ordinance~~ <u>A zoning regulation</u> ~~adopted pursuant to this section~~[424] shall not require that a lot greater than 10 acres in size have frontage on a public road or county-approved private road, or be served by public water or sewer lines, in order to be developed for single-family residential purposes.

(c) *Agricultural areas in municipal extraterritorial jurisdiction.*[425] ~~As used in this subsection, "bona fide farm purposes" is as described in G.S. 153A-340.~~[426] Property that is located in ~~the geographic area of~~[427] a municipality's extraterritorial <u>planning and development regulation</u> jurisdiction and that is used for bona fide farm purposes is exempt from ~~exercise of~~ the municipality's <u>zoning regulation to the same extent bona fide farming activities are exempt from county zoning pursuant to this section.</u>[428] As used in this subsec-

---

422. S.L. 2017-108 deleted a fifth item, a U.S. Department of Agriculture farm ID number, from this list.

423. This paragraph regarding agritourism was added by S.L. 2017-108. S.L. 2017-108 also deleted the provision allowing county zoning regulation of large-scale swine farms.

424. This language has been deleted as superfluous.

425. Portions of this subsection have been relocated from previous G.S. 160A-360(k) regarding farm uses in municipal extraterritorial areas.

426. This sentence has been deleted as unnecessary, given consolidation of city and county provisions related to zoning and agricultural uses.

427. Simplifies language.

428. This revision clarifies that the same county zoning exemption applicable to bona fide farming applies to city zoning within a city's extraterritorial jurisdiction (ETJ). This provides the same zoning and other

tion, "property" means a single tract of property or an identifiable portion of a single tract. Property that ~~is located in the geographic area of a municipality's extraterritorial jurisdiction and that~~ ceases to be used for bona fide farm purposes shall become subject to exercise of the municipality's extraterritorial <u>planning and development regulation</u> jurisdiction under this ~~Article~~ <u>Chapter</u>. For purposes of complying <u>with state or federal law,</u> ~~44 C.F.R. Part 60, Subpart A,~~[429] property that is exempt from the exercise of <u>municipal</u> extraterritorial <u>planning and development regulation</u> jurisdiction pursuant to this subsection shall be subject to the county's floodplain <u>regulation</u> ~~ordinance~~ or all floodplain regulation provisions of the county's unified development ordinance.

~~to the extraterritorial jurisdiction under this Article property that is located in the geographic area of a municipality's extraterritorial jurisdiction and that (l)   A municipality may provide in its zoning ordinance that an accessory building of a bona fide farm as defined by G.S. 153A-340(b) has the same exemption from the building code as it would have under county zoning. as provided by Part 3 of Article 18 of Chapter 153A of the General Statutes.~~[430]

~~This subsection applies only to the City of Raleigh and the Towns of Apex, Cary, FuquayVarina, Garner, Holly Springs, Knightdale, Morrisville, Rolesville, Wake Forest, Wendell, and Zebulon.~~

(d) *Accessory farm buildings.* A municipality may provide in its zoning <u>regulation</u> ~~ordinance~~ that an accessory building of a "bona fide farm" ~~as defined by G.S. 153A-340(b)~~ has the same exemption from the building code as it would have under county zoning ~~as provided by Part 3 of Article 18 of Chapter 153A of the General Statutes.~~[431]

~~This subsection applies only to the City of Raleigh and the Towns of Apex, Cary, Fuquay-Varina, Garner, Holly Springs, Knightdale, Morrisville, Rolesville, Wake Forest, Wendell, and Zebulon.~~[432]

(e) *City regulations in voluntary agricultural districts.*[433] A city may amend the <u>development regulations</u> ~~ordinances~~ applicable within its planning <u>and development regulation</u> jurisdiction to provide flexibility to farming operations that are located within a city or county voluntary agricultural district or enhanced voluntary agricultural district adopted under Article 61 of Chapter 106 of the General Statutes. Amendments to applicable <u>development regulations</u> ~~ordinances~~ may include provisions regarding on-farm sales, pick-your-own operations, road signs, agritourism, and other activities incident to farming. ~~For purposes of this section, the term "farming" shall have the same meaning as set forth in G.S. 106-581.1.~~[434]

---

development-regulation treatment for farmland in a municipal ETJ as would be provided if the property were in county jurisdiction.

429. This language citing specific federal regulations has been replaced by generalized language to avoid the potential for inaccuracy, as that citing reference may be modified in the future.

430. This provision has been relocated to the subsection immediately following this subsection. The authorization regarding accessory buildings and the building code previously applied only in Wake County municipalities.

431. This language has been deleted as unnecessary, given consolidation of city and county provisions related to zoning and agricultural uses.

432. This deletion gives all cities the option of exempting accessory farm buildings from city building code review.

433. This subsection has been relocated from G.S. 160A-383.2. Deletions were made to language that became unnecessary, given the consolidation of city and county provisions related to zoning and agricultural uses.

434. This language has been deleted as superfluous.

§ 160D-9-4. Airport zoning.[435] [160D-904]

Any ~~city~~ local government may enact and enforce airport zoning regulations pursuant to this Chapter or as authorized by Article 4 of Chapter 63 of the General Statutes. Airport zoning regulations for real property within six miles of any cargo airport complex site subject to regulation by the North Carolina Global TransPark Authority are governed by G.S. 63A-18.[436]

§ 160D-9-5. ~~Reasonable accommodation of~~ Amateur radio antennas.[437] [160D-905]

A ~~city~~ local government ordinance based on health, safety, or aesthetic considerations that regulates the placement, screening, or height of the antennas or support structures of amateur radio operators must reasonably accommodate amateur radio communications and must represent the minimum practicable regulation necessary to accomplish the purpose of the ~~city~~ local government. A ~~city~~ local government may not restrict antennas or antenna support structures of amateur radio operators to heights of 90 feet or lower unless the restriction is necessary to achieve a clearly defined health, safety, or aesthetic objective of the ~~city~~ local government.

§ 160D-9-6. Family care homes.[438] [160D-907]

(a) The General Assembly finds ~~has declared in Article 1 of this Chapter that~~ it is the public policy of this State to provide persons with disabilities with the opportunity to live in a normal residential environment.

(b) As used in this section ~~Article~~:

(1) "Family care home" means a home with support and supervisory personnel that provides room and board, personal care and habilitation services in a family environment for not more than six resident persons with disabilities.

(2) "Person with disabilities" means a person with a temporary or permanent physical, emotional, or mental disability including but not limited to mental retardation, cerebral palsy, epilepsy, autism, hearing and sight impairments, emotional disturbances and orthopedic impairments but not including mentally ill persons who are dangerous to others as defined in G.S. 122C-3(11)b.

(c) A family care home shall be deemed a residential use of property for zoning purposes and shall be a permissible use in all residential districts ~~of all political subdivisions~~. No ~~political subdivision~~ local government may require that a family care home, its owner, or operator obtain, because of the use, ~~a conditional use permit,~~ a special use permit, ~~special exception~~ or variance from any such zoning regulation ~~ordinance or plan~~; provided, however, that a ~~political subdivision~~ local government may prohibit a family care home from being located within a one-half mile radius of an existing family care home.

(d) A family care home shall be deemed a residential use of property for the purposes of determining charges or assessments imposed by ~~political subdivisions~~ local governments or businesses for water, sewer, power, telephone service, cable television, garbage and trash collection, repairs or improvements to roads, streets, and sidewalks, and other services, utilities, and improvements.

§ 160D-9-7. Fence Wraps.[439] [160D-908]

Fence wraps displaying signage when affixed to perimeter fencing at a construction site are exempt from zoning regulation pertaining to signage under this Article until the certificate of occupancy is issued for the final portion of any construction at that site or 24 months from the time the fence wrap was installed, whichever is shorter. If construction is not completed at the end of 24 months from the time the fence wrap was installed, the local government may regulate the signage but shall continue to allow fence wrapping

---

435. This revision adds a cross-reference to the 1941 Model Airport Zoning Act. Most cities and counties have now incorporated airport-zoning provisions into their zoning ordinances, but several still have separate airport-zoning provisions (particularly in unzoned portions of counties). Conforming amendments to that 1941 statute are set out in Section 4 of this bill.

436. This provision preserves the current jurisdictional relationship between local zoning and zoning adopted by the Global TransPark Authority.

437. This section has been relocated from G.S. 160A-383.3 and 153A-341.2.

438. This section has been relocated from G.S. 168-20 to 168-22.

439. This provision was added as G.S. 160A-381(j) and 153A-340(n) by S.L. 2015-246, § 4.

materials to be affixed to the perimeter fencing. No fence wrap affixed pursuant to this section may display any advertising other than advertising sponsored by a person directly involved in the construction project and for which monetary compensation for the advertisement is not paid or required.

§ 160D-9-8. Fraternities and sororities.[440] [160D-909]

A zoning regulation or unified development ordinance may not differentiate in terms of the regulations applicable to fraternities or sororities between those fraternities or sororities that are approved or recognized by a college or university and those that are not.

§ 160D-9-9. ~~Zoning regulations for m~~ Manufactured homes.[441] [160D-910]

(a) The General Assembly finds ~~and declares~~ that manufactured housing offers affordable housing opportunities for low and moderate income residents of this State who could not otherwise afford to own their own home. The General Assembly further finds that some local governments have adopted zoning regulations ~~which~~ that severely restrict the placement of manufactured homes. It is the intent of the General Assembly in enacting this section that ~~cities~~ local governments reexamine their land use practices to assure compliance with applicable statutes and case law, and consider allocating more residential land area for manufactured homes based upon local housing needs.

(b) For purposes of this section, the term "manufactured home" is defined as provided in G.S. 143-145(7).

(c) A ~~city~~ local government may not adopt or enforce zoning regulations or other provisions ~~which~~ that have the effect of excluding manufactured homes from the entire zoning jurisdiction or ~~which~~ that exclude manufactured homes based on the age of the home.[442]

(d) A ~~city~~ local government may adopt and enforce appearance and dimensional criteria for manufactured homes. Such criteria shall be designed to protect property values, to preserve the character and integrity of the community or individual neighborhoods within the community, and to promote the health, safety and welfare of area residents. The criteria shall be adopted by ordinance.

(e) In accordance with the ~~city's~~ local government's comprehensive plan and based on local housing needs, a ~~city~~ local government may designate a manufactured home overlay district within a residential district. Such overlay district may not consist of an individual lot or scattered lots, but shall consist of a defined area within which additional requirements or standards are placed upon manufactured homes.

(f) Nothing in this section shall be construed to preempt or supersede valid restrictive covenants running with the land. The terms "mobile home" and "trailer" in any valid restrictive covenants running with the land shall include the term "manufactured home" as defined in this section.

§ 160D-9-10. Modular homes. [160D-911]

Modular homes, as defined in G.S. 105-164.3(21b), shall comply with the design and construction standards set forth in G.S. 143-139.1.[443]

§ 160D-9-11. Outdoor advertising.[444] [160D-912]

(a) As used in this section, the term "off-premises outdoor advertising" includes off-premises outdoor advertising visible from the main-traveled way of any road.

440. This section has been relocated from G.S. 160A-382 and 153A-340(k).

441. This section has been relocated from G.S. 160A-383.1 and 153A-341.1.

442. This revision reflects the rule established in *Five C's, Inc. v. Pasquotank County*, 195 N.C. App. 410, 672 S.E.2d 737 (2009).

443. This cross-reference to the design standards for modular homes has been added for clarification and informational purposes.

444. This section has been relocated from G.S. 160A-199 and 153A-143.

(b) A ~~city~~ local government may require the removal of an off-premises outdoor advertising sign that is nonconforming under a local ordinance and may regulate the use of off-premises outdoor advertising within ~~the~~ its planning and development regulation jurisdiction ~~of the city~~ in accordance with the applicable provisions of this Chapter[445] and ~~in accordance with~~ subject to G.S. 136-131.1 and 136-131.2.[446]

(c) A ~~city~~ local government shall give written notice of its intent to require removal of off-premises outdoor advertising by sending a letter by certified mail to the last known address of the owner of the outdoor advertising and the owner of the property on which the outdoor advertising is located.

(d) No ~~city~~ local government may enact or amend an ordinance of general applicability to require the removal of any nonconforming, lawfully erected off-premises outdoor advertising sign without the payment of monetary compensation to the owners of the off-premises outdoor advertising, except as provided below. The payment of monetary compensation is not required if:

(1) The ~~city~~ local government and the owner of the nonconforming off-premises outdoor advertising enter into a relocation agreement pursuant to subsection (g) of this section.

(2) The ~~city~~ local government and the owner of the nonconforming off-premises outdoor advertising enter into an agreement pursuant to subsection (k) of this section.

(3) The off-premises outdoor advertising is determined to be a public nuisance or detrimental to the health or safety of the populace.

(4) The removal is required for opening, widening, extending or improving streets or sidewalks, or for establishing, extending, enlarging, or improving any of the public enterprises listed in G.S. 160A-311, and the ~~city~~ local government allows the off-premises outdoor advertising to be relocated to a comparable location.

(5) The off-premises outdoor advertising is subject to removal pursuant to statutes, ordinances, or regulations generally applicable to the demolition or removal of damaged structures.

This subsection shall be construed subject to and without any reduction in the rights afforded owners of outdoor advertising signs along interstate and federal aid primary highways in this State as provided in Article 13, Chapter 136.

(e) Monetary compensation is the fair market value of the off-premises outdoor advertising in place immediately prior to its removal and without consideration of the effect of the ordinance or any diminution in value caused by the ordinance requiring its removal. Monetary compensation shall be determined based on:

(1) The factors listed in G.S. 105-317.1(a); and

(2) The listed property tax value of the property and any documents regarding value submitted to the taxing authority.

(f) If the parties are unable to reach an agreement under subsection (e) of this section on monetary compensation to be paid by the ~~city~~ local government to the owner of the nonconforming off-premises outdoor advertising sign for its removal, and the ~~city~~ local government elects to proceed with the removal of the sign, the ~~city~~ local government may bring an action in superior court for a determination of the monetary compensation to be paid. In determining monetary compensation, the court shall consider the factors set forth in subsection (e) of this section. Upon payment of monetary compensation for the sign, the ~~city~~ local government shall own the sign.

(g) In lieu of paying monetary compensation, a ~~city~~ local government may enter into an agreement with the owner of a nonconforming off-premises outdoor advertising sign to relocate and reconstruct the sign. The agreement shall include the following:

---

445. These provisions on removal of nonconforming outdoor advertising were previously located within the general-police-power Articles of G.S. Chapters 153A and 160A. Relocation to Chapter 160D assures use of a process for adopting and amending ordinances that is consistent with the process for adopting and amending all development regulations. Note that the revision does not alter the substantive provisions of the statute.

446. Clarification. This revision adds cross-references to provisions in the Outdoor Advertising Control Act regarding local government authority to require the removal of signs and regulate sign modernization.

(1) Provision for relocation of the sign to a site reasonably comparable to or better than the existing location. In determining whether a location is comparable or better, the following factors shall be taken into consideration:

    a. The size and format of the sign.

    b. The characteristics of the proposed relocation site, including visibility, traffic count, area demographics, zoning, and any uncompensated differential in the sign owner's cost to lease the replacement site.

    c. The timing of the relocation.

(2) Provision for payment by the ~~city~~ <u>local government</u> of the reasonable costs of relocating and reconstructing the sign including:

    a. The actual cost of removing the sign.

    b. The actual cost of any necessary repairs to the real property for damages caused in the removal of the sign.

    c. The actual cost of installing the sign at the new location.

    d. An amount of money equivalent to the income received from the lease of the sign for a period of up to 30 days if income is lost during the relocation of the sign.

(h) For the purposes of relocating and reconstructing a nonconforming off-premises outdoor advertising sign pursuant to subsection (g) of this section, a ~~city~~ <u>local government</u>, consistent with the welfare and safety of the community as a whole, may adopt a resolution or adopt or modify its ordinances to provide for the issuance of a permit or other approval, including conditions as appropriate, or to provide for dimensional, spacing, setback, or use variances as it deems appropriate.

(i) If a ~~city~~ <u>local government</u> has offered to enter into an agreement to relocate a nonconforming off-premises outdoor advertising sign pursuant to subsection (g) of this section, and within 120 days after the initial notice by the ~~city~~ <u>local government</u> the parties have not been able to agree that the site or sites offered by the ~~city~~ <u>local government</u> for relocation of the sign are reasonably comparable to or better than the existing site, the parties shall enter into binding arbitration to resolve their disagreements. Unless a different method of arbitration is agreed upon by the parties, the arbitration shall be conducted by a panel of three arbitrators. Each party shall select one arbitrator and the two arbitrators chosen by the parties shall select the third member of the panel. The American Arbitration Association rules shall apply to the arbitration unless the parties agree otherwise.

(j) If the arbitration results in a determination that the site or sites offered by the ~~city~~ <u>local government</u> for relocation of the nonconforming sign are not comparable to or better than the existing site, and the ~~city~~ <u>local government</u> elects to proceed with the removal of the sign, the parties shall determine the monetary compensation under subsection (e) of this section to be paid to the owner of the sign. If the parties are unable to reach an agreement regarding monetary compensation within 30 days of the receipt of the arbitrators' determination, and the ~~city~~ <u>local government</u> elects to proceed with the removal of the sign, then the ~~city~~ <u>local government</u> may bring an action in superior court for a determination of the monetary compensation to be paid by the ~~city~~ <u>local government</u> to the owner for the removal of the sign. In determining monetary compensation, the court shall consider the factors set forth in subsection (e) of this section. Upon payment of monetary compensation for the sign, the ~~city~~ <u>local government</u> shall own the sign.

(k) Notwithstanding the provisions of this section, a ~~city~~ <u>local government</u> and an off-premises outdoor advertising sign owner may enter into a voluntary agreement allowing for the removal of the sign after a set period of time in lieu of monetary compensation. A ~~city~~ <u>local government</u> may adopt an ordinance or resolution providing for a relocation, reconstruction, or removal agreement.

(l) A ~~city~~ <u>local government</u> has up to three years from the effective date of an ordinance enacted under this section to pay monetary compensation to the owner of the off-premises outdoor advertising provided the affected property remains in place until the compensation is paid.

(m) This section does not apply to any ordinance in effect on July 1, 2004.[447] ~~the effective date of this section~~. A ~~city~~ <u>local government</u> may amend an ordinance in effect on July 1, 2004 ~~the effective date of this section~~ to extend application of the ordinance to off-premises outdoor advertising located in territory

---

447. Clarification, simplification. The effective date of this section was July 17, 2004.

acquired by annexation or located in the extraterritorial jurisdiction of the city. A ~~city~~ local government may repeal or amend an ordinance in effect on July 1, 2004 ~~the effective date of this section~~ so long as the amendment to the existing ordinance does not reduce the period of amortization in effect on the effective date of this section.[448]

(n) The provisions of this section shall not be used to interpret, construe, alter or otherwise modify the exercise of the power of eminent domain by an entity pursuant to Chapter 40A or Chapter 136 of the General Statutes.

(o) Nothing in this section shall limit a ~~city's~~ local government's authority to use amortization as a means of phasing out nonconforming uses other than off-premises outdoor advertising.

§ 160D-9-12. Public buildings.[449] ~~Part applicable to buildings constructed by State and its subdivisions; exception.~~ [160D-913]

All ~~of the provisions of this Part~~ local government zoning regulations are ~~hereby made~~ applicable to the erection, construction, and use of buildings by the State of North Carolina and its political subdivisions.

Notwithstanding the provisions of any general or local law or ordinance, except as provided in Article 9, Part 4 of this Chapter,[450] no land owned by the State of North Carolina may be included within an overlay district~~, or a special use or conditional use district,~~ or a conditional zoning district without approval of the Council of State or its delegee.[451]

§ 160D-9-13. Solar collectors.[452] [160D-914]

(a) Except as provided in subsection (c) of this section, no ~~city~~ local government ~~ordinance~~ development regulation shall prohibit, or have the effect of prohibiting, the installation of a solar collector that gathers solar radiation as a substitute for traditional energy for water heating, active space heating and cooling, passive heating, or generating electricity for a residential property, and no person shall be denied permission by a ~~city~~ local government to install a solar collector that gathers solar radiation as a substitute for traditional energy for water heating, active space heating and cooling, passive heating, or generating electricity for a residential property. As used in this section, the term "residential property" means property where the predominant use is for residential purposes.

(b) This section does not prohibit ~~an ordinance~~ a development regulation regulating the location or screening of solar collectors as described in subsection (a) of this section, provided the ~~ordinance~~ regulation does not have the effect of preventing the reasonable use of a solar collector for a residential property.

(c) This section does not prohibit ~~an ordinance~~ a development regulation that would prohibit the location of solar collectors as described in subsection (a) of this section that are visible by a person on the ground:

(1) On the facade of a structure that faces areas open to common or public access;
(2) On a roof surface that slopes downward toward the same areas open to common or public access that the facade of the structure faces; or
(3) Within the area set off by a line running across the facade of the structure extending to the property boundaries on either side of the facade, and those areas of common or public access faced by the structure.

(d) In any civil action arising under this section, the court may award costs and reasonable attorneys' fees to the prevailing party.

---

448. The law as codified will substitute "January 1, 2021" for "the effective date of this section."

449. This section has been relocated from G.S. 160A-392 and 153A-347.

450. This revision preserves a prior provision in G.S. 160A-400.9(f) regarding public buildings in historic districts.

451. This revision makes the terminology for references to districts consistent and allows the Council of State to delegate review and approval of these zoning decisions to staff in situations or categories deemed appropriate by the Council.

452. This section has been relocated from G.S. 160A-201 and 153A-144.

§ 160D-9-14. Temporary health care structures.[453] [160D-915]

   (a) The following definitions apply in this section:

   (1) Activities of daily living. – Bathing, dressing, personal hygiene, ambulation or locomotion, transferring, toileting, and eating.

   (2) Caregiver. – An individual 18 years of age or older who (i) provides care for a mentally or physically impaired person and (ii) is a first or second degree relative of the mentally or physically impaired person for whom the individual is caring.

   (3) First or second degree relative. – A spouse, lineal ascendant, lineal descendant, sibling, uncle, aunt, nephew, or niece and includes half, step, and in-law relationships.

   (4) Mentally or physically impaired person. – A person who is a resident of this State and who requires assistance with two or more activities of daily living as certified in writing by a physician licensed to practice in this State.

   (5) Temporary family health care structure. – A transportable residential structure, providing an environment facilitating a caregiver's provision of care for a mentally or physically impaired person, that (i) is primarily assembled at a location other than its site of installation, (ii) is limited to one occupant who shall be the mentally or physically impaired person, (iii) has no more than 300 gross square feet, and (iv) complies with applicable provisions of the State Building Code and G.S. 143-139.1(b). Placing the temporary family health care structure on a permanent foundation shall not be required or permitted.

   (b) A ~~city~~ local government shall consider a temporary family health care structure used by a caregiver in providing care for a mentally or physically impaired person on property owned or occupied by the caregiver as the caregiver's residence as a permitted accessory use in any single-family residential zoning district on lots zoned for single-family detached dwellings.

   (c) A ~~city~~ local government shall consider a temporary family health care structure used by an individual who is the named legal guardian of the mentally or physically impaired person a permitted accessory use in any single-family residential zoning district on lots zoned for single-family detached dwellings in accordance with this section if the temporary family health care structure is placed on the property of the residence of the individual and is used to provide care for the mentally or physically impaired person.

   (d) Only one temporary family health care structure shall be allowed on a lot or parcel of land. The temporary family health care structures under subsections (b) and (c) of this section shall not require a special use permit or be subjected to any other local zoning requirements beyond those imposed upon other authorized accessory use structures, except otherwise provided in this section. Such temporary family health care structures shall comply with all setback requirements that apply to the primary structure and with any maximum floor area ratio limitations that may apply to the primary structure.

   (e) Any person proposing to install a temporary family health care structure shall first obtain a permit from the ~~city~~ local government. The ~~city~~ local government may charge a fee of up to one hundred dollars ($100.00) for the initial permit and an annual renewal fee of up to fifty dollars ($50.00). The ~~city~~ local government may not withhold a permit if the applicant provides sufficient proof of compliance with this section. The ~~city~~ local government may require that the applicant provide evidence of compliance with this section on an annual basis as long as the temporary family health care structure remains on the property. The evidence may involve the inspection by the ~~city~~ local government of the temporary family health care structure at reasonable times convenient to the caregiver, not limited to any annual compliance confirmation, and annual renewal of the doctor's certification.

   (f) Notwithstanding subsection (i) of this section, any temporary family health care structure installed under this section may be required to connect to any water, sewer, and electric utilities serving the property and shall comply with all applicable State law, local ordinances, and other requirements, including ~~Part 5 of this Article~~ Article 11 of this Chapter, as if the temporary family health care structure were permanent real property.

---

453. This section has been relocated from G.S. 160A-383.5 and 153A-341.3.

(g) No signage advertising or otherwise promoting the existence of the temporary health care structure shall be permitted either on the exterior of the temporary family health care structure or elsewhere on the property.

(h) Any temporary family health care structure installed pursuant to this section shall be removed within 60 days in which the mentally or physically impaired person is no longer receiving or is no longer in need of the assistance provided for in this section. If the temporary family health care structure is needed for another mentally or physically impaired person, the temporary family health care structure may continue to be used, or may be reinstated on the property within 60 days of its removal, as applicable.

(i) The ~~city~~ local government may revoke the permit granted pursuant to subsection (e) of this section if the permit holder violates any provision of this section or G.S. 160A-202. The ~~city~~ local government may seek injunctive relief or other appropriate actions or proceedings to ensure compliance with this section or G.S. 160A-202.

(j) Temporary family health care structures shall be treated as tangible personal property for purposes of taxation.

§ 160D-9-15. ~~Designation of~~ Streets and transportation. [160D-916]

(a) *Street setbacks and curb cut regulations.*[454] Local governments may establish street setback and driveway connection regulations pursuant to G.S. 160A-306 and 160A-307 and as a part of development regulations adopted pursuant to this Chapter. If adopted pursuant to this Chapter, the regulations are also subject to the provisions of G.S. 160A-306 and 160A-307.

(b) *Transportation corridor official maps.*[455] Any ~~city~~ local government may establish official transportation corridor ~~official~~ maps and may enact and enforce ordinances pursuant to Article 2E of Chapter 136 of the General Statutes.

§ 160D-9-16. Bee hives.[456] [160D-906]

Restrictions on bee hives in local development regulations shall be consistent with the limitations of G.S. 106-645.

§ 160D-9-17 to 9-19. Reserved [160D-917 to 919]

---

454. This revision continues the current statutory scheme of (1) allowing street-setback regulations to be adopted pursuant to the specific provisions contained in Article 15 of G.S. Chapter 160A (which had previously been extended to counties by G.S. 153A-326) or (2) incorporating such regulations as part of the development regulations authorized by Chapter 160D. The revision clarifies that if setback regulations are incorporated into a development regulation, the provisions and limitations of the cited sections are still applicable.

455. This subsection has been relocated from G.S. 160A-458.4. It will be deleted in 2020, as authorization for these maps was repealed by S.L. 2019-35.

456. The statutory cross-reference in this subsection was created by S.L. 2015-246, § 8. It was added for clarification and informational purposes. When codified, the Revisor of Statutes will renumber this section to become G.S. 160D-906 in order to maintain the alphabetical order of particular uses listed in this Part.

Part 2. Environmental Regulations

§ 160D-9-20. Local environmental regulations.[457] [160D-920]

(a) Local governments are authorized to exercise the powers conferred by Article 8 of Chapter 160A and Article 6 of Chapter 153A to adopt and enforce local ordinances pursuant to this Part to the extent necessary to comply with state and federal law, rules and regulations, or permits consistent with the interpretations and directions of the state or federal agency issuing the permit.[458]

(b) Local environmental regulations adopted pursuant to this Part are not subject to the variance provisions of G.S. 160D-7-5 unless that is specifically authorized by the local ordinance.[459]

§ 160D-9-21. ~~Restriction of certain f~~ Forestry activities ~~prohibited~~.[460] [160D-921]

(a) The following definitions apply to this section:

(1) Development. - Any activity, including timber harvesting, that is associated with the conversion of forestland to nonforest use.

(2) Forest management plan. - A document that defines a landowner's forest management objectives and describes specific measures to be taken to achieve those objectives. A forest management plan shall include silvicultural practices that both ensure optimal forest productivity and environmental protection of land by either commercially growing timber through the establishment of forest stands or by ensuring the proper regeneration of forest stands to commercial levels of production after the harvest of timber.

(3) Forestland. - Land that is devoted to growing trees for the production of timber, wood, and other forest products.

(4) Forestry. - The professional practice embracing the science, business, and art of creating, conserving, and managing forests and forestland for the sustained use and enjoyment of their resources, materials, or other forest products.

(5) Forestry activity. - Any activity associated with the growing, managing, harvesting, and related transportation, reforestation, or protection of trees and timber, provided that such activities comply with existing State rules and regulations pertaining to forestry.

(b) A ~~city~~ local government shall not adopt or enforce any ordinance, rule, regulation, or resolution that regulates either:

(1) Forestry activity on forestland that is taxed on the basis of its present-use value as forestland under Article 12 of Chapter 105 of the General Statutes.

(2) Forestry activity that is conducted in accordance with a forest management plan that is prepared or approved by a forester registered in accordance with Chapter 89B of the General Statutes.

---

457. Environmental regulations previously included in Article 18 of G.S. Chapter 153A and Article 19 of Chapter 160A have been incorporated into this Part of Chapter 160D, as have other environmental regulations that require adoption of local development ordinances. Environmental regulations that only involve local administration of state regulatory programs, such as for Coastal Area Management Act minor development permits, are not incorporated and remain in their current statutory locations. The provision in G.S. 160D-9-1 stating that this Article of Chapter 160D does not expand, diminish, or alter the scope of authority granted in other articles is applicable to this part.

458. Some of the local regulations adopted under this Part of G.S. Chapter 160D are, in part, authorized and enforced under the powers granted in the general-police-power Articles of Chapters 160A and 153A; this cross-reference preserves that arrangement. Failure to explicitly cross-reference these authorities could lead to noncompliance with state and federal environmental requirements for local governments.

459. Allowing variances under the standards set out in G.S. 160D-7-5 would be contrary to state and federal regulatory requirements for some of these environmental programs.

460. This section has been relocated from G.S. 160A-458.5 and 153A-452.

(c) This section shall not be construed to limit, expand, or otherwise alter the authority of a ~~city~~ local government to:

(1) Regulate activity associated with development. A ~~city~~ local government may deny a building permit or refuse to approve a site or subdivision plan for either a period of up to:

    a. Three years after the completion of a timber harvest if the harvest results in the removal of all or substantially all of the trees that were protected under ~~city~~ local government regulations governing development from the tract of land for which the permit or approval is sought.

    b. Five years after the completion of a timber harvest if the harvest results in the removal of all or substantially all of the trees that were protected under ~~city~~ local government regulations governing development from the tract of land for which the permit or approval is sought and the harvest was a willful violation of the ~~city~~ local government regulations.

(2) Regulate trees pursuant to any local act of the General Assembly.

(3) Adopt ordinances that are necessary to comply with any federal or State law, regulation, or rule.

(4) Exercise its planning or zoning authority under this ~~Article~~ Chapter.

(5) Regulate and protect streets ~~under Article 15 of this Chapter.~~

§ 160D-9-22. Erosion and sedimentation control.[461] [160D-922]

Any ~~city~~ local government may enact and enforce erosion and sedimentation control regulations ~~ordinances~~ as authorized by Article 4 of Chapter 113A of the General Statutes and ~~in such enactment and enforcement~~ shall comply with all applicable provisions of ~~Article 4~~ that Article and ~~with Article 6 of this~~ to the extent not inconsistent with that Article, with this Chapter.

§ 160D-9-23. ~~Floodway~~ Floodplain regulations.[462] [160D-923]

Any local government ~~city~~ may enact and enforce ~~floodway~~ floodplain regulation or flood damage prevention regulations[463] ~~ordinances~~ as authorized by Part 6 of Article 21 of Chapter 143 of the General Statutes and ~~in such enactment and enforcement~~ shall comply with all applicable provisions of ~~Part 6~~ that Part and, to the extent not inconsistent with that Article, with this Chapter.

§ 160D-9-24. Mountain ridge protection.[464] [160D-924]

~~City~~ Any local government may enact and enforce a mountain ridge protection regulations ~~ordinances~~ pursuant to Article 14 of Chapter 113A of the General Statutes, and ~~in such enactment and enforcement~~ shall comply with all applicable provisions of ~~Article 14~~ that Article and to the extent not inconsistent with that Article, with this Chapter unless the ~~city~~ local government has removed itself from the coverage of Article 14 of Chapter 113A through the procedure provided by law.

§ 160D-9-25. Stormwater control.[465] [160D-925]

(a) A ~~city~~ local government may adopt and enforce a stormwater control regulation ~~ordinance~~ to protect water quality and control water quantity. A ~~city~~ local government may adopt a stormwater management regulation ~~ordinance~~ pursuant to this Chapter, its charter, other applicable laws, or any combination of these powers.

(b) A federal, State, or local government project shall comply with the requirements of a ~~city~~ local government stormwater control regulation ~~ordinance~~ unless the federal, State, or local government agency has a National Pollutant Discharge Elimination System (NPDES) stormwater permit that applies to the project. A ~~city~~ local government may take enforcement action to compel a State or local government agency to comply with a stormwater control regulation ~~ordinance~~ that implements the National Pollutant Discharge

---

461. This section has been relocated from G.S. 160A-458.
462. This section has been relocated from G.S. 160A-458.1.
463. This revision incorporates contemporary terminology.
464. This section has been relocated from G.S. 160A-458.2 and 153A-448.
465. This section has been relocated from G.S. 160A-459 and 153A-454.

Elimination System (NPDES) stormwater permit issued to the ~~city~~ local government. To the extent permitted by federal law, including Chapter 26 of Title 33 of the United States Code, a ~~city~~ local government may take enforcement action to compel a federal government agency to comply with a stormwater control regulation. ~~ordinance.~~

(c) A ~~city~~ local government may implement illicit discharge detection and elimination controls, construction site stormwater runoff controls, and post-construction runoff controls through an ordinance or other regulatory mechanism to the extent allowable under State law.

(d) A ~~city~~ local government that holds a National Pollutant Discharge Elimination System (NPDES) permit issued pursuant to G.S. 143-214.7 may adopt ~~an ordinance,~~ a regulation, applicable within its ~~corporate limits and~~ its planning and development regulation jurisdiction, to establish the stormwater control program necessary for the ~~city~~ local government to comply with the permit. A ~~city~~ local government may adopt ~~an ordinance~~ a regulation that bans illicit discharges within its ~~corporate limits and its~~ planning and development regulation jurisdiction. A ~~city~~ local government may adopt ~~an ordinance,~~ a regulation, applicable within its ~~corporate limits and its~~ planning and development regulation jurisdiction, that requires (i) deed restrictions and protective covenants to ensure that each project, including the stormwater management system, will be maintained so as to protect water quality and control water quantity and (ii) financial arrangements to ensure that adequate funds are available for the maintenance and replacement costs of the project.

(e) Unless the ~~city~~ local government requests the permit condition in its permit application, the Environmental Management Commission may not require as a condition of a National Pollutant Discharge Elimination System (NPDES) stormwater permit issued pursuant to G.S. 143-214.7 that a city implement the measure required by 40 Code of Federal Regulations § 122.34(b)(3)(1 July 2003 Edition) in its extraterritorial jurisdiction.

§ 160D-9-26. Water supply watershed management.[466] [160D-926]

Any local government may enact and enforce a water supply watershed management and protection regulation pursuant to G.S. 143-214.5 and shall comply with all applicable provisions of that statute and to the extent not inconsistent with that statute, with this Chapter.

§ 160D-9-27 to 9-29. Reserved. [160D-927 to 929]

Part 3. Wireless Telecommunication Facilities

§ 160D-9-30. Purpose and compliance with federal law.[467] [160D-930]

(a) The purpose of this section is to ensure the safe and efficient integration of facilities necessary for the provision of advanced mobile broadband and wireless telecommunications services throughout the community and to ensure the ready availability of reliable wireless service to the public, government agencies, and first responders, with the intention of furthering the public safety and general welfare.

(b) The deployment of wireless infrastructure is critical to ensuring first responders can provide for the health and safety of all residents of North Carolina and that, consistent with section 6409 of the ~~federal~~ Middle Class Tax Relief and Job Creation Act of 2012, 47 U.S.C. § 1455(a), ~~which creates~~ a national wireless emergency communications network for use by first responders that in large measure will be dependent on facilities placed on existing wireless communications support structures.[468] Therefore, it is the policy of this State to facilitate the placement of wireless communications support structures in all areas of North Carolina. The following standards shall apply to a ~~city's~~ local government's actions, as a regulatory body, in the regulation of the placement, construction, or modification of a wireless communications facility.

---

466. This revision cross-references the water-supply watershed management and protection programs mandated as cooperative state and local programs by G.S. 143-214.5.

467. This section has been relocated from G.S. 160A-400.50 and 153A-349.50. This Part of G.S. Chapter 160D was amended by S.L. 2017-159, and those amendments have been incorporated into this part. Statutory cross-references to G.S. 160A throughout this part have been updated to cross-reference Chapter 160D.

468. Stylistic edits have been made here for readability.

(c) The placement, construction, or modification of wireless communications facilities shall be in conformity with the Federal Communications Act, 47 U.S.C. § 332 as amended, section 6409 of the ~~federal~~ Middle Class Tax Relief and Job Creation Act of 2012, 47 U.S.C. § 1455(a), and in accordance with the rules promulgated by the Federal Communications Commission.

(d) This Part shall not be construed to authorize a city to require the construction or installation of wireless facilities or to regulate wireless services other than as set forth herein.[469]

§ 160D-9-31. Definitions.[470] [160D-931]

The following definitions apply in this Part.

(1) Antenna. - Communications equipment that transmits, receives, or transmits and receives electromagnetic radio signals used in the provision of all types of wireless communications services.

(2) Applicable codes. –The North Carolina State Building Code and any other uniform building, fire, electrical, plumbing, or mechanical codes adopted by a recognized national code organization together with State or local amendments to those codes enacted solely to address imminent threats of destruction of property or injury to persons.

(3) Application. - A request ~~that is~~ submitted by an applicant to the ~~city~~ local government for a permit to collocate wireless facilities or to approve the installation, modification, or replacement of a utility pole, city utility pole, or wireless support facility.

(4) Base station. - A station at a specific site authorized to communicate with mobile stations, generally consisting of radio receivers, antennas, coaxial cables, power supplies, and other associated electronics.

(5) Building permit. - An official administrative authorization issued by the ~~city~~ local government prior to beginning construction consistent with the provisions of G.S. 160D-11-10.

(6) City right-of-way. –A right-of-way owned, leased, or operated by a city, including any public street or alley that is not a part of the State highway system.

(7) City utility pole. –A pole owned by a city in the city right-of-way that provides lighting, traffic control, or a similar function.

(8) Collocation. - The placement, installation, maintenance, modification, operation, or replacement of wireless facilities on, under, within, or on the surface of the earth adjacent to existing structures, including utility poles, city utility poles, water towers, buildings, and other structures capable of structurally supporting the attachment of wireless facilities in compliance with applicable codes. The term 'collocation" does not include the installation of new utility poles, city utility poles, or wireless support structures.

(9) Communications facility. –The set of equipment and network components, including wires and cables and associated facilities used by a communications service provider to provide communications service.

(10) Communications service. –Cable service as defined in 47 U.S.C. § 522(6), information service as defined in 47 U.S.C. § 153(24), telecommunications service as defined in 47 U.S.C. § 153(53), or wireless services.

(11) Communications service provider. –A cable operator as defined in 47 U.S.C. § 522(5); a provider of information service, as defined in 47 U.S.C. § 153(24); a telecommunications carrier, as defined in 47 U.S.C. § 153(51); or a wireless provider.

(12) Eligible facilities request. - A request for modification of an existing wireless tower or base station that involves collocation of new transmission equipment or replacement of transmission equipment but does not include a substantial modification.

(13) Equipment compound. - An area surrounding or near the base of a wireless support structure within which a wireless facility is located.

469. This subsection was added by S.L. 2017-159.
470. This section has been relocated from G.S. 160A-400.51 and 153A-349.51. Additional definitions added by S.L. 2017-159 have been incorporated.

(14) Fall zone. - The area in which a wireless support structure may be expected to fall in the event of a structural failure, as measured by engineering standards.

(15) Land development regulation. - Any ordinance enacted pursuant to this ~~Part~~ Chapter.

(16) Micro wireless facility. –A small wireless facility that is no larger in dimension than 24 inches in length, 15 inches in width, and 12 inches in height and that has an exterior antenna, if any, no longer than 11 inches.

(17) Search ring. - The area within which a wireless support facility or wireless facility must be located in order to meet service objectives of the wireless service provider using the wireless facility or wireless support structure.

(18) Small wireless facility. –A wireless facility that meets both of the following qualifications:

a. Each antenna is located inside an enclosure of no more than six cubic feet in volume or, in the case of an antenna that has exposed elements, the antenna and all of its exposed elements, if enclosed, could fit within an enclosure of no more than six cubic feet.

b. All other wireless equipment associated with the facility has a cumulative volume of no more than 28 cubic feet. For purposes of this sub-subdivision, the following types of ancillary equipment are not included in the calculation of equipment volume: electric meters, concealment elements, telecommunications demarcation boxes, ground-based enclosures, grounding equipment, power transfer switches, cut-off switches, vertical cable runs for the connection of power and other services, or other support structures.

(19) Substantial modification. - The mounting of a proposed wireless facility on a wireless support structure that substantially changes the physical dimensions of the support structure. The burden is on the local government to demonstrate that a mounting that does not meet the listed criteria constitutes a substantial change to the physical dimensions of the wireless support structure. A mounting is presumed to be a substantial modification if it meets any one or more of the criteria listed below.

a. Increasing the existing vertical height of the structure by the greater of (i) more than ten percent (10%) or (ii) the height of one additional antenna array with separation from the nearest existing antenna not to exceed 20 feet.

b. Except where necessary to shelter the antenna from inclement weather or to connect the antenna to the tower via cable, adding an appurtenance to the body of a wireless support structure that protrudes horizontally from the edge of the wireless support structure the greater of (i) more than 20 feet or (ii) more than the width of the wireless support structure at the level of the appurtenance.

c. Increasing the square footage of the existing equipment compound by more than 2,500 square feet.

(20) Utility pole. - A structure that is designed for and used to carry lines, cables, wires, lighting facilities, or small wireless facilities for telephone, cable television, electricity, lighting, or wireless services.

(21) Water tower. - A water storage tank, a standpipe, or an elevated tank situated on a support structure originally constructed for use as a reservoir or facility to store or deliver water.

(22) Wireless facility. –Equipment at a fixed location that enables wireless communications between user equipment and a communications network, including (i) equipment associated with wireless communications and (ii) radio transceivers, antennas, wires, coaxial or fiber-optic cable, regular and backup power supplies, and comparable equipment, regardless of technological configuration. The term includes small wireless facilities. The term shall not include any of the following:

a. The structure or improvements on, under, within, or adjacent to which the equipment is collocated.

b. Wireline backhaul facilities.

c. Coaxial or fiber-optic cable that is between wireless structures or utility poles or city utility poles or that is otherwise not immediately adjacent to or directly associated with a particular antenna.

(23) Wireless infrastructure provider. –Any person with a certificate to provide telecommunications service in the State who builds or installs wireless communication transmission equipment, wireless facilities, or wireless support structures for small wireless facilities but that does not provide wireless services.

(24) Wireless provider. –A wireless infrastructure provider or a wireless services provider.

(25) Wireless services. –Any services, using licensed or unlicensed wireless spectrum, including the use of Wi-Fi, whether at a fixed location or mobile, provided to the public using wireless facilities.

(26) Wireless services provider.[471] –A person who provides wireless services.

(27) Wireless support structure. - A new or existing structure, such as a monopole, lattice tower, or guyed tower that is designed to support or capable of supporting wireless facilities. A utility pole or a city utility pole is not a wireless support structure.

§ 160D-9-32. Local authority.[472] [160D-932]

A ~~city~~ local government may plan for and regulate the siting or modification of wireless support structures and wireless facilities in accordance with land development regulations and in conformity with this Part. Except as expressly stated, nothing in this Part shall limit a ~~city~~ local government from regulating applications to construct, modify, or maintain wireless support structures, or construct, modify, maintain, or collocate wireless facilities on a wireless support structure based on consideration of land use, public safety, and zoning considerations, including aesthetics, landscaping, structural design, setbacks, and fall zones, or State and local building code requirements, consistent with the provisions of federal law provided in G.S. 160D-9-30. For purposes of this Part, public safety includes, without limitation, federal, State, and local safety regulations but does not include requirements relating to radio frequency emissions of wireless facilities.

§ 160D-9-33. Construction of new wireless support structures or substantial modifications of wireless support structures.[473] [160D-933]

~~(a) Repealed.~~

(a) Any person that proposes to construct a new wireless support structure or substantially modify a wireless support structure within the planning and ~~land-use~~ development regulation jurisdiction of a ~~city~~ local government must do both of the following:

        (1) Submit a completed application with the necessary copies and attachments to the appropriate planning authority.

        (2) Comply with any local ordinances concerning land use and any applicable permitting processes.

(b) A ~~city's~~ local government's review of an application for the placement or construction of a new wireless support structure or substantial modification of a wireless support structure shall only address public safety, land development, or zoning issues. In reviewing an application, the ~~city~~ local government may not require information on or evaluate an applicant's business decisions about its designed service, customer demand for its service, or quality of its service to or from a particular area or site. A ~~city~~ local government may not require information that concerns the specific need for the wireless support structure, including if the service to be provided from the wireless support structure is to add additional wireless coverage or additional wireless capacity. A ~~city~~ local government may not require proprietary, confidential, or other business information to justify the need for the new wireless support structure, including propagation maps and telecommunication traffic studies. In reviewing an application, the ~~city~~ local government may review the following:

---

471. This definition was deleted from the bill as introduced as superfluous. It was reinserted by House committee substitute to conform to existing law. The numbering of the provisions was clarified when the bill was codified.

472. This section has been relocated from G.S. 160A-400.51A and 153A-349.51A.

473. This section has been relocated from G.S. 160A-400.52 and 153A-349.52.

(1) Applicable public safety, land use, or zoning issues addressed in its adopted regulations, including aesthetics, landscaping, land-use based location priorities, structural design, setbacks, and fall zones.

(2) Information or materials directly related to an identified public safety, land development, or zoning issue including evidence that no existing or previously approved wireless support structure can reasonably be used for the wireless facility placement instead of the construction of a new wireless support structure; that residential, historic, and designated scenic areas cannot be served from outside the area; or that the proposed height of a new wireless support structure or initial wireless facility placement or a proposed height increase of a substantially modified wireless support structure, or replacement wireless support structure is necessary to provide the applicant's designed service.

(3) A ~~city~~ local government may require applicants for new wireless facilities to evaluate the reasonable feasibility of collocating new antennas and equipment on an existing wireless support structure or structures within the applicant's search ring. Collocation on an existing wireless support structure is not reasonably feasible if collocation is technically or commercially impractical or the owner of the existing wireless support structure is unwilling to enter into a contract for such use at fair market value. ~~Cities~~ Local governments may require information necessary to determine whether collocation on existing wireless support structures is reasonably feasible.

~~(d) Repealed.~~

(c) The ~~city~~ local government shall issue a written decision approving or denying an application under this section within a reasonable period of time consistent with the issuance of other ~~land-use permits~~ development approvals in the case of other applications, each as measured from the time the application is deemed complete.

(d) A ~~city~~ local government may fix and charge an application fee, consulting fee, or other fee associated with the submission, review, processing, and approval of an application to site new wireless support structures or to substantially modify wireless support structures or wireless facilities that is based on the costs of the services provided and does not exceed what is usual and customary for such services. Any charges or fees assessed by a ~~city~~ local government on account of an outside consultant shall be fixed in advance and incorporated into a permit or application fee and shall be based on the reasonable costs to be incurred by the ~~city~~ local government in connection with the regulatory review authorized under this section. The foregoing does not prohibit a ~~city~~ local government from imposing additional reasonable and cost-based fees for costs incurred should an applicant amend its application. On request, the amount of the consultant charges incorporated into the permit or application fee shall be separately identified and disclosed to the applicant. The fee imposed by a ~~city~~ local government for review of the application may not be used for either of the following:

(1) Travel time or expenses, meals, or overnight accommodations incurred in the review of an application by a consultant or other third party.

(2) Reimbursements for a consultant or other third party based on a contingent fee basis or a results-based arrangement.

(e) The ~~city~~ local government may condition approval of an application for a new wireless support structure on the provision of documentation prior to the issuance of a building permit establishing the existence of one or more parties, including the owner of the wireless support structure, who intend to locate wireless facilities on the wireless support structure. A ~~city~~ local government shall not deny an initial ~~land-use or zoning permit~~ development approval based on such documentation. A ~~city~~ local government may condition a ~~permit~~ development approval on a requirement to construct facilities within a reasonable period of time, which shall be no less than 24 months.

(f) The ~~city~~ local government may not require the placement of wireless support structures or wireless facilities on ~~city~~ local government owned or leased property, but may develop a process to encourage the placement of wireless support structures or facilities on ~~city~~ local government owned or leased property, including an expedited approval process.

(g) This section shall not be construed to limit the provisions or requirements of any historic district or landmark regulation adopted pursuant to ~~Part 3C of~~ this Article.

§ 160D-9-34. Collocation and eligible facilities requests of wireless support structures.[474] [160D-934]

(a) Pursuant to section 6409 of the ~~federal~~ Middle Class Tax Relief and Job Creation Act of 2012, 47 U.S.C. § 1455(a), a ~~city~~ local government may not deny and shall approve any eligible facilities request as provided in this section. Nothing in this Part requires an application and approval for routine maintenance or limits the performance of routine maintenance on wireless support structures and facilities, including in-kind replacement of wireless facilities. Routine maintenance includes activities associated with regular and general upkeep of transmission equipment, including the replacement of existing wireless facilities with facilities of the same size. A ~~city~~ local government may require an application for collocation or an eligible facilities request.

(b) A collocation or eligible facilities request application is deemed complete unless the ~~city~~ local government provides notice that the application is incomplete in writing to the applicant within 45 days of submission or within some other mutually agreed upon time frame. The notice shall identify the deficiencies in the application which, if cured, would make the application complete. A ~~city~~ local government may deem an application incomplete if there is insufficient evidence provided to show that the proposed collocation or eligible facilities request will comply with federal, State, and local safety requirements. A ~~city~~ local government may not deem an application incomplete for any issue not directly related to the actual content of the application and subject matter of the collocation or eligible facilities request. An application is deemed complete on resubmission if the additional materials cure the deficiencies indicated.

(c) The ~~city~~ local government shall issue a written decision approving an eligible facilities request application within 45 days of such application being deemed complete. For a collocation application that is not an eligible facilities request, the ~~city~~ local government shall issue its written decision to approve or deny the application within 45 days of the application being deemed complete.

(d) A ~~city~~ local government may impose a fee not to exceed one thousand dollars ($1,000) for technical consultation and the review of a collocation or eligible facilities request application. The fee must be based on the actual, direct, and reasonable administrative costs incurred for the review, processing, and approval of a collocation application. A ~~city~~ local government may engage a third-party consultant for technical consultation and the review of a collocation application. The fee imposed by a ~~city~~ local government for the review of the application may not be used for either of the following:

(1) Travel expenses incurred in a third-party's review of a collocation application.

(2) Reimbursement for a consultant or other third party based on a contingent fee basis or results-based arrangement.

~~(b), (c) Repealed.~~

§ 160D-9-35. Collocation of small wireless facilities.[475] [160D-935]

(a) Except as expressly provided in this Part, a city shall not prohibit, regulate, or charge for the collocation of small wireless facilities.

(b) A city may not establish a moratorium on (i) filing, receiving, or processing applications or (ii) issuing permits or any other approvals for the collocation of small wireless facilities.

(c) Small wireless facilities that meet the height requirements of G.S. 160D-9-36(b)(2) shall only be subject to administrative review and approval under subsection (d) of this section if they are collocated (i) in a city right-of-way within any zoning district or (ii) outside of city rights-of-way on property other than single-family residential property.

(d) A city may require an applicant to obtain a permit to collocate a small wireless facility. A city shall receive applications for, process, and issue such permits subject to the following requirements:

(1) A city may not, directly or indirectly, require an applicant to perform services unrelated to the collocation for which approval is sought. For purposes of this subdivision, "services unrelated to the collocation," includes in-kind contributions to the city such as the reservation of fiber, conduit, or pole space for the city.

---

474. This section has been relocated from G.S. 160A-400.53 and 153A-349.53.
475. This section has been relocated from G.S. 160A-400.54, created by S.L. 2017-159.

(2) The wireless provider completes an application as specified in form and content by the city. A wireless provider shall not be required to provide more information to obtain a permit than communications service providers that are not wireless providers.

(3) A permit application shall be deemed complete unless the city provides notice otherwise in writing to the applicant within 30 days of submission or within some other mutually agreed upon time frame. The notice shall identify the deficiencies in the application which, if cured, would make the application complete. The application shall be deemed complete on resubmission if the additional materials cure the deficiencies identified.

(4) The permit application shall be processed on a nondiscriminatory basis and shall be deemed approved if the city fails to approve or deny the application within 45 days from the time the application is deemed complete or a mutually agreed upon time frame between the city and the applicant.

(5) A city may deny an application only on the basis that it does not meet any of the following: (i) the city's applicable codes; (ii) local code provisions or regulations that concern public safety, objective design standards for decorative utility poles, city utility poles, or reasonable and nondiscriminatory stealth and concealment requirements, including screening or landscaping for ground-mounted equipment; (iii) public safety and reasonable spacing requirements concerning the location of ground-mounted equipment in a right-of-way; or (iv) the historic preservation requirements in subsection 160D-9-36(i). The city must (i) document the basis for a denial, including the specific code provisions on which the denial was based and (ii) send the documentation to the applicant on or before the day the city denies an application. The applicant may cure the deficiencies identified by the city and resubmit the application within 30 days of the denial without paying an additional application fee. The city shall approve or deny the revised application within 30 days of the date on which the application was resubmitted. Any subsequent review shall be limited to the deficiencies cited in the prior denial.

(6) An application must include an attestation that the small wireless facilities shall be collocated on the utility pole, city utility pole, or wireless support structure and that the small wireless facilities shall be activated for use by a wireless services provider to provide service no later than one year from the permit issuance date, unless the city and the wireless provider agree to extend this period or a delay is caused by a lack of commercial power at the site.

(7) An applicant seeking to collocate small wireless facilities at multiple locations within the jurisdiction of a city shall be allowed at the applicant's discretion to file a consolidated application for no more than 25 separate facilities and receive a permit for the collocation of all the small wireless facilities meeting the requirements of this section. A city may remove small wireless facility collocations from a consolidated application and treat separately small wireless facility collocations (i) for which incomplete information has been provided or (ii) that are denied. The city may issue a separate permit for each collocation that is approved.

(8) The permit may specify that collocation of the small wireless facility shall commence within six months of approval and shall be activated for use no later than one year from the permit issuance date, unless the city and the wireless provider agree to extend this period or a delay is caused by a lack of commercial power at the site.

(e) Subject to the limitations provided in G.S. 160A-296(a)(6),[476] a city may charge an application fee that shall not exceed the lesser of (i) the actual, direct, and reasonable costs to process and review applications for collocated small wireless facilities; (ii) the amount charged by the city for permitting of any similar activity; or (iii) one hundred dollars ($100.00) per facility for the first five small wireless facilities addressed in an application, plus fifty dollars ($50.00) for each additional small wireless facility addressed in the application. In any dispute concerning the appropriateness of a fee, the city has the burden of proving that the fee meets the requirements of this subsection.

---

476. The referenced limiting phrase was added by S.L. 2018-145. The phrase was inadvertently omitted from the bill as introduced; it was added by House committee substitute.

(f) Subject to the limitations provided in G.S. 160A-296(a)(6),[477] a city may impose a technical consulting fee for each application, not to exceed five hundred dollars ($500.00), to offset the cost of reviewing and processing applications required by this section. The fee must be based on the actual, direct, and reasonable administrative costs incurred for the review, processing, and approval of an application. A city may engage an outside consultant for technical consultation and the review of an application. The fee imposed by a city for the review of the application shall not be used for either of the following:

(1) Travel expenses incurred in the review of a collocation application by an outside consultant or other third party.

(2) Direct payment or reimbursement for an outside consultant or other third party based on a contingent fee basis or results-based arrangement.

In any dispute concerning the appropriateness of a fee, the city has the burden of proving that the fee meets the requirements of this subsection.

(g) A city may require a wireless services provider to remove an abandoned wireless facility within 180 days of abandonment. Should the wireless services provider fail to timely remove the abandoned wireless facility, the city may cause such wireless facility to be removed and may recover the actual cost of such removal, including legal fees, if any, from the wireless services provider. For purposes of this subsection, a wireless facility shall be deemed abandoned at the earlier of the date that the wireless services provider indicates that it is abandoning such facility or the date that is 180 days after the date that such wireless facility ceases to transmit a signal, unless the wireless services provider gives the city reasonable evidence that it is diligently working to place such wireless facility back in service.

(h) A city shall not require an application or permit or charge fees for (i) routine maintenance; (ii) the replacement of small wireless facilities with small wireless facilities that are the same size or smaller; or (iii) installation, placement, maintenance, or replacement of micro wireless facilities that are suspended on cables strung between existing utility poles or city utility poles in compliance with applicable codes by or for a communications service provider authorized to occupy the city rights-of-way and who is remitting taxes under G.S. 105-164.4(a)(4c) or G.S. 105-164.4(a)(6).

(i) Nothing in this section shall prevent a city from requiring a work permit for work that involves excavation, affects traffic patterns, or obstructs vehicular traffic in the city right-of-way.

§ 160D-9-36. Use of public right-of-way.[478] [160D-936]

(a) A city shall not enter into an exclusive arrangement with any person for use of city rights-of-way for the construction, operation, marketing, or maintenance of wireless facilities or wireless support structures or the collocation of small wireless facilities.

(b) Subject to the requirements of G.S. 160D-9-35, a wireless provider may collocate small wireless facilities along, across, upon, or under any city right-of-way. Subject to the requirements of this section, a wireless provider may place, maintain, modify, operate, or replace associated utility poles, city utility poles, conduit, cable, or related appurtenances and facilities along, across, upon, and under any city right-of-way. The placement, maintenance, modification, operation, or replacement of utility poles and city utility poles associated with the collocation of small wireless facilities, along, across, upon, or under any city right-of-way shall be subject only to review or approval under G.S. 160D-9-35(d) if the wireless provider meets all the following requirements:

(1) Each new utility pole and each modified or replacement utility pole or city utility pole installed in the right-of-way shall not exceed 50 feet above ground level.

(2) Each new small wireless facility in the right-of-way shall not extend more than 10 feet above the utility pole, city utility pole, or wireless support structure on which it is collocated.

(c) Nothing in this section shall be construed to prohibit a city from allowing utility poles, city utility poles, or wireless facilities that exceed the limits set forth in subdivision (1) of subsection (b) of this section.

---

477. The referenced limiting phrase was added by S.L. 2018-145. The phrase was inadvertently omitted from the bill as introduced; it was added by House committee substitute.

478. This section has been relocated from G.S. 160A-400.55, created by S.L. 2017-159.

(d) Applicants for use of a city right-of-way shall comply with a city's undergrounding requirements prohibiting the installation of above-ground structures in the city rights-of-way without prior zoning approval, if those requirements (i) are nondiscriminatory with respect to type of utility, (ii) do not prohibit the replacement of structures existing at the time of adoption of the requirements, and (iii) have a waiver process.

(d1) Notwithstanding subsection (d) of this section, in no instance in an area zoned single-family residential where the existing utilities are installed underground may a utility pole, city utility pole, or wireless support structure exceed forty (40) feet above ground level, unless the city grants a waiver or variance approving a taller utility pole, city utility pole, or wireless support structure.

(e) Except as provided in this part, a city may assess a right-of-way charge under this section for use or occupation of the right-of-way by a wireless provider, subject to the restrictions set forth under G.S. 160A-296(a)(6). In addition, charges authorized by this section shall meet all of the following requirements:

(1) The right-of-way charge shall not exceed the direct and actual cost of managing the city rights-of-way and shall not be based on the wireless provider's revenue or customer counts.

(2) The right-of-way charge shall not exceed that imposed on other users of the right-of-way, including publicly, cooperatively, or municipally owned utilities.

(3) The right-of-way charge shall be reasonable and nondiscriminatory.

Nothing in this subsection is intended to establish or otherwise affect rates charged for attachments to utility poles, city utility poles, or wireless support structures. At its discretion, a city may provide free access to city rights-of-way on a nondiscriminatory basis in order to facilitate the public benefits of the deployment of wireless services.

(f)Nothing in this section is intended to authorize a person to place, maintain, modify, operate, or replace a privately owned utility pole or wireless support structure or to collocate small wireless facilities on a privately owned utility pole, a privately owned wireless support structure, or other private property without the consent of the property owner.

(g) A city may require a wireless provider to repair all damage to a city right-of-way directly caused by the activities of the wireless provider, while occupying, installing, repairing, or maintaining wireless facilities, wireless support structures, city utility poles, or utility poles and to return the right-of-way to its functional equivalence before the damage. If the wireless provider fails to make the repairs required by the city within a reasonable time after written notice, the city may undertake those repairs and charge the applicable party the reasonable and documented cost of the repairs. The city may maintain an action to recover the costs of the repairs.

(h)This section shall not be construed to limit local government authority to enforce historic preservation zoning regulations consistent with Part 4 of Article 9 of this Chapter, the preservation of local zoning authority under 47 U.S.C. § 332(c)(7), the requirements for facility modifications under 47 U.S.C. § 1455(a), or the National Historic Preservation Act of 1966, 54 U.S.C. § 300101, et seq., as amended, and the regulations, local acts, and city charter provisions adopted to implement those laws.

(i) A wireless provider may apply to a city to place utility poles in the city rights-of-way, or to replace or modify utility poles or city utility poles in the public rights-of- way, to support the collocation of small wireless facilities. A city shall accept and process the application in accordance with the provisions of G.S. 160D-9-35(d), applicable codes, and other local codes governing the placement of utility poles or city utility poles in the city rights-of-way, including provisions or regulations that concern public safety, objective design standards for decorative utility poles or city utility poles, or reasonable and nondiscriminatory stealth and concealment requirements, including those relating to screening or landscaping, or public safety and reasonable spacing requirements. The application may be submitted in conjunction with the associated small wireless facility application.

§ 160A-9-37. Access to city utility poles to install small wireless facilities.[479] [160D-937]

(a) A city may not enter into an exclusive arrangement with any person for the right to collocate small wireless facilities on city utility poles. A city shall allow any wireless provider to collocate small wireless facilities on its city utility poles at just, reasonable, and nondiscriminatory rates, terms, and conditions,

---

479. This section has been relocated from G.S. 160A-400.56, created by S.L. 2017-159.

but in no instance may the rate exceed fifty dollars ($50.00) per city utility pole per year. The North Carolina Utilities Commission shall not consider this subsection as evidence in a proceeding initiated pursuant to G.S. 62-350(c).

(b) A request to collocate under this section may be denied only if there is insufficient capacity or for reasons of safety, reliability, and generally applicable engineering principles, and those limitations cannot be remedied by rearranging, expanding, or otherwise reengineering the facilities at the reasonable and actual cost of the city to be reimbursed by the wireless provider. In granting a request under this section, a city shall require the requesting entity to comply with applicable safety requirements, including the National Electrical Safety Code and the applicable rules and regulations issued by the Occupational Safety and Health Administration.

(c) If a city that operates a public enterprise as permitted by Article 16 of Chapter 160A has an existing city utility pole attachment rate, fee, or other term with an entity, then, subject to termination provisions, that attachment rate, fee, or other term shall apply to collocations by that entity or its related entities on city utility poles.

(d) Following receipt of the first request from a wireless provider to collocate on a city utility pole, a city shall, within 60 days, establish the rates, terms, and conditions for the use of or attachment to the city utility poles that it owns or controls. Upon request, a party shall state in writing its objections to any proposed rate, terms, and conditions of the other party.

(e) In any controversy concerning the appropriateness of a rate for a collocation attachment to a city utility pole, the city has the burden of proving that the rates are reasonably related to the actual, direct, and reasonable costs incurred for use of space on the pole for such period.

(f) The city shall provide a good-faith estimate for any make-ready work necessary to enable the city utility pole to support the requested collocation, including pole replacement if necessary, within 60 days after receipt of a complete application. Make-ready work, including any pole replacement, shall be completed within 60 days of written acceptance of the good-faith estimate by the applicant. For purposes of this section, the term "make-ready work" means any modification or replacement of a city utility pole necessary for the city utility pole to support a small wireless facility in compliance with applicable safety requirements, including the National Electrical Safety Code, that is performed in preparation for a collocation installation.

(g) The city shall not require more make-ready work than that required to meet applicable codes or industry standards. Fees for make-ready work shall not include costs related to preexisting or prior damage or noncompliance. Fees for make-ready work, including any pole replacement, shall not exceed actual costs or the amount charged to other communications service providers for similar work and shall not include any consultant fees or expenses.

(h) Nothing in this Part shall be construed to apply to an entity whose poles, ducts, and conduits are subject to regulation under section 224 of the Communications Act of 1934, 47 U.S.C. § 151, et seq., as amended, or under G.S. 62-350.

(i) This section shall not apply to an excluded entity. Nothing in this section shall be construed to affect the authority of an excluded entity to deny, limit, restrict, or determine the rates, fees, terms, and conditions for the use of or attachment to its utility poles, city utility poles, or wireless support structures by a wireless provider. This section shall not be construed to alter or affect the provisions of G.S. 62-350, and the rates, terms, or conditions for the use of poles, ducts, or conduits by communications service providers, as defined in G.S. 62-350, are governed solely by G.S. 62-350. For purposes of this section, "excluded entity" means (i) a city that owns or operates a public enterprise pursuant to Article 16 of Chapter 160A consisting of an electric power generation, transmission, or distribution system or (ii) an electric membership corporation organized under Chapter 117 of the General Statutes that owns or controls poles, ducts, or conduits, but which is exempt from regulation under section 224 of the Communications Act of 1934, 47 U.S.C. § 151 et seq., as amended.

§ 160D-9-38. Applicability.[480] [160D-938]

(a) A city shall not adopt or enforce any ordinance, rule, regulation, or resolution that regulates the design, engineering, construction, installation, or operation of any small wireless facility located in an interior structure or upon the site of any stadium or athletic facility. This subsection does not apply to a stadium or athletic facility owned or otherwise controlled by the city. This subsection does not prohibit the enforcement of applicable codes.

(b) Nothing contained in this Part shall amend, modify, or otherwise affect any easement between private parties. Any and all rights for the use of a right-of-way are subject to the rights granted pursuant to an easement between private parties.

(c) Except as provided in this Part or otherwise specifically authorized by the General Statutes, a city may not adopt or enforce any regulation on the placement or operation of communications facilities in the rights-of-way of State-maintained highways or city rights-of-way by a provider authorized by State law to operate in the rights-of-way of State-maintained highways or city rights-of-way and may not regulate any communications services.

(d) Except as provided in this Part or specifically authorized by the General Statutes, a city may not impose or collect any tax, fee, or charge to provide a communications service over a communications facility in the right-of-way.

(e) The approval of the installation, placement, maintenance, or operation of a small wireless facility pursuant to this Part does not authorize the provision of any communications services or the installation, placement, maintenance, or operation of any communications facility, including a wireline backhaul facility, other than a small wireless facility, in the right-of-way.

§ 160D-9-39. Reserved. [160D-939]

Part 4. Historic Preservation

§ 160D-9-40. Legislative findings.[481] [160D-940]

The ~~historical~~ heritage of our State is one of our most valued and important assets. The conservation and preservation of historic districts and landmarks stabilize and increase property values ~~in their areas~~ and strengthen the overall economy of the State.[482] This Part authorizes ~~cities and counties~~ local governments ~~of the State~~ within their respective ~~zoning~~ planning and development regulation jurisdictions and by means of listing, regulation, and acquisition:

(1) To safeguard the heritage of the city or county by preserving any district or landmark therein that embodies important elements of its culture, history, architectural history, or prehistory; and

(2) To promote the use and conservation of such district or landmark for the education, pleasure and enrichment of the residents of the city or county and the State as a whole.

~~§ 160A-400.2. Exercise of powers by counties as well as cities.~~[483]

~~The term "municipality" or "municipal" as used in G.S. 160A-400.1 through 160A-400.14 shall be deemed to include the governing board or legislative board of a county, to the end that counties may exercise the same powers as cities with respect to the establishment of historic districts and designation of landmarks.~~

---

480. This section has been relocated from G.S. 160A-400.57, created by S.L. 2017-159.

481. This section has been relocated from G.S. 160A-400.1. The entire statutory Part in which G.S. 160A-400.1 is located is also applicable to counties pursuant to G.S. 160A-400.2.

482. This revision was made to streamline and simplify language.

483. This section was deleted as unnecessary, given the merger of city and county provisions in G.S. Chapter 160D.

§ 160D-9-41. Historic Preservation Commission.[484] [160D-941]

Before it may designate one or more landmarks or historic districts, a ~~municipality~~ <u>local government</u> shall establish or designate a historic preservation commission <u>in accordance with G.S. 160D-3-3.</u>[485] ~~The municipal governing board shall determine the number of the members of the commission, which shall be at least three, and the length of their terms, which shall be no greater than four years. A majority of the members of such a commission shall have demonstrated special interest, experience, or education in history, architecture, archaeology, or related fields. All the members shall reside within the territorial jurisdiction of the municipality as established pursuant to G.S. 160A-360. The commission may appoint advisory bodies and committees as appropriate.~~

~~In lieu of establishing a historic preservation commission, a municipality may designate as its historic preservation commission, (i) a separate historic districts commission or a separate historic landmarks commission established pursuant to this Part to deal only with historic districts or landmarks respectively, (ii) a planning board established pursuant to this Article, or (iii) a community appearance commission established pursuant to Part 7 of this Article. In order for a commission or board other than the preservation commission to be designated, at least three of its members shall have demonstrated special interest, experience, or education in history, architecture, or related fields. At the discretion of the municipality the ordinance may also provide that the preservation commission may exercise within a historic district any or all of the powers of a planning board or a community appearance commission.~~

~~A county and one or more cities in the county may establish or designate a joint preservation commission. If a joint commission is established or designated, the county and cities involved shall determine the residence requirements of members of the joint preservation commission.~~

§ 160D-9-42. Powers of the Historic Preservation Commission.[486] [160D-942]

A preservation commission established pursuant to this ~~Part~~ <u>Chapter</u> may, within the ~~zoning~~ <u>planning and development regulation</u> jurisdiction of the ~~municipality~~ <u>local government</u>:

(1) Undertake an inventory of properties of historical, prehistorical, architectural, and/or cultural significance;

(2) Recommend to the ~~municipal~~ governing board areas to be designated by ordinance as "Historic Districts"; and individual structures, buildings, sites, areas, or objects to be designated by ordinance as "Landmarks";

(3) Acquire by any lawful means the fee or any lesser included interest, including options to purchase, to properties within established districts or to any such properties designated as landmarks; to hold, manage, preserve, restore and improve ~~the same~~ <u>such properties</u>, and to exchange or dispose of the property by public or private sale, lease or otherwise, subject to covenants or other legally binding restrictions ~~which~~ <u>that</u> will secure appropriate rights of public access and promote the preservation of the property;

(4) Restore, preserve and operate historic properties;

(5) Recommend to the governing board that designation of any area as a historic district or part thereof, or designation of any building, structure, site, area, or object as a landmark, be revoked or removed for cause;

(6) Conduct an educational program ~~with respect to~~ <u>regarding</u> historic properties and districts within its jurisdiction;

(7) Cooperate with the State, federal, and local governments in pursuance of the purposes of this Part. The governing board or the commission when authorized by the governing board may contract with the State, or the United States of America, or any agency of either, or with any other organization provided the terms are not inconsistent with State or federal law;

(8) Enter, solely in performance of its official duties and only at reasonable times, upon private lands for examination or survey thereof. However, no member, employee or agent of the commission

---

484. This section has been relocated from G.S. 160A-400.7.
485. The remainder of this section has been relocated to G.S. 160D-3-4.
486. This section has been relocated from G.S. 160A-400.8.

may enter any private building or structure without the express consent of the owner or occupant thereof;

(9) Prepare and recommend the official adoption of a preservation element as part of the ~~municipality's~~ local government's comprehensive plan;

(10) Review and act upon proposals for alterations, demolitions, or new construction within historic districts, or for the alteration or demolition of designated landmarks, pursuant to this Part; and

(11) Negotiate at any time with the owner of a building, structure, site, area, or object for its acquisition or its preservation, when such action is reasonably necessary or appropriate.

~~§ 160A-400.3. Character of historic district defined.~~[487]

~~Historic districts established pursuant to this Part shall consist of areas which are deemed to be of special significance in terms of their history, prehistory, architecture, and/or culture, and to possess integrity of design, setting, materials, feeling, and association.~~

§ 160D-9-43. Appropriations.[488] [160D-943]

A ~~city or county~~ governing board is authorized to make appropriations to a historic preservation commission established pursuant to this ~~Part~~ Chapter in any amount ~~that it may~~ determine necessary for the expenses of the operation of the commission, and may make available any additional amounts necessary for the acquisition, restoration, preservation, operation, and management of historic buildings, structures, sites, areas or objects designated as historic landmarks or within designated historic districts, or of land on which such buildings or structures are located, or to which they may be removed.

§ 160D-9-44. Designation of historic districts.[489] [160D-944]

(a) Any ~~municipal governing board~~ local government may, as part of a zoning ~~ordinance~~ regulation adopted pursuant to Article 7 or as a ~~or other ordinance~~ development regulation enacted or amended pursuant to ~~this~~ Article 6, designate and from time to time amend one or more historic districts within the area subject to the regulation. ~~ordinance.~~ Historic districts established pursuant to this Part shall consist of areas ~~which~~ that are deemed to be of special significance in terms of their history, prehistory, architecture, and/or culture, and to possess integrity of design, setting, materials, feeling, and association.[490]

Such ~~ordinance~~ development regulation may treat historic districts either as a separate use district classification or as districts ~~which~~ that overlay other zoning districts. Where historic districts are designated as separate use districts, the zoning regulation ~~ordinance~~ may include as uses by right or as ~~conditional~~ special uses those uses found by the Preservation Commission to have existed during the period sought to be restored or preserved, or to be compatible with the restoration or preservation of the district.

(b) No historic district or districts shall be designated under subsection (a) of this section until:

(1) An investigation and report describing the significance of the buildings, structures, features, sites or surroundings included in any such proposed district, and a description of the boundaries of such district has been prepared, and

(2) The Department of Cultural Resources, acting through the State Historic Preservation Officer or his or her designee, shall have made an analysis of and recommendations concerning such report and description of proposed boundaries. Failure of the department to submit its written analysis and recommendations to the ~~municipal~~ governing board within 30 calendar days after a written request for such analysis has been received by the Department of Cultural Resources shall relieve the ~~municipality~~ governing board of any responsibility for awaiting such analysis, and ~~said~~ the governing board may at any time thereafter take any necessary action to adopt or amend its zoning regulation. ~~ordinance.~~

(c) The ~~municipal~~ governing board may also, in its discretion, refer the report and proposed boundaries under subsection (b) of this section to any local preservation commission or other interested body

---

487. This section has been relocated to G.S. 160D-44(a).
488. This section has been relocated from G.S. 160A-400.12.
489. This section has been relocated from G.S. 160A-400.4.
490. This provision has been relocated from G.S. 160A-400.3.

for its recommendations prior to taking action to amend the zoning regulation ~~ordinance~~. With respect to any changes in the boundaries of such district subsequent to its initial establishment, or the creation of additional districts within the jurisdiction, the investigative studies and reports required by subdivision (1) of subsection (b) of this section shall be prepared by the preservation commission, and shall be referred to the ~~local planning agency~~ planning board for its review and comment according to procedures set forth in the zoning regulation. ~~ordinance.~~ Changes in the boundaries of an initial district or proposal for additional districts shall also be submitted to the Department of Cultural Resources in accordance with the provisions of subdivision (2) of subsection (b) of this section.

On receipt of these reports and recommendations, the ~~municipality~~ local government may proceed in the same manner as would otherwise be required for the adoption or amendment of any appropriate zoning regulation. ~~ordinance provisions.~~

(d) The provisions of G.S. 160D-9-10 apply to zoning or other ~~ordinances~~ development regulations pertaining to historic districts, and the authority under G.S. 160D-9-10(b) for the ordinance to regulate the location or screening of solar collectors may encompass requiring the use of plantings or other measures to ensure that the use of solar collectors is not incongruous with the special character of the district.

§ 160D-9-45. Designation of landmarks; ~~adoption of an ordinance; criteria for designation.~~[491] [160D-945]

Upon complying with G.S. 160D-9-46, the governing board may adopt and ~~from time to time~~ amend or repeal ~~an ordinance~~ a regulation designating one or more historic landmarks. No property shall be recommended for designation as a historic landmark unless it is deemed and found by the preservation commission to be of special significance in terms of its historical, prehistorical, architectural, or cultural importance, and to possess integrity of design, setting, workmanship, materials, feeling and/or association.

The regulation ~~ordinance~~ shall describe each property designated in the regulation, ~~ordinance,~~ the name or names of the owner or owners of the property, those elements of the property that are integral to its historical, architectural, or prehistorical value, including the land area of the property so designated, and any other information the governing board deems necessary. For each building, structure, site, area, or object so designated as a historic landmark, the regulation ~~ordinance~~ shall require that the waiting period set forth in this Part be observed prior to its demolition. For each designated landmark, the regulation ~~ordinance~~ may also provide for a suitable sign on the property indicating that the property has been so designated. If the owner consents, the sign shall be placed upon the property. If the owner objects, the sign shall be placed on a nearby public right-of-way.

§ 160D-9-46. Required landmark designation procedures.[492] [160D-946]

As a guide for the identification and evaluation of landmarks, the preservation commission shall undertake, at the earliest possible time and consistent with the resources available to it, an inventory of properties of historical, architectural, prehistorical, and cultural significance within its jurisdiction. Such inventories and any additions or revisions thereof shall be submitted as expeditiously as possible to the Office of Archives and History. No ~~ordinance~~ regulation designating a historic building, structure, site, area or object as a landmark nor any amendment thereto may be adopted, nor may any property be accepted or acquired by a preservation commission or the governing board ~~of a municipality,~~ until all of the following procedural steps have been taken:

(1) The preservation commission shall (i) prepare and adopt rules of procedure, and (ii) prepare and adopt principles and guidelines, not inconsistent with this Part, for altering, restoring, moving, or demolishing properties designated as landmarks.

(2) The preservation commission shall make or cause to be made an investigation and report on the historic, architectural, prehistorical, educational or cultural significance of each building, structure, site, area or object proposed for designation or acquisition. Such investigation or report shall be forwarded to the Office of Archives and History, North Carolina Department of Cultural Resources.

---

491. This section has been relocated from G.S. 160A-400.5.
492. This section has been relocated from G.S. 160A-400.6.

(3)   The Department of Cultural Resources, acting through the State Historic Preservation Officer shall, ~~either~~ upon request of the department or at the initiative of the preservation commission, be given an opportunity to review and comment upon the substance and effect of the designation of any landmark pursuant to this Part. Any comments shall be provided in writing. If the Department does not submit its comments or recommendation in connection with any designation within 30 days following receipt by the Department of the investigation and report of the preservation commission, the commission and any ~~city or county~~ governing board shall be relieved of any responsibility to consider such comments.

(4)   The preservation commission and the governing board shall hold a joint ~~public~~ legislative hearing or separate ~~public~~ legislative hearings on the proposed regulation. ~~ordinance. Reasonable notice of the time and place thereof shall be given.~~ Notice of the hearing shall be made as provided by G.S. 160D-6-1.[493] ~~All meetings of the commission shall be open to the public, in accordance with the North Carolina Open Meetings Law, Chapter 143, Article 33C.~~[494]

(5)   Following the ~~joint public hearing or separate public~~ hearings, the governing board may adopt the regulation ~~ordinance~~ as proposed, adopt the regulation ~~ordinance~~ with any amendments it deems necessary, or reject the proposed regulation. ~~ordinance.~~

(6)   Upon adoption of the regulation. ~~ordinance,~~ the owners and occupants of each designated landmark shall be given written ~~notification~~ notice of such designation within a reasonable time. ~~insofar as reasonable diligence permits.~~ One copy of the regulation ~~ordinance~~ and all amendments thereto shall be filed by the preservation commission in the office of the register of deeds of the county in which the landmark or landmarks are located. In the case of any landmark property lying within the ~~zoning~~ planning and development regulation jurisdiction of a city, a second copy of the regulation ~~ordinance~~ and all amendments thereto shall be kept on file in the office of the city or town clerk and be made available for public inspection at any reasonable time. A third copy of the regulation ~~ordinance~~ and ~~all~~ any amendments ~~thereto~~ shall be given to the ~~city or county~~ local government building inspector. The fact that a building, structure, site, area or object has been designated a landmark shall be clearly indicated on all tax maps maintained by the ~~county or city~~ local government for such period as the designation remains in effect.

(7)   Upon the adoption of the landmarks regulation ~~ordinance~~ or any amendment thereto, it shall be the duty of the preservation commission to give notice thereof to the tax supervisor of the county in which the property is located. The designation and any recorded restrictions upon the property limiting its use for preservation purposes shall be considered by the tax supervisor in appraising it for tax purposes.

§ 160D-9-47. Certificate of appropriateness required.[495] [160D-947]

(a) *Certificate required.* From and after the designation of a landmark or a historic district, no exterior portion of any building or other structure (including masonry walls, fences, light fixtures, steps and pavement, or other appurtenant features), nor above-ground utility structure nor any type of outdoor advertising sign shall be erected, altered, restored, moved, or demolished on such landmark or within such district until after an application for a certificate of appropriateness as to exterior features has been submitted to and approved by the preservation commission. The ~~municipality~~ local government shall require such a certificate to be issued by the commission prior to the issuance of a building permit ~~or other permit~~[496]

---

493. The legislative hearing requires the same notice as is required for hearings on adopting or amending a zoning ordinance. This revision provides for a uniform, consistent public-hearing notice requirement.

494. Deleted, as mandated compliance with open meetings law does not require inclusion of a specific reference in statute.

495. This section has been relocated from G.S. 160A-400.9.

496. This subsection retains the requirement that a certificate of appropriateness must be issued before a building permit can be issued, but it allows local governments flexibility in the process used to issue other permits, such as special-use permits.

granted for the purposes of constructing, altering, moving, or demolishing structures, which certificate may be issued subject to reasonable conditions necessary to carry out the purposes of this Part. A certificate of appropriateness shall be required whether or not a building or other permit is required.

For purposes of this Part, "exterior features" shall include the architectural style, general design, and general arrangement of the exterior of a building or other structure, including the kind and texture of the building material, the size and scale of the building, and the type and style of all windows, doors, light fixtures, signs, and other appurtenant fixtures. In the case of outdoor advertising signs, "exterior features" shall be construed to mean the style, material, size, and location of all such signs. Such "exterior features" may, in the discretion of the local governing board, include historic signs, color, and significant landscape, archaeological, and natural features of the area.

Except as provided in (b) below, the commission shall have no jurisdiction over interior arrangement. The commission ~~and~~ shall take no action under this section except to prevent the construction, reconstruction, alteration, restoration, moving, or demolition of buildings, structures, appurtenant fixtures, outdoor advertising signs, or other significant features in the district ~~which~~ that would be incongruous with the special character of the landmark or district. In making decisions on certificates of appropriateness, the commission shall apply the rules and standards adopted pursuant to subsection (c) of this section,

(b) *Interior spaces*. Notwithstanding subsection (a) of this section, jurisdiction of the commission over interior spaces shall be limited to specific interior features of architectural, artistic or historical significance in publicly owned landmarks; and of privately owned historic landmarks for which consent for interior review has been given by the owner. Said consent of an owner for interior review shall bind future owners and/or successors in title, provided such consent has been filed in the office of the register of deeds of the county in which the property is located and indexed according to the name of the owner of the property in the grantee and grantor indexes. The landmark designation shall specify the interior features to be reviewed and the specific nature of the commission's jurisdiction over the interior.

(c) *Rules and standards*. Prior to any action to enforce a landmark or historic district regulation, ~~ordinance,~~ the commission shall (i) prepare and adopt rules of procedure, and (ii) prepare and adopt principles and ~~guidelines~~ standards[497] not inconsistent with this Part to guide the commission in determining congruity with the special character of the landmark or district for new construction, alterations, additions, moving and demolition. The landmark or historic district regulation ~~ordinance~~ may provide, subject to prior adoption by the preservation commission of detailed standards, for ~~the~~ staff review and approval as an administrative decision ~~by an administrative official~~ of applications for a certificate of appropriateness for ~~or of~~ minor works or activity as defined by the regulation; ~~ordinance;~~ provided, however, that no application for a certificate of appropriateness may be denied without formal action by the preservation commission. Other than these administrative decisions on minor works, decisions on certificates of appropriateness are quasi-judicial and shall follow the procedures of G.S. 160D-4-6.[498] ~~Prior to issuance or denial of a certificate of appropriateness the commission shall take such steps as may be reasonably required in the ordinance and/or rules of procedure to inform the owners of any property likely to be materially affected by the application, and shall give the applicant and such owners an opportunity to be heard. In cases where the commission deems it necessary, it may hold a public an evidentiary hearing concerning the application. All meetings of the commission shall be open to the public, in accordance with the North Carolina Open Meetings Law, Chapter 143, Article 33C.~~[499]

---

497. This revision clarifies terminology to assure consistency with other sections of G.S. Chapter 160D. The standards mentioned are binding for decisions on quasi-judicial certificate of appropriateness decisions. The term "guidelines" could imply that the standards are advisory in nature rather than the necessary adequate guiding standards for decision making.

498. This language provides clarity and uniformity by mandating use of the standard process for all quasi-judicial decisions under this Article of G.S. Chapter 160D rather than retaining similar, but different, procedures for this particular type of quasi-judicial decision.

499. Deleted, as mandated compliance with open meetings law does not require inclusion of a specific reference in statute.

(d) *Time for review*. All applications for certificates of appropriateness shall be reviewed and acted upon within a reasonable time, not to exceed 180 days from the date the application for a certificate of appropriateness is filed, as defined by the <u>regulation</u> ~~ordinance~~ or the commission's rules of procedure. As part of its review procedure, the commission may view the premises and seek the advice of the Division of Archives and History or such other expert advice as it may deem necessary under the circumstances.

(e) *Appeals*.

(i) <u>Appeals of administrative decisions allowed by regulation may be made to the commission.</u>

(ii) <u>All decisions of the commission in granting or denying a certificate of appropriateness may, if so provided in the regulation, be appealed to the board of adjustment in the nature of certiorari within times prescribed for appeals of administrative decisions in G.S. 160D-4-5(c).[500] To the extent applicable, the provisions of G.S. 160D-14-2 shall apply to appeals in the nature of certiorari to the board of adjustment.</u>

(iii) <u>Appeals from the board of adjustment may be made pursuant to G.S. 160D-14-2.</u>

(iv) <u>If the regulation does not provide for an appeal to the board of adjustment, appeals of decisions on certificates of appropriateness may be made to superior court as provided in G.S. 160D-14-2.</u> ~~An appeal may be taken to the Board of Adjustment from the commission's action in granting or denying any certificate which appeals (i) may be taken by any aggrieved party,[501] (ii)~~

(v) <u>Petitions for judicial review</u> shall be taken within times prescribed <u>for appeal of quasi-judicial decisions in G.S. 160D-14-4.[502]</u> ~~by the preservation commission by general rule, and (iii) shall be in the nature of certiorari.[503]~~ <u>Any</u> Appeals ~~from the Board of Adjustment's decision~~ in any such case shall be heard by the superior court of the county in which the ~~municipality~~ <u>local government</u> is located.

(f) *Public buildings*. All of the provisions of this Part are hereby made applicable to construction, alteration, moving and demolition by the State of North Carolina, its political subdivisions, agencies and instrumentalities, provided however they shall not apply to interiors of buildings or structures owned by the State of North Carolina. The State and its agencies shall have a right of appeal to the North Carolina Historical Commission or any successor agency assuming its responsibilities under G.S. 121-12(a) from any decision of a local preservation commission. The <u>North Carolina Historical</u> Commission shall render its decision within 30 days from the date that the notice of appeal by the State is received by it. The current edition of the Secretary of the Interior's Standards for Rehabilitation and Guidelines for Rehabilitating Historic Buildings shall be the sole principles and guidelines used in reviewing applications of the State for certificates of appropriateness. The decision of the <u>North Carolina Historical</u> Commission shall be final and binding upon both the State and the preservation commission.

~~§ 160D-400.11. Remedies.~~[504]

~~In case any building, structure, site, area or object designated as a historic landmark or located within a historic district designated pursuant to this Part is about to be demolished whether as the result of deliberate neglect or otherwise, materially altered, remodeled, removed or destroyed, except in compliance with the ordinance or other provisions of this Part, the city or county, the historic preservation commission, or~~

---

500. Earlier drafts of this bill deleted the option of appealing to the board of adjustment and provided only for direct appeal to superior court, as is the process with other quasi-judicial decisions. Some local governments preferred to retain board of adjustment review prior to judicial review. That option has been retained, but it is available only if the local government incorporates that process into their historic preservation regulations. Otherwise, appeals of decisions on certificates of appropriateness will be made directly to superior court, as is the case with other quasi-judicial decisions.

501. This provision has been deleted as unnecessary, given the uniform provisions on standing in G.S. 160D-14-1.

502. G.S. 160D-14-4 establishes a uniform time period of thirty days within which to seek judicial review for all quasi-judicial decisions made under Chapter 160D.

503. This language has been deleted as surplusage, given the cross-reference to G.S. 160D-15-1.

504. This section has been relocated to G.S. 160D-4-4(c) in order to consolidate enforcement provisions.

~~other party aggrieved by such action may institute any appropriate action or proceedings to prevent such unlawful demolition, destruction, material alteration, remodeling or removal, to restrain, correct or abate such violation, or to prevent any illegal act or conduct with respect to such building, structure, site, area or object. Such remedies shall be in addition to any others authorized by this Chapter for violation of an municipal ordinance.~~

§ 160D-9-48. Certain changes not prohibited.[505] [160D-948]

Nothing in this Part shall be construed to prevent the ordinary maintenance or repair of any exterior architectural feature in a historic district or of a landmark ~~which~~ <u>that</u> does not involve a change in design, material or appearance thereof, nor to prevent the construction, reconstruction, alteration, restoration, moving or demolition of any such feature ~~which~~ <u>that</u> the building inspector or similar official shall certify is required by the public safety because of an unsafe or dangerous condition. Nothing in this Part shall be construed to prevent a property owner from making any use of his property that is not prohibited by other law. Nothing in this Part shall be construed to prevent a) the maintenance, or b) in the event of an emergency the immediate restoration, of any existing above-ground utility structure without approval by the preservation commission.

§ 160D-9-49. Delay in demolition of landmarks and buildings within historic district.[506] [160D-949]

(a) An application for a certificate of appropriateness authorizing the relocation, demolition or destruction of a designated landmark or a building, structure or site within the district may not be denied except as provided in subsection (c). However, the effective date of such a certificate may be delayed for a period of up to 365 days from the date of approval. The maximum period of delay authorized by this section shall be reduced by the <u>preservation</u> commission where it finds that the owner would suffer extreme hardship or be permanently deprived of all beneficial use of or return from such property by virtue of the delay. During such period the preservation commission shall negotiate with the owner and with any other parties in an effort to find a means of preserving the building or site. If the preservation commission finds that a building or site within a district has no special significance or value toward maintaining the character of the district, it shall waive all or part of such period and authorize earlier demolition, or removal.

If the <u>preservation</u> commission or planning board has voted to recommend designation of a property as a landmark or designation of an area as a district, and final designation has not been made by the ~~local~~ governing board, the demolition or destruction of any building, site, or structure located on the property of the proposed landmark or in the proposed district may be delayed by the <u>preservation</u> commission or planning board for a period of up to 180 days or until the ~~local~~ governing board takes final action on the designation, whichever occurs first.

(b) The governing board ~~of any municipality~~ may enact ~~an ordinance~~ <u>a regulation</u> to prevent the demolition by neglect of any designated landmark or any building or structure within an established historic district. Such <u>regulation</u> ~~ordinance~~ shall provide appropriate safeguards to protect property owners from undue economic hardship.

(c) An application for a certificate of appropriateness authorizing the demolition or destruction of a building, site, or structure determined by the State Historic Preservation Officer as having statewide significance as defined in the criteria of the National Register of Historic Places may be denied except where the <u>preservation</u> commission finds that the owner would suffer extreme hardship or be permanently deprived of all beneficial use or return by virtue of the denial.

---

505. This section has been relocated from G.S. 160A-400.13.
506. This section has been relocated from G.S. 160A-400.14.

§ 160D-9-50. Demolition by neglect to contributing structures outside local historic districts.[507] [160D-950]

Notwithstanding G.S. 160D-9-49 or any other provision of law, the governing board of any municipality may apply its demolition-by-neglect regulations ordinances to contributing structures located outside the local historic district within an adjacent central business district. The governing board may modify and revise its demolition by neglect regulations ordinances as necessary to implement this section and to further its intent. This section is applicable to any local government municipality with a population in excess of 100,000,[508] provided such municipality local government (i) has designated portions of the central business district and its adjacent historic district as an Urban Progress Zone as defined in G.S. 143B-437.09 and (ii) is recognized by the State Historic Preservation Office and the U.S. Department of the Interior as a Certified Local Government in accordance with the National Historic Preservation Act of 1966, as amended (16 U.S.C. § 470, et seq.), and the applicable federal regulations (36 C.F.R. Part 61), but is located in a county that has not received the same certification.

§ 160D-9-51. Conflict with other laws.[509] [160D-951]

Whenever any regulation ordinance adopted pursuant to this Part requires a longer waiting period or imposes other higher standards with respect to a designated historic landmark or district than are established under any other statute, charter provision, or regulation, this Part shall govern. Whenever the provisions of any other statute, charter provision, ordinance or regulation require a longer waiting period or impose other higher standards than are established under this Part, such other statute, charter provision, ordinance or regulation shall govern.

§ 160A-400.16. Reserved for future codification purposes.

§ 160A-400.17. Reserved for future codification purposes.

§ 160A-400.18. Reserved for future codification purposes.

§ 160A-400.19. Reserved for future codification purposes.

§ 160D-9-52 to 9-59. Reserved. [160D-952 to -959]

Part 5. Community Appearance Commissions

§ 160A-451. Membership and appointment of commission; joint commission.[510]

Each municipality and county in the State may create a special commission, to be known as the official appearance commission for the city or county. The commission shall consist of not less than seven nor more than 15 members, to be appointed by the governing body of the municipality or county for such terms, not to exceed four years, as the governing body may by ordinance provide. All members shall be residents of the municipality's or county's area of planning and zoning jurisdiction at the time of appointment. Where possible, appointments shall be made in such a manner as to maintain on the commission at all times a majority of members who have had special training or experience in a design field, such as architecture, landscape design, horticulture, city planning, or a closely related field. Members of the commission may be reimbursed for actual expenses incidental to the performance of their duties within the limits of any funds available to the commission, but shall serve without pay unless otherwise provided in the ordinance establishing the commission. Membership of the commission is declared to be an office that may be held concurrently with any other elective or appointive office pursuant to Article VI, Sec. 9, of the Constitution.

---

507. This section has been relocated from G.S. 160A-400.15.

508. In order to establish greater uniformity, this revision deletes a limitation that made this section applicable only to high-population cities.

509. This section has been relocated from G.S. 160A-400.10.

510. This section has been relocated to G.S. 160D-3-5.

A county and one or more cities in the county may establish a joint appearance commission. If a joint commission is established, the county and the city or cities involved shall determine the residence requirements for members of the joint commission.

§ 160D-9-60. Powers and duties of commission.[511] [160D-960]

The A community appearance commission, upon its appointment,[512] shall make careful study of the visual problems and needs of the municipality or county local government within its area of zoning planning and development regulation jurisdiction, and shall make any plans and carry out any programs that will, in accordance with the powers herein granted the provisions of this Part, enhance and improve the visual quality and aesthetic characteristics of the municipality or county local government. To this end, the governing board may confer upon the appearance commission the following powers and duties:

(1) To initiate, promote and assist in the implementation of programs of general community beautification in the municipality or county local government;

(2) To seek to coordinate the activities of individuals, agencies and organizations, public and private, whose plans, activities and programs bear upon the appearance of the municipality or county local government;

(3) To provide leadership and guidance in matters of area or community design and appearance to individuals, and to public and private organizations, and agencies;

(4) To make studies of the visual characteristics and problems of the municipality or county local government, including surveys and inventories of an appropriate nature, and to recommend standards and policies of design for the entire area, any portion or neighborhood thereof, or any project to be undertaken;

(5) To prepare both general and specific plans for the improved appearance of the municipality or county local government. These plans may include the entire area or any part thereof, and may include private as well as public property. The plans shall set forth desirable standards and goals for the aesthetic enhancement of the municipality or county local government or any part thereof within its area of planning and zoning development regulation jurisdiction, including public ways and areas, open spaces, and public and private buildings and projects;

(6) To participate, in any way deemed appropriate by the governing body board of the municipality or county local government and specified in the ordinance establishing the commission, in the implementation of its plans. To this end, the governing body board may include in the ordinance the following powers:

a. To request from the proper officials of any public agency or body, including agencies of the State and its political subdivisions, its plans for public buildings, facilities, or projects to be located within the local government's municipality or its area of planning and zoning development regulation jurisdiction. of the city or county.

b. To review these plans and to make recommendations regarding their aesthetic suitability to the appropriate agency, or to the municipal or county planning or governing board. All plans shall be reviewed by the commission in a prompt and expeditious manner, and all recommendations of the commission with regard to any public project shall be made in writing. Copies of the recommendations shall be transmitted promptly to the planning or governing board body of the city or county, and to the appropriate agency.

c. To formulate and recommend to the appropriate municipal planning or governing board the adoption or amendment of ordinances (including the zoning regulation, ordinance, subdivision regulations, and other local development regulations ordinances regulating the use of property) that will, in the opinion of the commission, serve to enhance the appearance of the municipality city or county and its surrounding areas.

d. To direct the attention of city or county local government officials to needed enforcement of any ordinance that may in any way affect the appearance of the city or county.

---

511. This section has been relocated from G.S. 160A-452. The entire statutory Part in which G.S. 160A-452 is located is also applicable to counties pursuant to G.S. 160A-451.

512. This language has been deleted as superfluous.

e. To seek voluntary adherence to the standards and policies of its plans.

f. To enter, in the performance of its official duties and at reasonable times, upon private lands and make examinations or surveys.

g. To promote public interest in and an understanding of its recommendations, studies, and plans, and to that end to prepare, publish and distribute to the public such studies and reports as will, in the opinion of the commission, advance the cause of improved ~~municipal or county~~ appearance.

h. To conduct public meetings and hearings, giving reasonable notice to the public thereof.

§ 160D-9-61. Staff services; advisory council.[513] [160D-961]

The commission may recommend to the ~~municipal or county~~ governing board suitable arrangements for the procurement or provision of staff or technical services for the commission, and the governing board may appropriate such amount as it deems necessary to carry out the purposes for which it was created. The commission may establish an advisory council or other committees.

§ 160D-9-62. Annual report.[514] [160D-962]

The commission shall, no later than April 15 of each year, submit to the ~~municipal or county~~ governing ~~body~~ _board_ a written report of its activities, a statement of its expenditures to date for the current fiscal year, and its requested budget for the next fiscal year. All accounts and funds of the commission shall be administered substantially in accordance with the requirements of the Municipal Fiscal Control Act or the County Fiscal Control Act.

§ 160D-9-63. Receipt and expenditure of funds.[515] [160D-963]

The commission may receive contributions from private agencies, foundations, organizations, individuals, the State or federal government, or any other source, in addition to any sums appropriated for its use by the ~~city or county~~ governing ~~body~~ _board_. It may accept and disburse these funds for any purpose within the scope of its authority as herein specified. All sums appropriated by the ~~city or county~~ _local government_ to further the work and purposes of the commission are deemed to be for a public purpose.

§ 160D-9-64 to 9-69. Reserved. [160D-964 to -669]

ARTICLE 10. DEVELOPMENT AGREEMENTS

§ 160D-10-1. Authorization ~~for development agreements~~.[516] [160D-1001]

(a) The General Assembly finds:

(1) ~~Large-scale development~~ _Development_[517] projects often occur in multiple phases ~~extending~~ over ~~a period of~~ _several_ years, requiring a long-term commitment of both public and private resources.

(2) Such ~~large-scale~~ developments often create ~~potential~~ community impacts and ~~potential~~ opportunities that are difficult ~~or impossible~~ to accommodate within traditional zoning processes.

(3) Because of their scale and duration, such ~~large-scale~~ projects often require careful ~~integration between~~ _coordination of_ public capital facilities planning, financing, and construction schedules and ~~the~~ phasing of the private development.

(4) ~~Because of their scale and duration,~~ Such ~~large-scale~~ projects involve substantial commitments of private capital ~~by developers~~, which developers are usually unwilling to risk

---

513. This section has been relocated from G.S. 160A-453.

514. This section has been relocated from G.S. 160A-454.

515. This section has been relocated from G.S. 160A-455.

516. This section has been relocated from G.S. 160A-400.20 and 153A-349.1. This revision makes stylistic changes for purposes of simplification and clarity.

517. This revision reflects amendments made to development-agreement statutes in 2015 to remove size and duration limitations.

without sufficient assurances that development standards will remain stable through the extended period of the development.

(5) ~~Because of their size and duration,~~ Such developments often permit communities and developers to experiment with different or nontraditional types of development concepts and standards, while still managing impacts on the surrounding areas.

(6) To better structure and manage development approvals for such ~~large-scale~~ developments and ensure their proper integration into local capital facilities programs, local governments need ~~the~~ flexibility ~~in negotiating~~ to negotiate such developments.

(b) Local governments ~~and agencies~~[518] may enter into development agreements with developers, subject to the procedures ~~and requirements~~ of this ~~Part~~ Article. In entering into such agreements, a local government may not exercise any authority or make any commitment not authorized by general or local act and may not impose any tax or fee not authorized by otherwise applicable law.

(c) This ~~Part~~ Article is supplemental to the powers conferred upon local governments and does not preclude or supersede rights and obligations established pursuant to other law regarding development approvals, site-specific ~~development~~ vesting plans, phased ~~development~~ vesting plans, or other provisions of law. A development agreement ~~adopted pursuant to this Chapter~~ shall not exempt the property owner or developer from compliance with the State Building Code or State or local housing codes that are not part of the local government's ~~planning, zoning, or subdivision~~ development regulations.[519] When the governing board approves the rezoning of any property associated with a development agreement executed and recorded pursuant to this Article, the provisions of G.S. 160D-6-5(a) apply.[520]

(d) Development authorized by a development agreement shall comply with all applicable laws, including all ordinances, resolutions, regulations, ~~comprehensive plans, land development regulations,~~ permits, policies, and ~~rules~~ laws ~~adopted by a local government~~ affecting the development of property, ~~and includes~~ including laws governing permitted uses of the property, density, intensity, design, and improvements.[521]

§ 160D-10-2. Definitions.[522] [160D-1002]

The following definitions apply in this Article: ~~Part:~~

~~(1) Comprehensive plan. - The comprehensive plan, land-use plan, small area plans, neighborhood plans, transportation plan, capital improvement plan, official map, and any other plans regarding land use and development that have been officially adopted by the governing board.~~

~~(2) Developer. - A person, including a governmental agency or redevelopment authority, who intends to undertake any development and who has a legal or equitable interest in the property to be developed.~~

(1) Development. - The planning for or carrying out of a building activity, the making of a material change in the use or appearance of any structure or property, or the dividing of land into two or more parcels. ~~"Development", as designated in a law or development permit, includes the planning for and all other activity customarily associated with it unless otherwise specified.~~ [523]When appropriate to the context, "development" refers to the planning for or the act of developing or to the result of development. Reference to a specific operation is not intended to mean that the operation or activity, when part of other operations or activities, is not development. Reference to particular operations is not intended to limit the generality of this item.

---

518. Clarification. Since only cities and counties have authority to adopt development regulations under this Article of G.S. Chapter 160D, only a city or county itself is authorized to enter into development agreements.

519. This sentence has been relocated from G.S. 160A-400.32 and 153A-349.1.

520. This revision incorporates a sentence added by S.L. 2017-10.

521. This subsection has been relocated from definitions sections in current law (G.S. 160A-400.21 and 153A-349.2) and expressly includes the limitation, set out in G.S. 160A-400.6 and 153A-349.7 (now G.S. 160D-10-7(a)), that the regulations in effect and applicable at the time of execution of the development agreement apply.

522. Deleted provisions in this section have been relocated to G.S. 160D-1-2.

523. This sentence was deleted as redundant, given the preceding sentence.

Appendix E. Annotated Text of Chapter 160D | 197

~~(4) Development permit. - A building permit, zoning permit, subdivision approval, special or conditional use permit, variance, or any other official action of local government having the effect of permitting the development of property.~~

~~(5) Governing body. - The city council of a municipality.[524]~~

~~(6) Land development regulations. - Ordinances and regulations enacted by the appropriate governing body for the regulation of any aspect of development and includes zoning, subdivision, or any other land development ordinances.~~

~~(7) Laws.[525] - All ordinances, resolutions, regulations, comprehensive plans, land development regulations, policies, and rules adopted by a local government affecting the development of property, and includes laws governing permitted uses of the property, density, design, and improvements.~~

~~(8) Local government. - Any municipality that exercises regulatory authority over and grants development permits for land development or which provides public facilities.~~

~~(9) Local planning board. - Any planning board established pursuant to G.S. 160A-361.~~

~~(10) Person. - An individual, corporation, business or land trust, estate, trust, partnership, association, two or more persons having a joint or common interest, State agency, or any legal entity.~~

~~(11) Property. - All real property subject to land-use regulation by a local government and includes any improvements or structures customarily regarded as a part of real property.~~

(2) Public facilities. - Major capital improvements, including, but not limited to, transportation, sanitary sewer, solid waste, drainage, potable water, educational, parks and recreational, and health systems and facilities.

§ 160D-10-3. ~~Local governments authorized to enter into development agreements;~~ Approval of governing ~~body~~ board required.[526] [160D-1003]

(a) A local government may establish procedures and requirements, as provided in this ~~Part~~ Article, to consider and enter into development agreements with developers. A development agreement must be approved by the governing ~~body~~ board of a local government ~~by ordinance~~ following the procedures specified in G.S. 160D-10-5.[527]

(b) The development agreement may, by ordinance, be incorporated, in whole or in part, into any ~~planning, zoning, or subdivision ordinance~~ development regulation adopted by the local government.[528] A development agreement may be considered concurrently with a zoning map or text amendment affecting the property and development subject to the development agreement.[529] A development agreement may be concurrently considered with and incorporate by reference a sketch plan or preliminary plat required under a subdivision regulation or a site plan or other development approval required under a zoning regulation.[530] If incorporated into a conditional district, the provisions of the development agreement shall be treated as ~~any other~~ a development regulation in the event of the developer's bankruptcy.

---

524. This subsection was deleted as surplusage, as this matter is covered in Article 1 of G.S. Chapter 160D.

525. The provisions of this definition have been incorporated into G.S. 160D-10-1(d).

526. This section has been relocated from G.S. 160A-400.22 and 153A-349.3.

527. This revision clarifies that a decision on a proposed development agreement is a legislative decision. While a development agreement is not an ordinance, this provision mandates that the same notice, hearing, and planning-board referral provisions of G.S. Chapter 160D Article 6 relative to rezonings be followed, given that those site-specific legislative decisions are the most nearly comparable actions to decisions on development agreements.

528. This revision reflects an amendment made by S.L. 2015-246, § 19.

529. This language explicitly authorizes the common practice of processing and considering concurrently a rezoning and a development agreement regarding a proposed development. The same process must be followed for each action, and often a rezoning is necessary for the proposed development. It is efficient and realistic to consider the two actions concurrently.

530. This revision facilitates the coordinated exercise of related development approvals for a project subject to a development agreement.

§ 160D-10-4. ~~Developed property must contain certain number of acres; permissible durations of agreements~~ <u>Size and duration</u>.[531] [160D-1004]

~~(a)~~ A local government may enter into a development agreement with a developer for the development of property as provided in this ~~Part~~ <u>Article</u> for developable property of any size.[532]~~, including property that is subject to an executed brownfields agreement pursuant to Part 5 of Article 9 of Chapter 130A of the General Statutes.~~[533] Development agreements shall be of a reasonable term specified in the agreement.[534]

§ 160D-10-5. Public hearing.[535] [160D-1005]

Before entering into a development agreement, a local government shall conduct a ~~public~~ <u>legislative</u>[536] hearing on the proposed agreement. <u>The notice provisions of G.S. 160D-6-2 applicable to zoning map</u> amendments shall be followed for this hearing.[537] ~~following the procedures set forth in G.S. 160A-364 regarding zoning ordinance adoption or amendment~~. The notice for the public hearing must specify the location of the property subject to the development agreement, the development uses proposed on the property, and must specify a place where a copy of the proposed development agreement can be obtained. ~~In the event that the development agreement provides that the local government shall provide certain public facilities, the development agreement shall provide that the delivery date of such public facilities will be tied to successful performance by the developer in implementing the proposed development (such as meeting defined completion percentages or other performance standards).~~[538]

§ 160D-10-6. ~~What development agreement must provide; what it may provide; major~~ <u>Content and</u> modification ~~requires public notice and hearing~~.[539] [160D-1006]

(a) A development agreement shall, at a minimum, include all of the following:
(1) A ~~legal~~ description of the property subject to the agreement and the names of its legal and equitable property owners.
(2) The duration of the agreement. However, the parties are not precluded from entering into subsequent development agreements that may extend the original duration period.
(3) The development uses permitted on the property, including population densities and building types, intensities, placement on the site, and design.
(4) A description of public facilities that will ~~service~~ <u>serve</u> the development, including who provides the facilities, the date any new public facilities, if needed, will be constructed, and a schedule to assure public facilities are available concurrent with the impacts of the development. In the event that the development agreement provides that the local government shall provide certain public facilities, the development agreement shall provide that the delivery date of such public facilities will be tied to successful performance by the developer in implementing the proposed development (such as meeting defined completion percentages or other performance standards).[540]
(5) A description, where appropriate, of any reservation or dedication of land for public purposes and any provisions ~~to protect~~ <u>agreed to by the developer that exceed existing laws related to protection of</u> environmentally sensitive property.

---

531. This section has been relocated from G.S. 160A-400.23 and 153A-349.4.
532. This revision reflects an amendment made by S.L. 2015-246, § 19.
533. This language has been deleted as superfluous, given a 2015 amendment to the statute deleting a minimum-size requirement for land subject to a development agreement.
534. This revision reflects an amendment made by S.L. 2015-246, § 19.
535. This section has been relocated from G.S. 160A-400.24 and 153A-349.5.
536. This language specifies the type of hearing to be conducted on proposed development agreements.
537. This revision simplifies hearing notice requirements through the use of a cross-reference to notice requirements for hearings on proposed rezonings.
538. This provision has been relocated to next section, G.S. 160D-10-6(a)(4).
539. This section has been relocated from G.S. 160A-400.25 and 153A-349.6.
540. This sentence has been relocated from G.S. 160A-400.24 and 153A-349.5.

(6)[541] ~~A description of all local development permits approved or needed to be approved for the development of the property together with a statement indicating that the failure of the agreement to address a particular permit, condition, term, or restriction does not relieve the developer of the necessity of complying with the law governing their permitting requirements, conditions, terms, or restrictions.~~

(6) A description, <u>where appropriate,</u> of any conditions, terms, restrictions, or other requirements ~~determined to be necessary by the local government~~[542] for the <u>protection of</u> public health, safety, or welfare ~~of its citizens~~.

(7) A description, where appropriate, of any provisions for the preservation and restoration of historic structures.

(b) A development agreement may <u>also</u> provide that the entire development or any phase of it be commenced or completed within a specified period of time. <u>If required by ordinance or in the agreement, the</u> ~~The~~ development agreement ~~must~~ <u>shall</u> provide a development schedule, including commencement dates and interim completion dates at no greater than five-year intervals; provided, however, the failure to meet a commencement or completion date shall not, in and of itself, constitute a material breach of the development agreement pursuant to G.S. 160D-10-8 but must be judged based upon the totality of the circumstances. ~~The development agreement may include other defined performance standards to be met by the developer.~~[543] The developer may request a modification in the dates as set forth in the agreement. ~~Consideration of a proposed major modification of the agreement shall follow the same procedures as required for initial approval of a development agreement.~~[544]

(c) If more than one local government is made party to an agreement, the agreement must specify which local government is responsible for the overall administration of the development agreement. <u>A local or regional utility authority may also be made a party to the development agreement.</u>[545]

(d) The development agreement also may cover any other matter<u>, including defined performance standards,</u>[546] not inconsistent with this ~~Part~~ <u>Chapter</u>.[547] <u>The development agreement may include mutually acceptable terms regarding provision of public facilities and other amenities and the allocation of financial responsibility for their provision, provided any impact mitigation measures offered by the developer beyond those that could be required by the local government pursuant to G.S. 160D-8-4 shall be expressly enumerated within the agreement, and provided the agreement may not include a tax or impact fee not otherwise authorized by law.</u>[548]

---

541. This subdivision has been deleted as unnecessary. A developer must secure all required state and local permits, and this requirement is explicitly stated in G.S. 160D-10-1(d). However, listing all required development approvals within a development agreement adds little educational or other value to the agreement and creates ambiguity and uncertainty as to the legal implications if a particular permit is inadvertently omitted from such a list.

542. This language has been deleted as surplusage.

543. This provision has been relocated to subsequent subsection of this section.

544. This provision has been relocated to subsequent subsection of this section.

545. This revision recognizes that agreements regarding the provision of infrastructure are often a critical aspect of a development agreement. A utility or other "agency" cannot create a development agreement unilaterally, an issue that has been clarified by the deletion of the term "agency" in G.S. 160D-10-1(b). A local government is an essential and necessary party to a development agreement. However, while the local government and the developer are the essential parties to the agreement, the entity providing utility services may need to be made a party in order to have binding agreements regarding utility services. When the entity providing utility services is not the local government itself, this revision explicitly allows utility authorities to be parties to the development agreement.

546. This provision has been relocated from earlier subsection of this section.

547. This revision updates a reference to reflect the fact that development agreements may address matters covered by the entirety of Chapter 160D, not just by this individual Article.

548. This revision clarifies that a developer and a local government can through negotiation agree to the provision of and cost-sharing for public facilities and other amenities related to development. However, in such situations, the revision requires that impact-mitigation measures (see proposed G.S. 160D-8-4(c))

(e) Consideration of a proposed major modification of the agreement shall follow the same procedures as required for initial approval of a development agreement.[549] What changes constitute a major modification may be determined by ordinance adopted pursuant to G.S. 160D-10.3 or as provided for in the development agreement.

(f) Any performance guarantees under the development agreement shall comply with G.S. 160D-8-4(d).[550]

§ 160D-10-7. Vesting.[551] ~~Law in effect at time of agreement governs development; exceptions.~~ [160D-1007]

(a) Unless the development agreement specifically provides for the application of subsequently enacted laws, the laws applicable to development of the property subject to a development agreement are those in force at the time of execution of the agreement.

(b) Except for grounds specified in G.S. 160D-1-8(e), a local government may not apply subsequently adopted ordinances or development policies to a development that is subject to a development agreement.

(c) In the event State or federal law is changed after a development agreement has been entered into and the change prevents or precludes compliance with one or more provisions of the development agreement, the local government may modify the affected provisions, upon a finding that the change in State or federal law has a fundamental effect on the development agreement. ~~, by ordinance after notice and a hearing.~~

(d) This section does not abrogate ~~any~~ vested rights otherwise preserved by law.[552] ~~by G.S. 160A-385 or G.S. 160A-385.1, or that may vest pursuant to common law or otherwise in the absence of a development agreement.~~

§ 160D-10-8. Breach and cure.[553] ~~Periodic review to assess compliance with agreement; material breach by developer; notice of breach; cure of breach or modification or termination of agreement.~~ [160D-1008]

(a) Procedures established pursuant to G.S. 160D-10-3 ~~must~~ may include a provision ~~for~~ requiring periodic review by the zoning administrator or other appropriate officer of the local government ~~at least every 12 months,~~[554] at which time the developer ~~must be required to~~ shall demonstrate good faith compliance with the terms of the development agreement.

(b) If ~~, as a result of a periodic review,~~ the local government finds and determines that the developer has committed a material breach of ~~the terms or conditions of~~ the agreement, the local government shall ~~serve notice in writing, within a reasonable time after the periodic review, upon~~ notify the developer in writing setting forth with reasonable particularity the nature of the breach and the evidence supporting the finding and determination, and providing the developer a reasonable time in which to cure the material breach.

(c) If the developer fails to cure the material breach within the time given, then the local government unilaterally may terminate or modify the development agreement; provided, the notice of termination or modification may be appealed to the board of adjustment in the manner provided by G.S. 160D-4-5.

---

beyond those that could be required under *Nollan v. California Coastal Commission*, 483 U.S. 825 (1987), and *Dolan v. City of Tigard*, 512 U.S. 374 (1994), be expressly set out in the agreement.

549. This provision has been relocated from an earlier subsection of this section.

550. This subsection was added by S.L. 2015-187.

551. This section has been relocated from G.S. 160A-400.26 and 153A-349.7.

552. Simplification. This revision preserves all vested rights, which are now codified at G.S. 160D-1-8.

553. This section has been relocated from G.S. 160A-400.27 and 153A-349.8.

554. This revision allows each local government to determine whether a periodic review is appropriate for a particular development agreement. Rather than specifying a certain statutory time period for review of all agreements, the revision increases flexibility by allowing each development agreement to specify an appropriate review period that takes into consideration the nature of the development and local circumstances.

(d) An ordinance adopted pursuant to G.S. 160D-10.3 or the development agreement may specify other penalties for breach in lieu of termination, including but not limited to, penalties allowed for violation of a development regulation. Nothing in this Article shall be construed to abrogate or impair the power of the local government to enforce applicable law.

(e) A development agreement shall be enforceable by any party to the agreement notwithstanding any changes in the development regulations made subsequent to the effective date of the development agreement. Any party to the agreement may file an action for injunctive relief to enforce the terms of a development agreement.[555]

§ 160D-10-9. Amendment or termination ~~cancellation~~.[556] ~~of development agreement by mutual consent of parties or successors in interest.~~ [160D-1009]

Subject to the provisions of G.S. 160D-10.6(e), a development agreement may be amended or ~~canceled~~ terminated by mutual consent of the parties. ~~to the agreement or by their successors in interest.~~

§ 160D-10-10. ~~Validity and duration of agreement entered into prior to~~ Change of jurisdiction.[557] ~~subsequent modification or suspension.~~ [160D-1010]

(a) Except as otherwise provided by this ~~Part~~ Article, any development agreement entered into by a local government before the effective date of a change of jurisdiction shall be valid for the duration of the agreement, or eight years from the effective date of the change in jurisdiction, whichever is earlier. The parties to the development agreement and the local government assuming jurisdiction have the same rights and obligations with respect to each other regarding matters addressed in the development agreement as if the property had remained in the previous jurisdiction.

(b) A local government assuming jurisdiction may modify or suspend the provisions of the development agreement if the local government determines that the failure of the local government to do so would place the residents of the territory subject to the development agreement, or the residents of the local government, or both, in a condition dangerous to their health or safety, or both.

§ 160D-10-11. Recordation.[558] ~~Developer to record agreement within 14 days; burdens and benefits inure to successors in interest.~~ [160D-1002]

~~Within 14 days after a local government enters into a development agreement,~~ The developer shall record the agreement with the register of deeds in the county where the property is located within 14 days after the local government and developer execute an approved development agreement. No development approvals may be issued until the development agreement has been recorded. The burdens of the development agreement are binding upon, and the benefits of the agreement shall inure to, all successors in interest to the parties to the agreement.

§ 160D-10-12. Applicability ~~to local government of constitutional and statutory~~ of procedures ~~for approval of~~ to approve debt.[559] [160D-1012]

In the event that any of the obligations of the local government in the development agreement constitute debt, the local government shall comply, at the time of the obligation to incur the debt and before the debt becomes enforceable against the local government, with any applicable constitutional and statutory procedures for the approval of this debt.

---

555. This revision explicitly acknowledges that parties to a development agreement may take action to enforce it.

556. This section has been relocated from G.S. 160A-400.28 and 153A-349.9.

557. This section has been relocated from G.S. 160A-400.29 and 153A-349.10

558. This section has been relocated from G.S. 160A-400.30 and 153A-349.11.

559. This section has been relocated from G.S. 160A-400.31 and 153A-349.12.

§ 160A-400.32. Relationship of agreement to building or housing code. [560]

A development agreement adopted pursuant to this Chapter shall not exempt the property owner or developer from compliance with the State Building Code or State or local housing codes that are not part of the local government's planning, zoning, or subdivision regulations.

ARTICLE 11. BUILDING CODE ENFORCEMENT

§ 160D-11-1. Definitions. [160D-1101] As used in this Article, the words:

(a) "Building"[561] or "buildings" include other structures.

(b) "Governing board" or "board of commissioners"[562] includes the Tribal Council of a federally recognized Indian Tribe.

(c) "Local government"[563] also means a federally recognized Indian Tribe, and as to such tribe includes lands held in trust for the tribe.

(d) "Public officer"[564] means the officer or officers who are authorized by regulations ordinances adopted hereunder to exercise the powers prescribed by the regulations ordinances and by this Article.

§ 160D-11-2. Building code administration Inspection department.[565] [160D-1102]

Every city in the State is hereby authorized to A local government may create an inspection department, and may appoint one or more inspectors who may be given the appropriate titles, such as building inspector, electrical inspector, plumbing inspector, housing inspector, zoning inspector, heating and air-conditioning inspector, fire prevention inspector, or deputy or assistant inspector, or such other titles as may be generally descriptive of the duties assigned. The department may be headed by a superintendent or director of inspections.[566] Every city local government shall perform the duties and responsibilities set forth in G.S. 160D-11-5 either by: (i) creating its own inspection department; (ii) creating a joint inspection department in cooperation with one or more other units of local government, pursuant to G.S. 160D-11-5 or Part 1 of Article 20 of this Chapter 160A; (iii) contracting with another unit of local government for the provision of inspection services pursuant to Part 1 of Article 20 of Chapter 160A; or (iv) arranging for the county in which it a city is located to perform inspection services within the city's jurisdiction as authorized by G.S. 160D-11-5 and G.S. 160D-2-2. Such action shall be taken no later than the applicable date in the schedule below, according to the city's population as published in the 1970 United States Census:

Cities over 75,000 population - July 1, 1979
Cities between 50,001 and 75,000 - July 1, 1981
Cities between 25,001 and 50,000 - July 1, 1983
Cities 25,000 and under - July 1, 1985.[567]

In the event that any city local government shall fails to provide inspection services by the date specified above or shall ceases to provide such services at any time thereafter, the Commissioner of Insurance shall arrange for the provision of such services, either through personnel employed by his the[568] department or through an arrangement with other units of government. In either event, the Commissioner shall have and may exercise within the city's local government's planning and development regulation jurisdiction all

---

560. This provision (applicable to cities and towns), along with G.S. 153A-349.13 (a mirror provision applicable to counties), has been relocated to G.S. 160D-10-1(c).

561. This provision has been relocated from G.S. 153A-350.

562. This provision has been relocated from G.S. 153A-350.1.

563. This provision has been relocated from G.S. 153A-350.1.

564. This provision has been relocated from G.S. 160A-442.

565. This section has been relocated from 160A-411 and 153-351(a), (a1).

566. Simplification.

567. This revision deletes, as obsolete, dates for establishing building code inspections, as all deadlines passed decades ago. It also deletes comparable provisions in G.S. 153A-351(a1) for counties.

568. Revised to reflect gender-neutral language.

powers made available to the ~~city council~~ governing board with respect to building inspection under this Article, and Part 1 of Article 20 of Chapter 160A. Whenever the Commissioner has intervened in this manner, the ~~city~~ local government may assume provision of inspection services only after giving the Commissioner two years' written notice of its intention to do so; provided, however, that the Commissioner may waive this requirement or permit assumption at an earlier date ~~if he finds~~ upon finding that such earlier assumption will not unduly interfere with arrangements ~~he has~~ made for the provision of those services.

§ 160D-11-3. Qualifications of inspectors.[569] [160D-1103]

~~On and after the applicable date set forth in the schedule in G.S. 160A-411,~~ No ~~city~~ local government shall employ an inspector to enforce the State Building Code ~~as a member of a city or joint inspection department~~ who does not have one of the following types of certificates issued by the North Carolina Code Officials Qualification Board attesting to ~~his~~ the inspector's qualifications to hold such position: (i) a probationary certificate~~, valid for one year only~~;[570] (ii) a standard certificate; or (iii) a limited certificate ~~which~~ that shall be valid only as an authorization ~~for him~~ to continue in the position held on the date specified in G.S. 143-151.13(c) and which shall become invalid if ~~he~~ the inspector does not successfully complete in-service training specified by the Qualification Board within the period specified in G.S. 143-151.13(c). An inspector holding one of the above certificates can be promoted to a position requiring a higher level certificate only upon issuance by the Board of a standard certificate or probationary certificate appropriate for such new position.

§ 160D-11-4. Duties and responsibilities.[571] [160D-1104]

(a) The duties and responsibilities of an inspection department and of the inspectors ~~therein~~ in it shall be to enforce within their planning and development regulation ~~territorial~~ jurisdiction State and local laws ~~and local ordinances and regulations~~[572] relating to:

(1) The construction of buildings and other structures;
(2) The installation of such facilities as plumbing systems, electrical systems, heating systems, refrigeration systems, and air-conditioning systems;
(3) The maintenance of buildings and other structures in a safe, sanitary, and healthful condition;
(4) Other matters that may be specified by the ~~city council~~ governing board.

(b) The duties and responsibilities set forth in subsection (a) of this section shall include the receipt of applications for permits and the issuance or denial of permits, the making of any necessary inspections in a timely manner, the issuance or denial of certificates of compliance, the issuance of orders to correct violations, the bringing of judicial actions against actual or threatened violations, the keeping of adequate records, and any other actions that may be required in order adequately to enforce those laws. The city council shall have the authority to enact reasonable and appropriate provisions governing the enforcement of those laws.

(c) In performing the specific inspections required by the North Carolina Building Code, the inspector shall conduct all inspections requested by the permit holder for each scheduled inspection visit. For each requested inspection, the inspector shall inform the permit holder of instances in which the work inspected fails to meet the requirements of the North Carolina Residential Code for One- and Two-Family Dwellings or the North Carolina Building Code.[573]

---

569. This section has been relocated from G.S. 160A-411.1 and 153A-351.1. This revision deletes, as obsolete, G.S. 153A-351(b) relative to electrical-inspector qualifications.

570. This revision retains the requirement that building inspectors have a valid certificate but does not specify a particular time limit for obtaining that certificate. As the state Code Qualifications Board may amend or regulate the time period for which probationary certificates are valid, there is no need to include a specific time period in this statute.

571. This section has been relocated from G.S. 160A-412 and 153A-352. Amendments made by S.L. 2015-145 have been incorporated.

572. This revision uses terminology from the county statute. No substantive change in the law was intended.

573. This subsection was amended by S.L. 2018-29.

(d) Except as provided in G.S. 160D-11-15 and G.S. 160D-12-7, a ~~city~~ local government may not adopt or enforce[574] a local ordinance or resolution or any other policy that requires regular, routine inspections of buildings or structures constructed in compliance with the North Carolina Residential Code for One- and Two-Family Dwellings in addition to the specific inspections required by the North Carolina Building Code without first obtaining approval from the North Carolina Building Code Council. The North Carolina Building Code Council shall review all applications for additional inspections requested by a ~~city~~ local government and shall, in a reasonable manner, approve or disapprove the additional inspections. This subsection does not limit the authority of the ~~city~~ local government to require inspections upon unforeseen or unique circumstances that require immediate action. In performing the specific inspections required by the North Carolina Residential Building Code, the inspector shall conduct all inspections requested by the permit holder for each scheduled inspection visit. For each requested inspection, the inspector shall inform the permit holder of instances in which the work inspected is incomplete or otherwise fails to meet the requirements of the North Carolina Residential Code for One- and Two-Family Dwellings or the North Carolina Building Code.[575]

(e) Each inspection department shall implement a process for an informal internal review of inspection decisions made by the department's inspectors. This process shall include, at a minimum, the following:

(1) Initial review by the supervisor of the inspector.

(2) The provision in or with each permit issued by the department of (i) the name, phone number, and e-mail address of the supervisor of each inspector and (ii) a notice of availability of the informal internal review process.

(3) Procedures the department shall follow when a permit holder or applicant requests an internal review of an inspector's decision.

Nothing in this subsection shall limit or abrogate any rights available under Chapter 150B of the General Statutes to a permit holder or applicant.

(f) If a specific building framing inspection as required by the North Carolina Residential Code for One- and Two-Family Dwellings results in 15 or more separate violations of that Code, the inspector shall forward a copy of the inspection report to the Department of Insurance.[576]

§ 160D-11-5. Other arrangements for inspections.[577] [160D-1105]

~~A city council may enter into and carry out contracts with another city, county, or combination thereof under which the parties agree to create and support a joint inspection department for the enforcement of State and local laws specified in the agreement. The governing boards of the contracting parties are authorized to make any necessary appropriations for this purpose.~~

~~In lieu of a joint inspection department, a city council may designate an inspector from any other city or county to serve as a member of its inspection department with the approval of the governing body of the other city or county.~~ A ~~city~~ local government may ~~also~~ contract with an individual who is not a ~~city or county~~ local government employee but who holds one of the applicable certificates as provided in G.S. 160D-11-3 or with the employer of an individual who holds one of the applicable certificates as provided in G.S. 160D-11-3. ~~The inspector, if designated from another city or county under this section, shall, while exercising the duties of the position, be considered a municipal employee. The city shall have the same potential liability, if any, for inspections conducted by an individual who is not an employee of the city as it does for an individual who is an employee of the city. The company or individual with whom the city contracts shall have errors and omissions and other insurance coverage acceptable to the city.~~

~~The city council of any city may request the board of county commissioners of the county in which the city is located to direct one or more county building inspectors to exercise their powers within part or all of the city's jurisdiction, and they shall thereupon be empowered to do so until the city council officially withdraws its request in the manner provided in G.S. 160A-360(g).~~

574. This provision was added by S.L. 2017-130.

575. An amendment to this subsection made by S.L. 2015-145 has been incorporated. S.L. 2017-130 added the language "or the North Carolina Building Code" to this subsection.

576. This subsection was added by S.L. 2018-29.

577. This section has been relocated from G.S. 160A-413 and 153A-353. The deleted portions of the subsection have been relocated to Article 4 of Chapter 160D, specifically, to G.S. 160D-4-2(c).

§ 160D-11-6. Alternate inspection method for component or element.[578] [160D-1106]

(a) Notwithstanding the requirements of this Article, a city shall accept and approve, accept, without further responsibility to inspect, a design or other proposal for a component or element in the construction of buildings from a licensed architect or licensed engineer provided all of the following apply:

    (1)   The submission design or other proposal is completed under valid seal of the licensed architect or licensed engineer.

    (2)   Field inspection of the installation or completion of a construction the component or element of the building is performed by a licensed architect or licensed engineer or a person under the direct supervisory control of the licensed architect or licensed engineer.

    (3)   The licensed architect or licensed engineer under subdivision (2) of this subsection provides the city with a signed written document stating the component or element of the building so inspected under subdivision (2) of this subsection is in compliance with the North Carolina State Building Code or the North Carolina Residential Code for One- and Two-Family Dwellings. The inspection certification required under this subdivision shall be provided by electronic or physical delivery and its receipt shall be promptly acknowledged by the city through reciprocal means.[579]

(b) Upon the acceptance and approval receipt of a signed written document by the city as required under subsection (a) of this section, notwithstanding the issuance of a certificate of occupancy, the city, its inspection department, and the inspectors shall be discharged and released from any liabilities, duties and responsibilities imposed by this Article with respect to or in common law from any claim arising out of or attributed to the component or element in the construction of the building for which the signed written document was submitted.

(c) Other than what may be required by subsection (a) of this section, no further certification by a licensed architect or licensed engineer shall be required for any component or element designed and sealed by a licensed architect or licensed engineer for the manufacturer of the component or element under the North Carolina State Building Code or the North Carolina Residential Code for One- and Two-Family Dwellings.

(d) As used in this section, the following definitions shall apply:

    (1)   Component. – Any assembly, subassembly, or combination of elements designed to be combined with other components to form part of a building or structure. Examples of a component include an excavated footing trench containing no concrete.[580]

    (2)   Element. – A combination of products designed to be combined with other elements to form all or part of a building component.

    (3)   Components and elements are not systems.

§ 160D-11-7. Mutual aid contracts.[581] [160D-1107]

(a) Any two or more cities or counties may enter into contracts with each other to provide mutual aid and assistance in the administration and enforcement of State and local laws pertaining to the North Carolina State Building Code. Mutual aid contracts may include provisions addressing the scope of aid provided, for reimbursement or indemnification of the aiding party for loss or damage incurred by giving aid, for delegating authority to a designated official or employee to request aid or to send aid upon request, and any other provisions not inconsistent with law.

(b) Unless the mutual aid contract says otherwise, while working with the requesting city or county under the authority of this section, a Code-enforcement official shall have the same jurisdiction, powers, rights, privileges, and immunities, including those relating to the defense of civil actions and payment of judgments, as the Code-enforcement officials of the requesting agency.

---

578. This section has been relocated from G.S. 160A-413.5, as created by S.L. 2018-29.

579. Amendments to this subdivision made by S.L. 2019-174 are to be incorporated in 2020.

580. Amendments to this subdivision made by S.L. 2019-174 are to be incorporated in 2020. One amendment adds "foundation" and "prepared underslab" to the list of examples in this subdivision.

581. This section has been relocated from G.S. 413.6, created by S.L. 2018-29.

(c) Nothing in this section shall deprive any party to a mutual aid contract under this section of its discretion to send or decline to provide aid to another party to the contract under any circumstances, whether or not obligated by the contract to do so. In no case shall a party to a mutual aid contract or any of its officials or employees be held to answer in any civil or criminal action for declining to send aid whether or not obligated by contract to do so.

§ 160A-414/153A-354. Financial support. [582]

~~The city council may appropriate for the support of the inspection department any funds that it deems necessary. It may provide for paying inspectors fixed salaries or it may reimburse them for their services by paying over part or all of any fees collected. It shall have power to fix reasonable fees for issuance of permits, inspections, and other services of the inspection department.~~

§ 160D-11-8. Conflicts of interest. [583] [160D-1108]

Staff members, agents or contractors responsible for building inspections shall comply with G.S. 160D-1-9(c). No member of an inspection department shall be financially interested or employed by a business that is financially interested in the furnishing of labor, material, or appliances for the construction, alteration, or maintenance of any building within the ~~city's~~ local government's planning and development regulation jurisdiction or any part or system thereof, or in the making of plans or specifications therefor, unless he is the owner of the building. No member of an inspection department or other individual or an employee of a company contracting with a ~~city~~ local government to conduct building inspections shall engage in any work that is inconsistent with his or her duties or with the interest of the ~~city~~ local government, as determined by the ~~city~~ local government. The ~~city~~ local government must find a conflict of interest if any of the following is the case:

(1) If the individual, company, or employee of a company contracting to perform building inspections for the ~~city~~ local government has worked for the owner, developer, contractor, or project manager of the project to be inspected within the last two years.

(2) If the individual, company, or employee of a company contracting to perform building inspections for the ~~city~~ local government is closely related to the owner, developer, contractor, or project manager of the project to be inspected.

(3) If the individual, company, or employee of a company contracting to perform building inspections for the ~~city~~ local government has a financial or business interest in the project to be inspected.

The provisions of this section do not apply to a firefighter whose primary duties are fire suppression and rescue, but who engages in some fire inspection activities as a secondary responsibility of the firefighter's employment as a firefighter, except no firefighter may inspect any work actually done, or materials or appliances supplied, by the firefighter or the firefighter's business within the preceding six years.

§ 160D-11-9. Failure to perform duties. [584] [160D-1109]

(a) If any member of an inspection department shall willfully fail to perform the duties required ~~of him~~ by law, or willfully shall improperly issue a building permit, or shall give a certificate of compliance without first making the inspections required by law, or willfully shall improperly give a certificate of compliance, ~~he~~ the member shall be guilty of a Class 1 misdemeanor.

---

582. This section has been relocated to Article 4 of Chapter 160D, specifically, to G.S. 160D-4-2(d). The provision regarding paying salaries from collected fees has been deleted in the relocated material as an unnecessary level of detail.

583. This section has been relocated from G.S. 160A-415 and 153A-355. Deleted provisions have been relocated to G.S. 160D-1-9(c).

584. This section has been relocated from G.S. 160A-416 and 153A-356. Amendments made by S.L. 2015-145 have been incorporated.

(b) A member of the inspection department shall not be in violation of this section when the local government, its inspection department, or one of the inspectors accepted a signed written document of compliance with the North Carolina State Building Code or the North Carolina Residential Code for One- and Two-Family Dwellings from a licensed architect or licensed engineer in accordance with G.S. 160D-11-4(d).

§ 160D-11-10. <u>Building permits</u>.[585] [160D-1110]

(a) Except as provided in subsection ~~(a2)~~ <u>(c)</u> of this section, no person shall commence or proceed with any of the following without first securing ~~from the inspection department with jurisdiction over the site of the work any and~~[586] all permits required by the State Building Code and any other State or local laws applicable to the work:

(1) The construction, reconstruction, alteration, repair, movement to another site, removal, or demolition of any building or structure.

(2) The installation, extension, or general repair of any plumbing system except that in any one- or two-family dwelling unit a permit shall not be required for the connection of a water heater that is being replaced, provided that the work is performed by a person licensed under G.S. 87-21, who personally examines the work at completion and ensures that a leak test has been performed on the gas piping, and provided the energy use rate or thermal input is not greater than that of the water heater ~~which~~ <u>that</u> is being replaced, there is no change in fuel, energy source, location, capacity, or routing or sizing of venting and piping, and the replacement is installed in accordance with the current edition of the State Building Code.

(3) The installation, extension, alteration, or general repair of any heating or cooling equipment system.

(4) The installation, extension, alteration, or general repair of any electrical wiring, devices, appliances, or equipment except that in any one- or two-family dwelling unit a permit shall not be required for repair or replacement of electrical lighting fixtures or devices, such as receptacles and lighting switches, or for the connection of an existing branch circuit to an electric water heater that is being replaced, provided that all of the following requirements are met:

a. With respect to electric water heaters, the replacement water heater is placed in the same location and is of the same or less capacity and electrical rating as the original.

b. With respect to electrical lighting fixtures and devices, the replacement is with a fixture or device having the same voltage and the same or less amperage.

c. The work is performed by a person licensed under G.S. 87-43.

d. The repair or replacement installation meets the current edition of the State Building Code, including the State Electrical Code.

However, a <u>building</u> permit is not required for the installation, maintenance, or replacement of any load control device or equipment by an electric power supplier, as defined in G.S. 62-133.8, or an electrical contractor contracted by the electric power supplier, so long as the work is subject to supervision by an electrical contractor licensed under Article 4 of Chapter 87 of the General Statutes. The electric power supplier shall provide such installation, maintenance, or replacement in accordance with (i) an activity or program ordered, authorized, or approved by the North Carolina Utilities Commission pursuant to G.S. 62-133.8 or G.S. 62-133.9 or (ii) a similar program undertaken by a municipal electric service provider, whether the installation, modification, or replacement is made before or after the point of delivery of electric service to the customer. The exemption under this subdivision applies to all existing installations.

~~(a1)~~ (b)[587] A <u>building</u> permit shall be in writing and shall contain a provision that the work done shall comply with the State Building Code and all other applicable State and local laws. Nothing in this section

---

585. This section has been relocated from G.S. 160A-417 and 153A-357.

586. Simplification.

587. Amendments to this subsection made by S.L. 2019-174 are to be incorporated in 2020. One amendment sets time limits for residential building plan reviews.

shall require a ~~city~~ local government to review and approve residential building plans submitted to the ~~city~~ local government pursuant to the North Carolina Residential Code. ~~Section 106 of the Administration Code and Policies R-110 of Volume VII of the North Carolina State Building Code;~~[588] provided that the ~~city~~ local government may review and approve such residential building plans as it deems necessary. No building permits shall be issued unless the plans and specifications are identified by the name and address of the author thereof, and if the General Statutes of North Carolina require that plans for certain types of work be prepared only by a licensed[589] architect or licensed engineer, no building permit shall be issued unless the plans and specifications bear the North Carolina seal of a licensed architect or of a licensed engineer. When any provision of the General Statutes of North Carolina or of any ordinance requires that work be done by a licensed specialty contractor of any kind, no building permit for the work shall be issued unless the work is to be performed by such a duly licensed contractor.

No permit issued under Articles 9 or 9C of Chapter 143 shall be required for any construction, installation, repair, replacement, or alteration performed in accordance with the current edition of the North Carolina State Building Code[590] costing fifteen thousand dollars ($15,000)[591] or less in any single family residence or farm building unless the work involves any of the following:

(1) The addition, repair or replacement of load bearing structures. However, no permit is required or replacement of windows, doors, exterior siding, or the pickets, railings, stair treads, and decking of porches and exterior decks.

(2) The addition or change in the design of plumbing. However, no permit is required for replacements otherwise meeting the requirements of this subsection that do not change size or capacity.

(3) The addition, replacement, or change in the design of heating, air conditioning, or electrical wiring, devices, appliances, or equipment, other than like-kind replacement of electrical devices and lighting fixtures.

(4) The use of materials not permitted by the North Carolina Residential Code for One- and Two-Family Dwellings.

(5) The addition (excluding replacement) of roofing.

~~(a2)~~ (d) A ~~city~~ local government shall not require more than one building permit for the complete installation or replacement of any natural gas, propane gas, or electrical appliance on an existing structure when the installation or replacement is performed by a person licensed under G.S. 87-21 or G.S. 87-43. The cost of the building permit for such work shall not exceed the cost of any one individual trade permit issued by that ~~city~~ local government, nor shall the ~~city~~ local government increase the costs of any fees to offset the loss of revenue caused by this provision.

~~(b)~~ (e) No building permit shall be issued pursuant to subsection (a) for any land-disturbing activity, as defined in G.S. 113A-52(6), or for any activity covered by G.S. 113A-57, unless an erosion and sedimentation control plan ~~has been approved by the Sedimentation Pollution Control Commission pursuant to G.S. 113A-54(d)(4) or by a local government pursuant to G.S. 113A-61~~ for the site of the activity or a tract of land including the site of the activity has been approved under the Sedimentation Pollution Control Act.

~~(c)~~ (f) No building permit shall be issued pursuant to subsection (a) of this section for any land-disturbing activity that is subject to, but does not comply with, the requirements of G.S. 113A-71.

~~(d)~~ (g) No building permit shall be issued pursuant to subdivision (1) of subsection (a) of this section where the cost of the work is thirty thousand dollars ($30,000) or more, other than for improvements to an existing single-family residential dwelling unit as defined in G.S. 87-15.5(7) that the owner occupies as a residence, or for the addition of an accessory building or accessory structure as defined in the North Carolina Uniform Residential Building Code, the use of which is incidental to that residential dwelling unit, unless the name, physical and mailing address, telephone number, facsimile number, and electronic mail

---

588. Updated citation.
589. Amendments to this subsection made by S.L. 2015-145 have been incorporated.
590. Amendments to this subsection made by S.L. 2016-113 have been incorporated.
591. Amendments to this subsection made by S.L. 2015-145 have been incorporated.

address of the lien agent designated by the owner pursuant to G.S. 44A-11.1(a) is conspicuously set forth in the permit or in an attachment thereto. The building permit may contain the lien agent's electronic mail address. The lien agent information for each permit issued pursuant to this subsection shall be maintained by the inspection department in the same manner and in the same location in which it maintains its record of building permits issued. Where the improvements to a real property leasehold are limited to the purchase, transportation, and setup of a manufactured home, as defined in G.S. 143-143.9(6), the purchase price of the manufactured home shall be excluded in determining whether the cost of the work is thirty thousand dollars ($30,000) or more.[592]

(h) No local government may withhold a building permit or certificate of occupancy that otherwise would be eligible to be issued under this section to compel, with respect to another property or parcel, completion of work for a separate permit or compliance with land use regulations under this Chapter unless otherwise authorized by law or unless the local government reasonably determines the existence of a public safety issue directly related to the issuance of a building permit or certificate of occupancy.[593]

(i) Violation of this section constitutes a Class 1 misdemeanor.

§ 160D-11-11. Expiration of building permits.[594] ~~Time limitations on validity of permits.~~ [160D-1111]

A building permit issued pursuant to ~~G.S. 160A-417/153A-357~~ this Article shall expire by limitation six months, or any lesser time fixed by ordinance of the city council, after the date of issuance if the work authorized by the permit has not been commenced. If after commencement the work is discontinued for a period of 12 months, the permit therefor shall immediately expire. No work authorized by any building permit that has expired shall thereafter be performed until a new permit has been secured.

§ 160D-11-12. Changes in work.[595] [160D-1112]

After a building permit has been issued, no changes or deviations from the terms of the application, plans and specifications, or the permit, except where changes or deviations are clearly permissible under the State Building Code, shall be made until specific written approval of proposed changes or deviations has been obtained from the inspection department.

§ 160D-11-13. Inspections of work in progress.[596] [160D-1113]

Subject to the limitation imposed by G.S. 160D-11-4(b), as the work pursuant to a building permit progresses, local inspectors shall make as many inspections thereof as may be necessary to satisfy them that the work is being done according to the provisions of any applicable State and local laws and of the terms of the permit. In exercising this power, members of the inspection department shall have a right to enter on any premises within the jurisdiction of the department at all reasonable hours for the purposes of inspection or other enforcement action, upon presentation of proper credentials. If a building permit has been obtained by an owner exempt from licensure under G.S. 87-1(b)(2), no inspection shall be conducted without the owner being ~~personally~~ present, unless the plans for the building were drawn and sealed by an architect licensed pursuant to Chapter 83A of the General Statutes.

§ 160D-11-14. Appeals of stop orders.[597] [160D-1114]

~~(a) Whenever any building or structure or part thereof is being demolished, constructed, reconstructed, altered, or repaired in a hazardous manner, or in substantial violation of any State or local building law, or in a manner that endangers life or property, the appropriate inspector may order the specific part of~~

---

592. This sentence was added by S.L. 2016-5.
593. This revision was added by S.L. 2015-187.
594. This section has been relocated from G.S. 160A-418 and 153A-358.
595. This section has been relocated from G.S. 160A-419 and 153A-359.
596. This section has been relocated from G.S. 160A-420 and 153A-360. Amendments to this section made by S.L. 2015-145 have been incorporated.
597. This section has been relocated from G.S. 160A-421 and 153A-361. Issuance of stop-work orders is addressed in G.S. 160D-4-4(b).

~~the work that is in violation or presents such a hazard to be immediately stopped. The stop order shall be in writing, directed to the person doing the work, and shall state the specific work to be stopped, the specific reasons therefor, and the conditions under which the work may be resumed.~~[598]

(a) ~~(b)~~ The owner or builder may appeal from a stop order involving alleged violation of the State Building Code or any approved local modification thereof to the North Carolina Commissioner of Insurance or his designee within a period of five days after the order is issued. Notice of appeal shall be given in writing to the Commissioner of Insurance or his designee, with a copy to the local inspector. The Commissioner of Insurance or his designee shall promptly conduct an investigation and the appellant and the inspector shall be permitted to submit relevant evidence. The Commissioner of Insurance or his designee shall as expeditiously as possible provide a written statement of the decision setting forth the facts found, the decision reached, and the reasons for the decision. Pending the ruling by the Commissioner of Insurance or his designee on an appeal no further work shall take place in violation of a stop order. In the event of dissatisfaction with the decision, the person affected shall have the options of:

(1) Appealing to the Building Code Council, or

(2) Appealing to the Superior Court as provided in G.S. 143-141.

(b) ~~(c)~~ The owner or builder may appeal from a stop order involving alleged violation of a local ~~zoning ordinance~~ development regulation as provided in G.S. 160D-4-5. ~~by giving notice of appeal in writing to the board of adjustment. The appeal shall be heard and decided within the period established by the ordinance, or if none is specified, within a reasonable time. No further work shall take place in violation of a stop order pending a ruling.~~[599]

~~(d) Violation of a stop order shall constitute a Class 1 misdemeanor.~~[600]

§ 160D-11-15. Revocation of <u>building</u> permits.[601] [160D-1115]

The appropriate inspector may revoke and require the return of any building permit by notifying the permit holder in writing stating the reason for the revocation. <u>Building</u> permits shall be revoked for any substantial departure from the approved application, plans, or specifications; for refusal or failure to comply with the requirements of any applicable State or local laws; or for false statements or misrepresentations made in securing the permit. Any <u>building</u> permit mistakenly issued in violation of an applicable State or local law may also be revoked.

§ 160D-11-16. Certificates of compliance.[602] [160D-1116]

At the conclusion of all work done under a <u>building</u> permit, the appropriate inspector shall make a final inspection, and if ~~he~~ <u>the inspector</u> finds that the completed work complies with all applicable State and local laws and with the terms of the permit, ~~he~~ <u>the inspector</u> shall issue a certificate of compliance. No new building or part thereof may be occupied, and no addition or enlargement of an existing building may be occupied, and no existing building that has been altered or moved may be occupied, until the inspection department has issued a certificate of compliance. A temporary certificate of occupancy or compliance may be issued permitting occupancy for a stated period of time of either the entire building or property or of specified portions of the building if the inspector finds that such building or property may safely be occupied prior to its final completion. ~~of the entire building.~~ Violation of this section shall constitute a Class 1 misdemeanor.[603] <u>A local government may require the applicant for a temporary certificate of occupancy to post suitable security to ensure code compliance.</u>

---

598. This subsection has been relocated to Article 4 of Chapter 160D, specifically, to G.S. 160D-4-4(b).

599. This provision has been relocated to Article 4 of Chapter 160D, specifically, to G.S. 160D-4-4(b).

600. This subsection has been relocated to Article 4 of Chapter 160D, specifically, to G.S. 160D-4-4(b).

601. This section has been relocated from G.S. 160A-422 and 153A-363. A more-general provision for revocation of other development permits is located in Article 4 of Chapter 160D, at G.S. 160D-4-4(f).

602. This section has been relocated from G.S. 160A-423 and 153A-363. Deleted provisions have been relocated to Article 4 of Chapter 160D, specifically, to G.S. 160D-4-3(g).

603. Amendments to this section made by S.L. 2019-174 are to be incorporated in 2020.

§ 160D-11-17. Periodic inspections.[604] [160D-1117]

(a) The inspection department may make periodic inspections, subject to the ~~council's~~ governing board's directions, for unsafe, unsanitary, or otherwise hazardous and unlawful conditions in buildings or structures within its ~~territorial~~ planning and development regulation jurisdiction. ~~Except as provided in subsection (b) of this section, the inspection department may make periodic inspections only when there is reasonable cause to believe that unsafe, unsanitary, or otherwise hazardous or unlawful conditions may exist in a residential building or structure. For purposes of this section, the term "reasonable cause" means any of the following: (i) the landlord or owner has a history of more than two verified violations of the housing ordinances or codes within a 12-month period; (ii) there has been a complaint that substandard conditions exist within the building or there has been a request that the building be inspected; (iii) the inspection department has actual knowledge of an unsafe condition within the building; or (iv) violations of the local ordinances or codes are visible from the outside of the property. In conducting inspections authorized under this section, the inspection department shall not discriminate between single-family and multifamily buildings.~~ In exercising this power, members of the department shall have a right to enter on any premises within the jurisdiction of the department at all reasonable hours for the purposes of inspection or other enforcement action, upon presentation of proper credentials. Inspections of dwellings shall follow the provisions of G.S. 160D-12-7. Nothing in this section shall be construed to prohibit periodic inspections in accordance with State fire prevention code or as otherwise required by State law.

~~(b) A city~~ local government ~~may require periodic inspections as part of a targeted effort within a geographic area that has been designated by the city council~~ governing board. ~~The municipality~~ local government ~~shall not discriminate in its selection of areas or housing types to be targeted and shall (i) provide notice to all owners and residents of properties in the affected area about the periodic inspections plan and information regarding a public hearing regarding the plan; (ii) hold a public hearing regarding the plan; and (iii) establish a plan to address the ability of low-income residential property owners to comply with minimum housing code standards.~~

~~(c) In no event may a city~~ local government ~~do any of the following: (i) adopt or enforce any ordinance that would require any owner or manager of rental property to obtain any permit or permission under~~ Article 11 or Article 12 of this Chapter[605] ~~from the city~~ local government ~~to lease or rent residential real property, except for those properties that have more than three verified violations in a 12-month period or upon the property being identified within the top 10% of properties with crime or disorder problems as set forth in a local ordinance; (ii) require that an owner or manager of residential rental property enroll or participate in any governmental program as a condition of obtaining a certificate of occupancy; or (iii) except as provided in subsection (d) of this section, levy a special fee or tax on residential rental property that is not also levied against other commercial and residential properties.~~

~~(d) A city~~ local government ~~may levy a fee for residential rental property registration under subsection (c) of this section for those rental units which have been found with more than two verified violations of local ordinances within the previous 12 months or upon the property being identified within the top 10% of properties with crime or disorder problems as set forth in a local ordinance. The fee shall be an amount that covers the cost of operating a residential registration program and shall not be used to supplant revenue in other areas. Cities~~ Local governments ~~using registration programs that charge registration fees for all residential rental properties as of June 1, 2011, may continue levying a fee on all residential rental properties as follows:~~

---

604. This section has been relocated from G.S. 160A-424 and 153A-364. The deleted provisions, which relate to inspections of existing residential buildings rather than inspections of new construction, were added to this section by S.L. 2011-281 and are relocated to Article 12 of Chapter 160D, specifically, to G.S. 160D-12-7. Note that the provisions in Article 11 of this same Chapter, beginning with this section and running through the end of the Article, do not deal with building permits for new construction but are older statutes related to the safety of existing buildings. Those older statutes apply to all buildings, not just residential structures, so their continued location in Article 11 is appropriate.

605. This revision clarifies that this limitation is intended to apply to the housing code and building code provisions of Chapter 160D.

(1) For properties with 20 or more residential rental units, the fee shall be no more than fifty dollars ($50.00) per year.

(2) For properties with fewer than 20 but more than three residential rental units, the fee shall be no more than twenty-five dollars ($25.00) per year.

(3) For properties with three or fewer residential rental units, the fee shall be no more than fifteen dollars ($15.00) per year.

§ 160D-11-18. Defects in buildings to be corrected.[606] [160D-1118]

When a local inspector finds any defects in a building, or finds that the building has not been constructed in accordance with the applicable State and local laws, or that a building because of its condition is dangerous or contains fire hazardous conditions, it shall be ~~his~~ the inspector's[607] duty to notify the owner or occupant of the building of its defects, hazardous conditions, or failure to comply with law. The owner or occupant shall each immediately remedy the defects, hazardous conditions, or violations of law in the property ~~he owns~~.

§ 160A-425.1: Repealed.

§ 160D-11-19. Unsafe buildings condemned ~~in localities~~.[608] [160D-1119]

(a) *Designation of Unsafe Buildings.* Every building that shall appear to the inspector to be especially dangerous to life because of its liability to fire or because of bad condition of walls, overloaded floors, defective construction, decay, unsafe wiring or heating system, inadequate means of egress, or other causes, shall be held to be unsafe, and the inspector shall affix a notice of the dangerous character of the structure to a conspicuous place on the exterior wall of the building.

(b) *Nonresidential Building or Structure.*[609] In addition to the authority granted in subsection (a) of this section, an inspector may declare a nonresidential building or structure within a community development target area to be unsafe if it meets both of the following conditions:

(1) It appears to the inspector to be vacant or abandoned.

(2) It appears to the inspector to be in such dilapidated condition as to cause or contribute to blight, disease, vagrancy, fire or safety hazard, to be a danger to children, or to tend to attract persons intent on criminal activities or other activities that would constitute a public nuisance.

(c) *Notice posted on structure.* If an inspector declares a nonresidential building or structure to be unsafe under subsection (b) of this section, the inspector must affix a notice of the unsafe character of the structure to a conspicuous place on the exterior wall of the building. For the purposes of this section, the term "community development target area" means an area that has characteristics of an urban progress zone under G.S. 143B-437.09, a "nonresidential redevelopment area" under G.S. 160A-503(10), or an area with similar characteristics designated by the ~~city council~~ governing board as being in special need of revitalization for the benefit and welfare of its citizens.

(d) *Applicability to residential structures.* A ~~municipality~~ local government may expand subsections (b) and (c) of this section to apply to residential buildings by adopting an ordinance. Before adopting such an ordinance, a ~~municipality~~ local government shall hold a ~~public~~ legislative hearing with published notice as provided by G.S. 160D-6-1. ~~and shall provide notice of the hearing at least 10 days in advance of the hearing.~~[610]

---

606. This section has been relocated from G.S. 160A-425 and 153A-365.

607. Revised to reflect gender-neutral language.

608. This section has been relocated from G.S. 160A-426 and 153A-366. Subsections (b) through (d), previously applicable only to cities, have been expanded for uniformity but are still applicable only within community-development target areas.

609. S.L. 2017-109 made subsections (b) through (d) applicable to counties.

610. This revision provides for uniform provisions for public hearings and notice for all legislative decisions.

§ 160D-11-20. Removing notice from condemned building.[611] [160D-1120]

If any person shall remove any notice that has been affixed to any building or structure by a local inspector of any ~~municipality~~ local government and that states the dangerous character of the building or structure, ~~he~~ that person[612] shall be guilty of a Class 1 misdemeanor.

§ 160D-11-21. Action in event of failure to take corrective action.[613] [160D-1121]

If the owner of a building or structure that has been condemned as unsafe pursuant to G.S. 160D-11-17[614] shall fail to take prompt corrective action, the local inspector shall give ~~him~~ written notice, by certified ~~or registered~~ mail to ~~his~~ the owner's last known address or by personal service:

(1) That the building or structure is in a condition that appears to meet one or more of the following conditions:
   a. Constitutes a fire or safety hazard.
   b. Is dangerous to life, health, or other property.
   c. Is likely to cause or contribute to blight, disease, vagrancy, or danger to children.
   d. Has a tendency to attract persons intent on criminal activities or other activities ~~which~~ that would constitute a public nuisance.

(2) That an administrative hearing will be held before the inspector at a designated place and time, not later than 10 days after the date of the notice, at which time the owner shall be entitled to be heard in person or by counsel and to present arguments and evidence pertaining to the matter; and

(3) That following the hearing, the inspector may issue such order to repair, close, vacate, or demolish the building or structure as appears appropriate.

If the name or whereabouts of the owner cannot after due diligence be discovered, the notice shall be considered properly and adequately served if a copy ~~thereof~~ is posted on the outside of the building or structure in question at least 10 days prior to the hearing and a notice of the hearing is published in a newspaper having general circulation in the ~~city~~ local government's area of jurisdiction at least once not later than one week prior to the hearing.

§ 160D-11-22. Order to take corrective action.[615] [160D-1122]

If, upon a hearing held pursuant to the notice prescribed in G.S. 160D-11-19, the inspector shall find that the building or structure is in a condition that constitutes a fire or safety hazard or renders it dangerous to life, health, or other property, ~~he~~ the inspector shall make an order in writing, directed to the owner of such building or structure, requiring the owner to remedy the defective conditions by repairing, closing, vacating, or demolishing the building or structure or taking other necessary steps, within such period, not less than 60 days, as the inspector may prescribe; provided, that where the inspector finds that there is imminent danger to life or other property, ~~he~~ the inspector may order that corrective action be taken in such lesser period as may be feasible.

§ 160D-11-23. Appeal; finality of order if not appealed.[616] [160D-1123]

Any owner who has received an order under G.S. 160D-11-20 may appeal from the order to the ~~city council~~ governing board by giving notice of appeal in writing to the inspector and to the ~~city~~ local government clerk within 10 days following issuance of the order. In the absence of an appeal, the order of the inspector shall be final. The ~~city council~~ governing board shall hear in accordance with G.S. 160D-4-6 and render a decision in an appeal within a reasonable time. The ~~city council~~ governing board may affirm, modify and affirm, or revoke the order.

---

611. This section has been relocated from G.S. 160A-427 and 153A-367.

612. Revised to reflect gender-neutral language.

613. This subsection has been relocated from G.S. 160A-428 and 153A-368. S.L. 2017-109 made amendments to conform G.S. 153A-368 to the municipal equivalent.

614. This cross-reference should be to G.S. 160D-11-19. It will be corrected in 2020.

615. This section has been relocated from G.S. 160A-429 and 153A-369.

616. This section has been relocated from G.S. 160A-430 and 153A-370.

§ 160D-11-24. Failure to comply with order.[617] [160D-1124]

If the owner of a building or structure fails to comply with an order issued pursuant to G.S. 160D-11-20 from which no appeal has been taken, or fails to comply with an order of the ~~city council~~ governing board following an appeal, ~~he~~ the owner shall be guilty of a Class 1 misdemeanor.

§ 160D-11-25. Enforcement.[618] [160D-1125]

(a) *Action Authorized*. Whenever any violation is denominated a misdemeanor under the provisions of this ~~Part~~ Article, the ~~city~~ local government, either in addition to or in lieu of other remedies, may initiate any appropriate action or proceedings to prevent, restrain, correct, or abate the violation or to prevent the occupancy of the building or structure involved.

~~(a1) Repealed by Session Laws 2009-263, s. 1, effective October 1, 2009.~~

(b) *Removal of Building*.[619] In the case of a building or structure declared unsafe under G.S. 160D-11-17 or an ordinance adopted pursuant to G.S. 160D-11-17,[620] a ~~city~~ local government may, in lieu of taking action under subsection (a), cause the building or structure to be removed or demolished. The amounts incurred by the ~~city~~ local government in connection with the removal or demolition shall be a lien against the real property upon which the cost was incurred. The lien shall be filed, have the same priority, and be collected in the same manner as liens for special assessments provided in Article 10 of ~~this~~ Chapter 160A of the General Statutes. If the building or structure is removed or demolished by the ~~city~~ local government, the ~~city~~ local government shall sell the usable materials of the building and any personal property, fixtures, or appurtenances found in or attached to the building. The ~~city~~ local government shall credit the proceeds of the sale against the cost of the removal or demolition. Any balance remaining from the sale shall be deposited with the clerk of superior court of the county where the property is located and shall be disbursed by the court to the person found to be entitled thereto by final order or decree of the court.

~~(b1)~~ (c) *Additional Lien*. The amounts incurred by ~~the~~ a ~~city~~ local government in connection with the removal or demolition shall also be a lien against any other real property owned by the owner of the building or structure and located within the ~~city limits~~ local government's planning and development regulation jurisdiction (and for municipalities without extraterritorial planning and development jurisdiction, within one mile of the city limits), except for the owner's primary residence. The provisions of subsection (b) of this section apply to this additional lien, except that this additional lien is inferior to all prior liens and shall be collected as a money judgment.

~~(c)~~ (d) *Nonexclusive Remedy*. Nothing in this section shall be construed to impair or limit the power of the ~~city~~ local government to define and declare nuisances and to cause their removal or abatement by summary proceedings, or otherwise.

§ 160D-11-26. Records and reports.[621] [160D-1126]

The inspection department shall keep complete and accurate records in convenient form of all applications received, permits issued, inspections and reinspections made, defects found, certificates of compliance or occupancy granted, and all other work and activities of the department. These records shall be kept in the manner and for the periods prescribed by the North Carolina Department of Cultural Resources. Periodic reports shall be submitted to the ~~city council~~ governing board and to the Commissioner of Insurance as they shall by ordinance, rule, or regulation require.

---

617. This section has been relocated from G.S. 160A-431 and 153A-371.

618. This section has been relocated from G.S. 160A-432 and 153A-372. For uniformity, this revision extends the applicability of subsections (b) through (d), currently applicable only to cities, to counties.

619. S.L. 2017-109 made amendments to conform G.S. 153A-372 to the municipal equivalent.

620. This cross-reference should be to G.S. 160D-11-19. It will be corrected in 2020.

621. This section has been relocated from G.S. 160A-433 and 153A-373.

§ 160D-11-27. Appeals ~~in general~~.[622] [160D-1127]

Unless otherwise provided by law, appeals from any order, decision, or determination by a member of a local inspection department pertaining to the State Building Code or other State building laws shall be taken to the Commissioner of Insurance or ~~his~~ the Commissioner's designee or other official specified in G.S. 143-139, by filing a written notice with ~~him~~ the Commissioner and with the inspection department within a period of 10 days after the order, decision, or determination. Further appeals may be taken to the State Building Code Council or to the courts as provided by law.

§ 160D-11-28. Fire limits. [160D-1128]

(a) *County fire limits.*[623] A county may by ordinance establish and define fire limits in any area within the county and not within a city. The limits may include only business and industrial areas. Within any fire limits, no frame or wooden building or addition thereto may be erected, altered, repaired, or moved (either into the fire limits or from one place to another within the limits) except upon the permit of the inspection department and approval of the Commissioner of Insurance. The ~~board of commissioners~~ governing board may make additional regulations necessary for the prevention, extinguishment, or mitigation of fires within the fire limits.

(b) *Municipal fire limits.*[624] The ~~city council~~ governing board of every incorporated city[625] shall pass one or more ordinances establishing and defining fire limits, which shall include the principal business portions of the city and which shall be known as primary fire limits. In addition, the ~~council~~ governing board may, in its discretion, establish and define one or more separate areas within the city as secondary fire limits.

(c) *Restrictions within municipal primary fire limits.*[626] Within the primary fire limits of any city, as established and defined by ordinance, no frame or wooden building or structure or addition thereto shall hereafter be erected, altered, repaired, or moved (either into the limits or from one place to another within the limits), except upon the permit of the local inspection department approved by the ~~city council~~ governing board and by the Commissioner of Insurance or his designee. The ~~city council~~ governing board may make additional regulations for the prevention, extinguishment, or mitigation of fires within the primary fire limits.

(d) *Restriction within municipal secondary fire limits.*[627] Within any secondary fire limits of any city or town, as established and defined by ordinance, no frame or wooden building or structure or addition thereto shall be erected, altered, repaired, or moved except in accordance with any rules and regulations established by ordinance of the areas.

(e) *Failure to establish municipal primary fire limits.*[628] If the ~~council~~ governing board of any city shall fail or refuse to establish and define the primary fire limits of the city as required by law, after having such failure or refusal called to their attention in writing by the State Commissioner of Insurance, the Commissioner shall have the power to establish the limits upon making a determination that they are necessary and in the public interest.

§ 160D-11-29. Regulation ~~Ordinance~~ authorized as to repair, closing, and demolition of nonresidential buildings or structures; order of public officer.[629] [160D-1129]

(a) *Authority.* The governing ~~body~~ board of the ~~city~~ local government may adopt and enforce ~~ordinances~~ regulations relating to nonresidential buildings or structures that fail to meet minimum standards of maintenance, sanitation, and safety established by the governing ~~body~~ board. The minimum standards

---

622. This section has been relocated from G.S. 160A-434 and 153A-374.
623. This subsection has been relocated from G.S. 153A-375.
624. This subsection has been relocated from G.S. 160A-435.
625. This revision intentionally left this subsection applicable only to cities, not to counties. The county provision is found in subsection (b) of this section.
626. This subsection has been relocated from G.S. 160A-436.
627. This subsection has been relocated from G.S. 160A-437.
628. This subsection has been relocated from G.S. 160A-438.
629. This section has been relocated from G.S. 160A-439, applicable to counties under G.S. 153A-372.1.

shall address only conditions that are dangerous and injurious to public health, safety, and welfare and identify circumstances under which a public necessity exists for the repair, closing, or demolition of such buildings or structures. The ~~ordinance~~ regulation shall provide for designation or appointment of a public officer to exercise the powers prescribed by the ~~ordinance,~~ regulation, in accordance with the procedures specified in this section. Such ~~ordinance~~ regulation shall ~~only~~ be applicable within the ~~corporate limits of the city~~ local government's entire planning and development regulation jurisdiction, or, limited to one or more designated zoning districts or municipal service districts.[630]

(b) *Investigation.* Whenever it appears to the public officer that any nonresidential building or structure has not been properly maintained so that the safety or health of its occupants or members of the general public are jeopardized for failure of the property to meet the minimum standards established by the governing ~~body~~ board, the public officer shall undertake a preliminary investigation. If entry upon the premises for purposes of investigation is necessary, such entry shall be made pursuant to a duly issued administrative search warrant in accordance with G.S. 15-27.2 or with permission of the owner, the owner's agent, a tenant, or other person legally in possession of the premises.

(c) *Complaint and Hearing.* If the preliminary investigation discloses evidence of a violation of the minimum standards, the public officer shall issue and cause to be served upon the owner of and parties in interest in the nonresidential building or structure a complaint. The complaint shall state the charges and contain a notice that an administrative hearing will be held before the public officer (or his or her designated agent) at a place within the county scheduled not less than 10 days nor more than 30 days after the serving of the complaint; that the owner and parties in interest shall be given the right to answer the complaint and to appear in person, or otherwise, and give testimony at the place and time fixed in the complaint; and that the rules of evidence prevailing in courts of law or equity shall not be controlling in hearings before the public officer.

(d) *Order.* If, after notice and hearing, the public officer determines that the nonresidential building or structure has not been properly maintained so that the safety or health of its occupants or members of the general public is jeopardized for failure of the property to meet the minimum standards established by the governing ~~body~~ board, the public officer shall state in writing findings of fact in support of that determination and shall issue and cause to be served upon the owner thereof an order. The order may require the owner to take remedial action, within a reasonable time specified, subject to the procedures and limitations herein.

(e) *Limitations on Orders.*

(1) An order may require the owner to repair, alter, or improve the nonresidential building or structure in order to bring it into compliance with the minimum standards established by the governing ~~body~~ board or to vacate and close the nonresidential building or structure for any use.

(2) An order may require the owner to remove or demolish the nonresidential building or structure if the cost of repair, alteration, or improvement of the building or structure would exceed fifty percent (50%) of its then current value. Notwithstanding any other provision of law, if the nonresidential building or structure is designated as a local historic landmark, listed in the National Register of Historic Places, or located in a locally designated historic district or in a historic district listed in the National Register of Historic Places and the governing ~~body~~ board determines, after a public hearing as provided by ordinance, that the nonresidential building or structure is of individual significance or contributes to maintaining the character of the district, and the nonresidential building or structure has not been condemned as unsafe, the order may require that the nonresidential building or structure be vacated and closed until it is brought into compliance with the minimum standards established by the governing ~~body~~ board.

(3) An order may not require repairs, alterations, or improvements to be made to vacant manufacturing facilities or vacant industrial warehouse facilities to preserve the original use. The

---

630. This revision provides uniformity by making jurisdiction for this authority consistent with jurisdiction for other planning and development regulations.

order may require such building or structure to be vacated and closed, but repairs may be required only when necessary to maintain structural integrity or to abate a health or safety hazard that cannot be remedied by ordering the building or structure closed for any use.

(f) *Action by Governing Board Upon Failure to Comply With Order.*

(1) If the owner fails to comply with an order to repair, alter, or improve or to vacate and close the nonresidential building or structure, the governing ~~body~~ <u>board</u> may adopt an ordinance ordering the public officer to proceed to effectuate the purpose of this section with respect to the particular property or properties that the public officer found to be jeopardizing the health or safety of its occupants or members of the general public. The property or properties shall be described in the ordinance. The ordinance shall be recorded in the office of the register of deeds and shall be indexed in the name of the property owner or owners in the grantor index. Following adoption of an ordinance, the public officer may cause the building or structure to be repaired, altered, or improved or to be vacated and closed. The public officer may cause to be posted on the main entrance of any nonresidential building or structure so closed a placard with the following words: "This building is unfit for any use; the use or occupation of this building for any purpose is prohibited and unlawful." Any person who occupies or knowingly allows the occupancy of a building or structure so posted shall be guilty of a Class 3 misdemeanor.

(2) If the owner fails to comply with an order to remove or demolish the nonresidential building or structure, the governing ~~body~~ <u>board</u> may adopt an ordinance ordering the public officer to proceed to effectuate the purpose of this section with respect to the particular property or properties that the public officer found to be jeopardizing the health or safety of its occupants or members of the general public. No ordinance shall be adopted to require demolition of a nonresidential building or structure until the owner has first been given a reasonable opportunity to bring it into conformity with the minimum standards established by the governing ~~body~~ <u>board</u>. The property or properties shall be described in the ordinance. The ordinance shall be recorded in the office of the register of deeds and shall be indexed in the name of the property owner or owners in the grantor index. Following adoption of an ordinance, the public officer may cause the building or structure to be removed or demolished.

(g) *Action by Governing Board Upon Abandonment of Intent to Repair.* If the governing ~~body~~ <u>board</u> has adopted an ordinance or the public officer has issued an order requiring the building or structure to be repaired or vacated and closed and the building or structure has been vacated and closed for a period of two years pursuant to the ordinance or order, the governing ~~body~~ <u>board</u> may make findings that the owner has abandoned the intent and purpose to repair, alter, or improve the building or structure and that the continuation of the building or structure in its vacated and closed status would be inimical to the health, safety, and welfare of the ~~municipality~~ <u>local government</u> in that it would continue to deteriorate, would create a fire or safety hazard, would be a threat to children and vagrants, would attract persons intent on criminal activities, or would cause or contribute to blight and the deterioration of property values in the area. Upon such findings, the governing ~~body~~ <u>board</u> may, after the expiration of the two-year period, enact an ordinance and serve such ordinance on the owner, setting forth the following:

(1) If the cost to repair the nonresidential building or structure to bring it into compliance with the minimum standards is less than or equal to fifty percent (50%) of its then current value, the ordinance shall require that the owner either repair or demolish and remove the building or structure within 90 days; or

(2) If the cost to repair the nonresidential building or structure to bring it into compliance with the minimum standards exceeds fifty percent (50%) of its then current value, the ordinance shall require the owner to demolish and remove the building or structure within 90 days.

In the case of vacant manufacturing facilities or vacant industrial warehouse facilities, the building or structure must have been vacated and closed pursuant to an order or ordinance for a period of five years before the governing ~~body~~ <u>board</u> may take action under this subsection. The ordinance shall be recorded in the office of the register of deeds in the county wherein the property or properties are located and shall be indexed in the name of the property owner in the grantor index. If the owner fails to comply with the ordinance, the public officer shall effectuate the purpose of the ordinance.

(h) *Service of Complaints and Orders*. Complaints or orders issued by a public officer pursuant to an ordinance adopted under this section shall be served upon persons either personally or by ~~registered or~~ certified mail so long as the means used are reasonably designed to achieve actual notice. When service is made by ~~registered or~~ certified mail, a copy of the complaint or order may also be sent by regular mail. Service shall be deemed sufficient if the ~~registered or~~ certified mail is refused, but the regular mail is not returned by the post office within 10 days after the mailing. If regular mail is used, a notice of the pending proceedings shall be posted in a conspicuous place on the premises affected. If the identities of any owners or the whereabouts of persons are unknown and cannot be ascertained by the public officer in the exercise of reasonable diligence, and the public officer makes an affidavit to that effect, the serving of the complaint or order upon the owners or other persons may be made by publication in a newspaper having general circulation in the ~~city~~ local government at least once no later than the time that personal service would be required under this section. When service is made by publication, a notice of the pending proceedings shall be posted in a conspicuous place on the premises affected.

(i) *Liens*.

(1) The amount of the cost of repairs, alterations, or improvements, or vacating and closing, or removal or demolition by the public officer shall be a lien against the real property upon which the cost was incurred, which lien shall be filed, have the same priority, and be collected as the lien for special assessment provided in Article 10 of Chapter 160A of the General Statutes.

(2) If the real property upon which the cost was incurred is located in an incorporated city, the amount of the costs is also a lien on any other real property of the owner located within the city limits except for the owner's primary residence. The additional lien provided in this subdivision is inferior to all prior liens and shall be collected as a money judgment.

(3) If the nonresidential building or structure is removed or demolished by the public officer, he or she shall offer for sale the recoverable materials of the building or structure and any personal property, fixtures, or appurtenances found in or attached to the building or structure and shall credit the proceeds of the sale, if any, against the cost of the removal or demolition, and any balance remaining shall be deposited in the superior court by the public officer, shall be secured in a manner directed by the court, and shall be disbursed by the court to the persons found to be entitled thereto by final order or decree of the court. Nothing in this section shall be construed to impair or limit in any way the power of the governing ~~body~~ board to define and declare nuisances and to cause their removal or abatement by summary proceedings or otherwise.

(j) *Ejectment*. If any occupant fails to comply with an order to vacate a nonresidential building or structure, the public officer may file a civil action in the name of the ~~city~~ local government to remove the occupant. The action to vacate shall be in the nature of summary ejectment and shall be commenced by filing a complaint naming as parties-defendant any person occupying the nonresidential building or structure. The clerk of superior court shall issue a summons requiring the defendant to appear before a magistrate at a certain time, date, and place not to exceed 10 days from the issuance of the summons to answer the complaint. The summons and complaint shall be served as provided in G.S. 42-29. The summons shall be returned according to its tenor, and if on its return it appears to have been duly served and if at the hearing the public officer produces a certified copy of an ordinance adopted by the governing ~~body~~ board pursuant to subsection (f) of this section to vacate the occupied nonresidential building or structure, the magistrate shall enter judgment ordering that the premises be vacated and all persons be removed. The judgment ordering that the nonresidential building or structure be vacated shall be enforced in the same manner as the judgment for summary ejectment entered under G.S. 42-30. An appeal from any judgment entered under this subsection by the magistrate may be taken as provided in G.S. 7A-228, and the execution of the judgment may be stayed as provided in G.S. 7A-227. An action to remove an occupant of a nonresidential building or structure who is a tenant of the owner may not be in the nature of a summary ejectment proceeding pursuant to this subsection unless the occupant was served with notice, at least 30 days before the filing of the summary ejectment proceeding, that the governing ~~body~~ board has ordered the public officer to proceed to exercise his duties under subsection (f) of this section to vacate and close or remove and demolish the nonresidential building or structure.

(k) *Civil Penalty*. The governing ~~body~~ board may impose civil penalties against any person or entity that fails to comply with an order entered pursuant to this section. However, the imposition of civil penalties shall not limit the use of any other lawful remedies available to the governing ~~body~~ board for the enforcement of any ordinances adopted pursuant to this section.

(l) *Supplemental Powers*. The powers conferred by this section are supplemental to the powers conferred by any other law. An ordinance adopted by the governing ~~body~~ board may authorize the public officer to exercise any powers necessary or convenient to carry out and effectuate the purpose and provisions of this section, including the following powers in addition to others herein granted:

(1) To investigate nonresidential buildings and structures in the ~~city~~ local government's planning and development regulation jurisdiction to determine whether they have been properly maintained in compliance with the minimum standards so that the safety or health of the occupants or members of the general public are not jeopardized.

(2) To administer oaths, affirmations, examine witnesses, and receive evidence.

(3) To enter upon premises pursuant to subsection (b) of this section for the purpose of making examinations in a manner that will do the least possible inconvenience to the persons in possession.

(4) To appoint and fix the duties of officers, agents, and employees necessary to carry out the purposes of the ordinances adopted by the governing ~~body~~ board.

(5) To delegate any of his or her functions and powers under the ordinance to other officers and agents.

(m) *Appeals*. The governing ~~body~~ board may provide that appeals may be taken from any decision or order of the public officer to the ~~city's~~ local government's housing appeals board or ~~zoning~~ board of adjustment. Any person aggrieved by a decision or order of the public officer shall have the remedies provided in G.S. 160D-12-8.

(n) *Funding*. The governing ~~body~~ board is authorized to make appropriations from its revenues necessary to carry out the purposes of this section and may accept and apply grants or donations to assist in carrying out the provisions of the ordinances adopted by the governing ~~body~~ board.

(o) *No Effect on Just Compensation for Taking by Eminent Domain*. Nothing in this section shall be construed as preventing the owner or owners of any property from receiving just compensation for the taking of property by the power of eminent domain under the laws of this State, nor as permitting any property to be condemned or destroyed except in accordance with the police power of the State.

(p) *Definitions*. As used in this section:

(1) "Parties in interest" means all individuals, associations, and corporations who have interests of record in a nonresidential building or structure and any who are in possession thereof.

(2) "Vacant industrial warehouse" means any building or structure designed for the storage of goods or equipment in connection with manufacturing processes, which has not been used for that purpose for at least one year and has not been converted to another use.

(3) "Vacant manufacturing facility" means any building or structure previously used for the lawful production or manufacturing of goods, which has not been used for that purpose for at least one year and has not been converted to another use.

"§ 160D-11-30. Vacant building receivership.[631] [160D-1130]

[to be added in 2020]

(a) Petition to Appoint a Receiver. – The governing body of a municipality or its delegated commission may petition the superior court for the appointment of a receiver to rehabilitate, demolish, or sell a vacant building, structure, or dwelling upon the occurrence of any of the following, each of which is deemed a nuisance per se:

(1) The owner fails to comply with an order issued pursuant to G.S. 160A-429, related to building or structural conditions that constitute a fire or safety hazard or render the building or structure dangerous to life, health, or other property, from which no appeal has been taken.

(2) The owner fails to comply with an order of the city council following an appeal of an inspector's order issued pursuant to G.S. 160A-429.

(3) The governing body of the municipality adopts any ordinance pursuant to subdivision (f)(1) of G.S. 160A-439, related to nonresidential buildings or structures that fail to meet minimum standards of maintenance, sanitation, and safety, and orders a public officer to continue enforcement actions prescribed by the ordinance with respect to the named nonresidential building or structure. The public officer may submit a petition on behalf of the governing body to the superior court for the appointment of a receiver, and if granted by the superior court, the petition shall be considered an appropriate means of complying with the ordinance. In the event the superior court does not grant the petition, the public officer and the governing body may take action pursuant to the ordinance in any manner authorized in G.S. 160A-439.

(4) The owner fails to comply with an order to repair, alter, or improve, remove, or demolish a dwelling issued under G.S. 160A-443, related to dwellings that are unfit for human habitation.

(5) Any owner or partial owner of a vacant building, structure, or dwelling, with or without the consent of other owners of the property, submits a request to the governing body in the form of a sworn affidavit requesting the governing body to petition the superior court for appointment of a receiver for the property pursuant to this section.

(b) Petition for Appointment of Receiver. – The petition for the appointment of a receiver shall include all of the following: (i) a copy of the original violation notice or order issued by the city or, in the case of an owner request to the governing body for a petition for appointment of a receiver, a verified pleading that avers that at least one owner consents to the petition; (ii) a verified pleading that avers that the required rehabilitation or demolition has not been completed; and (iii) the names of the respondents, which shall include the owner of the property, as recorded with the register of deeds, any mortgagee with a recorded interest in the property, and all other parties in interest, as defined in G.S. 160A-442(5). If the petition fails to name a respondent as required by this subsection, the proceeding may continue, but the receiver's lien for expenses incurred in rehabilitating, demolishing, or selling the vacant building, structure, or dwelling, as authorized by subsection (f) of this section, shall not have priority over the lien of that respondent.

(c) Notice of Proceeding. – Within 10 days after filing the petition, the city shall give notice of the pendency and nature of the proceeding by regular and certified mail to the last known address of all owners of the property, as recorded with the register of deeds, any mortgagee with a recorded interest in the property, and all other parties in interest, as defined in G.S. 160A-442(5). Within 30 days of the date on which the notice was mailed, an owner of the property, as recorded with the register of deeds, any mortgagee with a recorded interest in the property, and all other parties in interest, as defined in G.S. 160A-442(5), may apply to intervene in the proceeding and to be appointed as receiver. If the city fails to give notice to any owner of the property, as recorded with the register of deeds, any mortgagee with a recorded interest in the property, and all other parties in interest, as defined in G.S. 160A-442(5), as required by this subsection,

---

631. This section will be added to G.S. Chapter 160D in 2020. It has been relocated from G.S. 160A-439.1, created by S.L. 2018-65, and was inadvertently omitted from the edition of Chapter 160D adopted in 2019.

the proceeding may continue, but the receiver's lien for expenses incurred in rehabilitating, demolishing, or selling the vacant building, structure, or dwelling, as authorized by subsection (f) of this section, shall not have priority over the lien of that owner, as recorded with the register of deeds, any mortgagee with a recorded interest in the property, and all other parties in interest, as defined in G.S. 160A-442(5).

(d) Appointment of Receiver. – The court shall appoint a qualified receiver if the provisions of subsections (b) and (c) of this section have been satisfied. If the court does not appoint a person to rehabilitate or demolish the property pursuant to subsection (e) of this section, or if the court dismisses such an appointee, the court shall appoint a qualified receiver for the purpose of rehabilitating and managing the property, demolishing the property, or selling the property to a buyer. To be considered qualified, a receiver must demonstrate to the court (i) the financial ability to complete the purchase or rehabilitation of the property; (ii) the knowledge of, or experience in, the rehabilitation of vacant real property; (iii) the ability to obtain any necessary insurance; and (iv) the absence of any building code violations issued by the city on other real property owned by the person or any member, principal, officer, major stockholder, parent, subsidiary, predecessor, or others affiliated with the person or the person's business. No member of the petitioning city's governing body or a public officer of the petitioning city is qualified to be appointed as a receiver in that action. If, at any time, the court determines that the receiver is no longer qualified, the court may appoint another qualified receiver.

(e) Rehabilitation Not by Receiver. – The court may, instead of appointing a qualified receiver to rehabilitate or sell a vacant building, structure, or dwelling, appoint an owner, mortgagee, or other parties in interest in the property, as defined in G.S. 160A-442, to rehabilitate or demolish the property if that person (i) demonstrates the ability to complete the rehabilitation or demolition within a reasonable time, (ii) agrees to comply with a specified schedule for rehabilitation or demolition, and (iii) posts a bond in an amount determined by the court as security for the performance of the required work in compliance with the specified schedule. After the appointment, the court shall require the person to report to the court on the progress of the rehabilitation or demolition, according to a schedule determined by the court. If, at any time, it appears to the city or its delegated commission that the owner, mortgagee, or other person appointed under this subsection is not proceeding with due diligence or in compliance with the court-ordered schedule, the city or its delegated commission may apply to the court for immediate revocation of that person's appointment and for the appointment of a qualified receiver. If the court revokes the appointment and appoints a qualified receiver, the bond posted by the owner, mortgagee, or other person shall be applied to the receiver's expenses in rehabilitating, demolishing, or selling the vacant building, structure, or dwelling.

(f) Receiver Authority Exclusive. – Upon the appointment of a receiver under subsection (d) of this section and after the receiver records a notice of receivership in the county in which the property is located that identifies the property, all other parties are divested of any authority to collect rents or other income from or to rehabilitate, demolish, or sell the building, structure, or dwelling subject to the receivership. Any party other than the appointed receiver who actively attempts to collect rents or other income from or to rehabilitate, demolish, or sell the property may be held in contempt of court and shall be subject to the penalties authorized by law for that offense. Any costs or fees incurred by a receiver appointed under this section and set by the court shall constitute a lien against the property, and the receiver's lien shall have priority over all other liens and encumbrances, except taxes or other government assessments.

(g) Receiver's Authority to Rehabilitate or Demolish. – In addition to all necessary and customary powers, a receiver appointed to rehabilitate or demolish a vacant building, structure, or dwelling shall have the right of possession with authority to do all of the following:
   (1) Contract for necessary labor and supplies for rehabilitation or demolition.
   (2) Borrow money for rehabilitation or demolition from an approved lending institution or through a governmental agency or program, using the receiver's lien against the property as security.
   (3) Manage the property prior to rehabilitation or demolition and pay operational expenses of the property, including taxes, insurance, utilities, general maintenance, and debt secured by an interest in the property.
   (4) Collect all rents and income from the property, which shall be used to pay for current operating expenses and repayment of outstanding rehabilitation or demolition expenses.

> (5) Manage the property after rehabilitation, with all the powers of a landlord, for a period of up to two years and apply the rent received to current operating expenses and repayment of outstanding rehabilitation or demolition expenses.
>
> (6) Foreclose on the receiver's lien or accept a deed in lieu of foreclosure.

(h) Receiver's Authority to Sell. – In addition to all necessary and customary powers, a receiver appointed to sell a vacant building, structure, or dwelling shall have the authority to do all of the following: (i) sell the property to the highest bidder at public sale, following the same presale notice provisions that apply to a mortgage foreclosure under Article 2A of Chapter 45 of the General Statutes, and (ii) sell the property privately for fair market value if no party to the receivership objects to the amount and procedure. In the notice of public sale authorized under this subsection, it shall be sufficient to describe the property by a street address and reference to the book and page or other location where the property deed is registered. Prior to any sale under this subsection, the applicants to bid in the public sale or the proposed buyer in the private sale shall demonstrate the ability and experience needed to rehabilitate the property within a reasonable time. After deducting the expenses of the sale, the amount of outstanding taxes and other government assessments, and the amount of the receiver's lien, the receiver shall apply any remaining proceeds of the sale first to the city's costs and expenses, including reasonable attorneys' fees, and then to the liens against the property in order of priority. Any remaining proceeds shall be remitted to the property owner.

(i) Receiver Forecloses on Lien. – A receiver may foreclose on the lien authorized by subsection (f) of this section by selling the property subject to the lien at a public sale, following public notice and notice to interested parties in the manner as a mortgage foreclosure under Article 2A of Chapter 45 of the General Statutes. After deducting the expenses of the sale and the amount of any outstanding taxes and other government assessments, the receiver shall apply the proceeds of the sale to the liens against the property, in order of priority. In lieu of foreclosure, and only if the receiver has rehabilitated the property, an owner may pay the receiver's costs, fees, including reasonable attorneys' fees, and expenses or may transfer his or her ownership in the property to either the receiver or an agreed upon third party for an amount agreed to by all parties to the receivership as being the property's fair market value.

(j) Deed After Sale. – Following the court's ratification of the sale of the property under this section, the receiver shall sign a deed conveying title to the property to the buyer, free and clear of all encumbrances, other than restrictions that run with the land. Upon the sale of the property, the receiver shall at the same time file with the court a final accounting and a motion to dismiss the action.

(k) Receiver's Tenure. – The tenure of a receiver appointed to rehabilitate, demolish, or sell a vacant building, structure, or dwelling shall extend no longer than two years after the rehabilitation, demolition, or sale of the property. Any time after the rehabilitation, demolition, or sale of the property, any party to the receivership may file a motion to dismiss the receiver upon the payment of the receiver's outstanding costs, fees, and expenses. Upon the expiration of the receiver's tenure, the receiver shall file a final accounting with the court that appointed the receiver.

(l) Administrative Fee Charged. – The city may charge the owner of the building, structure, or dwelling subject to the receivership an administrative fee that is equal to five percent (5%) of the profits from the sale of the building, structure, or dwelling or one hundred dollars ($100.00), whichever is less."

§160A-440. ~~Reserved for future codification purposes.~~

ARTICLE 12. MINIMUM HOUSING <u>CODES</u>

§ 160D-12-1. <u>Authorization</u> ~~Exercise of police power authorized.~~[632] [160D-1201]

<u>(a) Occupied dwellings.</u> ~~It is hereby found and declared that~~ <u>T</u>he existence and occupation of dwellings ~~in this State~~ that are unfit for human habitation are inimical to the welfare and dangerous and injurious to the health <u>and</u> safety [633] of the people of this State.~~, and that~~ <u>A</u> public necessity exists for the repair, closing

---

632. This section has been relocated from G.S. 160A-441. Article 12 is, in its entirety, also applicable to counties pursuant to G.S. 160A-442.

633. Antiquated language has been deleted in this revision.

or demolition of such dwellings. Whenever any ~~city or county~~ local government ~~of this State~~ finds that there exists in the ~~city or county~~ planning and development regulation jurisdiction dwellings that are unfit for human habitation due to dilapidation, defects increasing the hazards of fire, accidents or other calamities, lack of ventilation, light or sanitary facilities, or due to other conditions rendering the dwellings unsafe or unsanitary, or dangerous or detrimental to the health, safety, morals, or otherwise inimical to the welfare of the residents of the ~~city or county~~ local government, power is ~~hereby~~ conferred upon the ~~city or county~~ local government to exercise its police powers to repair, close or demolish the dwellings consistent with the provisions of this Article. ~~in the manner herein provided. No ordinance enacted by the governing body of a county pursuant to this Part shall be applicable within the corporate limits of any city unless the city council of the city has by resolution expressly given its approval thereto.~~[634]

(b) *Abandoned structures.* ~~In addition, to the exercise of police power authorized herein,~~ Any ~~city~~ local government[635] may by ordinance provide for the repair, closing or demolition of any abandoned structure ~~which~~ that the ~~city council~~ governing board finds to be a health or safety hazard as a result of the attraction of insects or rodents, conditions creating a fire hazard, dangerous conditions constituting a threat to children or frequent use by vagrants as living quarters in the absence of sanitary facilities. ~~Such~~ The ordinance~~, if adopted,~~ may provide for the repair, closing or demolition of such structure pursuant to the same provisions and procedures as are prescribed ~~herein~~ by this Article[636] for the repair, closing or demolition of dwellings found to be unfit for human habitation.

§ 160A-12-2. Definitions.[637] [160D-1202]

The following terms shall have the meanings whenever used or referred to as indicated when used in this Part unless a different meaning clearly appears from the context:

(1) ~~"City" means any incorporated city or any county.~~

(2) ~~"Dwelling" means any building, structure, manufactured home or mobile home, or part thereof, used and occupied for human habitation or intended to be so used, and includes any outhouses and appurtenances belonging thereto or usually enjoyed therewith, except that it does not include any manufactured home or mobile home, which is used solely for a seasonal vacation purpose.~~

(3) ~~"Governing body" means the council, board of commissioners, or other legislative body, charged with governing a city or county.~~

(3a) ~~"Manufactured home" or "mobile home" means a structure as defined in G.S. 143-145(7).~~

(1) "Owner" means the holder of the title in fee simple and every mortgagee of record.

(2) "Parties in interest" means all individuals, associations and corporations who have interests of record in a dwelling and any who are in possession thereof.

(3) "Public authority" means any housing authority or any officer who is in charge of any department or branch of the government of the city, county, or State relating to health, fire, building regulations, or other activities concerning dwellings in the city.

(4) "Public officer" means the officer or officers who are authorized by ordinances adopted hereunder to exercise the powers prescribed by the ordinances and by this ~~Part~~ Article.

---

634. Simplification. This language was deleted as redundant of provisions in Article 2 of Chapter 160D, specifically, G.S. 160D-2-1 and 160D-2-2(f), regarding city-county jurisdiction.

635. This revision provides for consistent and uniform authority regarding abandoned structures by setting consistent authority for cities and counties.

636. Clarification.

637. This section has been relocated from G.S. 160A-442. It has been consolidated with the definitions in Article 1 of Chapter 160D.

§ 160D-12-3. Ordinance authorized as to repair, closing, and demolition; order of public officer.[638] [160D-1203]

Upon the adoption of an ordinance finding that dwelling conditions of the character described in G.S. 160D-12-1 exist ~~within a city~~, the ~~governing body of the city~~ governing board is ~~hereby~~ authorized to adopt and enforce ordinances relating to dwellings within the ~~city's territorial~~ planning and development regulation jurisdiction that are unfit for human habitation. These ordinances shall include the following provisions:

(1) *Designation of enforcement officer.* ~~That public officer~~ One or more public officers shall be designated ~~or appointed~~ to exercise the powers prescribed by the ordinance.

(2) *Investigation, complaint, hearing.* ~~That w~~Whenever a petition is filed with the public officer by a public authority or by at least five residents of the city jurisdiction charging that any dwelling is unfit for human habitation or ~~Whenever~~ when it appears to the public officer ~~(on his own motion)~~[639] that any dwelling is unfit for human habitation, the public officer shall, if ~~his~~ a preliminary investigation discloses a basis for such charges, issue and cause to be served upon the owner of and parties in interest in such dwellings a complaint stating the charges in that respect and containing a notice that ~~a~~ an administrative hearing will be held before the public officer (or ~~his~~ the officer's designated agent) at a place within the county in which the property is located. The hearing shall be ~~fixed~~ not less than 10 days nor more than 30 days after the serving of the complaint~~.; that~~ The owner and parties in interest shall be given the right to file an answer to the complaint and to appear in person, or otherwise, and give testimony at the place and time fixed in the complaint~~.; and that~~ The rules of evidence prevailing in courts of law ~~or equity~~ shall not be controlling in administrative hearings before the public officer.

(3) *Orders.* ~~That~~ If, after notice and hearing, the public officer determines that the dwelling under consideration is unfit for human habitation, ~~he~~ the officer[640] shall state in writing ~~his~~ findings of fact in support of that determination and shall issue and cause to be served upon the owner ~~thereof an order,~~ one of the two following orders, whichever is appropriate:

a. If the repair, alteration or improvement of the dwelling can be made at a reasonable cost in relation to the value of the dwelling, ~~(the ordinance of the city may fix a certain percentage of this value as being reasonable)~~,[641] requiring the owner, within the time specified, to repair, alter or improve the dwelling in order to render it fit for human habitation. The ordinance may fix a certain percentage of this value as being reasonable. The order may require that the property be vacated and closed only if continued occupancy during the time allowed for repair will present a significant threat of bodily harm, taking into account the nature of the necessary repairs, alterations, or improvements; the current state of the property; and any additional risks due to the presence and capacity of minors under the age of 18 or occupants with physical or mental disabilities. The order shall state that the failure to make timely repairs as directed in the order shall make the dwelling subject to the issuance of an unfit order under subdivision (4) of this section; or

b. If the repair, alteration or improvement of the dwelling cannot be made at a reasonable cost in relation to the value of the dwelling, ~~(the ordinance of the city may fix a certain percentage of this value as being reasonable)~~,[642] requiring the owner, within the time specified in the order, to remove or demolish such dwelling. The ordinance may fix a certain percentage of this value as being reasonable. However, notwithstanding any other provision of law, if the dwelling is located in a historic district ~~of the city~~ and the Historic District Commission determines, after a public hearing as provided by ordinance, that the dwelling is of particular significance or value toward maintaining the character of the district, and the dwelling has not been condemned as unsafe, the order may require that the dwelling be vacated and closed consistent with G.S. 160D-9-49.

---

638. This section has been relocated from G.S. 160A-443.

639. Surplusage and non-gender-neutral language have been deleted in this revision.

640. Revised to reflect gender-neutral language.

641. For purposes of clarity, this provision has been relocated within this subsection.

642. For purposes of clarity, this provision has been relocated within this subsection.

(4) *Repair, closing, and posting.* ~~That,~~ If the owner fails to comply with an order to repair, alter or improve or to vacate and close the dwelling, the public officer may cause the dwelling to be repaired, altered or improved or to be vacated and closed; that the public officer may cause to be posted on the main entrance of any dwelling so closed, a placard with the following words: "This building is unfit for human habitation; the use or occupation of this building for human habitation is prohibited and unlawful." Occupation of a building so posted shall constitute a Class 1 misdemeanor. The duties of the public officer set forth in this subdivision shall not be exercised until the governing ~~body~~ board shall have by ordinance ordered the public officer to proceed to effectuate the purpose of this Article with respect to the particular property or properties ~~which~~ that the public officer shall have found to be unfit for human habitation and which property or properties shall be described in the ordinance. This ordinance shall be recorded in the office of the register of deeds in the county ~~wherein~~ the property or properties are located and shall be indexed in the name of the property owner in the grantor index.

(5) *Demolition.* ~~That,~~ If the owner fails to comply with an order to remove or demolish the dwelling, the public officer may cause such dwelling to be removed or demolished. The duties of the public officer set forth in this subdivision shall not be exercised until the governing ~~body~~ board shall have by ordinance ordered the public officer to proceed to effectuate the purpose of this Article with respect to the particular property or properties ~~which~~ that the public officer shall have found to be unfit for human habitation and which property or properties shall be described in the ordinance. No such ordinance shall be adopted to require demolition of a dwelling until the owner has first been given a reasonable opportunity to bring it into conformity with the housing code. This ordinance shall be recorded in the office of the register of deeds in the county wherein the property or properties are located and shall be indexed in the name of the property owner in the grantor index.

(6) *Abandonment of intent to repair in* ~~*high population jurisdictions*~~.[643] If the dwelling has been vacated and closed for a period of one year pursuant to an ordinance adopted pursuant to subdivision (4) of this subsection or after a public officer issues an order or proceedings have commenced under the substandard housing regulations regarding a dwelling to be repaired or vacated and closed as provided in this subsection, then the governing board may find that the owner has abandoned the intent and purpose to repair, alter or improve the dwelling in order to render it fit for human habitation and that the continuation of the dwelling in its vacated and closed status would be inimical to the health, safety, and welfare of the local government in that the dwelling would continue to deteriorate, would create a fire and safety hazard, would be a threat to children and vagrants, would attract persons intent on criminal activities, would cause or contribute to blight and the deterioration of property values in the area, and would render unavailable property and a dwelling ~~which~~ that might otherwise have been made available to ease the persistent shortage of decent and affordable housing in this State, then in such circumstances, the governing board may, after the expiration of such one year period, enact an ordinance and serve such ordinance on the owner, setting forth the following:

1. If it is determined that the repair of the dwelling to render it fit for human habitation can be made at a cost not exceeding fifty percent (50%) of the then current value of the dwelling, the ordinance shall require that the owner either repair or demolish and remove the dwelling within 90 days; or

2. If it is determined that the repair of the dwelling to render it fit for human habitation cannot be made at a cost not exceeding fifty percent (50%) of the then current value of the dwelling, the ordinance shall require the owner to demolish and remove the dwelling within 90 days.

---

643. Stylistic changes to statutory format have been made for improved clarity. This language has been revised to provide for a uniform provision for all jurisdictions rather than retaining (1) the multiple procedures in the current statute, which are based on a jurisdiction's population, or (2) the specification of multiple jurisdictions in the statute.

This ordinance shall be recorded in the Office of the Register of Deeds in the county wherein the property or properties are located and shall be indexed in the name of the property owner in the grantor index. If the owner fails to comply with this ordinance, the public officer shall effectuate the purpose of the ordinance.

~~If the governing body board shall have adopted an ordinance as provided in subdivision (4) of this section, or the public officer shall have:~~

a. ~~\In a municipality located in counties which have a population in excess of 71,000 by the last federal census (including the entirety of any municipality located in more than one county at least one county of which has a population in excess of 71,000), other than municipalities with a population in excess of 190,000 by the last federal census, issued an order, ordering a dwelling to be repaired or vacated and closed, as provided in subdivision (3)a, and if the dwelling has been vacated and closed for a period of one year pursuant to the ordinance or order;~~

b. ~~In a municipality with a population in excess of 190,000 by the last federal census,~~

   (1) ~~issued an order~~ ~~or commenced proceedings under the substandard housing regulations regarding a dwelling to be repaired or vacated and closed, as provided in subdivision (3) a., and~~

   (2) ~~if the dwelling has been vacated and closed for a period of one year pursuant to the ordinance or after such proceedings have commenced,~~

~~then if the governing body~~ board shall ~~find that the owner has abandoned the intent and purpose to repair, alter or improve the dwelling in order to render it fit for human habitation and that the continuation of the dwelling in its vacated and closed status would be inimical to the health, safety, morals and welfare of the municipality~~ local government ~~in that the dwelling would continue to deteriorate, would create a fire and safety hazard, would be a threat to children and vagrants, would attract persons intent on criminal activities, would cause or contribute to blight and the deterioration of property values in the area, and would render unavailable property and a dwelling which might otherwise have been made available to ease the persistent shortage of decent and affordable housing in this State, then in such circumstances, the governing body~~ board ~~may, after the expiration of such one year period, enact an ordinance and serve such ordinance on the owner, setting forth the following:~~

a. ~~If it is determined that the repair of the dwelling to render it fit for human habitation can be made at a cost not exceeding fifty percent (50%) of the then current value of the dwelling, the ordinance shall require that the owner either repair or demolish and remove the dwelling within 90 days; or~~

b. ~~If it is determined that the repair of the dwelling to render it fit for human habitation cannot be made at a cost not exceeding fifty percent (50%) of the then current value of the dwelling, the ordinance shall require the owner to demolish and remove the dwelling within 90 days.~~

~~This ordinance shall be recorded in the Office of the Register of Deeds in the county wherein the property or properties are located and shall be indexed in the name of the property owner in the grantor index. If the owner fails to comply with this ordinance, the public officer shall effectuate the purpose of the ordinance.~~

~~This subdivision only applies to municipalities located in counties which have a population in excess of 71,000 by the last federal census (including the entirety of any municipality located in more than one county at least one county of which has a population in excess of 71,000).~~

~~This subdivision does not apply to the local government units listed in subdivision (5b) of this section.~~

(5b) ~~*Abandonment of intent to repair in specified jurisdictions.*~~ [644] ~~If the governing body board shall have adopted an ordinance as provided in subdivision (4) of this section, or the public officer shall have:~~

a. ~~In a municipality other than municipalities with a population in excess of 190,000 by the last federal census, issued an order, ordering a dwelling to be repaired or vacated and closed, as provided in subdivision (3)a, and if the dwelling has been vacated and closed for a period of one year pursuant to the ordinance or order;~~

---

644. This provision has been replaced by the uniform provisions for all jurisdictions in the previous subsection.

b. ~~In a municipality with a population in excess of 190,000 by the last federal census, commenced proceedings under the substandard housing regulations regarding a dwelling to be repaired or vacated and closed, as provided in subdivision (3)a., and if the dwelling has been vacated and closed for a period of one year pursuant to the ordinance or after such proceedings have commenced, then if the governing body~~ board ~~shall find that the owner has abandoned the intent and purpose to repair, alter or improve the dwelling in order to render it fit for human habitation and that the continuation of the dwelling in its vacated and closed status would be inimical to the health, safety, morals and welfare of the municipality in that the dwelling would continue to deteriorate, would create a fire and safety hazard, would be a threat to children and vagrants, would attract persons intent on criminal activities, would cause or contribute to blight and the deterioration of property values in the area, and would render unavailable property and a dwelling which might otherwise have been made available to ease the persistent shortage of decent and affordable housing in this State, then in such circumstances, the governing body may, after the expiration of such one year period, enact an ordinance and serve such ordinance on the owner, setting forth the following:~~

   a. ~~If it is determined that the repair of the dwelling to render it fit for human habitation can be made at a cost not exceeding fifty percent (50%) of the then current value of the dwelling, the ordinance shall require that the owner either repair or demolish and remove the dwelling within 90 days; or~~

   b. ~~If it is determined that the repair of the dwelling to render it fit for human habitation cannot be made at a cost not exceeding fifty percent (50%) of the then current value of the dwelling, the ordinance shall require the owner to demolish and remove the dwelling within 90 days.~~

~~This ordinance shall be recorded in the Office of the Register of Deeds in the county wherein the property or properties are located and shall be indexed in the name of the property owner in the grantor index. If the owner fails to comply with this ordinance, the public officer shall effectuate the purpose of the ordinance.~~

~~This subdivision applies to the Cities of Eden, Lumberton, Roanoke Rapids, and Whiteville, to the municipalities in Lee County, and the Towns of Bethel, Farmville, Newport, and Waynesville only.~~

(7)   *Liens.*

   a. That the amount of the cost of repairs, alterations or improvements, or vacating and closing, or removal or demolition by the public officer shall be a lien against the real property upon which the cost was incurred, which lien shall be filed, have the same priority, and be collected as the lien for special assessment provided in Article 10 of ~~this~~ Chapter 160A of the General Statutes.

   b. If the real property upon which the cost was incurred is located in an incorporated city, then the amount of the cost is also a lien on any other real property of the owner located within the city limits or within one mile thereof except for the owner's primary residence. The additional lien provided in this sub-subdivision is inferior to all prior liens and shall be collected as a money judgment.

   c. If the dwelling is removed or demolished by the public officer, ~~he~~ the local government[645] shall sell the materials of the dwelling, and any personal property, fixtures or appurtenances found in or attached to the dwelling, and shall credit the proceeds of the sale against the cost of the removal or demolition and any balance remaining shall be deposited in the superior court by the public officer, shall be secured in a manner directed by the court, and shall be disbursed by the court to the persons found to be entitled thereto by final order or decree of the court. Nothing in this section shall be construed to impair or limit in any way the power of the ~~city~~ local government to define and declare nuisances and to cause their removal or abatement by summary proceedings, or otherwise.

---

645. Revised to reflect gender-neutral language.

(8) *Civil action.* If any occupant fails to comply with an order to vacate a dwelling, the public officer may file a civil action in the name of the ~~city~~ local government to remove such occupant. The action to vacate the dwelling shall be in the nature of summary ejectment and shall be commenced by filing a complaint naming as ~~parties~~ defendant any person occupying such dwelling. The clerk of superior court shall issue a summons requiring the defendant to appear before a magistrate at a certain time, date and place not to exceed 10 days from the issuance of the summons to answer the complaint. The summons and complaint shall be served as provided in G.S. 42-29. ~~The summons shall be returned according to its tenor, and if on its return it~~ If the summons appears to have been duly served, and if at the hearing the public officer produces a certified copy of an ordinance adopted by the governing ~~body~~ board pursuant to subdivision (5) authorizing the officer to proceed to vacate the occupied dwelling, the magistrate shall enter judgment ordering that the premises be vacated and that all persons be removed. The judgment ordering that the dwelling be vacated shall be enforced in the same manner as the judgment for summary ejectment entered under G.S. 42-30. An appeal from any judgment entered hereunder by the magistrate may be taken as provided in G.S. 7A-228, and the execution of such judgment may be stayed as provided in G.S. 7A-227. An action to remove an occupant of a dwelling who is a tenant of the owner may not be in the nature of a summary ejectment proceeding pursuant to this paragraph unless such occupant was served with notice at least 30 days before the filing of the summary ejectment proceeding that the governing ~~body~~ board has ordered the public officer to proceed to exercise his duties under subdivisions (4) and (5) of this section to vacate and close or remove and demolish the dwelling.

(9) *Additional notices to affordable housing organizations.* ~~That~~ Whenever a determination is made pursuant to subdivision (3) of this section that a dwelling must be vacated and closed, or removed or demolished, under the provisions of this section, notice of the order shall be given by first-class mail to any organization involved in providing or restoring dwellings for affordable housing that has filed a written request for such notices. A minimum period of 45 days from the mailing of such notice shall be given before removal or demolition by action of the public officer, to allow the opportunity for any organization to negotiate with the owner to make repairs, lease, or purchase the property for the purpose of providing affordable housing. The public officer or clerk shall certify the mailing of the notices, and the certification shall be conclusive in the absence of fraud. Only an organization that has filed a written request for such notices may raise the issue of failure to mail such notices, and the sole remedy shall be an order requiring the public officer to wait 45 days before causing removal or demolition.

§ 160D-12-4. Heat source required.[646] [160D-1204]

(a) A ~~city~~ local government shall, by ordinance, require that ~~by January 1, 2000,~~[647] every dwelling unit leased as rental property within the city shall have, at a minimum, a central or electric heating system or sufficient chimneys, flues, or gas vents, with heating appliances connected, so as to heat at least one habitable room, excluding the kitchen, to a minimum temperature of 68 degrees Fahrenheit measured three feet above the floor with an outside temperature of 20 degrees Fahrenheit.

(b) If a dwelling unit contains a heating system or heating appliances that meet the requirements of subsection (a) of this section, the owner of the dwelling unit shall not be required to install a new heating system or heating appliances, but the owner shall be required to maintain the existing heating system or heating appliances in a good and safe working condition. Otherwise, the owner of the dwelling unit shall install a heating system or heating appliances that meet the requirements of subsection (a) of this section and shall maintain the heating system or heating appliances in a good and safe working condition.

---

646. This section has been relocated from G.S. 160A-443.1, currently applicable only to cities and not to counties; that distinction has been retained by this revision.

647. The required date passed more than a decade ago, and thus its inclusion is no longer needed in the statute.

(c) Portable kerosene heaters are not acceptable as a permanent source of heat as required by subsection (a) of this section but may be used as a supplementary source in single family dwellings and duplex units. An owner who has complied with subsection (a) shall not be held in violation of this section where an occupant of a dwelling unit uses a kerosene heater as a primary source of heat.

(d)[648] This section applies only to ~~cities~~ local governments with a population of 200,000 or over within their planning and development regulation jurisdiction, according to the most recent decennial federal census.

(e) Nothing in this section shall be construed as:

(1) Diminishing the rights of or remedies available to any tenant under a lease agreement, statute, or at common law; or

(2) Prohibiting a city from adopting an ordinance with more stringent heating requirements than provided for by this section.

§ 160D-12-5. Standards.[649] [160D-1205]

An ordinance adopted ~~by a city~~ under this ~~Part~~ Article shall provide that the public officer may determine that a dwelling is unfit for human habitation if ~~he~~ the officer[650] finds that conditions exist in the dwelling that render it dangerous or injurious to the health, safety, or welfare ~~or morals~~ of the occupants of the dwelling, the occupants of neighboring dwellings, or other residents of the ~~city~~ jurisdiction. Defective conditions may include the following (without limiting the generality of the foregoing): defects therein increasing the hazards of fire, accident, or other calamities; lack of adequate ventilation, light, or sanitary facilities; dilapidation; disrepair; structural defects; uncleanliness. The ordinances may provide additional standards to guide the public officers, ~~or his agents,~~ in determining the fitness of a dwelling for human habitation.

§ 160D-12-6. Service of complaints and orders.[651] [160D-1206]

(a) Complaints or orders issued by a public officer pursuant to an ordinance adopted under this ~~Part~~ Article shall be served upon persons either personally or by ~~registered or~~ certified mail. When service is made by ~~registered or~~ certified mail, a copy of the complaint or order may also be sent by regular mail. Service shall be deemed sufficient if the ~~registered or~~ certified mail is unclaimed or refused, but the regular mail is not returned by the post office within 10 days after the mailing. If regular mail is used, a notice of the pending proceedings shall be posted in a conspicuous place on the premises affected.

(b) If the identities of any owners or the whereabouts of persons are unknown and cannot be ascertained by the public officer in the exercise of reasonable diligence, or, if the owners are known but have refused to accept service by ~~registered or~~ certified mail, and the public officer makes an affidavit to that effect, then the serving of the complaint or order upon the owners or other persons may be made by publication in a newspaper having general circulation in the ~~city~~ jurisdiction at least once no later than the time at which personal service would be required under the provisions of this ~~Part~~ Article. When service is made by publication, a notice of the pending proceedings shall be posted in a conspicuous place on the premises thereby affected.

~~(b) Repealed.~~

§ 160D-12-7. Periodic inspections.[652] [160D-1207]

(a) Except as provided in subsection (b) of this section, the inspection department may make periodic inspections only when there is reasonable cause to believe that unsafe, unsanitary, or otherwise hazardous or unlawful conditions may exist in a residential building or structure. However, when the inspection department determines that a safety hazard exists in one of the dwelling units within a multifamily building,

---

648. Earlier editions this bill established a uniform rule for all jurisdictions by eliminating provisions that limited their application to large-population jurisdictions; the current bill edition maintains the status quo by retaining the current limit.

649. This section has been relocated from G.S. 160A-444.

650. Revised to reflect gender-neutral language.

651. This section has been relocated from G.S. 160A-445.

652. This section has been relocated from G.S. 160A-424 and 153A-364. Since these provisions are applicable to the inspection of existing residential buildings rather than to inspections of new construction,

which in the opinion of the inspector poses an immediate threat to the occupant, the inspection department may inspect, in the absence of a specific complaint and actual knowledge of the unsafe condition, additional dwelling units in the multifamily building to determine if that same safety hazard exists.[653] For purposes of this section, the term "reasonable cause" means any of the following: (i) the landlord or owner has a history of more than two verified violations of the housing ordinances or codes within a 12-month period; (ii) there has been a complaint that substandard conditions exist within the building or there has been a request that the building be inspected; (iii) the inspection department has actual knowledge of an unsafe condition within the building; or (iv) violations of the local ordinances or codes are visible from the outside of the property. In conducting inspections authorized under this section, the inspection department shall not discriminate between single-family and multifamily buildings or between owner-occupied and tenant-occupied buildings.[654] In exercising this power, members of the department shall have a right to enter on any premises within the jurisdiction of the department at all reasonable hours for the purposes of inspection or other enforcement action, upon presentation of proper credentials. Nothing in this section shall be construed to prohibit periodic inspections in accordance with State fire prevention code or as otherwise required by State law.

(b) A ~~city~~ local government may require periodic inspections as part of a targeted effort to respond to blighted or potentially blighted conditions[655] within a geographic area that has been designated by the ~~city council~~ governing board. However, the total aggregate of targeted areas in the ~~county~~ local government jurisdiction at any one time shall not be greater than one square mile or five percent (5%) of the area within the ~~county~~ local government jurisdiction, whichever is greater. A targeted area designated by the ~~county~~ local government shall reflect the local government's ~~county's~~ stated neighborhood revitalization strategy and shall consist of property that meets the definition of a "blighted area" or "blighted parcel" as those terms are defined in G.S. 160A-503(2) and G.S. 160A-503(2a), respectively, except that for purposes of this subsection the planning ~~commission~~ board is not required to make a determination as to the property.[656] The ~~municipality~~ local government shall not discriminate in its selection of areas or housing types to be targeted and shall (i) provide notice to all owners and residents of properties in the affected area about the periodic inspections plan and information regarding a public hearing regarding the plan; (ii) hold a public hearing regarding the plan; and (iii) establish a plan to address the ability of low-income residential property owners to comply with minimum housing code standards.

(c)[657] In no event may a ~~city~~ local government do any of the following: (i) adopt or enforce any ordinance that would require any owner or manager of rental property to obtain any permit or permission under Article 11 or Article 12 of this Chapter[658] from the ~~city~~ local government to lease or rent residential real property or to register rental property with the ~~county~~ local government, except for those individual properties that have more than four verified violations in a rolling 12-month period or two or more verified violations in a rolling 30-day period, or upon the property being identified within the top ten percent (10%) of properties with crime or disorder problems as set forth in a local ordinance; (ii) require that an owner or manager of residential rental property enroll or participate in any governmental program as a condition of obtaining a certificate of occupancy; (iii) levy a special fee or tax on residential rental property that is not also levied against other commercial and residential properties, unless expressly authorized by general law or applicable only to an individual rental unit or property described in clause (i) of this subsection and the fee does not exceed five hundred dollars ($500.00) in any 12-month period in which the unit or property is found to have verified violations; (iv) provide that any violation of a rental registration ordinance is punish-

the provisions' location within the housing code Article of G.S. Chapter 160D is more appropriate than their prior location within the building code Article.

653. This provision was added by S.L. 2016-122.

654. This provision was added by S.L. 2016-122.

655. This provision was added by S.L. 2016-122.

656. This provision was added by S.L. 2016-122.

657. Amendments to this subsection made by S.L. 2016-122 have been incorporated. This session law also deleted subsection (d) of this section.

658. This revision clarifies that this limitation is intended to apply to the housing code and building code provisions of Chapter 160D.

able as a criminal offense; or (v) require any owner or manager of rental property to submit to an inspection before receiving any utility service provided by the ~~city~~ local government. For purposes of this section, the term "verified violation" means all of the following:

(1) The aggregate of all violations of housing ordinances or codes found in an individual rental unit of residential real property during a 72-hour period.

(2) Any violations that have not been corrected by the owner or manager within 21 days of receipt of written notice from the ~~county~~ local government of the violations. Should the same violation occur more than two times in a 12-month period, the owner or manager may not have the option of correcting the violation. If the housing ~~ordinance or~~ code provides that any form of prohibited tenant behavior constitutes a violation by the owner or manager of the rental property, it shall be deemed a correction of the tenant-related violation if the owner or manager, within 30 days of receipt of written notice of the tenant-related violation, brings a summary ejectment action to have the tenant evicted.

~~(e)~~ [659] (d) If a property is identified by the ~~county~~ local government as being in the top ten percent (10%) of properties with crime or disorder problems, the ~~county~~ local government shall notify the landlord of any crimes, disorders, or other violations that will be counted against the property to allow the landlord an opportunity to attempt to correct the problems. In addition, the ~~county~~ local government and the county sheriff's office or city's police department shall assist the landlord in addressing any criminal activity, which may include testifying in court in a summary ejectment action or other matter to aid in evicting a tenant who has been charged with a crime. If the ~~county~~ local government or the county sheriff's office or city's police department does not cooperate in evicting a tenant, the tenant's behavior or activity at issue shall not be counted as a crime or disorder problem as set forth in the local ordinance, and the property may not be included in the top ten percent (10%) of properties as a result of that tenant's behavior or activity.

~~(f)~~ (e) If the ~~county~~ local government takes action against an individual rental unit under this section, the owner of the individual rental unit may appeal the decision to the housing appeals board or the zoning board of adjustment, if operating, or the planning board if created under G.S. ~~153A-321~~ 160D-3-1, or if neither is created, the governing board. The board shall fix a reasonable time for hearing appeals, shall give due notice to the owner of the individual rental unit, and shall render a decision within a reasonable time. The owner may appear in person or by agent or attorney. The board may reverse or affirm the action, wholly or partly, or may modify the action appealed from, and may make any decision and order that in the opinion of the board ought to be made in the matter.

§ 160D-12-8. Remedies.[660] [160D-1208]

(a)[661] ~~The governing body may provide for the creation and organization of a housing appeals board to which appeals may be taken from any decision or order of the public officer, or may provide for such appeals to be heard and determined by its zoning board of adjustment.~~

~~(b) The housing appeals board, if created, shall consist of five members to serve for three-year staggered terms. It shall have the power to elect its own officers, to fix the times and places for its meetings, to adopt necessary rules of procedure, and to adopt other rules and regulations for the proper discharge of its duties. It shall keep an accurate record of all its proceedings.~~

(a) An ordinance adopted pursuant to this Article may provide for a housing appeals board as provided by G.S. 160D-3-6. An appeal from any decision or order of the public officer is a quasi-judicial matter and may be taken by any person aggrieved thereby or by any officer, board or commission of the ~~city~~ local government. Any appeal from the public officer shall be taken within 10 days from the rendering of the decision or service of the order by filing with the public officer and with the housing appeals board a notice of appeal ~~which~~ that shall specify the grounds upon which the appeal is based. Upon the filing of any notice of appeal, the public officer shall forthwith transmit to the board all the papers constituting the record upon which the decision appealed from was made. When an appeal is from a decision of the public officer refusing

---

659. Prior subsection (d) was deleted by S.L. 2016-122.

660. This section has been relocated from G.S. 160A-446.

661. This subsection has been relocated to G.S. 160D-3-5.

to allow the person aggrieved thereby to do any act, ~~his~~ the decision shall remain in force until modified or reversed. When any appeal is from a decision of the public officer requiring the person aggrieved to do any act, the appeal shall have the effect of suspending the requirement until the hearing by the board, unless the public officer certifies to the board, after the notice of appeal is filed with ~~him~~ the officer, that because of facts stated in the certificate (a copy of which shall be furnished the appellant), a suspension of ~~his~~ the requirement would cause imminent peril to life or property. In that case the requirement shall not be suspended except by a restraining order, which may be granted for due cause shown upon not less than one day's written notice to the public officer, by the board, or by a court of record upon petition made pursuant to subsection (f) of this section.

(b) The housing appeals board shall fix a reasonable time for hearing appeals, shall give due notice to the parties, and shall render its decision within a reasonable time. Any party may appear in person or by agent or attorney. The board may reverse or affirm, wholly or partly, or may modify the decision or order appealed from, and may make any decision and order that in its opinion ought to be made in the matter, and to that end it shall have all the powers of the public officer, but the concurring vote of four members of the board shall be necessary to reverse or modify any decision or order of the public officer. The board shall have power also in passing upon appeals, when ~~practical difficulties or~~[662] unnecessary hardships would result from carrying out the strict letter of the ordinance, to adapt the application of the ordinance to the necessities of the case to the end that the spirit of the ordinance shall be observed, public safety and welfare secured, and substantial justice done.

(c) Every decision of the housing appeals board shall be subject to review by proceedings in the nature of certiorari instituted within 15 days of the decision of the board, but not otherwise.

(d) Any person aggrieved by an order issued by the public officer or a decision rendered by the housing appeals board may petition the superior court for an injunction restraining the public officer from carrying out the order or decision and the court may, upon such petition, issue a temporary injunction restraining the public officer pending a final disposition of the cause. The petition shall be filed within 30 days after issuance of the order or rendering of the decision. Hearings shall be had by the court on a petition within 20 days, and shall be given preference over other matters on the court's calendar. The court shall hear and determine the issues raised and shall enter such final order or decree as law and justice may require. It shall not be necessary to file bond in any amount before obtaining a temporary injunction under this subsection.

(e) If any dwelling is erected, constructed, altered, repaired, converted, maintained, or used in violation of this ~~Part~~ Article or of any ordinance or code adopted under authority of this Article or any valid order or decision of the public officer or board made pursuant to any ordinance or code adopted under authority of this ~~Part~~ Article, the public officer or board may institute any appropriate action or proceedings to prevent the unlawful erection, construction, reconstruction, alteration or use, to restrain, correct or abate the violation, to prevent the occupancy of the dwelling, or to prevent any illegal act, conduct or use in or about the premises of the dwelling.

§ 160D-12-9. Compensation to owners of condemned property.[663] [160D-1209]

Nothing in this ~~Part~~ Article shall be construed as preventing the owner or owners of any property from receiving just compensation for the taking of property by the power of eminent domain under the laws of this State, nor as permitting any property to be condemned or destroyed except in accordance with the police power of the State.

§ 160D-12-10. Additional powers of public officer.[664] [160D-1210]

An ordinance adopted by the governing ~~body of the city~~ board may authorize the public officer to exercise any powers necessary or convenient to carry out and effectuate the purpose and provisions of this ~~Part~~ Article, including the following powers in addition to others herein granted:

---

662. This language has been revised to align with updated zoning-variance language.
663. This section has been relocated from G.S. 160A-447.
664. This section has been relocated from G.S. 160A-448.

(1) To investigate the dwelling conditions in the ~~city~~ <u>local government's planning and development regulation jurisdiction</u> in order to determine which dwellings therein are unfit for human habitations;

(2) To administer oaths, affirmations, examine witnesses and receive evidence;

(3) To enter upon premises for the purpose of making examinations in a manner that will do the least possible inconvenience to the persons in possession;

(4) To appoint and fix the duties of officers, agents and employees necessary to carry out the purposes of the ordinances; and

(5) To delegate any of his functions and powers under the ordinance to other officers and other agents.

§ 160D-12-11. Administration of ordinance.[665] [160D-1211]

~~The governing body of any city~~ <u>A local government</u> adopting an ordinance under this ~~Part~~ <u>Article</u> shall, as soon as possible thereafter, prepare an estimate of the annual expenses or costs to provide the equipment, personnel and supplies necessary for periodic examinations and investigations of the dwellings ~~in the city~~ for the purpose of determining the fitness of dwellings for human habitation, and for the enforcement and administration of its ordinances adopted under this ~~Part~~ <u>Article</u>. The ~~city~~ <u>local government</u> is authorized to make appropriations from its revenues necessary for this purpose and may accept and apply grants or donations to assist it in carrying out the provisions of the ordinances.

§ 160D-12-12. Supplemental nature of Article.[666] [160D-1212]

Nothing in this ~~Part~~ <u>Article</u> shall be construed to abrogate or impair the powers of the courts or of any department of any ~~city~~ <u>local government</u> to enforce any provisions of its charter or its ordinances or regulations, nor to prevent or punish violations thereof. ~~; and~~ The powers conferred by this ~~Part~~ <u>Article</u> shall be ~~in addition and~~ supplemental to the powers conferred by any other law.

ARTICLE 13. ADDITIONAL AUTHORITY

Part 1. Open Space <u>Acquisition</u>[667]

§ 160D-13-1. Legislative intent.[668] [160D-1301]

It is the intent of the General Assembly ~~in enacting this Part~~[669] to provide a means whereby any ~~county or city in the State~~ <u>local government</u> may acquire, by purchase, gift, grant, devise, lease, or otherwise, and through the expenditure of public funds, the fee or any lesser interest or right in real property in order to preserve, through limitation of their future use, open spaces and areas for public use and enjoyment.

§ 160D-13-2. Finding of necessity.[670] [160D-1302]

The General Assembly finds that the rapid growth and spread of urban development in the State is encroaching upon, or eliminating, many open areas and spaces of varied size and character, including many having significant scenic or aesthetic values, which areas and spaces if preserved and maintained in their present open state would constitute important physical, social, esthetic, or economic assets to existing and impending urban development. The General Assembly declares that it is necessary for sound and proper urban development and in the public interest of the people of this State for any ~~county or city in the State~~ <u>local government</u> to expend or advance public funds for, or to accept by purchase, gift, grant, devise, lease, or

---

665. This section has been relocated from G.S. 160A-449.
666. This section has been relocated from G.S. 160A-450.
667. This Part has been relocated from G.S. 160A-401 to -410. These sections are also applicable to counties.
668. This section has been relocated from G.S. 160A-401.
669. Simplification.
670. This section has been relocated from G.S. 160A-402.

otherwise, the fee or any lesser interest or right in real property so as to acquire, maintain, improve, protect, limit the future use of, or otherwise conserve open spaces and areas within their respective jurisdictions as defined by this Article.

The General Assembly declares that the acquisition of interests or rights in real property for the preservation of open spaces and areas constitutes a public purpose for which public funds may be expended or advanced.

§ 160D-13-3. ~~Counties or cities~~ Local governments authorized to acquire and reconvey real property.[671] [160D-1303]

Any ~~county or city in the State~~ local government may acquire by purchase, gift, grant, devise, lease, or otherwise, the fee or any lesser interest, development right, easement, covenant, or other contractual right of or to real property within its respective jurisdiction, when it finds that the acquisition is necessary to achieve the purposes of this Part. Any ~~county or city in the State~~ local government may also acquire the fee to any property for the purpose of conveying or leasing the property back to its original owner or other person under covenants or other contractual arrangements that will limit the future use of the property in accordance with the purposes of this Part, but when this is done, the property may be conveyed back to its original owner but to no other person by private sale.

§ 160D-13-4. Joint action by governing bodies.[672] [160D-1304]

~~Any county or city in the State~~ A local government may enter into any agreement with any other ~~county or city in the State~~ local government for the purpose of jointly exercising the authority granted by this Part.

§ 160D-13-5. Powers of governing bodies.[673] [160D-1305]

~~Any county or city in the State~~ A local government, in order to exercise the authority granted by this Part, may:

(1) Enter into and carry out contracts with the State or federal government or any agencies thereof under which grants or other assistance are made to the ~~county or city in the State~~ local government;

(2) Accept any assistance or funds that may be granted by the State or federal government with or without a contract;

(3) Agree to and comply with any reasonable conditions imposed upon grants;

(4) Make expenditures from any funds so granted.

§ 160D-13-6. Appropriations authorized.[674] [160D-1306]

For the purposes set forth in this Part, a ~~county or city in the State~~ local government may appropriate funds not otherwise limited as to use by law.

§ 160D-13-7. Definitions.[675] [160D-1307]

(a) For the purpose of this Part an "open space" or "open area" is any space or area (i) characterized by great natural scenic beauty or (ii) whose existing openness, natural condition, or present state of use, if retained, would enhance the present or potential value of abutting or surrounding urban development, or would maintain or enhance the conservation of natural or scenic resources.

(b) For the purposes of this Part "open space" or "open area" and the "public use and enjoyment" of interests or rights in real property shall also include open space land and open space uses. The term "open

---

671. This section has been relocated from G.S. 160A-403.

672. This section has been relocated from G.S. 160A-404.

673. This section has been relocated from G.S. 160A-405.

674. This section has been relocated from G.S. 160A-406.

675. This section has been relocated from G.S. 160A-407. As the definitions set out in this section are particular to this Part of Chapter 160D, and because the terms can have less-precise or different definitions in ordinances and other statutes, the definitions have been left in the Part rather than incorporated in the general provisions applicable to the entire Chapter.

space land" means any undeveloped or predominantly undeveloped land in an urban area that has value for one or more of the following purposes: (i) park and recreational purposes, (ii) conservation of land and other natural resources, or (iii) historic or scenic purposes. The term "open space uses" means any use of open space land for (i) park and recreational purposes, (ii) conservation of land and other natural resources, or (iii) historic or scenic purposes.

§§ 160A-408 through 160A-410. Reserved for future codification purposes.

§ 160D-13-8 to 13-10. Reserved. [160D-1308 to -1310]

Part 2. Community Development and Redevelopment

§ 160D-13-11. Community development programs and activities.[676] [160D-1311]

(a) Any city local government is authorized to engage in, to accept federal and State grants and loans for, and to appropriate and expend funds for community development programs and activities. In undertaking community development programs and activities, in addition to other authority granted by law, a city local government may engage in the following activities:

(1) Programs of assistance and financing of rehabilitation of private buildings principally for the benefit of low and moderate income persons, or for the restoration or preservation of older neighborhoods or properties, including direct repair, the making of grants or loans, the subsidization of interest payments on loans, and the guaranty of loans;

(2) Programs concerned with employment, economic development, crime prevention, child care, health, drug abuse, education, and welfare needs of persons of low and moderate income.

(b) Any city council governing board may exercise directly those powers granted by law to municipal local government redevelopment commissions and those powers granted by law to municipal local government housing authorities, and may do so whether or not a redevelopment commission or housing authority is in existence in such city local government. Any city council governing board desiring to do so may delegate to any redevelopment commission or to any housing authority the responsibility of undertaking or carrying out any specified community development activities. Any city council governing board may by agreement undertake or carry out for each other any specified community development activities. Any city council governing board may contract with any person, association, or corporation in undertaking any specified community development activities. Any county or city board of health, county board of social services, or county or city board of education, may by agreement undertake or carry out for any city council governing board any specified community development activities.

(c) Any city council local government undertaking community development programs or activities may create one or more advisory committees to advise it and to make recommendations concerning such programs or activities.

(d) Any city council governing board proposing to undertake any loan guaranty or similar program for rehabilitation of private buildings is authorized to submit to its voters the question whether such program shall be undertaken, such referendum to be conducted pursuant to the general and local laws applicable to special elections in such city local government. No state or local taxes shall be appropriated or expended by a county pursuant to this section for any purpose not expressly authorized by G.S. 153A-149, unless the same is first submitted to a vote of the people as therein provided.[677]

(d1)(e) Any city local government may receive and dispense funds from the Community Development Block Grant Section 108 Loan Guarantee program, Subpart M, 24 CFR 570.700 et seq., either through application to the North Carolina Department of Commerce or directly from the federal government, in accordance with State and federal laws governing these funds. Any city local government that receives these funds directly from the federal government may pledge current and future CDBG funds for use as

---

676. This section has been relocated from G.S. 160A-456 and 153A-376.

677. This sentence has been relocated from G.S. 153A-376(c), which is applicable only to counties.

loan guarantees in accordance with State and federal laws governing these funds. A ~~city~~ local government may implement the receipt, dispensing, and pledging of CDBG funds under this subsection by borrowing CDBG funds and lending all or a portion of those funds to a third party in accordance with applicable laws governing the CDBG program.

~~Any city~~ local government that has pledged current or future CDBG funds for use as loan guarantees prior to the enactment of this subsection is authorized to have taken such action. A pledge of future CDBG funds under this subsection is not a debt or liability of the State or any political subdivision of the State or a pledge of the faith and credit of the State or any political subdivision of the State. The pledging of future CDBG funds under this subsection does not directly, indirectly, or contingently obligate the State or any political subdivision of the State to levy or to pledge any taxes.

~~(e) Repealed by Session Laws 1985, c. 665, s. 5.~~

~~(e1)~~(f) All program income from Economic Development Grants from the Small Cities Community Development Block Grant Program may be retained by recipient cities and counties in "economically distressed counties", as defined in G.S. 143B-437.01, for the purposes of creating local economic development revolving loan funds. Such program income derived through the use by cities of Small Cities Community Development Block Grant money includes but is not limited to: (i) payment of principal and interest on loans made by the county using Community Development Block Grant Funds; (ii) proceeds from the lease or disposition of real property acquired with Community Development Block Grant Funds; and (iii) any late fees associated with loan or lease payments in (i) and (ii) above. The local economic development revolving loan fund set up by the city shall fund only those activities eligible under Title I of the federal Housing and Community Development Act of 1974, as amended (P.L. 93-383), and shall meet at least one of the three national objectives of the Housing and Community Development Act. Any expiration of G.S. 143B-437.01 or G.S. 105-129.3 shall not affect this subsection as to designations of economically distressed counties made prior to its expiration.

§ 160D-13-12. Acquisition and disposition of property for redevelopment.[678] [160D-1312]

~~In addition to the powers granted by G.S. 160A-456, any city~~[679] Any local government is authorized, either as a part of a community development program or independently thereof, and without the necessity of compliance with the Urban Redevelopment Law, to exercise the following powers:

(1)   To acquire, by voluntary purchase from the owner or owners, real property ~~which~~ that is either:

    a.   Blighted, deteriorated, deteriorating, undeveloped, or inappropriately developed from the standpoint of sound community development and growth;

    b.   Appropriate for rehabilitation or conservation activities;

    c.   Appropriate for housing construction or the economic development of the community; or

    d.   Appropriate for the preservation or restoration of historic sites, the beautification of urban land, the conservation of open space, natural resources, and scenic areas, the provision of recreational opportunities, or the guidance of urban development;

(2)   To clear, demolish, remove, or rehabilitate buildings and improvements on land so acquired; and

(3)   To retain property so acquired for public purposes, or to dispose, through sale, lease, or otherwise, of any property so acquired to any person, firm, corporation, or governmental unit; provided, the disposition of such property shall be undertaken in accordance with the procedures of Article 12 of this Chapter 160A of the General Statutes, or the procedures of G.S. 160A-514, or any applicable local act or charter provision modifying such procedures; or subsection (4) of this section.

(4)   To sell, exchange, or otherwise transfer real property or any interest therein in a community development project area to any redeveloper at private sale for residential, recreational, commercial, industrial or other uses or for public use in accordance with the community development plan, subject to such covenants, conditions and restrictions as may be deemed to be in

---

678. This section has been relocated from G.S. 160A-457 and 153A-377.

679. Simplification.

the public interest or to carry out the purposes of this Article; provided that such sale, exchange or other transfer, and any agreement relating thereto, may be made only after approval of the ~~municipal~~ governing ~~body~~ board and after a public hearing; a notice of the public hearing shall be given once a week for two successive weeks in a newspaper having general circulation in the ~~municipality~~ local government's planning and development jurisdiction area, and the notice shall be published the first time not less than 10 days nor more than 25 days preceding the public hearing; and the notice shall disclose the terms of the sale, exchange or transfer. At the public hearing the appraised value of the property to be sold, exchanged or transferred shall be disclosed; and the consideration for the conveyance shall not be less than the appraised value.

§ 160D-13-13. Urban Development Action Grants.[680] [160D-1313]

~~In addition to the powers granted by G.S. 160A-456 and G.S. 160A-457, any city~~ Any local government is authorized, either as a part of a community development program or independently thereof, to enter into contracts or agreements with any person, association, or corporation to undertake and carry out specified activities in furtherance of the purposes of Urban Development Action Grants authorized by the Housing and Community Development Act of 1977 (P.L. 95-128) or any amendment ~~thereto which~~ that is a continuation of such grant programs by whatever designation, including the authority to enter into and carry out contracts or agreements to extend loans, loan subsidies, or grants to persons, associations, or corporations and to dispose of real or personal property by private sale in furtherance of such contracts or agreements.

Any enabling legislation contained in local acts ~~which~~ that refers to "Urban Development Action Grants" or the Housing and Community Development Act of 1977 (P.L. 95-128) shall be construed also to refer to any continuation of such grant programs by whatever designation.

§ 160D-13-14. Urban homesteading programs.[681] [160D-1314]

A ~~city~~ local government may establish a program of urban homesteading, in which residential property of little or no value is conveyed to persons who agree to rehabilitate the property and use it, for a minimum number of years, as their principal place of residence. Residential property is considered of little or no value if the cost of bringing the property into compliance with the ~~city's~~ local government's housing code exceeds sixty percent (60%) of the property's appraised value on the county tax records. In undertaking such a program a ~~city~~ local government may:

(1) Acquire by purchase, gift or otherwise, but not eminent domain, residential property specifically for the purpose of reconveyance in the urban homesteading program or may transfer to the program residential property acquired for other purposes, including property purchased at a tax foreclosure sale.

(2) Under procedures and standards established by the ~~city~~ local government, convey residential property by private sale under G.S. 160A-267 and for nominal monetary consideration to persons who qualify as grantees.

(3) Convey property subject to conditions that:
   a. Require the grantee to use the property as his or her principal place of residence for a minimum number of years,
   b. Require the grantee to rehabilitate the property so that it meets or exceeds minimum housing code standards,
   c. Require the grantee to maintain insurance on the property,
   d. Set out any other specific conditions (including, but not limited to, design standards) or actions that the ~~city~~ local government may require, and
   e. Provide for the termination of the grantee's interest in the property and its reversion to the ~~city~~ local government upon the grantee's failure to meet any condition so established.

(4) Subordinate the ~~city's~~ local government's interest in the property to any security interest granted by the grantee to a lender of funds to purchase or rehabilitate the property.

---

680. This section has been relocated from G.S. 160A-457.1.
681. This section has been relocated from G.S. 160A-457.2.

§ 160D-13-15. Downtown development projects.[682] [160D-1315]

(a) <u>Definition</u>. In this section, "downtown development project" means a capital project, in ~~the city's~~ <u>a</u> central business district, as that district is defined by the ~~city council~~ <u>governing board</u>, comprising one or more buildings and including both public and private facilities. By way of illustration but not limitation, such a project might include a single building comprising a publicly owned parking structure and publicly owned convention center and a privately owned hotel or office building.

(b) <u>Authorization</u>. If the ~~city council~~ <u>governing board</u> finds that it is likely to have a significant effect on the revitalization of the <u>jurisdiction</u>, ~~central business district,~~ the ~~city~~ <u>local government</u> may acquire, construct, own, and operate or participate in the acquisition, construction, ownership, and operation of a ~~downtown~~ <u>joint</u> development project or of specific facilities within such a project. The ~~city~~ <u>local government</u> may enter into binding contracts with one or more private developers with respect to acquiring, constructing, owning, or operating such a project. Such a contract may, among other provisions, specify the following:

(1) The property interests of both the ~~city~~ <u>local government</u> and the developer or developers in the project, provided that the property interests of the ~~city~~ <u>local government</u> shall be limited to facilities for a public purpose;

(2) The responsibilities of the ~~city~~ <u>local government</u> and the developer or developers for construction of the project;

(3) The responsibilities of the ~~city~~ <u>local government</u> and the developer or developers with respect to financing the project.

Such a contract may be entered into before the acquisition of any real property necessary to the project.

(c) <u>Eligible property</u>. A ~~downtown~~ <u>joint</u> development project may be constructed on property acquired by the developer or developers, on property directly acquired by the ~~city~~ <u>local government</u>, or on property acquired by the ~~city~~ <u>local government</u> while exercising the powers, duties, and responsibilities of a redevelopment commission pursuant to G.S. 160A-505 or G.S.160D-13-11.

(d) <u>Conveyance of property rights</u>. In connection with a ~~downtown~~ <u>joint</u> development project, the ~~city~~ <u>local government</u> may convey interests in property owned by it, including air rights over public facilities, as follows:

(1) If the property was acquired while the ~~city~~ <u>local government</u> was exercising the powers, duties, and responsibilities of a redevelopment commission, the ~~city~~ <u>local government</u> may convey property interests pursuant to the "Urban Redevelopment Law" or any local modification thereof.

(2) If the property was acquired by the ~~city~~ <u>local government</u> directly, the ~~city~~ <u>local government</u> may convey property interests pursuant to G.S. 160D-13-12, and Article 12 of Chapter 160A of the General Statutes does not apply to such dispositions.

(3) In lieu of conveying the fee interest in air rights, the ~~city~~ <u>local government</u> may convey a leasehold interest for a period not to exceed 99 years, using the procedures of subparagraphs (1) or (2) of this subsection, as applicable.

(e) <u>Construction</u>. The contract between the ~~city~~ <u>local government</u> and the developer or developers may provide that the developer or developers shall be responsible for construction of the entire ~~downtown~~ <u>joint</u> development project. If so, the contract shall include such provisions as the ~~city council~~ <u>governing board</u> deems sufficient to assure that the public facility or facilities included in the project meet the needs of the ~~city~~ <u>local government</u> and are constructed at a reasonable price. A project constructed pursuant to this paragraph is not subject to Article 8 of Chapter 143 of the General Statutes, provided that ~~city~~ <u>local government</u> funds constitute no more than fifty percent (50%) of the total costs of the ~~downtown~~ <u>joint</u> development project. Federal funds available for loan to private developers in connection with a ~~downtown~~ <u>joint</u> development project shall not be considered ~~city~~ <u>local government</u> funds for purposes of this subsection.

---

682. This section has been relocated from G.S. 160A-458.3. An earlier draft of the bill generalized this section by removing its applicability to central business districts. However, it was subsequently deemed appropriate to leave the current scope of the section's applicability unchanged.

(f) Operation. The ~~city~~ local government may contract for the operation of any public facility or facilities included in a ~~downtown~~ joint redevelopment project by a person, partnership, firm or corporation, public or private. Such a contract shall include provisions sufficient to assure that any such facility or facilities are operated for the benefit of the citizens of the ~~city~~ local government.

(g) Grant funds. To assist in the financing of its share of a ~~downtown~~ joint development project, the ~~city~~ local government may apply for, accept and expend grant funds from the federal or State governments.

§ 160D-13-16. Low-and moderate-income housing programs.[683] [160D-1316]

~~In addition to the powers, granted by G.S. 153A-376 and G.S. 153A-377, any county~~ Any local government is authorized to exercise the following powers:

(1) To engage in and to appropriate and expend funds for residential housing construction, new or rehabilitated, for sale or rental to persons and families of low and moderate income. Any ~~board of commissioners~~ governing board may contract with any person, association, or corporation to implement the provisions of this subdivision.

(2) To acquire real property by voluntary purchase from the owners to be developed by the ~~county~~ local government or to be used by the ~~county~~ local government to provide affordable housing to persons of low and moderate income.

(3) ~~Under procedures and standards established by the county,~~[684] To convey property by private sale to any public or private entity that provides affordable housing to persons of low or moderate income under procedures and standards established by the local government,. The ~~county~~ local government shall include as part of any such conveyance covenants or conditions that assure the property will be developed by the entity for sale or lease to persons of low or moderate income.

(4) ~~Under procedures and standards established by the county,~~ To convey residential property by private sale to persons of low or moderate income, in accordance with procedures and standards established by the local government, with G.S. 160A-267, and with any terms and conditions that the ~~board of commissioners~~ governing board may determine.

§ 160D-13-17 to 13-19. Reserved. [160D-1317 to -1319]

Part 3. Miscellaneous

§ 160D-13-20. Program to finance energy improvements.[685] [160D-1320]

(a) Purpose. The General Assembly finds it is in the best interest of the citizens of North Carolina to promote and encourage renewable energy and energy efficiency within the State in order to conserve energy, promote economic competitiveness, and expand employment in the State. The General Assembly also finds that a ~~city~~ local government has an integral role in furthering this purpose by promoting and encouraging renewable energy and energy efficiency within the ~~city's~~ local government's territorial jurisdiction. In furtherance of this purpose, a ~~city~~ local government may establish a program to finance the purchase and installation of distributed generation renewable energy sources or energy efficiency improvements that are permanently affixed to residential, commercial, or other real property.

(b) Financing Assistance. A ~~city~~ local government may establish a revolving loan fund and a loan loss reserve fund for the purpose of financing or assisting in the financing of the purchase and installation of distributed generation renewable energy sources or energy efficiency improvements that are permanently fixed to residential, commercial, or other real property. A ~~city~~ local government may establish other local government energy efficiency and distributed generation renewable energy source finance programs funded through federal grants. A ~~city~~ local government may use State and federal grants and loans and its

---

683. This section has been relocated from G.S. 153A-378.

684. The deleted language has been relocated to the end of this sentence to make it consistent with the structure in other subsections of this section.

685. This section has been relocated from G.S. 160A-459.1 and 153A-455.

general revenue for this financing. The annual interest rate charged for the use of funds from the revolving fund may not exceed eight percent (8%) per annum, excluding other fees for loan application review and origination. The term of any loan originated under this section may not be greater than 20 years.

(c) Definition. As used in this Article, "renewable energy source" has the same meaning as "renewable energy resource" in G.S. 62-133.8.

ARTICLE 14. JUDICIAL REVIEW

§ 160D-14-1. Declaratory judgments.[686] [160D-1401]

Challenges of legislative decisions of governing boards, including the validity and constitutionality of development regulations adopted pursuant to this Chapter, and actions authorized by G.S. 160D-1-8(c), 160D-1-8(g), and 160D-4-5(c) may be brought pursuant to Article 26 of Chapter 1 of the General Statutes.[687] The governmental unit making the challenged decision shall be named a party to the action.

§ 160D-14-2. Appeals in the nature of certiorari.[688] [160D-1402]

(a) *Applicability.* This section applies to appeals of quasi-judicial decisions of decision-making boards when that appeal is ~~to superior court and~~[689] in the nature of certiorari as required by this ~~Article~~ Chapter.

(b) *Filing the Petition.* An appeal in the nature of certiorari shall be initiated by filing ~~with the superior court~~ a petition for writ of certiorari with the superior court. The petition shall do all of the following:

(1) State the facts that demonstrate that the petitioner has standing to seek review.

(2) Set forth allegations sufficient to give the court and parties notice of the grounds upon which the petitioner contends that an error was made.

(3) Set forth with particularity the allegations and facts, if any, in support of allegations that, as the result of an impermissible conflict as described in G.S. 160D-1-9, or locally adopted conflict rules, the decision-making body was not sufficiently impartial to comply with due process principles.

(4) Set forth the relief the petitioner seeks.

(c) *Standing.*[690] A petition may be filed under this section only by a petitioner who has standing to challenge the decision being appealed. The following persons shall have standing to file a petition under this section:

(1) Any person ~~meeting~~ possessing any of the following criteria:

a. ~~Has~~ An ownership interest in the property that is the subject of the decision being appealed, a leasehold interest in the property that is the subject of the decision being appealed, or an interest created by easement, restriction, or covenant in the property that is the subject of the decision being appealed.

b. ~~Has~~ An option or contract to purchase the property that is the subject of the decision being appealed.

c. ~~Was~~ An applicant before the decision-making board whose decision is being appealed.[691]

(2) Any other person who will suffer special damages as the result of the decision being appealed.

---

686. This is a new provision. It adds an explicit reference to judicial review of legislative decisions to make this section parallel with provisions on judicial review of quasi-judicial decisions. This revision makes no substantive change to current law.

687. Article 26 of G.S. Chapter 1 is known as the Uniform Declaratory Judgment Act.

688. This section has been relocated from G.S. 160A-393 and 153A-349.

689. This language has been deleted as superfluous, given a provision in G.S. 160D-4-6(k) that sends all appeals of quasi-judicial decisions under Chapter 160D to superior court.

690. Amendments to this subsection made by Part I of S.L. 2019-111 are to be incorporated in 2020. One amendment adds a provision regarding mootness due to the loss of a property interest.

691. Amendments to this subsection made by Part I of S.L. 2019-111 are to be incorporated in 2020. One amendment in that bill adds a person aggrieved by a final decision to the list of parties entitled to enforce a development regulation.

(3) An incorporated or unincorporated association to which owners or lessees of property in a designated area belong by virtue of their owning or leasing property in that area, or an association otherwise organized to protect and foster the interest of the particular neighborhood or local area, so long as at least one of the members of the association would have standing as an individual to challenge the decision being appealed, and the association was not created in response to the particular development or issue that is the subject of the appeal.

(4) A ~~city~~ local government whose decision-making board has made a decision that the ~~council~~ governing board believes improperly grants a variance from or is otherwise inconsistent with the proper interpretation of ~~an ordinance~~ a development regulation adopted by that ~~council~~ governing board.

(d) *Respondent.* The respondent named in the petition shall be the ~~city~~ local government whose decision-making board made the decision that is being appealed, except that if the petitioner is a ~~city~~ local government that has filed a petition pursuant to subdivision (4) of subsection (d) of this section, then the respondent shall be the decision-making board. If the petitioner is not the applicant before the decision-making board whose decision is being appealed, the petitioner shall also name that applicant as a respondent. Any petitioner may name as a respondent any person with an ownership or leasehold interest in the property that is the subject of the decision being appealed who participated in the hearing, or was an applicant, before the decision-making board.

(e) *Writ of Certiorari.* Upon filing the petition, the petitioner shall present the petition and a proposed writ of certiorari to the clerk of superior court of the county in which the matter arose. The writ shall direct the respondent ~~city~~ local government, or the respondent decision-making board if the petitioner is a ~~city~~ local government that has filed a petition pursuant to subdivision (4) of subsection (d) of this section, to prepare and certify to the court the record of proceedings below within a specified date. The writ shall also direct that the petitioner shall serve the petition and the writ upon each respondent named therein in the manner provided for service of a complaint under Rule 4(j) of the Rules of Civil Procedure, except that, if the respondent is a decision-making board, the petition and the writ shall be served upon the chair of that decision-making board. Rule 4(j)(5)d. of the Rules of Civil Procedure shall apply in the event the chair of a decision-making board cannot be found. No summons shall be issued. The clerk shall issue the writ without notice to the respondent or respondents if the petition has been properly filed and the writ is in proper form. A copy of the executed writ shall be filed with the court.

Upon the filing of a petition for writ of certiorari, a party may request a stay of the execution or enforcement of the decision of the quasi-judicial board pending superior court review.[692] The court may grant a stay in its discretion, and on such conditions ~~which~~ that properly provide for the security of the adverse party. A stay granted in favor of a city or county shall not require a bond or other security.

(f) ~~*Answer*~~ *Response*[693] *to the Petition.* The respondent may, but need not, file ~~an answer~~ a response to the petition, except that, if the respondent contends for the first time that any petitioner lacks standing to bring the appeal, that contention must be set forth in ~~an answer~~ a response served on all petitioners at least 30 days prior to the hearing on the petition. If it is not served within that time period, the matter may be continued to allow the petitioners time to respond pursuant to subparagraph (j) of this section.

(g) *Intervention.* Rule 24 of the Rules of Civil Procedure shall govern motions to intervene as a petitioner or respondent in an action initiated under this section with the following exceptions:

(1) Any person described in subdivision (1) of subsection (d) of this section shall have standing to intervene and shall be allowed to intervene as a matter of right.

(2) Any person, other than one described in subdivision (1) of subsection (d) of this section, who seeks to intervene as a petitioner must demonstrate that the person would have had

---

692. Absent seeking and securing a stay, an applicant who has obtained a development approval may proceed at his or her own risk with the development pending an appeal, as is made explicit by proposed subsection (m)(1) of this section.

693. This revision adjusts the nomenclature to reflect "petitions" for review and "responses" to petitions for judicial review in the nature of certiorari, as opposed to "complaints" and "answers."

standing to challenge the decision being appealed in accordance with subdivisions (2) through (4) of subsection (d) of this section.

(3) Any person, other than one described in subdivision (d)(1) of this section, who seeks to intervene as a respondent must demonstrate that the person would have had standing to file a petition in accordance with subdivisions (2) through (4) of subsection (d) of this section if the decision-making board had made a decision that is consistent with the relief sought by the petitioner.

(h) *The Record.* The record shall consist <u>of the decision and</u>[694] all documents and exhibits submitted to the decision-making board whose decision is being appealed, together with the minutes of the meeting or meetings at which the decision being appealed was considered. Upon request of any party, the record shall also contain an audio or videotape of the meeting or meetings at which the decision being appealed was considered if such a recording was made. Any party may also include in the record a transcript of the proceedings, which shall be prepared at the cost of the party choosing to include it. The parties may agree, ~~or the court may direct,~~ that matters unnecessary to the court's decision be deleted from the record or that matters other than those specified herein be included. The record shall be bound and paginated or otherwise organized for the convenience of the parties and the court. A copy of the record shall be served by the ~~municipal~~ <u>local government</u> respondent, or the respondent decision-making board, upon all petitioners within three days after it is filed with the court.

(i) *Hearing on the Record.* The court shall hear and decide all issues raised by the petition by reviewing the record submitted in accordance with subsection ~~(h)~~ <u>(i)</u>[695] of this section. ~~Except that~~ The court may, in its discretion, allow the record to be supplemented with affidavits, testimony of witnesses, or documentary or other evidence if, and to the extent that, the record is not adequate to allow an appropriate determination of the following issues:[696]

(1) Whether a petitioner or intervenor has standing.

(2) Whether, as a result of impermissible conflict as described in G.S. 160D-1-9 or locally adopted conflict rules, the decision-making body was not sufficiently impartial to comply with due process principles.

(3) Whether the decision-making body erred for the reasons set forth in sub-subdivisions <u>(j) (1)(a) and (b)</u> ~~of subdivision (1) of subsection (k)~~ of this section.[697]

(j) *Scope of Review.*

(1) When reviewing the decision ~~of a decision-making board~~ under the provisions of this section, the court shall ensure that the rights of petitioners have not been prejudiced because the decision-making body's findings, inferences, conclusions, or decisions were:

   a. In violation of constitutional provisions, including those protecting procedural due process rights.

   b. In excess of the statutory authority conferred upon the ~~city~~ <u>local government</u> or the authority conferred upon the decision-making board by ordinance.

   c. Inconsistent with applicable procedures specified by statute or ordinance.

   d. Affected by other error of law.

   e. Unsupported by ~~substantial competent~~ <u>competent, material and substantial</u>[698] evidence in view of the entire record.

   f. Arbitrary or capricious.

---

694. This language clarifies that the decision being appealed is itself a part of the record.

695. This revision corrects a cross-reference error.

696. Amendments to this sentence made by Part I of S.L. 2019-111 are to be incorporated in 2020. One amendment requires the court to allow the record to be supplemented for specified issues.

697. An earlier draft of the bill added evidence on vested rights to this list. The codification of common law vested rights was not included in Chapter 160D. G.S. 160D-1-8(b)(1) provides for appeals of determinations regarding common law vested rights. Under G.S. 160D-1-8(b)(1), the zoning administrator makes an initial determination on claimed common law vested rights, with appeal to the board of adjustment and courts if that determination is disputed.

698. This revision aligns the language used in this subdivision with the terminology used in case law.

(2) When the issue before the court is whether the decision-making board erred in interpreting an ordinance, the court shall review that issue de novo. The court shall consider the interpretation of the decision-making board, but is not bound by that interpretation, and may freely substitute its judgment as appropriate.

(3) The term "competent evidence," as used in this subsection, shall not preclude reliance by the decision-making board on evidence that would not be admissible under the rules of evidence as applied in the trial division of the General Court of Justice if (i) the evidence was admitted without objection[699] or (ii) the evidence appears to be sufficiently trustworthy and was admitted under such circumstances that it was reasonable for the decision-making board to rely upon it. The term "competent evidence," as used in this subsection, shall not be deemed to include the opinion testimony of lay witnesses as to any of the following:

    a. The use of property in a particular way ~~would~~ affects the value of other property.

    b. The increase in vehicular traffic resulting from a proposed development ~~would~~ poses a danger to the public safety.

    c. Matters about which only expert testimony would generally be admissible under the rules of evidence.

(k) *Decision of the Court.* Following its review of the decision-making board in accordance with subsection (j) of this section, the court may affirm the decision, reverse the decision and remand the case with appropriate instructions, or remand the case for further proceedings. If the court does not affirm the decision below in its entirety, then the court shall ~~be guided by the following in determining~~ determine what relief should be granted to the petitioners:

(1) If the court concludes that the error committed by the decision-making board is procedural only, the court may remand the case for further proceedings to correct the procedural error.

(2) If the court concludes that the decision-making board has erred by failing to make findings of fact such that the court cannot properly perform its function, then the court may remand the case with appropriate instructions so long as the record contains substantial competent evidence that could support the decision below with appropriate findings of fact. However, findings of fact are not necessary when the record sufficiently reveals the basis for the decision below or when the material facts are undisputed and the case presents only an issue of law.

(3) If the court concludes that the decision by the decision-making board is not supported by ~~substantial competent~~ competent, material and substantial evidence in the record or is based upon an error of law, then the court may remand the case with an order that directs the decision-making board to take whatever action should have been taken had the error not been committed or to take such other action as is necessary to correct the error. Specifically:

    a. If the court concludes that a permit was wrongfully denied because the denial was not based on ~~substantial competent~~ competent, material and substantial evidence or was otherwise based on an error of law, the court may remand with instructions that the permit be issued, subject to reasonable and appropriate conditions.[700]

    b. If the court concludes that a permit was wrongfully issued because the issuance was not based on ~~substantial competent~~ competent, material and substantial evidence or was otherwise based on an error of law, the court may remand with instructions that the permit be revoked.[701]

---

699. An earlier draft of the bill proposed deleting this provision, but it was determined that the statute should remain in its current form.

700. Amendments to this subsection made by Part I of S.L. 2019-111 are to be incorporated in 2020. One amendment mandates remand to the decision-making board with instructions to issue the permit and specifies conditions that may be imposed.

701. Amendments to this subsection made by Part I of S.L. 2019-111 are to be incorporated in 2020. One amendment adds a directive to reverse any enforcement action (1) not supported by sufficient evidence or (2)

(l) *Effect of Appeal and Ancillary Injunctive Relief.*

(1) If a development approval is appealed, the applicant shall have the right to commence work while the appeal is pending. However, if the development approval is reversed by a final decision of any court of competent jurisdiction, the applicant shall not be deemed to have gained any vested rights on the basis of actions taken prior to or during the pendency of the appeal and must proceed as if no development approval had been granted.

(2) Upon motion of a party to a proceeding under this section, and under appropriate circumstances, the court may issue an injunctive order requiring any other party to that proceeding to take certain action or refrain from taking action that is consistent with the court's decision on the merits of the appeal.

(m) *Joinder.*[702] A declaratory judgment brought under G.S. 160D-14-1 or other civil action relating to the decision at issue may be joined with the petition for writ of certiorari and decided in the same proceeding.[703]

§ 160D-14-3. Appeals of decisions on subdivision plats.[704] [160D-1403]

(a) When a subdivision regulation ~~ordinance~~ adopted under this ~~Part~~ Chapter provides that the decision whether to approve or deny a preliminary or final subdivision plat is quasi-judicial,[705] ~~to be made by a city council the~~ governing board ~~or a planning board, other than a planning board comprised solely of members of a city~~ local government ~~planning staff, and the ordinance authorizes the council~~ governing ~~board or planning board to make a quasi-judicial decision in deciding whether to approve the subdivision plat,~~ then that ~~quasi-judicial~~ decision of the ~~council or planning~~ board shall be subject to review by the superior court by proceedings in the nature of certiorari. The provisions of ~~G.S. 160A-381(c), 160A-388(e)(2), and 160A-393~~ G.S. 160D-4-6 and this section shall apply to those appeals.

(b) When a subdivision regulation ~~ordinance~~ adopted under this ~~Part~~ Chapter provides that the decision whether to approve or deny a preliminary or final subdivision plat is administrative, then that decision of the board shall be subject to review by ~~and for all decisions made by the governing board, or ministerial, a city council governing board, planning board, or staff member is authorized to make only an administrative or ministerial decision in deciding whether to approve a preliminary or final subdivision plat, then any party aggrieved by that administrative or ministerial decision may seek to have the decision reviewed by~~ filing an action in superior court seeking appropriate declaratory or equitable relief within 30 days from receipt of the written notice of the decision, which shall be made as provided in G.S. 160D-4-3(b). ~~Such an action must be filed within the time frame specified in G.S. 160A-381(c) for petitions in the nature of certiorari.~~

(c) For purposes of this section, ~~an ordinance~~ a subdivision regulation shall be deemed to authorize a quasi-judicial decision if the ~~city council or planning board~~ decision-making entity under G.S. 160D-8-3(c) is authorized to decide whether to approve or deny the plat based not only upon whether the application complies with the specific requirements set forth in the regulation, ~~ordinance,~~ but also on whether the application complies with one or more generally stated standards requiring a discretionary decision to be made. ~~by the city council governing board or planning board.~~

§ 160D-14-4. Other civil actions.[706] [160D-1404]

Except as expressly stated, this Article does not limit the availability of civil actions otherwise authorized by law or alter the times in which they may be brought.

---

based on an error of law.

702. Amendments to this subsection made by Part I of S.L. 2019-111 are to be incorporated in 2020. In addition to joinder, these amendments also address mootness and estoppel.

703. This revision allows for efficient judicial review in those cases that raise certain issues properly addressed by a declaratory judgment and other issues properly addressed by appeals in the nature of certiorari. Appropriate claims would need to be filed for both types of actions, but the court is allowed to join the actions and consider both concurrently.

704. This section has been relocated from G.S. 160A-377 and 153A-336.

705. G.S. 160D-8-3 defines which entities can make quasi-judicial and administrative plat-review decisions.

706. This is a new provision. It explicitly provides that the forms of action specified in this Article of G.S. Chapter 160D are not exclusive.

§ 160D-14-5. Statutes of limitations.[707] [160D-1405]

(a) *Zoning map adoption or amendments*. A cause of action as to the validity of any regulation ~~ordinance~~ adopting or amending a zoning map ~~or approving a special use, conditional use, or conditional zoning district request~~[708] adopted under this ~~Article~~ Chapter or other applicable law or a development agreement adopted under Article 10 of this Chapter[709] shall accrue upon adoption of such ordinance and shall be brought within ~~two months~~ sixty days[710] as provided in G.S. 154.1.

(b) *Text adoption or amendment*. Except as otherwise provided in subsection (a) of this section, an action challenging the validity of ~~any~~ development regulation ~~zoning or unified development ordinance or any provision thereof~~ adopted under this ~~Article~~ Chapter or other applicable law shall be brought within one year of the accrual of such action. Such an action accrues when the party bringing such action first has standing to challenge the ordinance. A challenge to an ordinance on the basis of an alleged defect in the adoption process shall be brought within three years after the adoption of the ordinance.

(c) *Enforcement defense*. Nothing in this section or in G.S. 154(10) or G.S. 154.1 shall bar a party in an action involving the enforcement of a development regulation ~~zoning or unified development ordinance~~ from raising as a defense ~~to such enforcement action~~ in such proceedings the invalidity of the ordinance. Nothing in this section or in G.S. 154(10) or G.S. 154.1 shall bar a party who files a timely appeal from an order, requirement, decision, or determination made by an administrative official contending that such party is in violation of a development regulation ~~zoning or unified development ordinance~~ from raising in the judicial appeal the invalidity of such ordinance as a defense to such order, requirement, decision, or determination. A party in an enforcement action or appeal may not assert the invalidity of the ordinance on the basis of an alleged defect in the adoption process unless the defense is formally raised within three years of the adoption of the challenged ordinance.

(d) *Quasi-judicial decisions*.[711] Unless specifically provided otherwise, a petition for review of a quasi-judicial decision shall be filed with the clerk of superior court by the later of 30 days after the decision is effective or after a written copy thereof is given in accordance with G.S. 160D-4-6(j). ~~subdivision (1) of this subsection.~~ When first-class mail is used to deliver notice, three days shall be added to the time to file the petition.

(e) *Others*. Except as provided by this section, the statutes of limitations shall be as provided in Subchapter II of Chapter 1 of the General Statutes.[712]

Conforming Amendments to Other Statutes

SECTION 2.5(a).G.S. § 1-54 is amended to read as follows:

"§ 154. One year.

Within one year an action or proceeding –
(1)   Repealed by Session Laws 1975, c. 252, s. 5.
(2)   Upon a statute, for a penalty or forfeiture, where the action is given to the State alone, or in whole or in part to the party aggrieved, or to a common informer, except where the statute imposing it prescribes a different limitation.
(3)   For libel and slander.

---

707. This section has been relocated from G.S. 160A-364.1 and 153A-348.

708. This language has been deleted as surplusage.

709. This revision specifies a time period for challenging development agreements. As these agreements are most similar to rezoning decisions, the same statute of limitations is used.

710. Given that the lengths of months vary, "sixty days" is substantially similar to, but is a more consistent and precise period than, "two months."

711. This subsection has been relocated from G.S. 160A-388(e2).

712. This cross-reference is to the sections of the General Statutes that set statutes of limitations generally, G.S. 1-4 through -56. Those provisions, which include several specifically applicable to development regulations, are unchanged by this act.

(4)   Against a public officer, for the escape of a prisoner arrested or imprisoned on civil process.

(5)   For the year's allowance of a surviving spouse or children.

(6)   For a deficiency judgment on any debt, promissory note, bond or other evidence of indebtedness after the foreclosure of a mortgage or deed of trust on real estate securing such debt, promissory note, bond or other evidence of indebtedness, which period of limitation above prescribed commences with the date of the delivery of the deed pursuant to the foreclosure sale: Provided, however, that if an action on the debt, note, bond or other evidence of indebtedness secured would be earlier barred by the expiration of the remainder of any other period of limitation prescribed by this subchapter, that limitation shall govern.

(7)   Repealed by Session Laws 1971, c. 939, s. 2.

(7a)   For recovery of damages under Article 1A of Chapter 18B of the General Statutes.

(8)   As provided in G.S. 105377, to contest the validity of title to real property acquired in any tax foreclosure action or to reopen or set aside the judgment in any tax foreclosure action.

(9)   As provided in Article 14 of Chapter 126 of the General Statutes, entitled "Protection for Reporting Improper Government Activities".

(10)   Actions contesting the validity of any zoning or unified development ordinance or any provision thereof adopted under ~~Part 3 of Article 18 of Chapter 153A or Part 3 of Article 19 of Chapter 160A~~ Chapter 160D of the General Statutes or other applicable law, other than an ordinance adopting or amending a zoning map. ~~or approving a special use, conditional use, or conditional zoning district rezoning request.~~[713] Such an action accrues when the party bringing such action first has standing to challenge the ordinance; provided that, a challenge to an ordinance on the basis of an alleged defect in the adoption process shall be brought within three years after the adoption of the ordinance.

SECTION 2.5(b). G.S. § 1-54.1 is amended to read as follows:

"§ 154.1. Two months.

Within two months an action contesting the validity of any ordinance adopting or amending a zoning map. ~~or approving a special use, conditional use, or~~ conditional zoning district rezoning request under ~~Part 3 of Article 18 of Chapter 153A of the General Statutes or Part 3 of Article 19 of Chapter 160A~~ Article 7 ~~of Chapter 160D of the General Statutes or other applicable law.~~[714] Such an action accrues upon adoption of such ordinance or amendment. As used herein, the term "two months" shall be calculated as sixty days.

SECTION 2.5(c). G.S. § 63-31(a) is amended to read as follows:

"G.S. § 63-31. Adoption of airport zoning regulations.

(a) Every political subdivision may adopt, administer, and enforce, under the police power or as a land development regulation under Chapter 160D of the General Statutes, ~~and in the manner and upon the conditions hereinafter prescribed,~~ airport zoning regulations, which regulations shall divide the area surrounding any airport within the jurisdiction of said political subdivision into zones, and, within such zones, specify the land uses permitted, and regulate and restrict the height to which structures and trees may be erected or allowed to grow. In adopting or revising any such zoning regulations, the political subdivision shall consider, among other things, the character of the flying operations expected to be conducted at the airport, the nature of the terrain, the height of existing structures and trees above the level of the airport, the possibility of lowering or removing existing obstructions, and the views of the agency of the federal government charged with the fostering of civil aeronautics, as to the aerial approaches necessary to safe flying operations at the airport."

---

713. This language has been deleted as surplusage. The creation or amendment of these site-specific districts is only accomplished through a zoning-map adoption or amendment.

714. This language has been deleted as surplusage. The creation or amendment of these site-specific districts is only accomplished through a zoning-map adoption or amendment.

SECTION 2.5(d). G.S. § 63-32(b) is amended to read as follows:

"§ 63-32. Permits, new structures, etc., and variances.

(b) Variances. - Any person desiring to erect any structures, or increase the height of any structure, or permit the growth of any tree, or otherwise use his property, in violation of airport zoning regulations adopted under this Article, may apply to the board of appeals, as provided in G.S. 63-33, subsection (c), for a variance from the zoning regulations in question. Such variances <u>shall be considered pursuant to G.S. 160D-7-5(d) and</u> ~~be allowed where a literal application or enforcement of the regulations would result in practical difficulty or unnecessary hardship and the relief granted would not be contrary to the public interest but do substantial justice and~~ be in accordance with the spirit of the regulations and this Article."

SECTION 2.5(e). G.S. § 63-33 is amended to read as follows:

"§ 63-33. Procedure.

(a) Adoption of Zoning Regulations. - No airport zoning regulations shall be adopted, amended, or changed under this Article except by action of the legislative body of the political subdivision in question, or the joint board provided for in G.S. 63-31, subsection (c), <u>following the procedures set for adoption of development regulations in Article 6 of Chapter 160D of the General Statutes.</u> ~~after a public hearing in relation thereto, at which parties in interest and citizens shall have an opportunity to be heard. At least 10 days' notice of the hearing shall be published in an official paper, or a paper of general circulation, in the political subdivision or subdivisions in which the airport is located.~~

(b) Administration of Zoning Regulations - Administrative Agency. - The legislative body of any political subdivision adopting airport zoning regulations under this Article may delegate the duty of administering and enforcing such regulations to any administrative agency under its jurisdiction, or may create a new administrative agency to perform such duty, but such administrative agency shall not be or include any member of the board of appeals. The duties of such administrative agency shall include that of hearing and deciding all permits under G.S. 63-32, subsection (a), but such agency shall not have or exercise any of the powers delegated to the board of appeals.

(c) Administration of Airport Zoning Regulations - Board of Appeals. - Airport zoning regulations adopted under this Article shall provide for a board of appeals to have and exercise the following powers:

   (1) To hear and decide appeals from any order, requirement, decision, or determination made by the administrative agency in the enforcement of this Article ~~or of any ordinance adopted pursuant thereto~~;

   (2) To hear and decide special use permits ~~special exceptions to the terms of the ordinance~~ upon which such board may be required to pass under such ordinance;

   (3) To hear and decide specific variances ~~under G.S. 63-32, subsection (b)~~.

A ~~zoning~~ board of ~~appeals or~~ adjustment ~~already exists,~~ may be appointed as the board of appeals. Otherwise, the board of appeals shall consist of five members, each to be appointed for a term of three years and to be removable for cause by the appointing authority upon written charges and after public hearing.

<u>G.S. 160D-4-5 and 160D-4-6 shall be applicable to appeals, special use permits, and variance petitions made pursuant to this section.</u> ~~The board shall adopt rules in accordance with the provisions of any ordinance adopted under this Article. Meetings of the board shall be held at the call of the chairman and at such other times as the board may determine. The chairman, or in his absence the acting chairman, may administer oaths and compel the attendance of witnesses. All meetings of the board shall be public. The board shall keep minutes of its proceedings, showing the vote of each member upon each question, or, if absent or failing to vote, indicating such fact, and shall keep records of its examinations and other official actions, all of which shall immediately be filed in the office of the board and shall be a public record.~~

~~Appeals to the board may be taken by any person aggrieved, or by any officer, department, board, or bureau of the political subdivision affected, by any decision of the administrative agency. An appeal must be taken within a reasonable time, as provided by the rules of the board, by filing with the agency from which the appeal is taken and with the board, a notice of appeal specifying the grounds thereof. The agency from which the appeal is taken shall forthwith transmit to the board all the papers constituting the record upon which the action appealed from was taken.~~

~~An appeal shall stay all proceedings in furtherance of the action appealed from, unless the agency from which the appeal is taken certifies to the board, after the notice of appeal has been filed with it, that by reason of the facts stated in the certificate a stay would, in its opinion, cause imminent peril to life or property. In such case proceedings shall not be stayed otherwise than by a restraining order which may be granted by the board or by a court of record on application on notice to the agency from which the appeal is taken and on due cause shown.~~

~~The board shall fix a reasonable time for the hearing of the appeal, give public notice and due notice to the parties in interest, and decide the same within a reasonable time. Upon the hearing any party may appear in person or by agent or by attorney.~~

~~The board may, in conformity with the provisions of this Article, reverse or affirm, wholly or partly, or modify, the order, requirement, decision or determination appealed from and may make such order, requirement, decision or determination as ought to be made, and to that end shall have all the powers of the administrative agency from which the appeal is taken.~~

~~The concurring vote of a majority of the members of the board shall be sufficient to reverse any order, requirement, decision, or determination of the administrative agency, or to decide in favor of the applicant on any matter upon which it is required to pass under any such ordinance, or to effect any variation in such ordinance."~~

SECTION 2.5(f). G.S. § 63-34 is amended to read as follows:

"§ 63-34. Judicial review.

G.S. 160D-14-1 shall be applicable to judicial review of administrative and quasi-judicial decisions made pursuant to this Article.

~~(a) Any person aggrieved by any decision of the board of appeals, or any taxpayer, or any officer, department, board, or bureau of the political subdivision, may present to the superior court a verified petition setting forth that the decision is illegal, in whole or in part, and specifying the grounds of the illegality. Such petition shall be presented to the court within 30 days after the decision is filed in the office of the board. Such petition shall comply with the provisions of G.S. 160A-393.~~

~~(b) The allowance of the writ shall not stay proceedings upon the decision appealed from, but the court may, on application, on notice to the board and on due cause shown, grant a restraining order.~~

~~(c) The board of appeals shall not be required to return the original papers acted upon by it, but it shall be sufficient to return certified or sworn copies thereof or of such portions thereof as may be called for by the writ. The return shall concisely set forth such other facts as may be pertinent and material to show the grounds of the decision appealed from and shall be verified.~~

~~(d Repealed by Session Laws 2009-421, s. 3, effective January 1, 2010.~~

~~(e) Costs shall not be allowed against the board of appeals unless it appears to the court that it acted with gross negligence, in bad faith, or with malice, in making the decision appealed from."~~

SECTION 2.5(g). G.S. § 63-35 is amended to read as follows:

"§ 63-35. Enforcement and remedies.

G.S. 160D-4-4 shall be applicable to ordinances adopted pursuant to this Article. ~~Each violation of this Article or of any regulations, order, or ruling promulgated or made pursuant to this Article, shall constitute a Class 3 misdemeanor, and each day a violation continues to exist shall constitute a separate offense. In addition, the political subdivision within which the property is located may institute in any court of competent jurisdiction, an action to prevent, restrain, correct or abate any violation of this Article, or of airport zoning regulations adopted under this Article, or of any order or ruling made in connection with their administration or enforcement, and the court shall adjudge to the plaintiff such relief, by way of injunction (which may be mandatory) or otherwise, as may be proper under all the facts and circumstances of the case, in order fully to effectuate the purposes of this Article and of the regulations adopted and orders and rulings made pursuant thereto."~~

SECTION 2.5(h). G.S. § 143-215.57 is amended to read as follows:

"§ 143-215.57. Procedures in issuing permits.

(a) A local government may establish application forms and require maps, plans, and other information necessary for the issuance of permits in a manner consonant with the objectives of this Part. For this purpose a local government may take into account anticipated development in the foreseeable future that may be adversely affected by the obstruction, as well as existing development. They shall consider the effects of a proposed artificial obstruction in a stream in creating danger to life and property by:

    (1) Water that may be backed up or diverted by the obstruction.

    (2) The danger that the obstruction will be swept downstream to the injury of others.

    (3) The injury or damage at the site of the obstruction itself.

(b) In prescribing standards and requirements for the issuance of permits under this Part and in issuing permits, local governments shall proceed as in the case of an ordinance for the better government of the county or city as the case may be. Local government jurisdiction for these ordinances shall be as specified in Article 2 of Chapter 160D.[715] ~~A city may exercise the powers granted in this Part not only within its corporate boundaries but also within the area of its extraterritorial zoning jurisdiction. A county may exercise the powers granted in this Part at any place within the county that is outside the zoning jurisdiction of a city in the county. If a city does not exercise the powers granted in this Part in the city's extraterritorial zoning jurisdiction, the county may exercise the powers granted in this Part in the city's extraterritorial zoning jurisdiction. The county may regulate territory within the zoning jurisdiction of any city whose governing body, by resolution, agrees to the regulation. The governing body of a city may, upon one year's written notice, withdraw its approval of the county regulations, and those regulations shall have no further effect within the city's jurisdiction.~~

~~(c)~~ Article 4 of Chapter 160D shall be applicable to the administration, enforcement, and appeals regarding these ordinances. ~~The local governing body is hereby empowered to adopt regulations it may deem necessary concerning the form, time, and manner of submission of applications for permits under this Part. These regulations may provide for the issuance of permits under this Part by the local governing body or by an agency designated by the local governing body, as prescribed by the governing body. Every final decision granting or denying a permit under this Part shall be subject to review by the superior court of the county, with the right of jury trial at the election of the party seeking review. The time and manner of election of a jury trial shall be governed by G.S. 1A-1, Rule 38(b) of the Rules of Civil Procedure. Pending the final disposition of an appeal, no action shall be taken that would be unlawful in the absence of a permit issued under this Part.~~"

SECTION 2.5(i). G.S. § 143-215.58 is amended to read as follows:

"§ 143-215.58. Violations and penalties.

(a) Any willful violation of this Part or of any ordinance adopted (or of the provisions of any permit issued) under the authority of this Part shall constitute a Class 1 misdemeanor.

(a1) A local government may use all of the remedies available for the enforcement of ordinances under Chapters 153A, 160A, and 160D of the General Statutes to enforce an ordinance adopted pursuant to this Part.

(b) Failure to remove any artificial obstruction or enlargement or replacement thereof, that violates this Part or any ordinance adopted (or the provision of any permit issued) under the authority of this Part, shall constitute a separate violation of this Part for each day that the failure continues after written notice from the county board of commissioners or governing ~~body~~ board of a city.

(c) In addition to or in lieu of other remedies, the county board of commissioners or governing ~~body~~ board of a city may institute any appropriate action or proceeding to restrain or prevent any violation of this Part or of any ordinance adopted (or of the provisions of any permit issued) under the authority of this Part, or to require any person, firm or corporation that has committed a violation to remove a violating obstruction or restore the conditions existing before the placement of the obstruction."

---

715. Simplification. For planning- and development-regulation jurisdiction, this revision calls for the use of standard statutory provisions applicable to other local development regulations.

SECTION 2.5(j). G.S. § 130A-55(17) is amended to read as follows:

§ 130A-55. Corporate powers.

"(17) For the purpose of promoting and protecting the public health, safety and the general welfare of the State, a sanitary district board is authorized to establish as zoning units any portions of the sanitary district not under the control of the United States or this State or any agency or instrumentality of either, in accordance with the following:

a. No sanitary district board shall designate an area a zoning area until a petition signed by two-thirds of the qualified voters in the area, as shown by the registration books used in the last general election, and with a petition signed by two-thirds of the owners of real property in the area, as shown by the records in the office of the register of deeds for the county, is filed with the sanitary district board. The petition must be accompanied by a map of the proposed zoning area. The board shall hold a public hearing to obtain comment on the proposed creation of the zoning area. A notice of public hearing must be published in a newspaper of general circulation in the county at least two times, and a copy of the notice shall be posted at the county courthouse and in three other public places in the sanitary district.

b. When a zoning area is established within a sanitary district, the sanitary district board as to the zoning area shall have all rights, privileges, powers and duties granted to <u>local governments under Article 7, Chapter 160D</u> ~~municipal corporations under Part 3, Article 19, Chapter 160A~~ of the General Statutes. However, the sanitary district board shall not be required to appoint any zoning commission or board of adjustment. If neither a zoning commission nor board of adjustment is appointed, the sanitary district board shall have all rights.

c. A sanitary district board may enter into an agreement with any city, town or sanitary district for the establishment of a joint zoning commission.

d. A sanitary district board is authorized to use the income of the district and levy and collect taxes upon the taxable property within the district necessary to carry out and enforce the rules and provisions of this subsection.

e. This subsection shall apply only to sanitary districts which adjoin and are contiguous to an incorporated city or town and are located within three miles or less of the boundaries of two other cities or towns.

SECTION 2.5(k). G.S. § 143-214.5(d) is amended to read as follows:

§ 143-214.5. Water supply watershed protection.

"*(d) Mandatory Local Programs.* - The Department shall assist local governments to develop water supply watershed protection programs that comply with this section. Local government compliance programs shall include an implementing local ordinance and shall provide for maintenance, inspection, and enforcement procedures. As part of its assistance to local governments, the Commission shall approve and make available a model local water supply watershed management and protection ordinance. The model management and protection ordinance adopted by the Commission shall, at a minimum, include as options (i) controlling development density, (ii) providing for performance-based alternatives to development density controls that are based on sound engineering principles, and (iii) a combination of both (i) and (ii). Local governments shall administer and enforce the minimum management requirements. Every local government that has within its jurisdiction all or a portion of a water supply watershed shall submit a local water supply watershed management and protection ordinance to the Commission for approval. Local governments may adopt such ordinances pursuant to their general police power, power to regulate the subdivision of land, zoning power, or any combination of such powers. In adopting a local ordinance that imposes water supply watershed management requirements that are more stringent than those adopted by the Commission, a <u>local government must comply with Article 6, Chapter 160D of the General Statutes.</u> ~~county must comply with the notice provisions of G.S. 153A-343 and a municipality must comply with the notice provisions of G.S. 160A-384.~~ This section shall not be construed to affect the validity of any local ordinance adopted for the protection of water supply watersheds prior to completion of the review of the ordinance by the Commission or prior to the assumption by the Commission of responsibility for a local water supply watershed protection program. Local governments may create or designate agencies to administer and enforce such programs. The Commission shall approve a local program only if it determines that the requirements of the program equal or exceed the minimum statewide water supply watershed management requirements adopted pursuant to this section."

SECTION 2.5(I). G.S. § 113A-208 is amended to read as follows:

"§ 113A-208. Regulation of mountain ridge construction by counties and cities.

(a) Any county or city may adopt, effective not later than January 1, 1984, and may enforce an ordinance that regulates the construction of tall buildings or structures on protected mountain ridges by any person. The ordinance may provide for the issuance of permits to construct tall buildings on protected mountain ridges, the conditioning of such permits, and the denial of permits for such construction. Any ordinance adopted hereunder shall be based upon studies of the mountain ridges within the county, a statement of objectives to be sought by the ordinance, and plans for achieving these objectives. Any such county ordinance shall apply countywide except as otherwise provided in G.S. 160A-360 Article 2 of Chapter 160D of the General Statutes, and any such city ordinance shall apply citywide, to construction of tall buildings on protected mountain ridges within the city or county, as the case may be.

A city with a population of 50,000 or more may adopt, prior to January 1, 1986, an ordinance eliminating the requirement for an elevation of 3,000 feet, as permitted by G.S. 113A-206(6).

(b) Under the ordinance, permits shall be denied if a permit application (and shall be revoked if a project) fails to provide for:

(1) Sewering that meets the requirements of a public wastewater disposal system that it discharges into, or that is part of a separate system that meets applicable State and federal standards;

(2) A water supply system that is adequate for fire protection, drinking water and other projected system needs; that meets the requirements of any public water supply system that it interconnects with; and that meets any applicable State standards, requirements and approvals;

(3) Compliance with applicable State and local sedimentation control regulations and requirements; and

(4) Adequate consideration to protecting the natural beauty of the mountains, as determined by the local governing body board.

(c) Permits may be conditioned to insure proper operation, to avoid or mitigate any of the problems or hazards recited in the findings of G.S. 113A-207, to protect natural areas or the public health, and to prevent badly designed, unsafe or inappropriate construction.

(d) An ordinance adopted under the authority of this section applies to all protected mountain ridges as defined in G.S. 113A-206. A county or city may apply the ordinance to other mountain ridges within its jurisdiction if it finds that this application is reasonably necessary to protect against some or all of the hazards or problems set forth in G.S. 113A-207. Additionally, a city with a population of 50,000 or more may apply the ordinance to other mountain ridges within its extraterritorial planning jurisdiction if it finds that this application is reasonably necessary to protect against some or all of the hazards or problems set forth in G.S. 113A-207.

(e) Determinations by the county or city governing board of heights or elevations under this Article shall be conclusive In the absence of fraud. Any county or city that adopts a ridge ordinance under the authority of this section or other authority shall send a copy of the ordinance to the Secretary of Environment and Natural Resources.

(f) Any county or city that adopts an ordinance pursuant to this section shall follow the procedures of Article 6 of Chapter 160D of the General Statutes. must hold a public hearing before adopting the ordinance upon the question of adopting the ordinance or of allowing the construction of tall buildings on protected mountain ridges to be governed by G.S. 113A-209. The public hearing required by this section shall be held upon at least 10 days' notice in a newspaper of general circulation in the unit adopting the ordinance. Testimony at the hearing shall be recorded and any and all exhibits shall be preserved within the custody of the governing body. The testimony and evidence shall be made available for inspection and scrutiny by any person.

(g) Any resident of a county or city that adopted an ordinance pursuant to this section, or of an adjoining county, may bring a civil action against the ordinance-adopting unit, contesting the ordinance as not meeting the requirements of this section. If the ordinance is found not to meet all of the requirements of this section, the county or city shall be enjoined from enforcing the ordinance and the provisions of G.S. 113A-209 shall apply. Nothing in this Article authorizes the State of North Carolina or any of its agencies to bring a civil action to contest an ordinance, or for a violation of this Article or of an ordinance adopted pursuant to this Article."

SECTION 2.5(m). G.S. § 113A-211(a) is amended to read as follows:

"§ 113A-211. Enforcement and penalties.

(a) Violations of this Article shall be subject to the same criminal sanctions, civil penalties and equitable remedies as provided by G.S. 160D-4-4. ~~violations of county ordinances under G.S. 153A-123~~."

SECTION 2.5(n). G.S. § 160A-75[716] is amended to read as follows:

§ 160A-75. Voting.

No member shall be excused from voting except upon matters involving the consideration of the member's own financial interest or official conduct or on matters on which the member is prohibited from voting under G.S. 14-234 or 160D-1-9. ~~160A-381(d), 160A-388(e)(2)~~. In all other cases, except votes taken under ~~G.S.160A-385~~ G.S. 160D-6-1, a failure to vote by a member who is physically present in the council chamber, or who has withdrawn without being excused by a majority vote of the remaining members present, shall be recorded as an affirmative vote. The question of the compensation and allowances of members of the council is not a matter involving a member's own financial interest or official conduct.

An affirmative vote equal to a majority of all the members of the council not excused from voting on the question in issue, including the mayor's vote in case of an equal division, shall be required to adopt an ordinance, take any action having the effect of an ordinance, authorize or commit the expenditure of public funds, or make, ratify, or authorize any contract on behalf of the city. In addition, no ordinance nor any action having the effect of any ordinance (except an ordinance on which a public hearing must be held pursuant to G.S. 160D-6-1 before the ordinance may be adopted)[717] may be finally adopted on the date on which it is introduced except by an affirmative vote equal to or greater than two thirds of all the actual membership of the council, excluding vacant seats and not including the mayor unless the mayor has the right to vote on all questions before the council. For purposes of this section, an ordinance shall be deemed to have been introduced on the date the subject matter is first voted on by the council.

SECTION 2.5.(o). [718] G.S. 136-18 reads as rewritten:

"§ 136-18. Powers of Department of Transportation.

The said Department of Transportation is vested with the following powers:

...

(10) To make proper and reasonable rules, regulations and ordinances for the placing or erection of telephone, telegraph, electric and other lines, above or below ground, wireless facilities, signboards, fences, gas, water, sewerage, oil, or other pipelines, and other similar obstructions that may, in the opinion of the Department of Transportation, contribute to the hazard upon any of the said highways or in any way interfere with the same, and to make reasonable rules and regulations for the proper control thereof. And whenever the order of the said Department of Transportation shall require the removal of, or changes in, the location of telephone, telegraph,

---

716. This revision incorporates amendments made by S.L. 2015-160 and updates cross-references to Chapter 160D.

717. This revision was adapted from G.S. 153A-45. It provides city-county uniformity for the process of making legislative decisions on development regulations. It adopts county provision requiring only a simple majority on first reading for adoption, amendment, or repeal of development regulations, given the mandatory public hearing with prior published notice prior to governing board consideration of such ordinances.

718. This is a conforming amendment added by House committee substitute.

electric or other lines, wireless facilities, signboards, fences, gas, water, sewerage, oil, or other pipelines, or other similar obstructions, the owners thereof shall at their own expense, except as provided in G.S. 136-19.5(c), move or change the same to conform to the order of said Department of Transportation. Any violation of such rules and regulations or noncompliance with such orders shall constitute a Class 1 misdemeanor. For purposes of this subdivision, "wireless facilities" shall have the definition set forth in G.S. 160A-400.51.G.S. 160D-9-31.

....."

SECTION 2.5.(p). [719] **G.S. 136-18.3A reads as rewritten:**

"§ 136-18.3A. Wireless communications infrastructure.

(a) The definitions set forth in G.S. 160A-400.51 G.S. 160D-9-31 shall apply to this section.

....."

Repeal of Prior Statutes Replaced by Chapter 160D

SECTION 2.2. Article 18 of Chapter 153A of the General Statutes is repealed.[720]

SECTION 2.3. Article 19 of Chapter 160A of the General Statutes is repealed.[721]

SECTION 2.6(a). G.S. 153A-102.1 is repealed.[722]

SECTION 2.6(b). G.S. 160A-4.1 is repealed.[723]

SECTION 2.6(c). G.S. 160A-181.1 is repealed.[724]

SECTION 2.6(d). G.S. 153A-143 is repealed.[725]

SECTION 2.6(e). G.S. 160A-199 is repealed.[726]

SECTION 2.6(f). G.S. 153A-144 is repealed.[727]

SECTION 2.6(g). G.S. 160A-201 is repealed.[728]

SECTION2.6(h). G.S. 153A-452 is repealed.[729]

SECTION 2.6(i). G.S. 153A-455 is repealed.[730]

SECTION 2.6(j). Article 3 of Chapter 168 is repealed.[731]

---

719. This is a conforming amendment added by House committee substitute.

720. The previous provisions on local government planning and development regulation, Article 18 in G.S. Chapter 153A and Article 19 in Chapter 160A, are replaced by a single Chapter 160D that applies to both counties and cities. See Appendix C and Appendix D for depictions of where sections previously located in Chapters 153A and 160A are located within the proposed Chapter 160D.

721. The comments set out in note 718, *supra*, apply here.

722. This section has been relocated to G.S. 160D-8-5. It deals with notice of changes in subdivision fees.

723. This section has been relocated to G.S. 160D-8-5. It deals with notice of changes in subdivision fees.

724. This section has been relocated to G.S. 160D-9-2. It deals with regulation of adult businesses.

725. This section has been relocated to G.S. 160D-9-9. It deals with regulation of manufactured housing.

726. This section has been relocated to G.S. 160D-9-9. It deals with regulation of manufactured housing.

727. This section has been relocated to G.S. 160D-9-12. It deals with regulation of public buildings.

728. This section has been relocated to G.S. 160D-9-12. It deals with regulation of public buildings.

729. This section has been relocated to G.S. 160D-9-21. It deals with regulation of forestry activity.

730. This section has been relocated to G.S. 160D-13-20. It deals with energy-facility financing.

731. This section has been relocated to G.S. 160D-9-6. It deals with zoning regulation regarding the location of family care homes.

Relocation of Provisions in Repealed Statutes Not Incorporated into Chapter 160D

SECTION 2.7. Article 23 of Chapter 153A of the General Statues is amended by adding the following new sections to read:

"153A- 457. Submission of statement concerning improvements. [732]

A county may by ordinance require that when a property owner improves property at a cost of more than twenty-five hundred dollars ($2,500) but less than five thousand dollars ($5,000), the property owner must, within 14 days after the completion of the work, submit to the county assessor a statement setting forth the nature of the improvement and the total cost thereof."

"§ 153A-458. Authorization to provide grants.[733]

(a) A county may provide grants to unaffiliated qualified private providers of highspeed Internet access service, as that term is defined in G.S. 160A-340(4), for the purpose of expanding service in unserved areas for economic development in the county. The grants shall be awarded on a technology neutral basis, shall be open to qualified applicants, and may require matching funds by the private provider. A county shall seek and consider request for proposals from qualified private providers within the county prior to awarding a broadband grant and shall use reasonable means to ensure that potential applicants are made aware of the grant, including, at a minimum, compliance with the notice procedures set forth in G.S. 160A-340.6(c). The county shall use only unrestricted general fund revenue for the grants. For the purposes of this section, a qualified private provider is a private provider of high-speed Internet access service in the State prior to the issuance of the grant proposal. Nothing in this section authorizes a county to provide highspeed Internet broadband service."

Savings Clause, Transition Provisions, and Effective Dates

SECTION 2.8. If any provision of this act or its application is held invalid, the invalidity does not affect other provisions or applications of this act that can be given effect without the invalid provisions or application, and to this end the provisions of this act are severable.

SECTION 2.9(a). Any otherwise valid permit or development approval made prior to January 1, 2021 shall not be invalid based on inconsistency with the provisions of this Act. The validity of any plan adopted prior to January 1, 2021 is not affected by a failure to comply with the procedural requirements of G.S. 160D-5-1(b).

SECTION 2.9(b). Any special use district or conditional use district zoning district that is valid and in effect as of January 1, 2021 shall be deemed a conditional zoning district consistent with the terms of this Act and the special or conditional use permits issued concurrently with establishment of those districts shall be valid as specified in Section 8.1. Any valid "conditional use permit" issued prior to January 1, 2021 shall be deemed a "special use permit" consistent with the provisions of this Act.

SECTION 2.9(c). Any local government that has adopted zoning regulations but that has not adopted a comprehensive plan shall adopt such a plan no later than July 1, 2022 in order to retain the authority to adopt and apply zoning regulations.[734]

SECTION 2.10. If Part II of this act becomes law in 2019, it is the intent of the General Assembly that legislation contained in Part I of this act or in other acts enacted in the 2019 Regular Session of the General Assembly, or that affects statutes repealed and replaced by similar provisions in Chapter 160D of the General

---

732. This section has been relocated from G.S. 153A-325, previously located within repealed Article 18 of G.S. Chapter 153A.

733. This section has been relocated from G.S. 153A-349.60, previously located within repealed Article 18 of G.S. Chapter 153A.

734. Under this provision, any local government without a land use plan is given a full year to prepare and adopt a plan in order to retain authority to adopt zoning regulations. The plan requirement and related provisions relative to planning are set forth in G.S. 160D-5-1.

Statutes, as enacted by Part II of this act, also be incorporated into Chapter 160D of the General Statutes.[735] It is the further intent of the General Assembly that legislation contained in the telecommunications provisions of Part II of this act makes no substantive policy changes from the statutes repealed.[736] The North Carolina General Statutes Commission shall study the need for legislation to accomplish this intent and shall report its findings and recommendations, including any legislative proposals, to the 2020 Regular Session of the 2019 General Assembly upon its convening.

SECTION 3.2. Part II of this act becomes effective January 1, 2021 and applies to local government development regulation decisions made on or after that date. Part II of this act clarifies and restates the intent of existing law and applies to ordinances adopted before, on, and after the effective date.

---

735. This provision affirms that if amendments are made to the statutes repealed and relocated to Chapter 160D by other legislation enacted in 2019, those amendments will be incorporated into Chapter 160D prior to its effective date.

736. This sentence was added by 2019 House committee substitute to clarify that there were no substantive changes to existing law contained in Part 3 of Article 9 of G.S. Chapter 160D.